The Macmillan Dictionary of Religious Quotations

Margaret Pepper was born in Manchester but has lived most of her life in the West Country. The mother of four grown-up children, she was a nurse in the last war and has been active in church affairs and in the WI and the WRVS for many years. She lives in Devon.

D1399428

THE MACMILLAN DICTIONARY OF

RELIGIOUS QUOTATIONS

COMPILED & EDITED BY
MARGARET PEPPER

MACMILLAN

First published 1989 by André Deutsch Ltd

This edition published 1996 by Macmillan Reference Books
a division of Macmillan Publishers Limited
25 Eccleston Place, London SW1W 9NF
and Basingstoke

Associated companies throughout the world

ISBN 0-333-65378-5

9 8 7 6 5 4 3 2 1

A CIP catalogue record for this book is available from the British Library

Printed and bound in Great Britain by
Cox & Wyman Ltd, Reading, Berkshire

To Frank Pepper, my husband, without whose professional help and encouragement the book would never have got started.

ACKNOWLEDGEMENTS

It would have been impossible to compile this book without the help and advice of many kind friends who brought to my attention numerous items I would otherwise have missed. I would particularly like to thank the Right Revd George Carey; the Right Revd Brother Michael SSF; the Right Revd Peter Ball CGA; the Right Revd Kenneth Pillar; the Right Revd Richard Llewellin; the Ven. John Richards; Archimandrite Barnabas; the Rabbi Julia Neuberger; the Revd Preb. John Harper; the Revd Dr Richard Legg; the Revd Derek Hooper; the Revd Michael Stagg; the Revd John Perry; the Revd John Dibb-Smith; Sister Barbara SC; Lady Alethea Eliot; Valerie Cons; Carolyn Legg; Marjorie Ruhrmund; Ray Seddon, Christian Science Publications; John Miller; Christopher Potter; John Pepper; and Lucy Taylor for kindly typing the manuscript.

INTRODUCTION

This book began as a personal collection of favourite religious quotations, for my own use, to fill a gap on my bookshelf because there was nothing to be found which quite answered the purpose.

When the possibility of publication was mooted, it was necessary to turn a private anthology into a collection with much wider appeal. I have tried to include ideas from a broad range of religious thinking, past and present. The result will, I hope, sometimes strike a chord, sometimes provoke and sometimes amuse.

At a time when religious movements throughout the world are growing stronger and when religious and secular leaders are showing less hesitation than for years in sharing their concerns, I hope this book will give some indication of the rich sources which feed this current vitality.

Margaret Pepper
North Minack, Cornwall

ABANDONMENT

1 My heart I give you, Lord, eagerly and entirely.
    John Calvin Personal motto

2 I am not afraid that God will destroy the world, but I am
afraid that he may abandon it to wander blindly in the
sophisticated wasteland of contemporary civilisation.
    Carlo Carretto *In Search of the Beyond*

ABIDING

3 Abide with us, for it is toward evening, and the day is far
spent.
    Holy Bible St Luke Chap. 24 v. 29

4 Hold Thou Thy Cross before my closing eyes;
Shine through the gloom, and point me to the skies;
Heaven's morning breaks, and earth's vain shadows flee;
In life, in death, O Lord, abide with me.
    Henry F. Lyte Hymn 'Abide With Me'

ABORTION

5 Abortion leads to an appalling trivialisation of the art of
procreation.
    Dr Donald Coggan, when Archbishop of York Speech to
    the Shaftesbury Society 2 October 1973

6 We cannot treat the human embryo as cheap and worthless
without passing judgement on all human life, including our
own.
    Monica Furlong *Christian Uncertainties*

7 We are fighting abortion by adoption. We have sent word to
the clinics, to the hospitals, to the police stations. 'Please do
not destroy the child. We will take the child.'
    Mother Teresa of Calcutta Nobel Peace Prize Lecture 1979

ABRAHAM

1 'Oh' God said to Abraham 'Kill me a son'
Abraham says 'Man, you must be putting me on.'
    Bob Dylan 'Highway 61 Revisited' (song)

2 Charles Darwin, the Abraham of scientific men, a searcher as
obedient to the command of truth as was the Patriarch
obedient to the command of God.
    John Tyndall *Fragments of Science* 'Science and Man'

3 Thou liest in Abraham's bosom all the year;
And worshipp'st at the Temple's inner shrine,
God being with thee when we know it not.
    William Wordsworth 'It is a Beauteous Evening'

ABSENCE

4 That which you most love in a friend may be clearer in his
absence.
    Kahlil Gibran *The Prophet*

5 Absence in love is like water upon fire, a little quickens, but
much extinguishes it.
    Hannah More *Tracts*

ABSOLUTION

6 He pardoneth and absolveth all them that truly repent and
unfeignedly believe his holy Gospel.
    Book of Common Prayer Order of Morning Prayer
    The Absolution or Remission of Sins

7 Ful swetely herde he confessioun,
And plesaunt was his absolucioun.
    Geoffrey Chaucer *Canterbury Tales* Prologue

8 The blackest sin is cleared with absolution.
    William Shakespeare *The Rape of Lucrece*

9 Forgive! How many will say 'forgive', and find
A sort of absolution in the sound
To hate a little longer!
    Alfred, Lord Tennyson 'Sea Dreams'

10 There is strife between human ways and God's ways; damned
by you, we are absolved by God.
    Tertullian *Apologeticus*

ABSTINENCE

1 The abstinent run away from the things they desire, but carry
their desires with them.
Bhagavad Gita

2 Called to the temple of impure delight,
He that abstains, and he alone, does right.
If a wish wander that way, call it home;
He cannot long be safe whose wishes roam.
William Cowper 'The Progress of Error'

3 Refined himself to Soul, to curb the Sense;
And made almost a Sin of Abstinence.
John Dryden 'The Character of a Good Parson'

4 Abstinence is whereby a man refraineth from anything which
he may lawfully take.
Sir Thomas Elyot *The Governor*

5 Touch not; taste not; handle not.
Holy Bible Colossians Chap. 2 v. 21

6 It ought to give pause to the most fanatical teetotaller that the
only humans worth saving in the Flood were a family of
vintners.
Dr Bernard Rudofsky 'Now I Lay Me Down to Eat'

ABSURDITY

7 As a man is so's his God
Explains why God's so often absurd.
Giles and Melville Harcourt *Short Prayers for a Long Day*

8 Taboos, where humour is concerned, are an admission of
doubt and derive from a sense of weakness and insecurity. The
truly religious take no offence when attention is drawn to the
absurdity necessarily inherent in the dogmas to which they
subscribe and the ceremonies in which they participate.
Malcolm Muggeridge *Tread Softly for You Tread on My Jokes*

ABUNDANCE

9 My cup runneth over.
Holy Bible Psalm 23 v. 5

10 Out of the abundance of the heart the mouth speaketh.
Holy Bible St Matthew Chap. 12 v. 34

ABUSE

1   When a simpleton abused him, Buddha listened to him in silence, but when the man had finished asked him, 'Son, if a man declined to accept a present offered to him, to whom would it belong?' The man answered, 'To him who offered it.' 'My son,' Buddha said, 'I decline to accept your abuse. Keep it for yourself.'

   Will Durant *The Story of Civilisation*

ACCEPTANCE

2   When I believe, I am no longer a mere man, I am already a son of God.

   Carlo Carretto *Summoned by Love*

3   Just as I am, thou wilt receive,
   Wilt welcome, pardon, cleanse, relieve:
   Because thy promise I believe,
   O Lamb of God, I come.

   Charlotte Elliott *Hymns Ancient and Modern* 'Just as I am'

4   Weep if you must,
   Parting is here —
   But life goes on,
   So sing as well.

   Joyce Grenfell *Joyce Grenfell Requests the Pleasure*

5   For what has been — thanks!
   For what shall be — yes!

   Dag Hammarskjöld

6   Give me grace ever to desire and to will what is most acceptable to thee and most pleasing in thy sight.

   Thomas à Kempis

7   The spirit of rejection finds its support in the consciousness of separateness; the spirit of acceptance finds its base in the consciousness of unity.

   Rabindranath Tagore *Letters to a Friend*

ACCOMPLISHMENT

8   I have fought a good fight, I have finished my course, I have kept the faith.

   Holy Bible 2 Timothy Chap. 4 v. 7

ACHIEVEMENT

1 Thou shalt ever joy at eventide if you spend the day fruitfully.
   Thomas à Kempis *The Imitation of Christ*

2 No great achievement is possible without persistent work.
   Bertrand Russell

ACTION

3 The quality of life is determined by its activities.
   Aristotle *Nicomachean Ethics*

4 No one doth well what he doth against his will.
   St Augustine of Hippo Quoted *Butler's Lives of the Saints*

5 Action should culminate in wisdom.

6 Freedom from activity is never achieved by abstaining from action.
   Bhagavad Gita

7 Action springs not from thought, but from a readiness for responsibility.
   Dietrich Bonhoeffer *Letters and Papers from Prison*

8 Man is his own star, and the soul that can
   Render an honest and a perfect man
   Commands all light, all influence, all fate;
   Nothing to him falls early, or too late.
   Our acts, our angels are, or good or ill,
   Our fatal shadows that walk by us still.
   John Fletcher *The Honest Man's Fortune*

9 Make the least ado about your greatest gifts. Be content to act, and leave the talking to others.
   Baltasar Gracian *The Oracle*

10 We do ourselves wrong and too meanly estimate the holiness above us when we deem that any act or enjoyment good in itself is not good to do religiously.
   Nathaniel Hawthorne *The Marble Faun*

11 To dispose a soul to action we must upset its equilibrium.
   Eric Hoffer *The Ordeal of Change*

12 Act only on that maxim whereby you can at the same time will that it should become a universal law.
   Immanuel Kant *Critique of Practical Reason*

1 Never be entirely idle; but either be reading, or writing, or praying, or meditating, or endeavouring something for the public good.
   Thomas à Kempis *The Imitation of Christ*

2 Boast not of what thou would'st have done, but do
   What then thou would'st.
   John Milton *Samson Agonistes*

3 Activity may lead to evil; but inactivity cannot be led to good.
   Hannah More *Tracts*

4 Our nature consists in motion, complete inaction is death.
   Blaise Pascal *Pensées*

5 Tomorrow God isn't going to ask
   What did you dream?
   What did you think?
   What did you plan?
   What did you preach?
   He's going to ask *What did you do?*
   Michel Quoist *With Open Heart*

6 Not all of those to whom we do good love us, neither do all those to whom we do evil hate us.
   Joseph Roux *Meditations of a Parish Priest*

7 'Let God do it all', someone will say; but if man folds his arms, God will go to sleep.
   Miguel de Unamuno *The Tragic Sense of Life*

8 Meditation and action —
   He who knows these two together,
   Through action leaves death behind and through meditation gains immortality.
   The Upanishads

ADAM AND EVE

9 The luckiest man was Adam — he had no mother-in-law.
   Sholom Aleichem Quoted A. Marks *I've Taken a Page in the Bible*

10 When Adam dolve and Eve span
   Who was then the gentleman.
   John Ball Speech at Blackheath Wat Tyler's Rebellion
   12 June 1381

1 You see dear, it is not true that woman was made from man's rib, she was really made from his funny bone.
   J.M. Barrie *What Every Woman Knows*

2 When Eve saw her reflection in a pool, she sought Adam and accused him of infidelity.
   Ambrose Bierce

3 I wish Adam had died with all his ribs in his body.
   Dion Boucicault

4 Humanity was Adam's only gift
   He scattered it wide
   Seeding God everywhere.
   Valerie Cons *Land's Ender*

5 For women, with a mischief to their kind,
   Pervert with bad advice our better mind;
   A woman's counsel brought us first to woe,
   And made her man his Paradise forego.
   John Dryden 'The Cock and the Fox'

6 Adam 'ad 'em.
   Strickland Gillilan 'Lines on the Antiquity of Microbes'
   (claimed to be the world's shortest poem)

7 And the man said, The woman thou gavest to be with me, she gave me of the tree, and I did eat.
   Holy Bible Genesis Chap. 3 v. 12

8 As in Adam all die, even so in Christ shall all be made alive.
   Holy Bible 1 Corinthians Chap. 15 v. 22

9 When Eve upon the first of men
   The apple pressed with specious cant,
   Oh! what a thousand pities then
   That Adam was not Adamant!
   Thomas Hood 'A Reflection'

10 All the world was Adam once, with Eve by his side.
   Jean Ingelow 'Like a Laverock in the Lift'

11 Adam, whilst he spake not, had paradise at will.
   William Langland *The Vision of Piers Plowman*

12 Adam, the goodliest man of men since born
   His sons; the fairest of her daughters Eve.
   John Milton *Paradise Lost*

1   Our grandsire Adam, ere of Eve possessed,
Alone, and ev'n in paradise unbless'd,
With mournful looks the blissful scene survey'd
And wander'd in the solitary shade:
The Maker saw, took pity, and bestow'd
Woman, the last, the best reserv'd of God.
   Alexander Pope 'January and May'

2   And Adam was a gardener.
   William Shakespeare *Henry VI Part II* Act IV Sc. 2

3   There is no ancient gentlemen but gardeners, ditchers, and
grave-makers; they hold up Adam's profession.
   William Shakespeare *Hamlet* Act V Sc. 1

4   Adam and Eve had many advantages, but the principal one
was that they escaped teething.
   Mark Twain

5   I sometimes think that if Adam and Eve had been merely
engaged, she would not have talked with the serpent, and the
world would have been saved an infinity of misery.
   H.G. Wells 'Selected Conversations with an Uncle'

6   Think how poor Mother Eve was brought
To being as God's afterthought.
   Anna Wickham 'To Men'

ADAPTABILITY

7   Man is a pliable animal, a being who gets accustomed to
everything.
   Feodor Dostoevsky *The House of the Dead*

ADMIRATION

8   I think that God's works are so beautiful that I am amazed
that people can admire them but deny that they have a
Maker.
   Commissioner Catherine Bramwell-Booth *My Faith* Ed. Mary
   E. Callan

9   No nobler feeling than this of admiration for one higher than
himself dwells in the breast of man.
   Thomas Carlyle *Heroes and Hero Worship* 'The Hero as
   Divinity'

ADOLESCENCE

1 Adolescence, physical, emotional and intellectual, is a sign
from God that this is the time of preparation, the time to
prepare for union with another person.

2 The adolescent is a child who is in the process of receiving
from the hands of God, through the intermediary of his
parents, personal care of and responsibility for his body, his
affections, and his mind.
   Michel Quoist *The Christian Response*

ADORATION

3 Down in Adoration falling
Lo, the Sacred Host we hail!
Lo, o'er ancient forms deporting,
Newer rites of grace prevail;
Faith for all defects supplying
Where the feeble senses fail.
   St Thomas Aquinas 'A Hymn of Vespers on the Feast of
   Corpus Christi'

4 When we cannot by searching find the bottom, we must sit
down at the brink and adore the depths.
   Matthew Arnold *Commentary*

5 Praised be You, my Lord, through our Sister Mother Earth,
who sustains us, governs us, and who produces varied fruits
with coloured flowers and herbs.

Praised be You, my Lord, through Brother Wind and through
the air, cloudy and serene, and every kind of weather.

Praised be You, my Lord, through Sister Moon and the stars
in heaven: you formed them clear and precious and beautiful.

Praised be You, my Lord, through Brother Fire, through
whom You light the night and he is beautiful and playful and
robust and strong.

Praised be You, my Lord, with all your creatures, especially
Sir Brother Sun, who is the day and through whom you give us
light. And he is beautiful and radiant with great splendours
and bears likeness of You, Most High One.
   St Francis of Assisi *The Canticle of Brother Sun*

1 If we would understand Divine things, we must cultivate an
attitude of humble adoration. Who does not begin by kneeling
down, runs every possible risk.
Ernest Hello *Life, Science and Art*

2 It is magnificent to be clothed like the lilies of the field ... but
the supreme glory is to be nothingness in adoration.
Søren Kierkegaard Quoted Antonia Sertikanges *Rectitude*

3 Open wide the windows of our spirits and fill us full of light;
open wide the door of our hearts, that we may receive and
entertain Thee with all our powers of adoration.
Christina Rossetti

4 Man is most truly himself, as the Eastern Church well knows,
not when he toils but when he adores. And we are learning
more and more that all the innocent joy in life may be a form
of adoration.
Vida P. Scudder *The Privilege of Age*

5 The adoration to which you are avowed is not an affair of red
hassocks and authorized hymn books; but a burning and
consuming fire.

6 This is adoration: not a difficult religious exercise, but an
attitude of the soul.
Evelyn Underhill *The Love of God*

7 It is a beauteous evening, calm and free;
The holy time is quiet as a nun
Breathless with adoration.
William Wordsworth 'It is a Beauteous Evening'

ADULTERY

8 Whosoever looketh on a woman to lust after her hath
committed adultery with her already in his heart.
Holy Bible St Matthew Chap. 5 v. 28

ADVENTIST

9 The dead sleep until the day of the Last Judgement, when
the heavens will be opened, Christ will come in glory, the
wicked will be annihilated or sent to Hell, and the good
redeemed.
E. Royston Pike *The Encyclopaedia of Religion*

ADVERSITY

1 The beauty of the soul shines out when a man bears with composure one heavy mischance after another, not because he does not feel them, but because he is a man of high and heroic temper.
   Aristotle *Nicomachean Ethics*

2 It was a high speech of Seneca (after the manner of the Stoics) that 'the good things which belong to prosperity are to be wished, but the good things that belong to adversity are to be admired.'

3 Prosperity is the blessing of the Old Testament. Adversity is the blessing of the New.

4 Prosperity doth best discover vice, but adversity doth best discover virtue.
   Francis Bacon *Essays* 'Of Adversity'

5 In every kind of adversity the bitterest part of a man's affliction is to remember he once was happy.
   Boethius *The Consolation of Philosophy*

6 There are three modes of bearing the ills of life; by indifference, by philosophy and by religion.
   Charles Caleb Colton *Lacon*

7 If thou faint in the day of adversity, thy strength is small.
   Holy Bible Proverbs Chap. 24 v. 10

8 Man is born unto trouble, as the sparks fly upward.
   Holy Bible Job Chap. 5 v. 7

9 Adversity is the state in which a man most easily becomes acquainted with himself, being especially free from admirers then.
   Samuel Johnson Quoted Boswell's *Life of Johnson*

10 He knows not his own strength who hath not met adversity.
   Ben Jonson *Timber* 'Explorata'

11 For a man to rejoice in adversity is not grievous to him who loves; for so to joy is to joy in the cross of Christ.
   Thomas à Kempis *The Imitation of Christ*

12 Adversity reminds men of religion.
   Livy *History*

1 In adversity a man is saved by hope.
   Menander *Fragments*

2 The Good are better made by Ill,
   As odours crushed are sweeter still.
   Samuel Rogers *Jacqueline*

3 Behold a noble sight to which God may direct his gaze.
   Behold a thing worthy of a God — a brave man matched in
   conflict with adversity.
   Seneca *On Providence*

ADVICE

4 Don't use God for a conversation stopper.
   John Habgood, Archbishop of York

5 Go to the ant, thou sluggard; consider her ways, and be wise.
   Holy Bible Proverbs Chap. 6 v. 6

6 A word spoken in due season, how good is it!
   Holy Bible Proverbs Chap. 15 v. 23

AFFECTION

7 Most people would rather get than give affection.
   Aristotle *Nicomachean Ethics*

8 He who is without affection either for good or evil is firmly
   fixed in perfect knowledge.
   Bhagavad Gita

9 Set your affection on things above, not on things on the earth.
   Holy Bible Colossians Chap. 3 v. 2

10 Affection has no price.
   St Jerome *Letters* No. 3

11 Affection hides three times as many virtues as charity does
   sins.
   Horace Mann

AFFLICTION

12 Nothing is more desirable than to be released from affliction,
   but nothing is more frightening than to be deprived of a
   crutch.
   James Baldwin *Nobody Knows My Name*

1   Affliction smarts most in the most happy state.
     Sir Thomas Browne *Christian Morals*

2   If afflictions refine some, they consume others.
     Thomas Fuller *Gnomologia*

3   God ne'er afflicts us more than our desert,
     Though He may seem to overact His part;
     Sometimes He strikes us more than flesh can bear,
     But yet still less than Grace can suffer here.
     Robert Herrick 'Affliction'

4   Feed him with bread of affliction and with water of affliction,
     until I come in peace.
     Holy Bible 1 Kings Chap. 22 v. 27 2 Chronicles Chap. 18 v. 26

5   I have chosen thee in the furnace of affliction.
     Holy Bible Isaiah Chap. 48 v. 10

6   He was afflicted, yet he opened not his mouth: he is brought
     as a lamb to the slaughter, and as a sheep before her shearers
     is dumb, so he openeth not his mouth.
     Holy Bible Isaiah Chap. 53 v. 7

7   For our light affliction, which is but for a moment, worketh for
     us a far more exceeding and eternal weight of a glory.
     Holy Bible 2 Corinthians Chap. 4 v. 17

8   There is no man in this world without some manner of
     tribulation or anguish, though he be king or pope.
     Thomas à Kempis *The Imitation of Christ*

9   Affliction is not sent in vain, young man,
     From that good God who chastens whom he loves.
     Robert Southey *Madoc in Wales*

10   God gives almonds to those who have no teeth.
     Spanish proverb

11   The Lord gets his best soldiers out of the highlands of
     affliction.
     Charles Haddon Spurgeon *Gleanings Among the Sheaves*

12   It is surprising that God should have given affliction the power
     to seize the very souls of the innocent and to take possession
     of them as their sovereign lord. At the very best he who is
     branded by affliction will only keep half his soul.
     Simone Weil *Modern Spirituality*

AFTERLIFE

1 And I shall thereupon
Take rest, ere I be gone
Once more on my adventure brave and new.
    Robert Browning 'Rabbi Ben Ezra'

2 That which is the foundation of all our hopes and all our fears;
all our hopes and fears which are of any consideration; I mean
a future life.
    Joseph Butler *Analogy of Religion*

3 I laugh, for hope hath happy place with me;
If my bark sinks 'tis to another sea.
    William Ellery Channing *A Poet's Hope*

4 But though life's valley be a vale of tears,
A brighter scene beyond that vale appears.
    William Cowper 'Conversation'

5 When the subject of Heaven and Hell was broached in
conversation one day, Cocteau politely declined to offer an
opinion. 'Excuse me for not answering,' he said, 'I have
friends in both places.'
    Clifton Fadiman *Little Brown Book of Anecdotes*

6 Hark, how the birds do sing,
And woods do ring!
All creatures have their joy, and man hath his.
Yet if we rightly measure,
Man's joy and pleasure
Rather hereafter, than in present, is.
    George Herbert 'Man's Medley'

7 We shall all be changed, in a moment, in the twinkling of an
eye.
    Holy Bible 1 Corinthians Chap. 15 vv. 51—52

8 The great world of light that lies
Behind all human destinies.
    Henry Wadsworth Longfellow 'To a Child'

9 Beyond this vale of tears
There is a life above
Unmeasured by the flight of years
And all that life is love.
    James Montgomery *The Issues of Life and Death*

The humble, meek, merciful, just, pious and devout souls are everywhere of one religion; and when death has taken off the mask they will know one another, though the divers liveries they wear here makes them strangers.

William Penn *Friends and the Christian Church*

2 There is something beyond the grave, death does not end all, and the pale ghost escapes from the vanquished pyre.

Sextus Propertius *Elegies*

3 Man says 'How is it possible, when I am dead, that I shall then be brought forth able?' Does he not remember that we have created him once, and he was nothing then.

The Qur'an

4 This life is but the passage of a day,
This life is but a pang and all is over;
But in the life to come which fades not away
Every love shall abide and every lover.

Christina Rossetti 'Saints and Angels'

5 In that sweet by and by we shall meet on that beautiful shore.

Ira David Sankey *Sacred Songs*

6 If you get to heaven before I do
Just bore a hole and pull me through.

Student song

7 The cry of the human for a life beyond the grave comes from that which is noblest in the soul of man.

Henry Van Dyke

8 He sins against this life, who slights the next.

Edward Young *Night Thoughts*

AGE

9 A man that is young in years may be old in hours.

Francis Bacon

10 No one is so old that he cannot live another year, or so young that he cannot die today.

Fernando de Rojas *La Celestina* Act IV

11 We grow in years more fragile in body, but morally stouter, and we can throw off the chill of a bad conscience almost at once.

Logan Pearsall Smith *All Trivia* 'Afterthoughts'

AGNOSTIC

1   I am all for the higher agnosticism: its better name is
    ignorance.
>   G.K. Chesterton *Orthodoxy*

2   John Grubby, who was short and stout
    And troubled with religious doubt,
    Refused about the age of three
    To sit upon the curate's knee.
>   G.K. Chesterton *The New Freethinker*

3   Those who deny Thee could not deny, if Thou didst not exist;
    and their denial is never complete, for if it were so, they would
    not exist.
>   T.S. Eliot *Murder In the Cathedral*

4   The various modes of worship, which prevailed in the Roman
    world, were all considered by the people as equally true; by
    the philosopher as equally false; and by the magistrate as
    equally useful.
>   Edward Gibbon *Decline and Fall of the Roman Empire*

5   I took thought and invented what I thought to be the
    appropriate title of 'agnostic'. It came into my head as
    suggestively antithetic to the 'Gnostic' of the church history
    who professed to know so much about the very things of which
    I was ignorant.
>   Thomas Henry Huxley *Nineteenth Century Magazine*
>   'Agnosticism' February 1889

6   You are not an agnostic, Paddy. You are just a fat slob who is
    too lazy to go to Mass.
>   Conor Cruise O'Brien, quoting an Irish Parish Priest
>   *Observer* 4 February 1979

AGONY

7   Jesus was in a garden, not of delight as the first Adam, in
    which he destroyed himself and the whole human race, but in
    one of agony, in which he saved himself and the whole human
    race.
>   Blaise Pascal *Pensées*

AGREEMENT

8   If all pulled in one direction the world would keel over.
>   Hanan J. Ayalti *Yiddish Proverbs*

ALMS

1 The rich have no more of the Kingdom of Heaven than they
have purchased by their alms.
  John Donne *Sermons* No. 59

2 Give no bounties; make equal laws; secure life and prosperity
and you need not give alms.
  Ralph Waldo Emerson *The Conduct of Life*

3 Give unto all, lest he whom thou deny'st
May chance to be no other man but Christ.
  Robert Herrick 'Alms'

4 When thou doest alms, let not thy left hand know what thy
right hand doeth.
  Holy Bible St Matthew Chap. 6 v. 3

5 Not what we give, but what we share, —
For the gift without the giver is bare;
Who gives himself with his alms feeds three, —
Himself, his hungering neighbour, and me.
  James Russell Lowell 'The Vision of Sir Launfal'

6 I had much rather not to live at all than to live by alms.
  Montaigne *Essays*

ALONENESS

7 The deepest need of man is the need to overcome his
separateness, to leave the prison of his aloneness.
  Erich Fromm *The Art of Loving*

8 And how am I to face the odds
Of man's bedevilment and God's?
I, a stranger and afraid
In a world I never made.
  A.E. Housman *Last Poems*

9 There's no such thing as a person alone. There are only people
bound to each other to the limits of humanity and time.
  Michel Quoist *With Open Heart*

ALTRUISM

10 A large part of altruism, even when it is perfectly honest, is
grounded upon the fact that it is uncomfortable to have
unhappy people about one.
  H.L. Mencken *Prejudices*

1   Human altruism which is not egoism is sterile.
    Marcel Proust *Remembrance of Things Past*

AMBITION

2   I had Ambition, by which sin
    The angels fell;
    I climbed and, step by step, O Lord,
    Ascended into Hell.
    Returning now to peace and quiet,
    And made more wise,
    Let my descent and fall, O Lord,
    Be into Paradise.
    W.H. Davies 'Ambition'

3   Nothing arouses ambition so much in the heart as the trumpet-
    clang of another's fame.
    Baltasar Gracian *The Art of Worldly Wisdom*

4   What shall it profit a man, if he shall gain the whole world,
    and lose his own soul?
    Holy Bible St Mark Chap. 8 v. 36

5   If men could regard the events of their own lives with more
    open minds they would frequently discover that they did not
    really desire the things they failed to obtain.
    André Maurois *The Art of Living*

6   To reign is worth ambition, though in Hell:
    Better to reign in Hell, than serve in Heaven.
    John Milton *Paradise Lost*

7   All sins have their origin in a sense of inferiority, otherwise
    called ambition.
    Cesare Pavese *The Burning Brand*

8   Men would be angels, angels would be gods.
    Alexander Pope *An Essay on Man*

9   Ambition is the grand enemy of all peace.
    John Cowper Powys *The Meaning of Culture*

10 Cromwell, I charge thee, fling away ambition:
    By that sin fell the angels. How can man then,
    The image of his Maker, hope to win by it?
    William Shakespeare *Henry VIII* Act III Sc. 2

1 In Heaven Ambition cannot dwell,
   Nor avarice in the vaults of Hell:
   Earthly these passions of the Earth,
   They perish where they have their birth.
   Robert Southey *The Curse of Kehama*

2 Ambition destroys its possessor.
   The Talmud

3 Vain the ambition of Kings
   Who seek by trophies and dead things
   To leave a living name behind
   And weave but nets to catch the wind.
   John Webster *The Devil's Law Case*

AMERICA

4 America is God's Crucible, the great Melting Pot where all the
   races of Europe are melting and reforming! God is making the
   American.
   Israel Zangwill *The Melting Pot*

ANARCHY

5 In those days there was no king in Israel: every man did that
   which was right in his own eyes.
   Holy Bible Judges Chap. 21 v. 25

ANGEL

6 A demon holds a book, in which are written the sins of a
   particular man; an angel drops on it from a phial a tear which
   the sinner had shed in doing a good action, and his sins are
   washed out.
   Alberic, monk of Monte Cassino

7 An angel can illumine the thought and mind of man by
   strengthening the power of vision, and by bringing within his
   reach some truth which the angel himself contemplates.
   St Thomas Aquinas Quoted Cecily Hallack *The Bliss of the Way*

8 God made the angels to show him splendour.
   Robert Bolt *A Man for All Seasons*

9 Dear and great Angel, wouldst thou only leave
   That child, when thou hast done with him, for me!
   Robert Browning 'The Guardian Angel'

1 Every man hath a good and a bad angel attending on him in
particular, all his life long.
> Robert Burton *The Anatomy of Melancholy*

2 The angels all were singing out of tune,
And hoarse with having little else to do,
Excepting to wind up the sun and moon,
Or curb a runaway young star or two.
> Lord Byron *The Vision of Judgement*

3 Angels can fly because they take themselves lightly.
> G.K. Chesterton *Orthodoxy*

4 We trust, in plumed procession,
For such the angels go,
Rank after rank, with even feet
And uniforms of snow.
> Emily Dickinson *Poems*

5 Once at the Angelus
(Ere I was dead),
Angels all glorious
Came to my bed;
Angels in blue and white
Crowned on the Head.
> Austin Dobson 'Good-night Babette'

6 If you pray truly, you will feel within yourself a great
assurance: and the angels will be your companions.
> Evagrius of Pontus Quoted *Seasons of the Spirit* Selected George
> Every, Richard Harries, Kallistos Ware

7 An angel whose muscles developed no more power weight for
weight than those of an eagle or a pigeon would require a
breast projecting for about four feet to house the muscles
engaged in working the wings, while to economise in weight,
its legs would have to be reduced to mere stilts.
> J.B.S. Haldane *Possible Worlds*

8 For he shall give his angels charge over thee, to keep thee in
all thy ways.
> *Holy Bible* Psalm 91 v. 11

9 'Angel' is the only word in the language which can never be
worn out. No other word would exist under the pitiless use
made of it by lovers.
> Victor Hugo *Les Misérables*

1 If a man is only a little lower than the angels, the angels should reform.
>   Mary Wilson Little

2 But all God's angels come to us disguised;
   Sorrow and sickness, poverty and death,
   One after other lift their frowning masks,
   And we behold the Seraph's face beneath,
   All radiant with the glory and the calm
   Of having looked upon the front of God.
>   James Russell Lowell 'On the Death of a Friend's Child'

3 An angel is a spiritual being created by God without a body, for the service of Christendom and the Church.
>   Martin Luther *Table Talk*

4 For God will deign
   To visit oft the dwellings of just men
   Delighted, and with frequent intercourse
   Thither will send his winged messengers
   On errands of supernal grace.

5 Speak ye who best can tell, ye Sons of Light,
   Angels, for ye behold him, and with songs
   And choral symphonies, day without night,
   Circle his throne rejoicing.
>   John Milton *Paradise Lost*

6 The helmed Cherubim
   The sworded Seraphim
   Are seen in glittering ranks with wings display'd.
>   John Milton 'On the Morning of Christ's Nativity'

7 When a man dies they who survive him ask what property he has left behind:

   The angel who bends over the dying man asks what good deeds he has sent before him.
>   *The Qur'an*

8 If some angel appeared to me without a carnal body and assured me that it was perfectly happy on prayer and music I should congratulate him, but shouldn't care to emulate him.
>   George Santayana *Letters*

9 Angels are bright still, though the brightest fell.
>   William Shakespeare *Macbeth* Act IV Sc. 3

1 Around our pillows golden ladders rise
   And up and down the skies
   With winged sandals shod
   The Angels come and go, the Messengers of God.
       R.H. Stoddard 'Hymn to the Beautiful'

2 Sweet souls around us watch us still,
   Press nearer to our side;
   Into our thoughts, into our prayers,
   With gentle helpings glide.
       Harriet Beecher Stowe 'The Other World'

3 To wish to act like angels while we are still in this world is
   nothing but folly.
       St Teresa of Avila Quoted Abbé Rodolphe Hoornaert
       St Teresa and Her Writings

4 It is not known precisely where angels dwell — whether in the
   air, the void or the planets. It has not been God's pleasure
   that we should be informed of their abode.
       Voltaire *Philosophical Dictionary* 'Angels'

5 There is no reason why good cannot triumph as often as evil.
   The triumph of anything is a matter of organisation. If there
   are such things as angels I hope they are organised along the
   lines of the Mafia.
       Kurt Vonnegut *Sirens of Titan*

6 With silence only as their benediction,
   God's angels come
   Where, in the shadow of a great affliction,
   The soul sits dumb!
       John Greenleaf Whittier 'To My Friend on the Death of
       His Sister'

7 Angels are men of a superior kind:
   Angels are men in lighter habit clad.
       Edward Young *Night Thoughts*

ANGER

8 A man that does not know how to be angry does not know
   how to be good.
       Henry Ward Beecher *Proverbs from a Plymouth Pulpit*

9 From anger, delusion arises, and from delusion bewilderment
   of memory. When memory is bewildered, intelligence is lost,

and when intelligence is lost, one falls down again into the material pool.
Bhagavad Gita

1 Speak when you are angry and you will make the best speech you will ever regret.
Ambrose Bierce *Devil's Dictionary*

2 A man is as big as the things that make him angry.
Winston Churchill

3 The sun must not set upon anger, much less will I let the sun set upon the anger of God towards me.
John Donne *Sermons*

4 There was never an angry man that thought his anger unjust.
St Francis de Sales *Introduction to the Devout Life*

5 Anger is one of the sinews of the soul: he that wants it hath a maimed mind.
Thomas Fuller *The Holy State and the Profane State of Anger*

6 He that is slow to anger is better than the mighty; and he that ruleth his spirit than he that taketh a city.
Holy Bible Proverbs Chap. 16 v. 32

7 To build one's activity on love and non-violence demands the greatest inner purification; one must constantly rid one's heart of inordinate desires, fears, and anxieties, but above all, one must cleanse oneself of anger.
William Johnston SJ Quoted *Love's Journey Done*

8 To be angry is to revenge the fault of others upon ourselves.
Alexander Pope *Thoughts on Various Subjects*

9 Anger begins in folly, and ends in repentance.
Pythagoras

10 Anger would inflict punishment on another; meanwhile, it tortures itself.
Publilius Syrus *Moral Sayings*

ANGLICANISM

11 When an Anglican is asked 'Where was your Church before the Reformation?' his best answer is to put the counter-question 'Where was your face before you washed it?'
Michael Ramsey, Archbishop of Canterbury Quoted James B. Simpson *The Hundredth Archbishop of Canterbury*

ANIMAL

1 Animals are not brethren, they are not underlings, they are other nations, caught up with ourselves in the net of life and time, fellow prisoners of the splendour and travail of the earth.
   Henry Boston *The Outermost House*

2 God made all the creatures and gave them our love and our fear,
   To give sign, we and they are his children, one family here.
   Robert Browning 'Saul'

3 Love the animals: God has given them the rudiments of thought and joy untroubled.
   Feodor Dostoevsky *The Brothers Karamazov*

4 Many years ago when an adored dog died a great friend, a bishop, said to me, 'You must always remember that, as far as the Bible is concerned, God only threw the humans out of Paradise.'
   Bruce Foyle *Pets and Their People*

5 In the nimble silence of my life, on the thread of my airy dreams, in the geometric tracery of my thoughts, I thank you, for ever, dear God.
   Carmen de Gasztold *The Beasts Choir* 'Spider'

6 Though I am far from denying that the counsels of Divine Goodness regarding dumb creatures are, for us, involved in deep obscurity, yet Scripture foretells for them a 'glorious liberty', and we are assured that the compassion of Heaven will not be wanting to them.
   John Keble *Lectures on Poetry*

7 I really don't think I could consent to go to Heaven if I thought there were to be no animals there.
   George Bernard Shaw *Androcles and the Lion*

8 Man is worse than an animal when he is an animal.
   Rabindranath Tagore *Stray Birds*

ANOINTING

9 You were rubbed with oil like an athlete, Christ's athlete, as though in preparation for an earthly wrestling-match, and you agreed to take on your opponent.
   St Ambrose *De Sacramentis*

1. The true charismatic congregation doesn't start the service until the anointing of the Spirit comes upon us. How do we know? — We know.

    Fr John Harper 'Sermons: St John-in-the-Fields, St Ives'

ANXIETY

2. If the twenty years after the first great war can be described as being a period of profound disillusionment, our own period should be perhaps described as being a time of deep disturbance. I do not mean the threat of a nuclear war, or the tragedies of conflicts, but rather the fear and anxiety of men and women who can see no aim or purpose in life.

    Fr Aelred, Prior of Ewell Monastery 'Letter to Friends'

3. Our whole life is taken up with anxiety for personal security, with preparations for living, so that we really never live at all.

    Leo Tolstoy *My Religion*

APATHY

4. Science may have found a cure for most evils, but it has found no remedy for the worst of them all — the apathy of human beings.

    Helen Keller *My Religion*

APOSTACY

5. If I were called upon to identify the principal trait of the entire twentieth century, I would be unable to find anything more precise than to repeat once again 'Men have forgotten God'.

6. We can only reach with determination for the warm hand of God, which we have so rashly and self-confidently pushed away.

    Alexander Solzhenitsyn Quoted Richard Harries *Morning Has Broken*

APPEARANCE

7. Fine words and an insinuating appearance are seldom associated with true virtue.

    Confucius *Analects*

8. Judge not according to the appearance.

    Holy Bible St John Chap. 7 v. 24

1 The Lord seeth not as man seeth; for man looketh on the outward appearance, but the Lord looketh on the heart.
> *Holy Bible* 1 Samuel Chap. 16 v. 7

2 We must try to love without imagining. To love the appearance in its nakedness without interpretation. What we love then is God.
> Simone Weil *Gravity and Grace*

APPLE

3 The apple was the first fruit of the world according to Genesis, but it was no Cox's Orange Pippin. God gave the crab apple and left the rest to man.
> Jane Grigson *Jane Grigson's Fruit Book*

ARCHBISHOP

4 A great-aunt of mine looked up from the correspondence columns of your paper and enquired, 'Who is this tiresome man Cantuar who is always interfering in religious matters?'
> Arthur Harrison Letter to *The Times* 23 February 1987

5 It is the unhappy lot of the Archbishop to have immense responsibility with very little power.
> Cosmo Gordon Lang, Archbishop of Canterbury Quoted
> D.R. Matthews *Daily Telegraph* 11 November 1971

6 Lord, I am coming as fast as I can.
> William Laud, Archbishop of Canterbury Last words from
> the scaffold

7 Archbishop: A Christian ecclesiastic of a rank superior to that attained by Christ.
> H.L. Mencken

8 The Archbishop of Canterbury, on a visit to Nigeria, was greeted by children waving balloons printed with his picture. As he approached the children were exhorted, 'Help the Anglican Communion: blow up the Archbishop of Canterbury.'
> Quoted *The Times* 'Diary' 21 January 1987

ARCHDEACON

9 It was, I believe, the famous wit Sydney Smith who defined an archdeacon as 'one who performs archidiaconal functions.'
> Rt Revd E.C. Bidwell *Evening News* 20 December 1938

1 My late husband, while Archdeacon of Canterbury, received a
letter addressed to 'The Vulnerable Bernard Pawley'. His
characteristic comment was 'How did they know?'
  Margaret Pawley Letter to *The Times* 3 March 1987

ARGUMENT

2 If any man have a quarrel against any: even as Christ forgave
you, so also do ye.
  Holy Bible Colossians Chap. 3 v. 13

3 Myself when young did eagerly frequent
Doctor and Saint, and heard great argument
About it and about: but evermore
Came out by the same door as in I went.
  Omar Khayyam *Rubaiyat* Trans. Edward Fitzgerald

ARMOUR

4 Put on the whole armour of God, that ye may be able to stand
against the wiles of the devil.
  Holy Bible Ephesians Chap. 6 v. 11

ART

5 Paintings are the Bible of the laity.
  Gratian *Decretum*

6 Religion is always a patron of the arts, but its taste is by no
means impeccable.
  Aldous Huxley *Tomorrow and Tomorrow and Tomorrow*

7 Artists in a way are religious anyhow. They have to be, if by
religion one means believing that life has some significance,
and some meaning, which is what I think it has. An artist
couldn't work without believing that.
  Henry Moore

8 Not everything has a name. Some things lead us into the realm
beyond words. Art thaws even the frozen, darkened soul,
opening it to lofty spiritual experience. Through Art we are
sometimes sent — indistinctly, briefly — revelations not to be
achieved by rational thought.
  Alexander Solzhenitsyn *One Word of Truth*

9 Because man is made in the image and likeness of God, there
is something divine about the act of painting an icon.
  St Theodore the Studite *Antirrheticus*

ASCENSION

1 The golden gates are lifted up,
  The doors are opened wide;
  The King of Glory is gone in
  Unto His Father's side.
  > Cecil Francis Alexander 'Lift Up Your Hearts'

2 As sign and wonder this exaltation is a pointer to the
  revelation that occurred in His resurrection, of Jesus Christ as
  the heart of all powers in heaven and earth.
  > Karl Barth *Credo*

3 The Ascension is a festival of the future of the world. The
  flesh is redeemed and glorified, for the Lord has risen for ever.
  We Christians are, therefore, the most sublime materialists.
  > Karl Rahner

4 The ascension of Christ is his liberation from all restrictions of
  time and space. It does not represent his removal from the
  earth, but his constant presence everywhere on earth.
  > Archbishop William Temple *Fellowship with God*

5 Hail the day that sees Him rise
  To His throne above the skies;
  Christ, a while to mortals given,
  Reascends His native Heaven.
  > Charles Wesley 'Ascension'

ASPIRATION

6 O Lord, I, a beggar, ask of Thee more than a thousand kings
  may ask of Thee. Each one has something he needs to ask of
  Thee; I have come to ask Thee to give me Thyself.
  > Al-Ansari Sufi spirituality

7 What you are must always displease you, if you would attain
  that which you are not.
  > St Augustine of Hippo *Sermons*

8 I am nothing, I have nothing, I desire nothing but the love of
  Jesus in Jerusalem.
  > Walter Hilton *Ladder of Perfection*

9 Set your affection on things above, not on things on the earth.
  > *Holy Bible* Colossians Chap. 3 v. 2

1 You never enjoy the world aright till the sea itself floweth in your veins, till you are clothed with the heavens and crowned with the stars.
   Thomas Traherne *Centuries of Meditations*

ASTRONOMY

2 Astronomy compels the soul to look upwards and leads us from this world to another.
   Plato *Dialogues*

3 An undevout astronomer is mad.
   Edward Young *Night Thoughts*

ATHANASIAN CREED

4 The Athanasian Creed is the most splendid ecclesiastical lyric ever poured forth by the genius of man.
   Benjamin Disraeli *Endymion*

ATHEISM

5 Man without God risks his life for impure causes and cannot avoid doing so. Atheist-humanism can define itself only by accepting the limits of human existence.
   Raymond Aron *Selected Essays*

6 I had rather believe all the fables in the legends and the Talmud and the Al-coran, than that this universal frame is without a mind.

7 They that deny a God destroy man's nobility; for certainly man is of kin to the beasts by his body; and if he be not of kin to God by his spirit, he is a base and ignoble creature.
   Francis Bacon *Essays* 'Of Atheism'

8 I am an atheist still, thank God.
   Luis Buñuel Quoted Ado Kyron *Luis Buñuel, an Introduction*

9 The writers against religion, whilst they oppose every other system, are wisely careful never to set up any of their own.
   Edmund Burke *A Vindication of Natural Society* Preface

10 Theist and Atheist — the fight between them is as to whether God shall be called God or have some other name.
   Samuel Butler *Note Books* 'Rebelliousness'

1 The man who regards his own life and that of his fellow
creatures as meaningless is not merely unfortunate, but almost
disqualified from life.
   Albert Einstein *The World as I See It* 'The Meaning of Life'

2 If there are no gods all our toil is without meaning.
   Euripides *Iphigenia in Aulis*

3 An atheist is a man with no invisible means of support.
   Henry Emerson Fosdick

4 Anti-clericalism and non-belief have their bigots just as
orthodoxy does.
   Julian Green *Journal*

5 The devil divides the world between atheism and superstition.
   George Herbert *Jacula Prudentum*

6 The fool hath said in his heart, There is no God.
   Holy Bible Psalm 14 v. 1

7 He hath denied the faith, and is worse than an infidel.
   Holy Bible 1 Timothy Chap. 5 v. 8

8 There seems to be a terrible misunderstanding on the part of a
great many people to the effect that when you cease to believe
you may cease to behave.
   Louis Kronenberger *Company Manners*

9 It is a public crime to act as if there is no God.
   Pope Leo XIII Encyclical *Immortalis Dei*

10 God is not dumb, that He should speak no more;
If thou hast wanderings in the wilderness
And find'st not Sinai, 'tis thy soul is poor.
   James Russell Lowell 'Bibliolatries'

11 There is no strength in unbelief. Even the unbelief of what is
false is no source of might. It is the truth shining from behind
that gives the strength to disbelieve.
   George MacDonald *The Marquis of Lossie*

12 The first requisite for the happiness of the people is the
abolition of religion.
   Karl Marx *A Criticism of the Hegelian Philosophy of Right*

13 The wildest scorner of his Maker's laws
Finds in a sober moment time to pause.
   William Cowper 'Tirocinium'

1 There are few so confirmed in Atheism, that a pressing danger or the neighbourhood of death will not force to a recognition of the divine power.
   Montaigne *Essays*

2 The sort of atheist who does not so much disbelieve in God as personally dislike him.
   George Orwell *Down and Out in Paris and London*

3 No one of them who took up in his youth with his opinion that there are no gods ever continued to old age faithful to his convictions.
   Plato *Dialogues*

4 Atheists put on a false courage and alacrity in the midst of their darkness and apprehensions, like children who, when they fear to go in to the dark, will sing with fear.
   Alexander Pope *Thoughts on Various Subjects*

5 God can stand being told by Professor Ayer and Marghanita Laski that he doesn't exist.
   J.B. Priestley *The BBC's Duty to Society*

6 The highest praise of God consists in the denial of Him by the atheist, who finds creation so perfect that he can dispense with a creator.
   Marcel Proust *Remembrance of Things Past*

7 I was told that the Chinese would bury me by the Western Lake and build a shrine to my memory. I have a slight regret that this did not happen as I might have become a god, which would have been very *chic* for an atheist.
   Bertrand Russell *Autobiography*

8 The existence of a world without a God seems to me less absurd than the presence of a God, existing in all his perfections, creating an imperfect man in order to make him run the risk of hell.
   Armand Salacrou *Theatre*

9 God's trustiest lieutenants often lack official credentials. They may be professed atheists who are also men of honour and high public spirit.
   George Bernard Shaw *Back to Methuselah* Preface

10 Atheism shows strength of mind, but only to a certain degree.
   Blaise Pascal

1   We are not to be guilty of that practical atheism, which, seeing
    no guidance for human affairs but its own limited foresight,
    endeavours itself to play the God, and decide what will be
    good for mankind and what bad.
        Herbert Spencer *Social Statics*

2   It's an interesting view of atheism, as a sort of crutch for those
    who can't stand the reality of God.
        Tom Stoppard *Jumpers*

3   The atheist who is moved by love is moved by the spirit of
    God; an atheist who lives by love is saved by his faith in the
    God whose existence (under that name) he denies.
        Archbishop William Temple

4   When the atheist is confronted with one of the natural
    outrages against the dignity and decency of life he is tempted
    to act for the moment as if God existed simply in order to have
    something on which to unloose his outraged feelings.
        Philip Toynbee *Observer* 'Death of a Mother' 17 April 1966

5   The worst moment for an atheist is when he feels grateful and
    doesn't know who to thank.
        Wendy Ward *Quote Unquote* Attributed by P. & J. Holton

6   Selfishness is the only real atheism.
        Israel Zangwill

ATOMIC ENERGY

7   If there had been no cliff the Gadarene Swine would have had
    nowhere to hurl themselves. The bomb constitutes a cliff, and
    we should be duly grateful for it.
        Malcolm Muggeridge *Sunday Times* 1 August 1965

8   There is no evil in the atom — only in men's souls.
        Adlai Stevenson Speech at Harvard 18 September 1952

9   The use of atomic energy proves that the road to Hell is paved
    with good inventors.
        Arthur White *Saturday Evening Post* 4 December 1948

ATONEMENT

10 Most men are led by interest; and the few
    Who are not, expiate the general sin,
    Involved in one suspicion with the base.
        Matthew Arnold *Merope*

1   Why should his unstain'd breast make good
    My blushes with his own heart-blood?
    O, my Saviour, make me see
    How dearly thou hast paid for me,
    That lost again my life may prove
    As then in death, so now in love.
        Richard Crashaw 'The Dear Bargain'

2   Jesus alone can make atonement because he is the
    atonement — the at-onement of God and man.
        Gonville ffrench-Beytagh *A Glimpse of Glory*

3   Behold the Lamb of God, which taketh away the sin of the
    world.
        Holy Bible St John Chap. 1 v. 29

4   The blood of Jesus Christ his Son cleanseth us from all sin.
        Holy Bible 1 John Chap. 1 v. 7

ATTENTION

5   The authentic and pure values — truth, beauty and
    goodness — in the activity of a human being are the result
    of one and the same act, a certain application of the full
    attention to the object.
        Simone Weil *Gravity and Grace*

AUTHORITY

6   For he taught them as one having authority, and not as the
    scribes.
        Holy Bible St Matthew Chap. 7 v. 29

7   I am a man under authority, having soldiers under me: and I
    say to this man, Go, and he goeth; and to another, Come, and
    he cometh.
        Holy Bible St Matthew Chap. 8 v. 9

8   With authority commandeth he even the unclean spirits, and
    they do obey him.
        Holy Bible St Mark Chap. 1 v. 27

AVARICE

9   Nobody can fight properly and boldly for the faith if he clings
    to a fear of being stripped of earthly possessions.
        St Peter Damian 'Sermon 13 on St George of England'

1 Extreme avarice misapprehends itself almost always; there is no passion which more often misses its aim, nor upon which the present has so much influence to the prejudice of the future.

   François, Duc de la Rochefoucauld *Maxims*

2 Avarice is a cursed vice: offer a man enough gold, and he will part with his own small hoard of food, however great his hunger.

   Lucan *On the Civil War*

3 Avarice is as destitute of what it has, as poverty of what it has not.

   Publilius Syrus *Moral Sayings*

AWE

4 Stand in awe, and sin not: commune with your own heart, and in your chamber, and be still.

   Book of Common Prayer Psalm 4 v. 4

5 The highest point a man can attain is not knowledge, or Virtue, or Goodness, or Victory, but something even greater, more heroic and more despairing: Sacred Awe!

   Nikos Kazantzakis *Zorba the Greek*

B

BAPTISM

1 Would an enquiry by experimental psychology show a higher standard of conduct on the part of those 'regenerated from original sin' than appears in others not subjected to baptism?

Ernest William Barnes, Bishop of Birmingham *The Rise of Christianity*

2 To be baptised is to be born according to Christ; it is to receive existence, to come into being out of nothing.

Nicolas Cabasilas *Life in Christ*

3 He [the devil] does not dare look at you directly because he sees the light blazing from your head and blinding his eyes.

St John Chrysostom Baptismal Homily

4 I wasn't christened in a church, but I was sprinkled from morning to night with the dew of grace.

Rufus Jones Quoted Mark Gibbard *Guides to Hidden Springs*

5 Do work-to-rulers realise that if the clergy followed their example babies would never be returned to their parents after baptism. There is no rubric so directing.

Peterborough *Daily Telegraph* 8 February 1962

BAPTIST

6 'You're a Christian?'

'Church of England,' said Mr Polly.

'H'm,' said the employer, a little checked. 'For good all round business work I should have preferred a Baptist.'

H.G. Wells *The History of Mr Polly*

BEATITUDE

7 To breathe is a beatitude.

H.F. Amiel *Journals*

1   The character which we find in the Beatitudes is, beyond
    all question, nothing less than our Lord's own character,
    put into words. It is the description set side by side with
    an example.
    Billy Graham *The Secret of Happiness* Preface to
    Revised Edition

2   What the Beatitudes say is that the poor, not the rich, are
    blessed; that the meek, not the strong, inherit the earth; that
    the merciful obtain mercy, the pure in heart see God and
    Heaven belongs to those who are persecuted for righteousness'
    sake.
    Malcolm Muggeridge *Jesus — The Man Who Lives*

BEAUTY

3   The first Puritans had a forbidding sort of holiness, and some
    of them had a great regard for the truth, but what about
    beauty? The empty niches, the ancient glass and beautiful
    buildings that they destroyed, all cry out against them.
    Fr Andrew SDC *Meditations for Every Day*

4   Beauty is one of the rare things that do not lead to doubt of
    God.
    Jean Anouilh *Becket*

5   Beauty, real beauty, is something very grave. If there is a
    God, He must be partly that.
    Jean Anouilh *The Rehearsal*

6   Beauty is the gift of God.
    Aristotle

7   I know a man who, when he saw a woman of striking beauty,
    praised the Creator for her. The sight of her lit within him the
    love of God.
    St John Climacus Quoted *The New Christian Year*

8   When you reach the heart of life you shall find beauty in all
    things, even in the eyes that are blind to beauty.
    Kahlil Gibran *Sand and Foam*

9   There is a daily round for beauty as well as for goodness.
    Caroline C. Graveson *The Art of Living*

10 Beauty is a fading flower.
    Holy Bible Isaiah Chap. 28 v. 1

1 God passes through the thicket of the world, and wherever his glance falls he turns all things to beauty.
   St John of the Cross *The Spiritual Canticle*

2 The human soul needs actual beauty more than bread.
   D.H. Lawrence *Selected Essays*

BEGINNING

3 In my beginning is my end.
   T.S. Eliot 'East Coker'

4 Better is the end of a thing than the beginning thereof.
   Holy Bible Ecclesiastes Chap. 7 v. 8

5 A journey of a thousand miles must begin with a single step.
   Lao-Tze *The Way of Lao-Tze*

6 In the beginning
   There was no death then, nor yet deathlessness.
   Of night or day, there was not any sign.
   The One breathed without breath, by its own impulse.
   Other than that there was nothing else at all.
   Rig-Veda Indian spirituality

BEHAVIOUR

7 You will rest from vain fancies if you perform every act in life as though it were your last.
   Marcus Aurelius *Meditations*

8 If a man be gracious and courteous to strangers, it shews he is a citizen of the world, and that his heart is no island cut off from other lands, but a continent that joins them.
   Francis Bacon

9 One must not always think so much about what one should do, but rather what one should be. Our works do not ennoble us; but we must ennoble our works.
   Meister Eckhart *Work and Being*

10 A man's ethical behaviour should be based effectually on sympathy, education and social ties and needs; no religious basis is necessary. Man would indeed be in a poor way if he had to be restrained by fear of punishment and hope of reward after death.
   Albert Einstein *New York Times Magazine* 'Religion and Science' 9 November 1930

1   Perhaps the straight and narrow path would be wider if more
    people used it.
    Kay Ingram *Saturday Evening Post* 23 December 1950

2   A man of religion should treat all beings as he himself would
    be treated.
    Jain spirituality

3   What is hateful to you, do not to your fellow men. That is the
    entire Law; all the rest is commentary.
    Jewish spirituality

4   It is not that doing is unimportant. It is rather that right doing
    springs from right being.
    Robert Llewelyn *A Doorway to Silence*

5   To have a respect for ourselves guides our morals; and to have
    a deference for others governs our manners.
    Laurence Sterne

6   Right intention is to the actions of a man what the soul is to
    the body, or the root to the tree.
    Jeremy Taylor

7   Our least deed, like the young of the land crab, wends its way
    to the sea of cause and effect as soon as born and makes a
    drop there to eternity.
    Henry David Thoreau *Journal*

8   We spend most of our lives conjugating three verbs: to want,
    to have and to do. But none of these verbs has any ultimate
    significance until it is transcended by and included in the
    fundamental verb — to be.
    Evelyn Underhill

9   Do all the good you can
    By all the means you can
    In all the ways you can
    In all the places you can
    To all the people you can
    As long as ever you can.
    John Wesley Rule of Conduct

10 That nature only is good when it shall not do to another
    whatever is not good for its own self.
    Zoroastrian spirituality

BELIEF

1 A belief is not true because it is useful.
    H.F. Amiel *Journal*

2 All things are possible to one who believes.
    St Bernard of Clairvaux

3 When you want to believe in something you also have to
    believe in everything that's necessary for believing in it.
    Ugo Betti *Struggle Till Dawn*

4 He's a Blockhead who wants a proof of what he can't
    Percieve,
    And he's a Fool who tries to make such a Blockhead believe.
    William Blake 'To Flaxman'

5 To believe only possibilities is not faith, but mere philosophy.
    Sir Thomas Browne *Religio Medici*

6 If people stop believing in religion they don't then believe in
    nothing, they believe in everything.
    G.K. Chesterton Quoted Katherine Whitehorn *Observer*
    16 September 1979

7 There is nothing that can help you understand your beliefs
    more than trying to explain them to an inquisitor.
    Frank Clark *Reader's Digest* July 1978

8 If every gnat that flies were an archangel, all that could but tell
    me is that there is a God, and the poorest worm that creeps
    tells me that.
    John Donne *Sermons* No. 57

9 The majority of people live below the level of belief or doubt.
    It takes application and a kind of genius to believe anything.
    T.S. Eliot *The Enemy*

10 A man must not swallow more beliefs than he can digest.
    Havelock Ellis *The Dance of Life*

11 A believer . . . is never disturbed because other persons do not
    see the fact which he sees.
    Ralph Waldo Emerson *Journals*

12 Belief consists in accepting the affirmations of the soul;
    unbelief in denying them.
    Ralph Waldo Emerson *Representative Men* 'Montaigne'

1 The care of God for us is a great thing; if a man believe it at heart, it plucks the burden of sorrow from him.
  Euripides *Hippolytus*

2 Each believes easily what he fears and what he desires.
  Jean de la Fontaine *Fables* 'The Wolf and The Fox'

3 He does not believe that does not love according to his beliefs.
  Thomas Fuller *Gnomologia*

4 A little credulity helps one on through life very smoothly.
  Mrs Gaskell

5 Mass movements can arise without belief in a God, but not without belief in a devil.
  Eric Hoffer *The Time Believer*

6 Jesus said unto him, If thou canst believe, all things are possible to him that believeth.
  Holy Bible St Mark Chap. 9 v. 23

7 I am the resurrection, and the life: he that believeth in me, though he were dead, yet shall he live.
  Holy Bible St John Chap. 11 v. 25

8 Jesus saith unto him, Thomas, because thou hast seen me, thou hast believed: blessed are they that have not seen, and yet have believed.
  Holy Bible St John Chap. 20 v. 29

9 No one of you is a believer until he desires for his brother that which he desires for himself.
  Islamic spirituality

10 Believe that life is worth living, and your belief will help create the fact.
  William James *The Will to Believe*

11 My dear child, you must believe in God in spite of what the clergy tell you.
  Dr Jowett to Margot Asquith Quoted in her *Autobiography*

12 May we not worry but believe in thee, our great Parent.
  Bunjiro Kawate Shintoism

13 Faith means just that blessed unrest, deep and strong, which so urges the believer onward that he cannot settle at ease in the world and anyone who was quite at ease would cease to be a believer.
  Søren Kierkegaard *Gospel of Suffering*

1 When you go to heaven you have to say sorry to the holy gost for not believing in him. I don't believe in gosts so I'm not goin there.
> Kim, aged 7 Quoted Nanette Newman *Lots of Love*

2 The constant assertion of belief is an indication of fear.
> Krishnamurti *The Penguin Khrishnamurti Reader*

3 I certainly think that belief in God did give shaping and pattern to life for which I can see no conceivable substitute and to that extent my life is poorer than that of a believer.
> Marghanita Laski

4 The believer may well have less use for books on religion than the unbeliever — for how can a man honestly disbelieve unless he has done himself the justice of discovering in what it is he does not believe?
> Lionel McColver *The Personal Library*

5 If you don't believe in God, all you have to believe in is decency. Decency is very good. Better decent than indecent. But I don't think it's enough.
> Harold Macmillan Quoted Alistair Horne *Sunday Times* 4 January 1987

6 It is easier to believe than to doubt.
> E.D. Martin *The Meaning of a Liberal Education*

7 The world goes on because a few men in each generation believe in it utterly, accept it unquestioningly; they underwrite it with their lives.
> Henry Miller *The Air-Conditioned Nightmare*

8 What distinguishes the majority of men from the few is their inability to act according to their beliefs.
> Henry Miller *The Cosmological Eye*

9 Nothing is so firmly believed as what we least know.
> Montaigne

10 You're not free
until you've been made captive by/supreme belief.
> Marianne Moore 'Spenser's Ireland'

11 I believe in one God and no more, and I hope for happiness beyond this life. I believe in the equality of man; and I believe that religious duties consist in doing justice, loving mercy and in endeavouring to make our fellow creatures happy.
> Thomas Paine *The Age of Reason*

1   It is your own assent to yourself, and the constant voice of
    your own reason, and not of others, that should make you
    believe.
       Blaise Pascal *Pensées*

2   Man makes holy what he believes as he makes beautiful what
    he loves.
       Ernest Renan *Studies in Religious History*

3   We are incredibly heedless in the formation of our beliefs, but
    find ourselves filled with an illicit passion for them when
    anyone proposes to rob us of their companionship.
       James Harvey Robinson *The Mind in the Making*

4   In view of the widespread silliness of the majority of mankind
    a widespread belief is more likely to be foolish than sensible.
       Bertrand Russell *Marriage and Morals*

5   Man is a credulous animal and must believe something. In the
    absence of good grounds for belief, he will be satisfied with
    bad ones.
       Bertrand Russell *Unpopular Essays*

6   We ought to struggle earnestly to increase our beliefs. Every
    addition to them is an extension of life, both in breadth and
    depth.
       Mark Rutherford *Last Pages from a Journal*

7   The brute necessity of believing something so long as life lasts
    does not justify any belief in particular.
       George Santayana *Scepticism and Animal Faith*

8   It is not disbelief that is dangerous to our society, it is belief.
       George Bernard Shaw *Androcles and the Lion*

9   I believe in the reality of God as the centre of human
    aspiration and history. What I believe about man, made in the
    image of God, derives first and foremost from what I believe
    about God.
       David Sheppard *Bias to the Poor*

10 Dame Edith Sitwell when asked why she had come to faith
    said she had looked at the pattern of a frosted flower on a
    window-pane, she had studied shells, feathers, petals and
    grasses; and she knew without a doubt there must be a cause
    ... 'I have come to believe that the cause is God.'
       Dame Edith Sitwell Quoted *Christian Poetry*

1 Few really believe. The most only believe that they believe, or even make believe.

> John Lancaster Spalding *Thoughts and Theories of Life and Education*

2 Florence Nightingale's conception of God was certainly not orthodox. She felt towards Him as she might have felt towards a glorified sanitary engineer; and in some of her speculations she seems hardly to distinguish between the Deity and the Drains.

> Lytton Strachey *Eminent Victorians*

3 By and large gentlemen believe in God because, by and large, they are confident God believes in them.

> Douglas Sutherland *The English Gentleman*

4 We have only to believe. And the more threatening and irreducible reality appears, the more firmly and desperately must we believe. Then, little by little, we shall see the universal horror unbend, and then smile upon us, and then take us in its more than human arms.

> Pierre Teilhard de Chardin *The Divine Milieu*

5 I believe in the Church, one Holy Catholic and Apostolic Church; and nowhere does it exist.

> Archbishop William Temple

6 While men believe in the infinite, some ponds will be thought to be bottomless.

> Henry David Thoreau

7 To believe in God is to yearn for his existence and furthermore, it is to act as if he did exist.

> Miguel de Unamuno *The Tragic Sense of Life*

8 People are going mad and talking balls to psychiatrists, not because of accidents to the chamber-pot in the nursery, but because there is no logical structure to their beliefs.

> Evelyn Waugh Letter to John Betjeman 22 December 1946

9 The Christian believes that he was created to know, love, and serve God in this world and to be happy with Him in the next. That is the sole reason for his existence.

> Evelyn Waugh *Month* November 1949

10 What ardently we wish we soon believe.

> Edward Young *Night Thoughts*

BELLS

1   The Bell calls others to Church, but itself never minds the
sermon.
    Benjamin Franklin *Poor Richard*

2   Bells call others, but themselves enter not into Church.
    George Herbert *Jacula Prudentum*

3   The bells they sound on Bredon,
    And still the steeples hum.
    'Come all to church good people,' —
    Oh, noisy bells be dumb;
    I hear you, I will come.
       A.E. Housman *A Shropshire Lad*

4   Bells, the music bordering nearest heaven.
    Charles Lamb *Essays of Elia* 'New Year's Eve'

5   Bell! thou soundest merrily,
    When the bridal party
    To the church doth hie!
    Bell! thou soundest solemnly,
    When on Sabbath morning
    Fields deserted lie.
       Henry Wadsworth Longfellow 'Song of the Bell'

6   For bells are the voice of the Church;
    They have tones that touch and search
    The hearts of young and old.
       Henry Wadsworth Longfellow 'The Bells of San Blas'

7   What passing bells for those who die as cattle?
    Only the monstrous anger of the guns.
       Wilfred Owen *War Poems*

8   And now the chapel's silver bell you hear,
    That summons you to all the pride of prayer:
    Light quirks of music, broken and uneven,
    Make the soul dance upon a jig to Heaven.
       Alexander Pope *Moral Essays*

BEREAVEMENT

9   Him who is dead and gone honour with remembrance, not
with tears.
    St John Chrysostom *Commentaries*

1 The buried are not lost, but gone before.
    Ebenezer Elliott *The Excursion*

2 It was sea and islands now. Atlantis had sunk.
    C.S. Lewis, on the death of his mother *Surprised by Joy*

3 Passionate grief does not link us with the dead, but cuts us off
    from them.
    C.S. Lewis *A Grief Observed*

4 Moderate lamentation is the right of the dead; excessive grief
    the enemy to the living.
    William Shakespeare *All's Well That Ends Well* Act I Sc. 1

5 Ah Christ, that it were possible
    For one short hour to see
    The souls we loved, that they might tell us
    What and where they be.
    Alfred, Lord Tennyson *Maud*

BETRAYAL

6 All a man can betray is his conscience.
    Joseph Conrad *Under Western Eyes*

BIBLE

7 Thousands have gone to heaven who have never read one
    page of the Bible.
    Francis A. Baker *Sermons*

8 I was reading the Bible in many different languages, and I saw
    that it cannot really be translated, the real meaning cannot be
    given in another language. It is only in Hebrew that you feel
    the full meaning of it — all the associations which a different
    word has.
    David Ben-Gurion Quoted James Nelson *Wisdom*

9 God is the celebrity. Author of the World's Best Seller. We
    have made God into the biggest celebrity of all, to contain our
    own emptiness.

10 Our highest praise is to call the Bible 'The World's Best Seller'
    and it has become more and more difficult to say whether it
    has become a best seller because it is great, or vice versa.
    Daniel J. Boorstein *The Image*

1   I have sometimes seen more in a line of the Bible than I could
    well tell how to stand under, yet at another time the whole
    Bible hath been to me as dry as a stick.
    John Bunyan *Grace Abounding to the Chief of Sinners*

2   The Bible is like the poor; we have it always with us, but we
    know very little about it.
    Samuel Butler *Notebooks*

3   In the poorest cottage are Books; is one Book wherein for
    several thousands of years the spirit of man has found light,
    and nourishment and an interpreting response to whatever is
    deepest in him.
    Thomas Carlyle *Essays* 'Corn-Law Rhymes'

4   What built St Paul's Cathedral? Look at the heart of the
    matter, it was that divine Hebrew Book — the word partly of
    the man, Moses, an outlaw tending his Midianitish herds, four
    thousand years ago, in the wilderness of Sinai! It is the
    strangest of things, yet nothing is truer.
    Thomas Carlyle *Heroes and Hero Worship* 'The Hero as Man
    of Letters'

5   The New Testament is the Thesaurus of sacred wisdom
    compared to which there is no book or monument that
    deserves to be named.
    John Jay Chapman *Memoirs and Milestones*

6   I have found in the Bible words for my inmost thoughts, songs
    for my joy, utterance for my hidden griefs and pleadings for
    my shame and feebleness.
    Samuel Taylor Coleridge Quoted Mary Hodgkin *A Diary
    for the Thankful-Hearted*

7   A glory gilds the sacred page,
    Majestic like the sun;
    It gives a light to every age,
    It gives, but borrows none.
    William Cowper *Olney Hymns*

8   Then for the style, majestic and divine,
    It speaks no less than God in every line.
    John Dryden *Religio Laici*

9   Those who talk of the Bible as a 'monument of English prose'
    are merely admiring it as a monument over the grave of
    Christianity.
    T.S. Eliot *Religion and Literature*

1   Had the Bible been in clear straightforward language, had the
ambiguities and contradictions been edited out, and had the
language been constantly modernised to accord with
contemporary taste it would almost certainly have been, or
become, a work of lesser influence.
    John Kenneth Galbraith *Economics, Peace and Laughter*

2   It is a plain old book, modest as nature itself, and as simple,
too; a book of an unpretending workaday appearance, like the
sun that warms or the bread that nourishes us. And the name
of this book is simply — the Bible.
    Heinrich Heine *Scintillations*

3   The Holy Bible is an abyss. It is impossible to explain how
profound it is, impossible to explain how simple it is.
    Ernest Hello *Life, Science and Art*

4   It was a common saying among the Puritans 'Brown bread and
the Gospel is good fare.'
    Matthew Henry *Commentaries* 'Isaiah'

5   Shallows where a lamb could wade and depths where an
elephant could drown.
    Matthew Henry *Commentaries* 'Solomon's Song'

6   They sewed fig leaves together, and made themselves
breeches.
    Holy Bible Genesis Chap. 3 v. 7 From the English Bible,
    Geneva 1560, known as the Breeches Bible

7   The existence of the Bible is the greatest blessing which
humanity has ever experienced.
    Immanuel Kant

8   There is a book, who runs may read,
    Which heavenly truth imparts;
    And all the love its scholars need,
    Pure eyes and Christian hearts.
    John Keble *The Christian Year*

9   When you read God's word, you must constantly be saying to
yourself, 'It is talking to me, and about me.'
    Søren Kierkegaard *For Self Examination*

10 A man may learn from his Bible to be a more thorough
gentleman than if he had been brought up in all the drawing
rooms in London.
    Charles Kingsley *The Water Babies*

1 The English Bible, a book which if everything else in our language should perish, would alone suffice to show the whole extent of its beauty and power.
   Thomas Babington Macaulay *Essays* 'On Dryden'

2 The books of the Bible were written over a long period of time. It took God longer to write the Bible than it has taken him to build the British Empire.
   William C. MacDonald *Modern Evangelism*

3 The Old Testament is tribal in its provinciality; its god is a local god, and its village police and sanitary regulations are erected into eternal laws.
   John Macy *The Spirit of American Literature*

4 The number one book of the ages was written by a committee, and it was called the Bible.
   Louis B. Mayer

5 What is home without a Bible?
   'Tis a home where daily bread
   For the body is provided
   But the soul is never fed.
   C.D. Meigs 'Home Without a Bible'

6 By the reading of Scripture I am so renewed that all nature seems renewed around me and with me.
   Thomas Merton *The Sign of Jonas*

7 You can learn more about human nature by reading the Bible than by living in New York.
   William Lyon Phelps Quoted *New York Times* 19 October 1953

8 Within that awful volume lies
   The Mystery of Mysteries!
   Happiest they of human race,
   To whom God has granted grace
   To read, to fear, to hope, to pray,
   To lift the latch and force the way;
   And better had they ne'er been born,
   Who read to doubt, or read to scorn.
   Sir Walter Scott *The Monastery*

9 Dear Lord, this Book of thine
   Informs me where to go,
   For grace to pardon all my sin,
   And makes me holy, too.

1   How glad the heathens would have been,
    That worship idols wood and stone,
    If they the book of God had seen,
    Of Jesus and his gospel known.

2   The stars that in their courses roll
    Have much instruction given;
    But thy good Word informs my soul
    How I may climb to heaven.
           Isaac Watts *Hymns and Spiritual Songs*

BIGOTRY

3   The man who never alters his opinion is like standing water,
    and breeds reptiles of the mind.
           William Blake *The Marriage of Heaven and Hell*

4   Bigotry may be roughly defined as the anger of men who have
    no opinions.
           G.K. Chesterton *Heretics*

5   Religion is as effectively destroyed by bigotry as by
    indifference.
           Ralph Waldo Emerson *Journal*

6   How it infuriates a bigot when he is forced to drag into the
    light his dark convictions.
           Logan Pearsall Smith *All Trivia* 'Afterthoughts'

7   Bigotry tries to keep truth safe in its hand with the grip that
    kills it.
           Rabindranath Tagore *Fireflies*

BIRTH

8   We brought nothing into this world and it is certain we can
    carry nothing out.
           Holy Bible 1 Timothy Chap. 6 v. 7

9   By God's birth
    All common birth is holy; birth
    Is all at Christmas time, and wholly blest.
           Anne Ridler 'Christmas and Common Birth'

10   Not in utter nakedness,
    But trailing clouds of glory do we come
    From God, who is our home.
           William Wordsworth 'Ode on Intimations of Immortality'

BISHOP

1   *With* you I am a Christian, and *for* you I am a bishop.
    St Augustine of Hippo Quoted Carlo Carretto *Summoned by Love*

2   An editor of *Crockford's* once deplored the practice, then new, of bishops making crosses against their signature. I seem to recall that his comment was 'Noughts would be more appropriate.'
    John Biggs-Davison MP Letter to *The Times* 25 February 1987

3   'People get nervous when they think they have to call me "my Lord",' said an Irish bishop. 'Especially the poor nuns. One was giving me a cup of coffee. As she pushed the sugar bowl towards me she said, "How many lords my lump?"'
    Kevin Buckley *Reader's Digest* June 1982

4   The popularity of George Whitefield was such that the Privy Council debated whether steps should be taken to prevent his vast evangelical rallies. Lord Chesterfield suggested, 'Make him a bishop, then you will silence him at once.'
    Edmund Fuller *Anecdotes*

5   He had been a bishop so long that no one knew now what he thought about death, or indeed about anything except the Prayer Book, any change in which he deprecated with determination.
    John Galsworthy *Maid in Waiting*

6   The greatest mistake the bishops make is in thinking they are the Church. The Church is the laity.
    Lord Hailsham Quoted Susan Barnes *Behind the Image*

7   The Bishop of London reported to the General Synod that before attending a church function recently he said he would bring his pastoral staff. 'And how many seats will you want?' came the reply.
    Peterborough *Daily Telegraph*

8   How can a bishop marry? How can he flirt? The most he can say is 'I will see you in the vestry after the service.'

9   The most solemn and terrible duty of a bishop is the entertainment of the clergy.
    Sydney Smith Quoted Hesketh Pearson *The Smith of Smiths*

1   The Sandringham gamekeeper who had taken Bishop Herbert of Norwich out shooting said of him, 'He was just like any other gentleman, except that when he missed he said "Bother".'
    Colin Stephenson *Merrily on High*

2   A bishop keeps on saying at eighty what he was told to say when he was a boy of eighteen.
    Oscar Wilde

BITTERNESS

3   If you are bitter at heart, sugar in the mouth will not help you.
    Jewish proverb

BLAME

4   A reproof entereth more into a wise man than an hundred stripes into a fool.
    Holy Bible Proverbs Chap. 17 v. 10

BLASPHEMY

5   Watch over yourselves that you may never swear. I invoked God my helper and he afforded me his succour not to swear. Now nothing is more easy to me than not to swear.
    St Augustine of Hippo Quoted *Butler's Lives of the Saints*

6   He that blasphemeth the name of the Lord, he shall surely be put to death.
    Holy Bible Leviticus Chap. 24 v. 16

7   Woe is me! for I am undone; because I am a man of unclean lips, and I dwell in the midst of a people of unclean lips.
    Holy Bible Isaiah Chap. 6 v. 5

8   Should each blasphemer quite escape the rod,
    Because the insult's not to man, but God?
    Alexander Pope

9   All great truths begin as blasphemies.
    George Bernard Shaw *Annajanska*

10 Think'st thou in temporal speech God's Name may uttered be?
    It is unspeakable to all eternity.
    Angelus Silesius *The Spiritual Maxims of Angelus Silesius*

BLESSEDNESS

1   Blessed are those who saw Christ in the flesh. But still more blessed are we who see his image portrayed in the Gospels, and hear his voice speaking from them.

St Tikhon of Zadonsk Quoted N. Gordetzky *Inspirer of Dostoevsky*

BLESSED VIRGIN MARY

2   I saw our Blessed Lady — grounded in Humility she was filled with grace and all virtues, and is thus higher than all other creatures.

Julian of Norwich *Revelations of Divine Love*

3   The poverty of Mary, living out her unseen, humble and quite ordinary existence and sharing life with common humanity in an insignificant little village, is altogether the sign of the grace and glory of the Lord's greatness.

4   To speak of Mary is to speak of the Church. The two are united in one fundamental vocation — maternity.

Max Thurian *Mary, Mother of the Lord*

BLESSING

5   Be the eye of God dwelling with you
The foot of Christ in guidance with you
The shower of the Spirit pouring on you
Richly and generously.

Alexander Carmichael *Carmina Gadelica*

6   Bless the four corners of this little house
And be the lintel blessed;
And bless the hearth, and bless the board
And bless each place of rest.

Arthur Guiterman *House Blessing*

7   The Lord bless thee, and keep thee: the Lord make his face to shine upon thee, and be gracious unto thee: the Lord lift up his countenance upon thee, and give thee peace.

Holy Bible Numbers Chap. 6 vv. 24—26

8   Blessed be he that cometh in the name of the Lord.

Holy Bible Psalm 118 v. 26

1   Myself in constant good health, and in a most handsome and thriving condition, Blessed be Almighty God for it.

      Samuel Pepys *Diary*

2   Grant to them, Lord, eternal rest, and may your perpetual light shine on them as on us. May it shine on them now as the light of faith, and then in eternity, as the light of blessed life.

      Karl Rahner *The Eternal Years*

BLESSINGS

3   They in heaven prize blessings when they have them. They on earth do not prize them when they have them. They in hell prize them but do not have them.

      Thomas Traherne Quoted *The Wisdom of the English Mystics*

BODY

4   The body you receive in the sacrament accomplished its purpose by nailing to a tree. You are to become this body, you are to be nailed ... the nails that hold you are God's commandments.

      Austin Farrer *The Crown of the Year*

BOREDOM

5   It is not surprising that boredom — in human beings so often the mask of fear — is a problem in marriage as it is in prayer.

      Monica Furlong *Christian Uncertainties*

6   Withdraw thy foot from thy neighbour's house; lest he be weary of thee, and so hate thee.

      Holy Bible Proverbs Chap. 25 v. 17

7   Boredom is a vital problem for the moralist since half the sins of mankind are caused by fear of it.

      Bertrand Russell *The Conquest of Happiness*

8   One can be bored until boredom becomes a mystical experience.

      Logan Pearsall Smith *All Trivia* 'Afterthoughts'

BORROWING

9   The borrower is servant to the lender.

      Holy Bible Proverbs Chap. 22 v. 7

BREAD

1 Cast thy bread upon the waters: for thou shalt find it after
  many days.
  Holy Bible Ecclesiastes Chap. 11 v. 1

2 Man shall not live by bread alone, but by every word that
  proceedeth out of the mouth of God.
  Holy Bible St Matthew Chap. 4 v. 4

BROADCASTING

3 A dramatist employed to write stories from the Bible in radio
  form was astonished at the end of a broadcast to hear the
  announcer say, 'Will Cain kill Abel? Tune in at the same time
  tomorrow and find out.'
  Albert R. Perkins *Vogue* Magazine 1943

BROTHERHOOD

4 Chapuys: After all, we are brothers in Christ, you and I.
  More: A characteristic we share with the rest of humanity. You
  live in Cheapside, Signor? To make contact with a brother
  in Christ you have only to open your window and empty a
  chamber pot. There was no need to come to Chelsea.
  Robert Bolt *A Man for All Seasons*

5 Of a truth, men are mystically united; a mysterious bond of
  brotherhood makes all men one.
  Thomas Carlyle *Essays* 'Goethe's Works'

6 That all men should be brothers is the dream of people who
  have no brothers.
  Charles Chincholles *Pensées de Tout le Monde*

7 Yes, you'd know him for a heathen
  If you judged him by the hide,
  But bless you he's my brother,
  For he's just like me inside.
  Robert Freeman 'The Heathen'

8 A low capacity for getting along with those near to us often
  goes hand in hand with a high receptivity to the idea of the
  brotherhood of man.
  Eric Hoffer *The Ordeal of Change*

9 Am I my brother's keeper?
  Holy Bible Genesis Chap. 4 v. 9

1 Behold, how good and how pleasant it is for brethren to dwell together in unity!
  Holy Bible Psalm 133 v. 1

2 Have we not all one father? hath not one God created us?
  Holy Bible Malachi Chap. 2 v. 10

3 Be kindly affectioned one to another with brotherly love.
  Holy Bible Romans Chap. 12 v. 10

4 If a man say, I love God, and hateth his brother, he is a liar: for he that loveth not his brother whom he hath seen, how can he love God whom he hath not seen?
  Holy Bible 1 John Chap. 4 v. 20

5 There is always a type of man who says he loves his fellow man, and expects to make a living out of it.
  Edgar Watson Howe *Ventures in Common Sense*

6 The brotherhood of man is evoked by particular men according to their circumstances. But it seldom extends to all men. In the name of freedom and brotherhood we are prepared to blow up the other half of the world and be blown up in our turn.
  R.D. Laing *The Politics of Experience*

7 The crest and crowning of all good,
  Life's final star, is Brotherhood.
  Edwin Markham 'Brotherhood'

8 There is a destiny which makes us brothers,
  None goes away alone.
  Edwin Markham 'A Creed'

9 Heaven forming each on other to depend,
  A master, or a servant, or a friend,
  Bids each on other for assistance call,
  Till one man's weakness grows the strength of all.
  Alexander Pope *An Essay on Man*

10 We cannot possibly let ourselves get frozen into regarding everyone we do not know as an absolute stranger.
  Albert Schweitzer *Memories of Childhood and Youth*

11 Throw out the life-line across the dark wave,
  There is a brother whom someone must save.
  Edward Smith Ufford 'Throw Out the Lifeline'

BURDEN

1 For my yoke is easy, and my burden is light.
   Holy Bible St Matthew Chap. 11 v. 30

2 Bear ye one another's burdens.
   Holy Bible Galatians Chap. 6 v. 2

3 The burden is equal to the horse's strength.
   The Talmud

BURIAL

4 Earth, receive an honoured guest:
   William Yeats is laid to rest.
   Let the Irish vessel lie
   Emptied of its poetry.
   W.H. Auden 'In Memory of W.B. Yeats'

5 We therefore commit [t]his body to the ground; earth to earth,
   ashes to ashes, dust to dust; in sure and certain hope of the
   resurrection to eternal life, through our Lord, Jesus Christ.
   Book of Common Prayer At the Burial of the Dead

6 The last act is bloody, however fine the rest of the play. They
   throw earth over your head and it is finished for ever.
   Blaire Pascal Quoted A. Krailsheimer *Pascal*

CARING

1 Christianity has taught us to care. Caring is the greatest thing,
caring matters most.
   Friedrich von Hügel *Letters from Baron von Hügel to a Niece*

CATHEDRAL

2 Cathedrals — luxury liners laden with souls
Holding to the east their hulls of stone.
   W.H. Auden *On This Island*

CATHOLICISM

3 As long as Catholicism lasts it will feel the need for reform, for
a more perfect assimilation of its actuality to the ideal which
illumines its path.
   Karl Adam *The Spirit of Catholicism*

4 He was of the faith chiefly in the sense that the church he
currently did not attend was Catholic.
   Kingsley Amis *One Fat Englishman*

5 One Catholick and Apostolick Church.
   Book of Common Prayer Nicene Creed

6 Catholicism, which is as genuinely human as Christ Himself is
human, is the religion for all those who know that the springs
of mirth and holy laughter lie deeper than the sources of the
world's tears.
   Cornelius Clifford *Introibo*

7 True Catholicity is commensurate with the wants of the human
mind, but persons are often to be found who are surprised that
they cannot persuade all men to follow them, and cannot
destroy dissent, by preaching a portion of the Divine system,
instead of the whole of it.
   John Henry, Cardinal Newman *Oxford University Sermons*

1   Woodlice are catholic little creatures because their habitat is
    universal, they are found under various sub-species in pretty
    well every country in the world.
       Martin Thornton *A Joyous Heart*

2   Catholicism is successful in producing rather a fine type of
    woman, but it is not so happy with men. The men have a need
    to shake off something which the Church hangs on them, and
    unless they do, they are ineffective as thinkers.
       Alfred North Whitehead *Dialogues*

CELIBACY

3   If every man gave up women in God's name
    Where in God's name would be the men
    To give up women in a generation's time.
       Christopher Fry *Curtmantle*

4   I could not live after *both* the flesh and the spirit.
       Gandhi

5   Even people who think themselves quite advanced believe that
    only the sexually starved exist on wholesome moral influence.
       Bertrand Russell Letter to A.S. Neill 31 January 1931

CEMETERY

6   A cemetery saddens us because it is the only place in the world
    in which we do not have to meet our dead again.
       François Mauriac *Cain, Where is Your Brother?* 'All Souls Day'

CHALICE

7   Once we had wooden chalices and golden priests. Now we
    have golden chalices and wooden priests.
       Ralph Waldo Emerson

CHALLENGE

8   It became so clear to me that it must be either obedience to
    the Divine challenge or failure to grow in the spiritual life, that
    all desire for smoking suddenly left me, and from that day to
    this I have never even wanted to take it up again; some greater
    desire had mastered the old habit, it was a desire to know
    God.
       J. Rowntree Gillett *Spiritual Experiences of Friends*

CHANCE

1 A certain man drew a bow at a venture, and smote the king of Israel.
   Holy Bible 1 Kings Chap. 22 v. 34

CHANCES

2 What is the use of working out chances? There are no chances against God.
   Georges Bernanos *The Diary of a Country Priest*

CHAOS

3 Where envying and strife is, there is confusion and every evil work.
   Holy Bible James Chap. 3 v. 16

CHARACTER

4 One's own character is such a puzzle. Here I am, a comfortable middle-aged rabbi, blessed with central heating, and a food processor, and aspiring to a microwave, devouring books on suffering, affliction and asceticism as I go to work in the morning.
   Rabbi Lionel Blue *Kitchen Blues*

5 All that is good in you comes from God, all that is bad, spoilt and corrupt comes from yourself.
   Jean-Pierre de Caussade SJ *Self-Abandonment to Divine Providence*

6 As he thinketh in his heart, so is he.
   Holy Bible Proverbs Chap. 23 v. 7

7 Character is simply habit long continued.
   Plutarch

8 A man should endeavour to be as pliant as a reed, yet as hard as cedar wood.
   The Talmud

CHARITY

9 In common with many Christians of the classic type he felt sincerely safer and more at ease when he had given away all he had, like a man passing a ball in a game.
   Margery Allingham *Tiger in the Smoke*

1 Charity is never a waste of time. Tonight I have given up my
   prayer in order to write to you.
       St Thomas Aquinas

2 The living need charity more than the dead.
       George Arnold *The Jolly Old Pedagogue*

3 If charity cost no money and benevolence no heartache, the
   world would be full of philanthropists.
       Hanan J. Ayalti *Yiddish Proverbs*

4 He that defers his charity until he is dead is, if a man weighs it
   rightly, rather liberal of another man's than his own.
       Francis Bacon *Apophthegms*

5 The desire for power caused the angels to fall; the desire for
   knowledge in excess caused man to fall, but in charity there is
   no excess, neither can angel nor man come in danger by it.
       Francis Bacon *Essays* 'Of Goodness'

6 A man who sees another man on the street corner with only a
   stump for an arm will be so shocked the first time he'll give
   him sixpence. But the second time it'll only be a threepenny
   bit. And if he sees him a third time he will cold-bloodedly
   have him handed over to the police.
       Bertolt Brecht *The Threepenny Opera*

7 But how shall we expect charity towards others, when we are
   uncharitable to ourselves? Charity begins at home, is the voice
   of the world, yet is every man his greatest enemy, and, as it
   were, his own executioner.

8 For this I think charity, to love God for Himself and our
   neighbour for God.
       Sir Thomas Browne *Religio Medici*

9 He that bestows his goods upon the poor,
   Shall have as much again, and ten times more.
       John Bunyan *The Pilgrim's Progress*

10 No sound ought to be heard in the church but the healing
   voice of Christian charity.
       Edmund Burke *Reflections on the Revolution in France*

11 Too many have dispensed with generosity to practise
   charity.
       Albert Camus *The Fall*

1 Human love is a straight line, the union of two points in the space of the creature. Charity is a triangle.
   Carlo Carretto *The God Who Comes*

2 Charity is, indeed, a great thing, and a gift of God, and when it is rightly ordered likens us unto God himself, as far as that is possible; for it is charity which makes the man.
   St John Chrysostom *True Almsgiving*

3 Loving one another with the charity of Christ, let the love you have in your hearts be shown outwardly in your deeds so that compelled by such an example, the sisters may also grow in the love of God and charity for one another.
   St Clare of Assisi *The Testament of St Clare*

4 Charity means nothing else but to love God for himself above all creatures, and to love one's fellowmen for God's sake as one loves oneself.
   The Cloud of Unknowing

5 Did universal charity prevail, earth would be heaven — and hell a fable.
   Charles Caleb Colton *Lacon*

6 A man of humanity is one who, in seeking to establish himself, finds a foothold for others and who, desiring attainment for himself, helps others to attain.
   Confucius *Analects*

7 No rich man's largesse may suffice his soul
   Nor are the plundered succoured by a dole.
   Edmund Vance Cooke *Book of Extenuations*

8 True charity makes others' wants their own.
   Robert Daborne

9 Isn't it better to have men being ungrateful than to miss the chance to do good?
   Denis Diderot *Discourses*

10 Recall the face of the poorest and the most helpless man whom you have seen, and ask yourself if the step you contemplate is going to be of any use to him.
   Inscription on the place of Gandhi's cremation at Rajghat

11 Verily I say unto you, Inasmuch as ye have done it unto one of the least of these my brethren, ye have done it unto me.
   Holy Bible St Matthew Chap. 25 v. 40

1 Though I speak with the tongues of men and of angels, and
have not charity, I am become as sounding brass, or a tinkling
cymbal.
Holy Bible 1 Corinthians Chap. 13 v. 1

2 Charity suffereth long, and is kind; charity envieth not; charity
vaunteth not itself, is not puffed up.
Holy Bible 1 Corinthians Chap. 13 v. 4

3 And now abideth faith, hope, charity, these three; but the
greatest of these is charity.
Holy Bible 1 Corinthians Chap. 13 v. 13

4 Charity shall cover the multitude of sins.
Holy Bible 1 Peter Chap. 4 v. 8

5 The cliché 'charity begins at home' has done more damage
than any other in the English language.
Archbishop Trevor Huddleston Letter to *The Times*
8 September 1980

6 Soft-handed Charity,
Tempering her gifts that seem so free
By time and place,
Till not a woe the bleak world see
But finds her grace.
John Keble *The Christian Year* 'The Sunday After
Ascension Day'

7 He is truly great who hath great charity.
Thomas à Kempis *The Imitation of Christ*

8 Christian beneficence takes a large sweep; that circumference
cannot be small of which God is the centre.
Hannah More

9 Charity that is always beginning at home stays there.
Austin O'Malley *Keystones of Thought*

10 I as little fear that God will damn a man who has charity, as I
hope that the priests can save one who has not.
Alexander Pope *Thoughts on Various Subjects*

11 In faith and hope the world will disagree,
But all mankind's concern is charity.
Alexander Pope *An Essay on Man*

12 God's servant making a snug living
By guiding Mammon in smug giving.
Keith Preston 'Professional Welfare Worker'

1 Charity, decent, modest, easy, kind,
Softens the high, and rears the abject mind;
Knows with just reins and gentle hand to guide
Betwixt vile shame and arbitrary pride.

2 Soft peace she brings, wherever she arrives;
She builds our quiet, as she forms our lives;
Lays the rough paths of peevish Nature even,
And opens in each heart a little Heaven.
Matthew Prior 'Charity'

3 Lots of people think they are charitable if they give away their
old clothes and things they don't want.
Myrtle Reed *Old Rose and Silver*

4 The dignity of the individual demands that he be not reduced
to vassalage by the largesse of others.
Antoine de Saint-Exupéry *Flight to Arras*

5 . . . charity,
Which renders good for bad, blessings for curses.
William Shakespeare *King Richard III* Act 1 Sc. 2

6 Charity itself fulfils the law,
And who can sever love from charity?
William Shakespeare *Love's Labour's Lost* Act IV Sc. 3

7 !f we fail to feed the needy, we do not have God's love, no
matter what we say. Regardless of what we do or say at 11 am
on a Sunday morn, affluent people who neglect the poor are
not people of God.
Ronald Sider *Rich Christians in an Age of Hunger*

8 Feel for others — in your pocket.
Charles Haddon Spurgeon *Salt Cellars*

9 True charity is the desire to be useful to others without
thought of recompense.
Emanuel Swedenborg *Heavenly Arcana*

10 Loving kindness is greater than laws; and the charities of life
are more than all ceremonies.
The Talmud

11 To do him any wrong was to beget
A kindness from him, for his heart was rich;
Of such fine mould that if you sowed therein
The seed of Hate it blossomed Charity.
Alfred, Lord Tennyson *Queen Mary*

1 No one would remember the Good Samaritan if he had only
good intentions. He had money as well.
  Margaret Thatcher MP Quoted Kenneth Skelton, Bishop of
  Lichfield, at a Diocesan Synod 5 March 1983

2 It is not the shilling I give you that counts, but the warmth that
it carries with it from my hand.
  Miguel de Unamuno *Essays and Soliloquies*

3 One might lay down as a postulate: All conceptions of God
which are incompatible with the movement of pure charity are
false.
  Simone Weil *Letter to a Priest*

CHASTITY

4 The essence of chastity is not the suppression of lust, but the
total orientation of one's life towards a goal.
  Dietrich Bonhoeffer *Letters and Papers from Prison*

5 Too chaste an adolescence makes for a dissolute old age.
  André Gide *Journals*

6 Chastity enables a soul to breathe pure air in the foulest places.
  Joseph Joubert *Pensées*

7 Chastity without charity lies chained in hell:
It is but an unlighted lamp.
Many chaplains are chaste, but where is their charity?
There are no harder, hungrier men than men of the Church.
  William Langland *The Vision of Piers the Plowman*

8 There is no getting away from it: the old Christian rule is
'Either marriage, with complete faithfulness to your partner,
or else total abstinence.' Chastity is the most unpopular of our
Christian virtues.
  C.S. Lewis *Mere Christianity*

9 'Tis chastity, my brother, chastity.
She that has that is clad in complete steel,
And, like a quiver'd nymph with arrows keen,
May trace huge forests and unharbour'd heaths,
Infamous hills and sandy perilous wilds,
Where, through the sacred rays of chastity,
No savage fierce, bandit or mountaineer,
Will dare to soil her virgin purity.
  John Milton *Comus*

1   Coffee is not necessary to ministers of the reformed faith as
    to Catholic priests. The latter are not allowed to marry, and
    coffee is said to induce chastity.
        Charlotte-Elisabeth, Duchesse d'Orléans *Letters*

2   She is chaste whom nobody has asked.
        Ovid *Amores* Book I

3   The woman who has lost her honour can refuse nothing.
        Tacitus *Annals* Book IV

4   Chastity is a wealth that comes from abundance of love.
        Rabindranath Tagore Quoted *Holy Waters* Indian Psalm
        Meditations Text by Martin Kämpchen

5   The little respect paid to chastity in the male world is, I am
    persuaded, the grand source of many of the physical and moral
    evils that torment mankind, as well as of the vices and follies
    that destroy women.
        Mary Wollstonecraft *A Vindication of the Rights of Woman*

CHILD

6   Love children especially, for like the angels they too are
    sinless, and they live to soften and purify our hearts, and, as it
    were, to guide us. Woe to him who offends a child!
        Feodor Dostoevsky *The Brothers Karamazov*

7   Lo, children are an heritage of the Lord: and the fruit of the
    womb is his reward. As arrows are in the hand of a mighty
    man; so are children of the youth. Happy is the man that hath
    his quiver full of them.
        Holy Bible Psalm 127 vv. 3–5

8   He that spareth his rod hateth his son.
        Holy Bible Proverbs Chap. 13 v. 24

9   Train up a child in the way that he should go: and when he is
    old, he will not depart from it.
        Holy Bible Proverbs Chap. 22 v. 6

10 As is the mother, so is her daughter.
        Holy Bible Ezekiel Chap. 16 v. 44

11 Suffer the little children to come unto me, and forbid them
    not: for of such is the kingdom of God.
        Holy Bible St Mark Chap 10 v. 14 St Luke Chap. 18 v. 16

1   It were better for him that a millstone were hanged about his
neck, and he cast into the sea, than that he should offend one
of these little ones.
> *Holy Bible* St Luke Chap. 17 v. 2

2   The supreme reality of our time is our individuality as children
of God and the common vulnerability of this planet.
> John F. Kennedy Address to the Irish Parliament 28 June 1963

3   Children are God's apostles, day by day
Sent forth to preach of love, and hope, and peace.
> James Russell Lowell 'On the Death of a Friend's Child'

4   A parent should never make distinctions between his children.
> *The Talmud*

CHOICE

5   Every act is an act of self-sacrifice. When you choose anything
you reject everything else — just as when you marry one
woman you give up all the others.
> G.K. Chesterton *Orthodoxy*

6   We choose our joys and sorrows long before we experience
them.
> Kahlil Gibran *Sand and Foam*

7   Many be called, but few chosen.
> *Holy Bible* St Matthew Chap. 20 v. 16

CHRIST – HIS INFLUENCE

8   Christ came when all things were growing old. He made them
new.
> St Augustine of Hippo *Sermons*

9   I say, the acknowledgement of God in Christ
Accepted by thy reason, solves for thee
All questions in the earth and out of it.
> Robert Browning 'A Death in the Desert'

10   In every pang that rends the heart
The Man of Sorrows has a part.
> Michael Bruce 'Christ Ascended'

11   The difference between Socrates and Jesus Christ?
The great Conscious: the immeasurable great unconscious.
> Thomas Carlyle *Journal*

1   I believe that he [Jesus] belongs not only to Christianity but to the entire world, to all races and all people.
     Gandhi

2   In darkness there is no choice. It is light that enables us to see the differences between things: and it is Christ that gives us light.
     J.C. and A.W. Hare *Guesses at Truth*

3   For where two or three are gathered together in my name, there am I in the midst of them.
     Holy Bible St Matthew Chap. 18 v. 20

4   And the Spirit and the bride say, Come. And let him that heard say, Come. And let him that is athirst come. And whosoever will, let him take the water of life freely.
     Holy Bible Revelation Chap. 22 v. 17

5   Apart from Christ we know neither what our life nor our death is; we do not know what God is nor what we ourselves are.
     Blaise Pascal *Pensées*

6   Jesus never claims to be God, personally, yet he always claims to bring God, completely.
     Bishop John Robinson *Honest to God*

7   His love, at once, and dread, instruct our thought;
As man he suffered, and as God he taught.
     Edmund Waller *Of Divine Love*

CHRIST – HIS LIFE

8   The Christ-child stood at Mary's knee,
His hair was like a crown,
And all the flowers looked up at Him,
And all the stars looked down.
     G.K. Chesterton 'A Christmas Carol'

9   The way in which, amid the political and social unrest of his time, Christ keeps aloof from politics, is truly sublime.
     Thomas Masaryk *The Spirit of Russia*

10   Jesus had no organisation, no headed notepaper, no funds, no registered premises, no distinguished patrons or officers, except only a treasurer – the ill-famed Judas Iscariot.
     Malcolm Muggeridge *Jesus, the Man Who Loves*

1   Though his earthly state was negligible and far below the level
    at which death duties become payable, his posthumous
    circumstances put him in the millionaire class. This astonishing
    career, from a carpenter's son to an accepted position on
    God's right hand, exemplified Lord Beaverbrook's favourite
    proposition that dazzling opportunities await whoever has the
    shrewdness, energy and pertinacity to see and seize them. Not
    even the sky is the limit.
        Malcolm Muggeridge *Tread Softly for You Tread on My Jokes*

2   He might be described as an underprivileged, colonial,
    working-class victim of political and religious persecution.
        HRH Prince Philip, Duke of Edinburgh *A Question of
        Balance*

3   Two thousand years ago there was One here on this earth who
    lived the grandest life that ever has been lived yet – a life
    that every thinking man with deeper or shallower meaning has
    agreed to call divine.
        F.W. Robertson *Lectures and Addresses*

CHRIST – HIS NATURE

4   Thou art the King of Glory, O Christ. Thou art the everlasting
    Son of the Father.
        Book of Common Prayer Order of Morning Prayer 'Te Deum'

5   I'm sure Christ wore a mezuzah. He certainly didn't wear a
    cross.
        Cesar Chavez

6   I believe there is no one lovelier, deeper, more sympathetic
    and more perfect than Jesus – not only is there no one else
    like him, but there could never be anyone like him.
        Feodor Dostoevsky

7   We must not have Christ Jesus, the Lord of Life, put any more
    in the stable amongst the horses and asses, but he must now
    have the best chamber.
        George Fox *God and Man*

8   Jesus Christ was not a Conservative. That is a racing certainty.
        Eric Heffer MP *Observer* 'Sayings of the Week'
        20 February 1983

9   This is my beloved Son, in whom I am well pleased.
        Holy Bible St Matthew Chap. 3 v. 17

1 Jesus Christ, the same yesterday, and today, and for ever.
   Holy Bible Hebrews Chap. 13 v. 8

2 All His glory and beauty come from within, and there He
   delights to dwell. His visits there are frequent, His
   conversation sweet, His comforts refreshing: His peace passing
   all understanding.
   Thomas à Kempis *The Imitation of Christ*

3 Not splendour but the penal flesh
   Taken for love, that moves us most.
   Anne Ridler 'Deus Absconditus'

4 Whether you think Jesus was God or not, you must admit that
   he was a first-rate political economist.
   George Bernard Shaw *Androcles and the Lion* Preface

5 Jesus alone IS; the rest IS NOT.
   St Thérèse of Lisieux Quoted *By Love Alone* Ed. Michael
   Hollings

CHRISTIAN

6 When all are Christians, none are.
   R.H. Benson Quoted Martin L. Smith *Benson of Cowley*

7 Christians and camels receive their burdens kneeling.
   Ambrose Bierce *Devil's Dictionary*

8 It is our business, as readers of literature, to know what we
   like. It is our business as Christians as *well* as readers of
   literature, to know what we ought to like. It is our business as
   honest men not to assume that what we like is what we ought
   to like.
   T.S. Eliot *Selected Essays*

9 A real Christian is a person who can give his pet parrot to a
   town gossip.
   Billy Graham

10 A Christian is God Almighty's Gentleman.
   J.C. and A.W. Hare *Guesses at Truth*

11 And the disciples were called Christians first in Antioch.
   Holy Bible Acts Chap. 12 v. 26

12 The main business of a Christian soul is to go through the
   world turning its water into wine.
   Andrew Lang Quoted Cecily Hallack *The Bliss of the Way*

1   The Christian whose life is all sadness, and whose only hope
lies beyond the grave, may be sure there is something amiss in
his life or in his method.
    Basil W. Maturin *Laws of Spiritual Life*

2   The Christian is one who has forever given up the hope of
being able to think of himself as a good man.
    Leslie Newbigin *Christian Freedom in the Modern World*

3   Nowadays, the world is full of tame Christians; in
consequence, the churches are empty of life, if not of people.
    Philip Rieff *The Triumph of the Therapeutic*

4   A strong Christian is not part of a system, or a creature of
habit. He is a revolutionary, in the good sense of the word. He
revolts against all injustices, but especially against those which
do not affect himself.
    Cardinal Saliege *Who Shall Bear the Flame*

5   The true Christian is in all countries a pilgrim and a stranger.
    George Santayana *Winds of Doctrine*

6   In his estimation the most Christian deed he ever performed
was to use the hairpin an old lady took from her hair to prise
out the winkles she served him for tea.
    Carolyn Scott, of the Rev. H.R.L. Sheppard, in *Dick Sheppard*

7   The nearest he gets to being a Christian is stirring his tea with
an apostle spoon.
    Peter Spence 'To the Manor Born' BBC TV 25 December 1979

8   We are not criticised for being Christians, but for not being
Christian enough.
    Cardinal Suenens Quoted Kenneth Pillar in letter to Margaret
    Pepper 1987

9   A Christian is an oak flourishing in winter.
    Thomas Traherne *Centuries of Meditations*

10 Some Christians are like candles that have been lit once and
then put away in a cupboard to be eaten by mice.
    Henry Van Dyke *The Friendly Year*

11 A Christian is a man who feels
Repentance on a Sunday
For what he did on Saturday
And is going to do on Monday.
    Thomas Russel Ybarra 'The Christian'

1 A Christian is the highest style of man.
   Edward Young *Night Thoughts*

CHRISTIANITY

2 Two things about the Christian religion must surely be clear to anybody with eyes in his head. One is that men cannot do without it; the other, that they cannot do with it as it is.
   Matthew Arnold

3 There was never law, or sect, or opinion did not so much magnify goodness, as the Christian religion doth.
   Francis Bacon *Essays* 'Of Goodness'

4 There's not much practical Christianity in the man who lives on better terms with angels and seraphs than with his children, servants and neighbours.
   Henry Ward Beecher

5 Every time in history that man has tried to turn crucified truth into coercive truth he has betrayed the fundamental principle of Christianity.
   Nicolas Berdyaev *Dostoevsky*

6 The energy and combativeness of Christian nations comes, I suspect, from the doctrine of sin, particularly Original Sin, and the kind of struggle that must go on for redemption (or for money).
   Gerald Brenan Letter to Bertrand Russell 1 June 1935

7 Christianity flourishes in proportion to the misery and insecurity of life. Prosperity kills it because at its most sincere it is a cry from the depths.
   Gerald Brenan *Thoughts in a Dry Season*

8 I especially liked Gibbon on the Christians. They really had nothing to offer except bishops and the after-life, but they pushed on and came through well.
   R.A. Butler Quoted John Mortimer *In Character*

9 Only through Christianity can one acquire a healthy kind of worldly-mindedness.
   Herbert Butterfield *The Origins of History*

10 Carlyle said that men were mostly fools. Christianity, with a surer and more reverend realism, says that they are all fools.
   G.K. Chesterton *Heretics*

1 The primary paradox of Christianity is that the ordinary
   condition of man is not his sane or sensible condition; that the
   normal itself is an abnormality.
   > G.K. Chesterton *Orthodoxy*

2 Christianity is the summons of divine Love for man to be
   Christlike — to emulate the words and the works of our great
   Master.
   > Mary Baker Eddy *The First Church of Christ, Scientist and
   > Miscellany*

3 Two inestimable advantages Christianity has given us; first, the
   Sabbath, the jubilee of the whole world; and secondly, the
   institution of preaching.
   > Ralph Waldo Emerson 'The Address Before the Divinity Class,
   > Cambridge 1838'

4 Christianity is a religion of motives — ways of acting and
   reasons for acting, more than actions.
   > Frederick W. Faber *Notes on Doctrinal and Spiritual Subjects*

5 Philosophy makes us wiser, but Christianity makes us better,
   men.
   > Henry Fielding *Tom Jones*

6 He who shall introduce into public affairs the principle of
   primitive Christianity will change the face of the world.
   > Benjamin Franklin Letter to the French Ministry March 1778

7 The Christian life is not a way 'out', but a way 'through' life.
   > Billy Graham

8 Christianity is a revolutionary idealism which estranges
   revolutionaries by its idealism and conservatives by its drastic
   revaluation of earthly goods.
   > Dean W.R. Inge *Freedom, Love and Truth*

9 The doctrines which flowed from the lips of Jesus himself are
   within the comprehension of a child; but thousands of volumes
   have not yet explained the Platonisms engrafted on them.

10 Of all the systems of morality, ancient or modern, which have
    come under my observation, none appear to me so pure as
    that of Jesus.
    > Thomas Jefferson *Collected Writings*

11 Christianity is the highest perfection of humanity.
    > Samuel Johnson Quoted Boswell's *Life of Johnson*

1   A wise man will always be a Christian, because the perfection
    of wisdom is to know where lies tranquillity of mind, and how
    to attain it, which Christianity teaches.
    > Walter Savage Landor *Imaginary Conversations* 'Marvell and
    > Parker'

2   Christianity is a statement which, if false, is of NO
    importance, and, if true, of INFINITE importance. The one
    thing it cannot be is moderately important.
    > C.S. Lewis

3   I wonder when Christianity will have sufficiently decayed for
    the fact to be driven into men's heads that pleasure is not
    hurtful nor pain beneficial.
    > W. Somerset Maugham *A Writer's Notebook*

4   No Resurrection. No Christianity.
    > Michael Ramsey, Archbishop of Canterbury

5   In the ethic of Christianity it is the relation of the soul to God
    that is important, not the relation of man to his fellow man.
    > Bertrand Russell *Marriage and Morals*

6   People may say what they like about the decay of Christianity;
    the religious system that produced green Chartreuse can never
    totally die.
    > Saki (H.H. Munro) *Reginald on Christmas Presents*

7   Christianity is perhaps approaching one of those long winters
    that overtake it from time to time. Romantic Christendom —
    picturesque, passionate, unhappy episode — may be coming to
    an end. Such a catastrophe would be no reason for despair.
    > George Santayana *Character and Opinion in the United States*

8   Popular Christianity has for its emblem a gibbet, for its chief
    sensation a sanguinary execution after torture, for its central
    mystery an insane vengeance bought off by a trumpery
    expiation. But there is a nobler and profounder Christianity
    which affirms the sacred mystery of equality and forbids the
    glaring futility and folly of vengeance.
    > George Bernard Shaw *Major Barbara* Preface

9   Christ cannot live his life today in this world without our
    mouth, without our eyes, without our going and coming,
    without our heart. When we love, it is Christ loving through us.
    > Cardinal Suenens

1 My experience is that Christianity dispels more mystery than it involves. With Christianity it is twilight in the world; without it, night.
   Madame Swetchine *The Writings of Madame Swetchine*

2 Christianity is pre-eminently the religion of slaves. Slaves cannot help belonging to it, and I am among them.
   Simone Weil *The Need for Roots*

3 Christ's place is indeed with the poets ... What God was to the pantheist, Man was to Him.
   Oscar Wilde *De Profundis*

CHRISTIAN SCIENCE

4 When I read my Christian Science lesson in the morning I feel I can go out and raise the dead. But what happens? I go out and raise the devil.
   Lady Astor Quoted John Grigg *Nancy Astor: Portrait of a Pioneer*

5 In the year 1866 I discovered the Christ Science, or Divine Laws of Life, Truth and Love and named my discovery CHRISTIAN SCIENCE.
   Mary Baker Eddy Pamphlet

6 Christian Science is the law of God, the law of good, interpreting and demonstrating the Divine Principle and rule of the Universal Harmony.
   Mary Baker Eddy *Rudimental Divine Science*

7 If Christianity is not scientific, and Science is not God, then there is no invariable law, and truth becomes an accident.

8 Jesus of Nazareth was the most scientific man that ever trod the globe. He plunged beneath the material surface of things, and found the spiritual causes.

9 Sickness, sin and death, being inharmonious, do not originate in God nor belong to his Government.
   Mary Baker Eddy *Science and Health with Key to the Scriptures*

10 If the doctors knew a little more about religion, and the clergy a little more about medicine, it wouldn't matter which you consulted, as long as you had a good nurse.
   William Nicholson, apropos Christian Science Quoted Rupert Hart-Davis *The Lyttelton—Hart-Davis Letters* 4 March 1956

CHRISTMAS

1   I have often thought, said Sir Roger, it happens very well that
Christmas should fall out in the middle of winter.
      Joseph Addison *The Spectator* No. 269

2   This most tremendous tale of all,
Seen in a stained-glass window's hue,
A Baby in an ox's stall.
      John Betjeman 'Christmas'

3   No trumpet blast profaned
The home in which the Prince of Peace was born.
No bloody streamlet stained
Earth's silver rivers on that sacred morn.
      William Cullen Bryant 'Christmas in 1875'

4   Christmas is a festival unknown to most of the world's
population.
      Jeremy Bulger *Radio Times* 3 February 1979

5   There fared a mother driven forth
Out of an inn to roam;
In the place where she was homeless
All men are at home.
The crazy stable close at hand,
With shaking timber and shifting sand,
Grew a stronger thing to abide and stand
Than the square stones of Rome.
      G.K. Chesterton 'The House of Christmas'

6   Our children await Christmas presents like politicians getting
election returns.
      Marceline Cox *Ladies Home Journal* December 1950

7   The Christmas season has come to mean the period when the
public plays Santa Claus to the merchants.
      John Haynes Holmes *Wisdom in Small Doses*

8   I heard the bells on Christmas Day
Their old familiar carols play,
And wild and sweet
The words repeat
Of peace on earth, goodwill to men!
      Henry Wadsworth Longfellow 'Christmas Bells'

1   There were only a few shepherds at the first Bethlehem.
The ox and the ass understood more of the first Christmas
than the high priests in Jerusalem. And it is the same today.
   Thomas Merton *The Seven Storey Mountain*

2   Putting stuffing in our turkey is Bronze Age, and you still find
it in the disembowelling rites of the Bush people.
   Stephen Potter *Supermanship*

3   What is Christmas without
snow? We need it
as bread of a cold
climate, ermine to trim
our sins with, a brief
sleeve for charity's
scarecrow to wear its heart
on, bold as a robin.
   R.S. Thomas 'Carol'

4   At Christmas play and make good cheer
For Christmas comes but once a year.
   Thomas Tusser *Five Hundred Points of Good Husbandry*

5   I hope your Christmas has had a little touch of Eternity in
among the rush and pitter and all. It always seems such a
mixture of this world and the next — but that after all is the
idea!
   Evelyn Underhill *Letters*

6   To perceive Christmas through its wrapping becomes more
difficult every year.
   E.B. White *The Second Tree from the Corner*

7   The good old heathen's feasting day, the profane man's
ranting day, the superstitious man's idol day and Satan's
working day.
   Hezekiah Woodward, a Puritan, in 1647

CHURCH

8   Sir Roger will suffer no one to sleep in [church] besides
himself . . . if he sees anybody else nodding, either wakes
them himself, or sends his servants to them.
   Joseph Addison *The Spectator* No. 112

9   For all in common she prays, for all in common she works, in
the temptations of all she is tried.
   St Ambrose

1 I have no objection to churches, so long as they do not
   interfere in God's work.
>   Brooks Anderson *Once Around the Sun*

2 Many come to bring their clothes to church rather than
   themselves.
        Anon

3 What an amazing capacity for disappointment the Church has.
        Nigel Balchin *Lord, I Was Afraid*

4 The Church's Restoration
   In eighteen-eighty-three
   Has left for contemplation
   Not what there used to be.
        John Betjeman 'Hymn'

5 Those who are content with the Church are just those who
   haven't imagination enough to be Christians.
        Charles Horton Cooley *Life and the Student*

6 He cannot have God for his father who has not the Church for
   his mother.
        St Cyprian *De Unitate Ecclesiae*

7 The hippopotamus's day
   Is passed in sleep; at night he hunts;
   God works in a mysterious way —
   The Church can sleep and feed at once.
        T.S. Eliot 'The Hippopotamus'

8 How beautiful to have the church always open, so that every
   tired wayfaring man may come in and be soothed by all that
   art can suggest of a better world when he is weary of this.
        Ralph Waldo Emerson *Journals*

9 When once thy foot enters the Church, be bare.
   God is more there than thou.
        George Herbert *The Temple* 'The Church Porch'

10 Except the Lord build the house, they labour in vain that build
   it.
        Holy Bible Psalm 127 v. 1

11 And I say also unto thee, That thou art Peter, and upon this
   rock I will build my church; and the gates of hell shall not
   prevail against it.
        Holy Bible St Matthew Chap. 16 v. 18

1   Now are they many members, yet but one body.
    Holy Bible 1 Corinthians Chap. 12 v. 20

2   A Church is God between four walls.
    Victor Hugo *Ninety Three*

3   The only place a new hat can be carried into with safety is a
    church, for there is plenty of room there.
    Leigh Hunt

4   The Church which is married to the Spirit of its Age will be a
    widow in the next.
    Dean W.R. Inge

5   This gift of God was entrusted to the Church that all the
    members might receive of him and be made alive; and none
    are partakers of him who do not assemble with the Church but
    defraud themselves of life. For where the Church is there is
    the Spirit of God, and where the Spirit of God is, there is the
    Church and all grace.
    Irenaeus *Adversus Omnes Haereses*

6   To be of no church is dangerous. Religion . . . will glide by
    degrees out of the mind.
    Samuel Johnson *Lives of the English Poets* 'Milton'

7   The church must be reminded that it is not the master or
    servant of the state, but rather the conscience of the state.
    Martin Luther King *Strength to Love*

8   A church is a place in which gentlemen who have never been
    to Heaven brag about it to persons who will never get there.
    H.L. Mencken *Prejudices*

9   Churches in cities are most wonderful solitudes.
    Thomas Merton *The Sign of Jonas*

10 An inscription over a church door in Cheshire: 'This is the
    House of God. This is the gate of heaven. (This door is locked
    in the winter months.)'
    Peterborough *Daily Telegraph*

11 Who builds a church to God, and not to fame,
    Will never mark the marble with his name.
    Alexander Pope *Moral Essays*

12 A great many more men would want to go to Church if there
    was a law against it.
    Reflections of a Bachelor

1   When you go to church you should actively seek something.
    You must not go like an empty basket, waiting passively to be
    filled.
        Roger William Riis *American Mercury* January 1941

2   The great door sighs. It opens and a child
    Enters the church and kneels in the front pew.
    The maker of the Universe has smiled:
    He made the Church for this one interview.
        Daniel Sargent *God's Ambuscade: The Village Church*

3   I would rather smell incense than varnish in the House of God.
        Rev. H.R.L. Sheppard Quoted Carolyn Scott *Dick Sheppard*

4   The oldest and greatest monopolist of all, Holy Church
    herself; the monopolist in God.
        John Strachey *The Coming Struggle for Power*

5   When he [a Gentleman] reads the lesson he does so with great
    gusto, with particular emphasis on those parts of the Old
    Testament that refer to fornicators and sinners.
        Douglas Sutherland *The English Gentleman*

6   See the Gospel Church secure
    And founded on a Rock!
    All her promises are sure;
    Her bulwarks who can shock?
        Charles Wesley 'The Church'

7   I look upon all the world as my parish.
        John Wesley *Journal*

8   People don't go to Church, but they feel better because it's
    there.
        Jonathan Lynn and Anthony Jay 'Yes, Prime Minister' BBC TV
        1988

CHURCHGOING

9   There is little good in filling churches with people who go out
    exactly the same as they came in; the call of the Church is not
    to fill churches but to fill heaven.
        Fr Andrew SDC *The Way of Victory*

10 The British churchman goes to church as he goes to the
    bathroom, with the minimum of fuss and no explanation if he
    can help it.
        Ronald Blythe *The Age of Illusion*

1 He was himself a robust rationalist, but he went to church to set his tenants an example. Of what, it would have puzzled him to say.

    G.K. Chesterton *The Man Who Knew Too Much*

CHURCH OF ENGLAND

2 The Church of England, that fine flower of our Island genius for compromise; that system, peculiar to these shores, which deflects the currents of religious passion down the canals of moderation.

    Robert Bolt *A Man for All Seasons*

3 The Church of England is the perfect church for people who don't go to church.

    Gerald Priestland 'Priestland's Progress' BBC Radio 4
    19 November 1981

4 The gentleman goes to church at regular intervals with his wife and children. This is not because he feels in need of spiritual guidance, but to set a good example to those whose chance of entering the Kingdom of Heaven is less certain.

    Douglas Sutherland *The English Gentleman*

CLEANLINESS

5 Let it be observed that cleanliness is no part of religion, that neither this nor any text of Scripture condemns neatness of apparel. Certainly this is a duty, not a sin. Cleanliness is indeed next to godliness.

    John Wesley *Sermons* 'On Dress'

CLERGY

6 It may be that only men who have no intense, personal, passionate life of their own drift into the ministry, and again, it may be that the ministerial habit itself tends to foster such impersonality, to crush out all the intense, tearing impulses that make the essence of the lives of most of us.

    Gamaliel Bradford *Letters*

7 What makes all doctrines plain and clear?
About two hundred pounds a year.
And that which was proved true before,
Prove false again? Two hundred more.

    Samuel Butler *Hudibras*

1 The clergyman is expected to be a kind of human Sunday.
   Samuel Butler *The Way of All Flesh*

2 I conceive that priests are extremely like other men, and neither the better nor the worse for wearing a gown or a surplice.
   Lord Chesterfield *Advice to His Son*

3 There would never be any stigma attached to a young man going into the church because the upper classes have to believe in God.
   Jilly Cooper *Class*

4 A clergyman's wife from St Albans recently had her application form for a Marks and Spencer credit card returned because it did not contain sufficient information. In answer to the question, 'Who is your husband's employer?' she had written 'God'.
   Daily Telegraph 22 July 1985

5 It is the best part of a man, I sometimes think, that revolts most against him being a minister. His good revolts from official goodness.
   Ralph Waldo Emerson *Journals*

6 Clergy are men, as well as other folk.
   Henry Fielding *Joseph Andrews*

7 When Dame Edith Evans was introduced to Billy Graham he told her, 'We in the ministry could learn a good deal from you about how to put our message across.' 'You in the ministry have an advantage over us,' replied Edith. 'You have long-term contracts.'
   Bryan Forbes *Ned's Girl*

8 A broad hat does not always cover a venerable head.
   Thomas Fuller *Gnomologia*

9 Priests are no more necessary to religion than politicians are to patriotism.
   John Haynes Holmes *The Sensible Man's View of Religion*

10 I am afraid the clergyman's God is too often head of the clerical profession.
   Dean W.R. Inge

11 The clergy should regard themselves as physicians of the soul.
   Dean W.R. Inge Quoted Ray Giles *Christian Herald* July 1941

1 People expect the clergy to have the grace of a swan, the friendliness of a sparrow, the strength of an eagle and the night hours of an owl — and some people expect such a bird to live on the food of a canary.
   Rev. Edward Jeffrey *Observer* 14 June 1964

2 That clergyman soon becomes an object of contempt, who being often asked out to dinner, never refuses to go.

3 Avoid, as you would the plague, a clergyman who is also a man of business.
   St Jerome *Letters* No. 52

4 I have always considered a clergyman as the father of a larger family than he is able to maintain.
   Samuel Johnson Quoted Boswell's *Life of Johnson*

5 My father made the walls resound,
   He wore his collar the wrong way round.
   Louis MacNeice 'Autobiography'

6 The minister, priest or rabbi is not to be regarded necessarily as one to whom religion has meant much: he is one for whom the expounding or administering of religion has meant much.
   Karl A. Menninger *The Human Mind*

7 Christianity was not founded by clergymen.
   Norman Vincent Peale *Faith for Today*

8 When W.A. Gilbert arrived at a provincial hotel to stay the night he was alarmed to find it filled by clergymen attending a theological conference. He confessed, 'I felt like a lion in a den of Daniels.'
   Hesketh Pearson *Gilbert and Sullivan*

9 Overheard at a Christmas party, from a girl discussing jobs with a local curate: 'But yours is such a *soul*-destroying job.'
   Peterborough *Daily Telegraph*

10 A parson should light fires in a dark room, and go on lighting them all his life.
   Rev. H.R.L. Sheppard Quoted Carolyn Scott *Dick Sheppard*

11 What bishops like best in their clergy is a dropping-down-deadness of manner.
   Sydney Smith *First Letter to Archdeacon Singleton*

1 Some ministers would make good martyrs. They are so dry,
   they would burn well.
      Charles Haddon Spurgeon

2 I never saw, heard, nor read, that the clergy were beloved in
   any nation where Christianity was the religion of the Country.
   Nothing can render them popular but some degree of
   persecution.
      Jonathan Swift *Thoughts on Religion*

3 A friend who wished to check some point on aeronautics
   asked in his library for books on Metropolitan Vickers. He
   was handed a copy of Crockford's Clerical Directory.
      The Times 'Diary' 7 January 1987

4 What village parson would not like to be a pope?
      Voltaire *Letters on the English*

5 Like so many vicars, he had a poor opinion of curates.
      P.G. Wodehouse *Mr Mulliner Speaking*

CLOTHING

6 But what went ye out to see? A man clothed in soft raiment?
   behold, they that wear soft clothing are in kings' houses.
      Holy Bible St Matthew Chap. 11 v. 8

7 Let us not be found, when our Master call us, stripping the
   lace off our waistcoats but the spirit of contention from our
   souls and tongues. Alas, sir, a man who cannot get to heaven
   in a green coat will not find his way thither sooner in a great
   one.
      Samuel Johnson

COMFORT

8 Come unto me all that travail and are heavy laden, and I will
   refresh you.
      Book of Common Prayer Order of Holy Communion
      St Matthew Chap. 11 v. 28

9 In a Word, as my Life was a Life of Sorrow one way, so it was
   a Life of Mercy another; and I wanted nothing to make it a
   Life of Comfort but to be able to make any sense of God's
   goodness to me and care over me in this condition to be my
   only consolation.
      Daniel Defoe *Robinson Crusoe*

1   Comfort ye, comfort ye my people, saith your God. Speak ye
    comfortably to Jerusalem.
    Holy Bible Isaiah Chap. 40 v. 1

2   As one whom his mother comforteth, so will I comfort you.
    Holy Bible Isaiah Chap. 66 v. 13

3   We through patience and comfort of the scriptures might have
    hope.
    Holy Bible Romans Chap. 15 v. 4

4   How sweet the Name of Jesus sounds
    In a believer's ear!
    It soothes his sorrows, heals his wounds,
    And drives away his fear!
    John Newton *Olney Hymns*

COMMANDMENTS

5   His Light gives wisdom and knowledge, and his Love gives
    power and strength, to run the ways of his commandments
    with delight.
    John Bellers *The Meeting for Worship*

6   If God had been a Liberal there wouldn't have been ten
    commandments. There would have been ten suggestions.
    Malcolm Bradbury and Christopher Bigsby *After-Dinner Game*
    (TV Play)

7   Fear God, and keep his commandments: for this is the whole
    duty of man.
    Holy Bible Ecclesiastes Chap. 12 v. 13

8   He said NOT
              'Thou shalt not be tempted:
              Thou shalt not be travailed:
              Thou shalt not be afflicted.'
    But he SAID
              'Thou shalt NOT be overcome.'
    Julian of Norwich

9   The Ten Commandments, when written on tablets of stone
    and given to man, did not then first begin to belong to him;
    they had their existence in man and lay as a seed hidden in the
    form and maker of his soul.
    William Law *The Spirit of Love*

1 When a man's in love he at once makes a pedestal of the Ten
Commandments and stands on top of it with his arms akimbo.
When a woman's in love she doesn't care two straws about
Thou Shalt or Thou Shalt Not.
W. Somerset Maugham *Lady Frederick*

2 Say what you like about the Ten Commandments, you must
always come back to the pleasant truth that there are only ten
of them.
H.L. Mencken

3 Live by the commandments. Do not die by them.
The Talmud

4 This is the age of bargain hunters. If it had been this way in
biblical times, we'd probably have been offered another
Commandment free if we had accepted the first ten.
Earl Wilson Quoted *Reader's Digest* September 1978

COMMITMENT

5 Go thy way, sell whatsoever thou hast, and give to the poor,
and thou shalt have treasure in heaven: and come, take up thy
cross and follow me.
Holy Bible St Mark Chap. 10 v. 21

6 Commitment to the poor is based on the Gospel: it does not
have to rely on some political manifesto.
Pope John Paul II Third Conference of Latin American
Bishops Puebla 1979

7 The profundity of a spiritual act is in direct proportion to its
author's commitment.
Henri de Lubac *Paradoxes*

8 In one form or another the Church is the only society which
points people to God through Jesus Christ. By Baptism and
the response of faith individuals exercise their membership
and in so doing commit themselves to God.
Bishop Peter Mumford *The Cornish Churchman*

9 The need for devotion to something outside ourselves is even
more profound than the need for companionship. If we are not
to go to pieces or wither away, we all must have some purpose
in life; for no man can live for himself alone.
Ross Parmenter *The Doctor and the Cleaning Woman* 'The Plant
on My Window'

COMMUNION

1 Always seek communion. It is the most precious thing men possess. In this respect, the symbol of the religious is indeed full of majesty. Where there is communion there is something that is more than human, there is surely something divine.
  Georges Duhamel *The Heart's Desire*

COMMUNITY

2 What life have you if you have not life together?
  There is no life that is not in community,
  And no community not lived in praise of God.
  T.S. Eliot *The Rock*

3 I know that a community of God-seekers is a shelter for man. But directly this grows into an institution it is apt to give ready access to the Devil by the back door.
  Rabindranath Tagore *Letters to a Friend*

COMPANIONS

4 Be the tail of lions rather than the head of foxes.
  The Talmud

COMPASSION

5 One cannot weep for the whole world, it is beyond human strength. One must choose.
  Jean Anouilh *Cecile*

6 Let everything be done in moderation.
  Let the weakness of the old and the very young be always taken into account.
  Let the weaker be helped so that they may not do their work in sadness.
  St Benedict *The Rule of St Benedict*

7 By compassion we make others' misery our own, and so, by relieving them, we relieve ourselves also.
  Sir Thomas Browne *Religio Medici*

8 Who go miles and miles to see the dubious stigmata on someone or other's hands, yet move not a step to contemplate the sore-covered hands of the poor?
  Carlo Carretto *Summoned by Love*

1 O Lord, baptise our hearts into a sense of the conditions and need of all men.

> George Fox, founder of the Quaker Society

2 'Twould ring the bells of heaven
The wildest peal for years
If Parson lost his senses
And people came to theirs
And he and they together
Knelt down with angry prayers
For tamed and shabby tigers
And dancing dogs and bears
And wretched blind pit ponies
And little hunted hares.

> Ralph Hodgson 'The Bells of Heaven'

3 No one need search for a programme of action or a crusade. The world and suffering humanity create the agenda for those who have eyes for human misery, ears for the stories of oppression and hearts to respond to the distress of our human family.

> Cardinal Basil Hume OSB *To Be a Pilgrim*

4 Every act of kindness and compassion done by any man for his fellow Christian is done by Christ working within him.

> Julian of Norwich *Revelations of Divine Love*

5 There is no wilderness so terrible, so beautiful, so arid, so fruitful, as the wilderness of compassion. It is the only desert that shall truly flourish like a lily.

> Thomas Merton

6 What value has compassion that does not take its object in its arms.

> Antoine de Saint-Exupéry *The Wisdom of the Sands*

7 God tempers the wind to the shorn lamb.

> Laurence Sterne

8 When a man has compassion for others, God has compassion for him.

> *The Talmud*

9 Difficult as it is really to listen to someone in affliction, it is just as difficult for him to know that compassion is listening to him.

> Simone Weil *Waiting on God*

COMPENSATION

1   When God wounds from on high he will follow with the
    remedy.
    Fernando de Rojas *La Celestina* Act X

COMPROMISE

2   The older generation, bigoted and neck-deep in compromise,
    wastes its time defending itself by passing laws against divorce,
    instead of bearing witness, out of deep faith, to the certainty
    of the gospel and the light that a true and freely given love
    always brings.
    Carlo Carretto *The God Who Comes*

CONCILIATION

3   A soft answer turneth away wrath.
    Holy Bible Proverbs Chap. 15 v. 1

4   Blessed are the peacemakers: for they shall be called the
    children of God.
    Holy Bible St Matthew Chap. 5 v. 9

5   Be swift to hear, slow to speak, slow to wrath.
    Holy Bible James Chap. 1 v. 19

CONDUCT

6   A right exterior conduct really has its secret in a true interior
    life.
    Fr Andrew SDC *Letters of Fr Andrew SDC*

7   When brothers go about, they should carry nothing for the
    journey, neither a knapsack nor a purse, nor bread, nor
    money. And whatever house they enter, let them first say:
    'Peace to this house'. And, remaining in that house they may
    eat and drink whatever their hosts have offered.
    St Francis of Assisi 'The Manner of the Brothers' Conduct'
    Francis and Clare Trans. Regis J. Armstrong OFM Cap. and
    Ignatius Bradley OFM

8   Circles are praised, not that abound
    In Largeness, but the exactly round;
    So life we praise, that does excel
    Not in much time, but acting well.
    Edmund Waller *Epigrams*

CONFESSION

1 The Roman Catholic Church, by using confession, makes people interested in themselves, and, feeling it right to be interested, it makes everyone form a kind of romantic picture of himself or herself.
   A.C. Benson *Diaries*

2 Confess your sins to the Lord and you will be forgiven; confess them to men and you will be laughed at.
   Josh Billings (Henry W. Shaw)

3 Open confession is good for the soul.
   Henry George Bohn *Handbook of Proverbs*

4 We have left undone those things which we ought to have done; and we have done those things which we ought not to have done.
   Book of Common Prayer From the General Confession

5 We confess our bad qualities to others out of fear of appearing naive or ridiculous by not being aware of them.
   Gerald Brenan *Thoughts in a Dry Season*

6 Come, now again thy woes impart,
   Tell all thy sorrows, all thy sin:
   We cannot heal the throbbing heart,
   Till we discern the wounds within.
   George Crabbe 'The Hall of Justice'

7 It used to irritate a friend of mine that when he went to confession he never got the chance to tell the priest the good things he had done.
   Monica Furlong *Christian Uncertainties*

8 Confession is the first step to repentance.
   Edmund Gayton *Festivous Notes on Don Quixote*

9 Should we all confess our sins to one another we would all laugh at one another for our lack of originality.
   Kahlil Gibran *Sand and Foam*

10 A fault confessed was half amended.
   Sir John Harrington *Epigrams*

11 We acknowledge our faults in order to repair by our sincerity the damage they have done us in the eyes of others.
   François, Duc de la Rochefoucauld *Maxims*

1 It is not the criminal things which are hardest to confess, but the ridiculous and shameful.
      Jean-Jacques Rousseau *Confessions*

2 Confess yourself to heaven;
Repent what's past; avoid what is to come.
      William Shakespeare *Hamlet* Act III Sc. 4

3 Confession of our faults is the next thing to innocence.
      Publilius Syrus *Moral Sayings*

4 Confession may be considered as a sort of exorcism in which Christ does battle against the powers of evil.
      Max Thurian *Confession*

CONFIDENCE

5 I have been young, and now am old: and yet saw I never the righteous forsaken, nor his seed begging their bread.
      Book of Common Prayer Psalm 37 v. 25

6 To those leaning on the sustaining infinite, today is big with blessings.
      Mary Baker Eddy *Science and Health with Key to the Scriptures*

7 Lord, I am not worthy that thou shouldest come under my roof; but speak the word only, and my servant shall be healed.
      Holy Bible St Matthew Chap. 8 v. 8

CONFIRMATION

8 The vicar reported an increased number of communicants in the year. He also said that the Death Watch Beetle had been confirmed in the Church.
      Newspaper report Quoted *Bibliophile* April 1987

CONFLICT

9 Christians are not called to win battles, but to find ways of being in battles.
      Bishop David Jenkins 'Spirituality for Conflict'

10 No doubt there are other important things in life besides conflict but there are not many things so inevitably interesting. The very saints interest us most when we think of them in conflict with the Devil.
      Robert Lynd *The Blue Lion*

1 No Kingdom has ever suffered as many civil wars as Christ's.
   Montesquieu *Letters*

CONFORMITY

2 For one man who thanks God that he is not as other men are,
   there are a few thousand who offer thanks that they are as
   other men, sufficiently as others to escape attention.
   John Dewey *Human Nature and Conflict*

3 Conformity is one of the most fundamental dishonesties of all.
   When we reject our specialness, water down our God-given
   individuality and uniqueness, we begin to lose our freedom.
   The conformist is in no way a free man. He has to follow the
   herd.
   Norman Vincent Peale *Man, Morals and Maturity*

CONGREGATION

4 How many times go we to comedies, to masques, to places of
   great and noble resort, nay even to church only to see the
   company?
   John Donne *Sermons*

5 To Mr Rawlinson's church. A very fine store of women there
   is in this church, more than I know anywhere else.
   Samuel Pepys *Diary*

6 One of the advantages of pure congregational singing is that
   you can join in the singing whether you have a voice or not.
   The disadvantage is that your neighbour can do the same.
   Charles Dudley Warner *Backlog Studies* 'Seventh Study'

7 Men and Women wanted to form a congregation — no
   experience necessary.
   Wayside pulpit Quoted Peterborough *Daily Telegraph*

CONQUEST

8 He whose conquest nobody can conquer, into whose conquest
   none can enter — by what track can you trace him, the
   awakened, whose limits are infinite, the trackless?
   Dhammapada Buddhist spirituality

9 Thou hast conquered, O Galilean.
   Julian the Apostate

CONSCIENCE

1   The conscience is a built-in feature
That haunts the sinner, helps the preacher.
Some sins it makes us turn and run from,
But most it simply takes the fun from.
>   Richard Armour *Saturday Evening Post* 'The Conscience'
>   12 May 1951

2   Conscience and reputation are two things. Conscience is due
to yourself and reputation is due to your neighbour.
>   St Augustine of Hippo *Confessions*

3   When a man is content with the testimony of his own
conscience, he does not care to shine with the light of
another's praise.
>   St Bernard of Clairvaux *Letters*

4   Stand in awe, and sin not: commune with your own heart, and
in your chamber, and be still.
>   *Book of Common Prayer* Psalm 4 v. 4

5   There is another man within me that is angry with me.
>   Sir Thomas Browne *Religio Medici*

6   The great beacon-light God sets in all,
The conscience of each bosom.
>   Robert Browning *Strafford* Act IV Sc. 2

7   You cannot make yourself feel something you do not feel, but
you can make yourself do right in spite of your feelings.
>   Pearl S. Buck *To My Daughter, with Love*
>   'My Neighbour's Son'

8   Conscience was born when man had shed his fur, his tail, his
pointed ears.
>   Sir Richard Burton *The Kasîdah*

9   Those whom God forsakes, the devil by his permission lays
hold on. Sometimes he persecutes them with that worm of
conscience, as he did Judas, Saul and others. The poets call it
Nemesis.
>   Robert Burton *Anatomy of Melancholy*

10   Conscience is thoroughly well bred and soon leaves off talking
to those who do not wish to hear it.
>   Samuel Butler *Notebooks*

1 But at sixteen the conscience rarely gnaws
   So much as when we call our old debts in
   At sixty years, and draw the accounts of evil,
   And find a deuced balance with the devil.
       Lord Byron *Don Juan*

2 Yet still there whispers the small voice within,
   Heard through gain's silence, and o'er glory's din;
   Whatever creed be taught, or land be trod,
   Man's conscience is the oracle of God.
       Lord Byron 'The Island'

3 Conscience is a cur that does not stop us from passing but that
   we cannot prevent from barking.
       Nicolas Chamfort *Maximes et Pensées*

4 A man that will enjoy a quiet conscience must lead a quiet life.
       Lord Chesterfield *Letters*

5 Your conscience is what your mother told you before you were
   six months old.
       Dr G.B. Chisholm *Ladies Home Journal* October 1949

6 Those of us who were brought up as Christians and who have
   lost our faith have retained the Christian sense of sin without
   the saving belief in redemption. This poisons our thought and
   so paralyses us in action.
       Cyril Connolly *The Unquiet Grave*

7 There is no hell like a bad conscience.
       John Crowne *The Ambitious Statesman* Act V Sc. 3

8 O faithful conscience delicately pure,
   How doth a little failing wound thee sore!

9 May heaven's grace so clear away the foam from thy
   conscience, that the river of thy thoughts may roll limpid
   henceforth.
       Dante *Divine Comedy* 'Purgatory'

10 Inexorable conscience holds his court, with still small voice the
   plot of guilt alarms.
       Erasmus Darwin *Mores Concluded*

11 Fear of death has gone farther with me in two minutes than
   my conscience would have gone in two months.
       John Dryden *Don Sebastian*

1 There is one thing alone that stands the brunt of life throughout its course, a quiet conscience.
   Euripides *Hippolytus*

2 A good conscience is a continual Christmas.
   Benjamin Franklin · *Poor Richard*

3 Conscience is the internal perception of the rejection of a particular wish operating within us.
   Sigmund Freud *Totem and Taboo*

4 The paradoxical — and tragic — situation of a man is that his conscience is weakest when he needs it most.
   Erich Fromm *Man For Himself*

5 A quiet conscience sleeps in thunder.

6 A guilty conscience never thinketh itself safe.
   Thomas Fuller *Gnomologia*

7 Conscience is a just but weak judge. Weakness leaves it powerless to execute its judgement.
   Kahlil Gibran *Thoughts and Meditations* 'A Story of a Friend'

8 The disease of an evil conscience is beyond the practice of all physicians of all the countries in the world.
   William Ewart Gladstone Speech at Plumstead 1878

9 Conscience is a coward, and those faults it has not strength enough to prevent, it seldom has justice enough to accuse.
   Oliver Goldsmith *The Vicar of Wakefield*

10 Most of us follow our conscience as we follow a wheelbarrow. We push it in front of us in the direction we want to go.
    Billy Graham

11 Some make a conscience of spitting in the church, yet rob the altar.
    George Herbert *Jacula Prudentum*

12 A man's conscience and his judgement is the same thing, and as the judgement, so the conscience, may be erroneous.
    Thomas Hobbes *Leviathan*

13 There is a spectacle more grand than the sea, it is heaven: there is a spectacle more grand than heaven, it is the conscience.
    Victor Hugo *Les Misérables*

1 When one has a conscience it is generally a bad one.
Eugene Ionesco *Fragments of a Journal*

2 Conscience was the barmaid of the Victorian soul ... It would permit, rather ungraciously perhaps, the indulgence of a number of carefully selected desires. Once the appointed limit was reached conscience would rap on the bar of the soul. 'Time's up, gentlemen,' she would say.
C.E.M. Joad *Under the Fifth Rib*

3 Conscience is a small, still voice that makes minority reports.
Franklin P. Jones *Saturday Evening Post* 'Put It This Way' 25 July 1959

4 The glory of good men is in their conscience and not in the mouths of men.

5 The testimony of a good conscience is the glory of a good man: have a good conscience and thou shalt ever have gladness. A good conscience may bear right many things and rejoices among adversities.
Thomas a Kempis *The Imitation of Christ*

6 A man's vanity tells him what is honour, a man's conscience what is justice.
Walter Savage Landor *Imaginary Conversations* 'Peter Leopold and President'

7 Conscience is a treacherous thing, and mine behaves badly whenever there is a serious danger of being found out.
Margaret Lane *A Calabash of Diamonds*

8 It is neither safe nor prudent to do anything against conscience.
Martin Luther *Table Talk*

9 Justice is the temporary thing which must at last come to an end, but the conscience is eternal and will never die.
Martin Luther *On Marriage*

10 The Anglo-Saxon conscience does not prevent the Anglo-Saxon from sinning. It merely prevents him from enjoying it.
Salvador de Madariaga Quoted David Frost and Anthony Jay *To England with Love*

11 A state of conscience is higher than a state of innocence.
Thomas Mann *I Believe* Ed. Clifton Fadiman

1 Conscience is the guardian in the individual of the rules which the community has evolved for its own preservation.
   W. Somerset Maugham *The Moon and Sixpence*

2 Conscience is a God to all mortals.
   Menander *Monostikoi*

3 Conscience is the inner voice which warns us that someone may be looking.
   H.L. Mencken *Prejudices*

4 O conscience, into what abyss of fears
   And horrors hast thou driven me.

5 Now conscience wakes despair
   That slumber'd, wakes the bitter memory
   Of what he was, what is, and what must be
   Worse; of worse deeds, worse sufferings must ensue.

6 And I will place within them as a guide
   My umpire Conscience, whom if they will hear,
   Light after light well used they shall attain,
   And to the end persisting, safe arrive.
   John Milton *Paradise Lost*

7 The laws of conscience, which we pretend are born of nature, are born of custom.
   Montaigne *Essays*

8 Conscience, the bosom-hell of guilty men!
   James Montgomery *Pelican Island*

9 There is only one way to achieve happiness on this terrestrial ball,
   And that is to have a clear conscience or none at all.
   Ogden Nash *I'm a Stranger Here Myself*

10 Conscience implies a relation between the soul and a something exterior ... a relation to an excellence which it does not possess, and to a tribunal over which it has no power.
   John Henry, Cardinal Newman *Oxford University Sermons*

11 Liberty of conscience is the first step towards having a religion.
   William Penn *The People's Ancient and Just Liberties Asserted*

12 There is no witness so dreadful, no accuser so terrible, as the conscience that dwells in the heart of every man.
   Polybius *History* Book XVIII

1   What conscience dictates to be done,
    Or warns me not to do,
    This, teach me more than Hell to shun,
    That, more than heaven pursue.
        Alexander Pope 'The Universal Prayer'

2   Conscience is the voice of the soul, the passions are the voice
    of the body.
        Jean-Jacques Rousseau *Émile*

3   The still small voice that makes you feel even smaller.
        J.A. Sanaker *Reader's Digest* February 1946

4   A man has less conscience when in love than in any other
    condition.
        Arthur Schopenhauer *Metaphysics of Love*

5   Living with a conscience is like driving a car with the brakes
    on.
        Budd Schulberg *What Makes Sammy Run*

6   Thus conscience does make cowards of us all.
        William Shakespeare *Hamlet* Act III Sc. 1

7   A peace above all earthly dignities,
    A still and quiet conscience.
        William Shakespeare *Henry VIII* Act III Sc. 2

8   My conscience hath a thousand several tongues,
    And every tongue brings in a several tale,
    And every tale condemns me for a villain.
        William Shakespeare *Richard III* Act V Sc. 3

9   I know thou art religious
    And hast a thing within thee called conscience,
    With twenty popish tricks and ceremonies
    Which I have seen thee careful to observe.
        William Shakespeare *Titus Andronicus* Act V Sc. 1

10 And conscience, that undying serpent, calls
    Her venomous brood to their nocturnal task.
        Percy Bysshe Shelley *Queen Mab*

11 Trust that man in nothing who has not a conscience in
    everything.
        Laurence Sterne *Tristram Shandy*

1   The conscience has morbid sensibilities; it must be employed but not indulged, like the imagination or the stomach.
    Robert Louis Stevenson *Ethical Studies*

2   And I know of the future judgement
    How dreadful so'er it be
    That to sit alone with my conscience
    Would be judgement enough for me.
    Charles William Stubbs *Alone with My Conscience*

3   Conscience is God's presence in man.
    Emanuel Swedenborg *Heavenly Arcana*

4   The best preacher is the heart; the best teacher is time; the best book is the world; the best friend is Jesus.
    The Talmud

5   In matters of conscience that is the best sense which every wise man takes in before he hath sullied his understanding with the designs of sophisters and interested persons.
    Jeremy Taylor *Ductor Dubitantium*

6   The nagging conscience learns to live with the evils it cannot cure.
    George Malcolm Thomson *Lord Castlerosse and His Times*

7   Ideas of what is right and wrong vary from age to age and from place to place, but the significant thing is that there *is* a distinction between right and wrong. The inner compulsion to do right and the shame we feel when we are aware of having done wrong are an experience of God.
    Leslie J. Tizard *Facing Life and Death*

8   What better bed than conscience good, to pass the night in sleep.
    Thomas Tusser *Posies for the Bed Chamber*

9   Some good must come by clinging to the right. Conscience is a man's compass, and though the needle sometimes deviates, though one perceives irregularities in directing one's course by it, still one must try to follow its direction.
    Vincent Van Gogh *Dear Theo*

10 He that loses his conscience has nothing left that is worth keeping.
    Isaac Walton *Compleat Angler*

1 Conscience, a terrifying little sprite
That bat-like winks by day and wakes by night.
   John Wolcot *The Lousiad*

CONSECRATION

2 All things are God's already; we can give him no right by consecrating any that he has not had before.
   John Selden *Table Talk* 'Consecrated Places'

CONSERVATION

3 Do not dishonour to the earth lest you dishonour the spirit of man.
   Henry Beson *The Outermost House*

4 Man thinks of himself as a creator instead of a user, and this delusion is robbing him, not only of his natural heritage, but perhaps of his future.
   Helen Hoover *The Long-Shadowed Forest*

5 We abuse land because we regard it as a commodity belonging to us. When we see land as a community to which we belong we may begin to use it with love and respect.
   Aldo Leopold Quoted Stewart I. Udell *The Quiet Crisis*

6 Everything is perfect coming from the hands of the Creator, everything degenerates in the hands of man.
   Jean-Jacques Rousseau *Émile*

CONSOLATION

7 Christianity, above all, consoles; but there are naturally happy souls who do not need consolation. Consequently Christianity begins by making such souls unhappy, for otherwise it would have no power over them.
   André Gide *Journals*

8 Formal religion was organised for slaves; it offered them consolation which earth did not provide.
   Elbert Hubbard *Philistine* Vol. 25

9 Nobody can have the consolation of religion or philosophy unless he has first experienced their desolations.
   Aldous Huxley *Collected Essays*

CONTEMPLATION

1 Nowhere can man find a quieter or more untroubled retreat than to his own soul.
   Marcus Aurelius *Meditations*

2 Place your mind before the mirrors of eternity!
   Place your soul in the brilliance of glory
   Place your heart in the figure of the divine substance
   And transform your whole being into the magic of the
      Godhead Itself through Contemplation.
   St Clare of Assisi *Francis and Clare* 'Third Letter to Blessed
   Agnes of Prague' Trans. Regis J. Armstrong OFM Cap. and
   Ignatius Bradley OFM

3 The higher part of contemplation is wholly caught up in darkness and in this cloud of unknowing, with an outreaching of love and a blind groping for the naked being of God, himself and him alone.
   The Cloud of Unknowing

4 Contemplatives are not useful, they are only indispensable.
   Ernest Dimnet *What We Live By*

5 In silence man can most readily preserve his integrity.
   Meister Eckhart *Directions for the Contemplative Life*

6 If I were to compare action of a much higher strain with a life of contemplation I should not venture to pronounce with much confidence in favour of the former.
   Ralph Waldo Emerson *Representative Men* 'Goethe'

7 Give me, kind Heaven, a private station,
   A mind serene for contemplation.
   John Gay *Fables*

8 In order to attain the Citadel of Contemplation you must begin by exercising yourself in the field of labour.
   St Gregory the Great

9 The longest journey is the journey inward ... The road to holiness necessarily passes through the world of action.
   Dag Hammarskjöld *Markings*

10 He that contemplates hath a day without night.
   George Herbert *The Temple*

11 Be still, and know that I am God.
   Holy Bible Psalm 46 v. 10

1   Contemplation is nothing else but a secret, peaceful, and loving infusion of God, which, if admitted, will set the soul on fire with the spirit of love.
    St John of the Cross *The Dark Night of the Soul*

2   The peace of the contemplative is at once the most beautiful and the most fruitful act of man.
    Stephen Mackenna *Journals and Letters*

3   Wisdom's best nurse is contemplation.
    John Milton *Comus*

4   But first and chiefest, with thee bring
    Him that yon soars on golden wing,
    Guiding the fiery-wheeled throne,
    The Cherub Contemplation.
    John Milton *Il Penseroso*

5   A church which starves itself and its members in the contemplative life deserves whatever spiritual leanness it may experience.
    Michael Ramsey, Archbishop of Canterbury *Canterbury Pilgrim*

6   Contemplation is a gift of God which is not necessary for salvation nor for earning our eternal reward, nor will anyone require you to possess it.
    St Teresa of Avila *The Way of Perfection*

7   If you contemplated Him in everything, contemplation of Him would veil all things from your sight.
    If you contemplated Him, they would not hide Him from you in the before and after and the time of things.
    The Wisdom of the Sufis Compiled by Kenneth Cragg

CONTENMENT

8   A person who is not disturbed by the incessant flow of desires can alone achieve peace, and not the man who strives to satisfy such desires.
    Bhagavad Gita

9   Sweet are the thoughts that savour of content;
    The quiet mind is richer than a crown.
    Robert Greene 'Farewell to Folly'

10 I have learned, in whatsoever state I am, therewith to be content.
    Holy Bible Philippians Chap. 4 v. 11

1 The best of blessings, a contented mind.
   Horace *Epistles*

2 He who is content can never be ruined.
   Lao-Tze *The Simple Way*

3 I am a true labourer: I earn that I eat, get that I wear; owe no man hate, envy no man's happiness; glad of other men's good, content with my harm.
   William Shakespeare *As You Like It* Act III Sc. 2

4 You never enjoy the world aright till the sea itself floweth in your veins, till you are clothed with the heavens and crowned with the stars; and perceive yourself to be the sole heir of the world, and more than so, because men are in it who are everyone sole heirs as well as you.
   Thomas Traherne *Centuries of Meditations*

CONTRACEPTION

5 It is quite lawful for a Catholic woman to avoid pregnancy by a resort to mathematics, though she is still forbidden to resort to physics and chemistry.
   H.L. Mencken *Minority Report*

CONTRITION

6 Mercy for praise — to be forgiven for fame
   He asked, and hoped, through Christ. Do thou the same!
   Samuel Taylor Coleridge 'Epitaph on Himself'

CONTROVERSY

7 Some feel that for a minister to be controversial because he unashamedly proclaims the Gospel is one thing, and quite acceptable, but for him to arouse ire because he espouses a particular secular cause, such as full employment or the halting of the nuclear arms race, is quite another.
   Christopher Catherwood *Five Evangelical Leaders*

8 Francis Atterbury, Bishop of Rochester (1662—1732), had a mind inexhaustibly rich in all resources of controversy, and familiar with all the artifices which make falsehood look like truth and ignorance like knowledge.
   Thomas Babington Macaulay *Life of Atterbury*

1 Matters of religion should never be matters of controversy. We neither argue with a lover about his taste, nor condemn him, if we are just, for knowing so human a passion.
George Santayana *The Life of Reason* 'Reason in Religion'

2 My grandfather was interested and amused by the controversies that raged round religion and thought that the kettle might be better than the pot, yet he had no wish to be boiled in either of them.
Cecil Torr *Small Talk of Wreyland*

CONVENT

3 A schoolgirl was asked in an examination paper to describe a convent. She wrote, 'A convent is a place where virgins are confined.' The inspector marked the paper, 'This is either a misconception or a clerical error.'
Sir Charles Wheeler Speech to the Royal Society of Arts

CONVERSATION

4 He that converses not, knows nothing.
Thomas Fuller *Gnomologia*

5 Silence and modesty are very valuable qualities in the art of conversation.
Montaigne *Essays*

6 They converse as those would who know that God hears.
Tertullian *Apologeticus*

CONVERSION

7 You come to God in many ways. A student I knew read the *Summa* of Thomas Aquinas, said 'that's it', threw up his career, changed his religion and became a priest. Julian of Norwich, in the Middle Ages, had a bad dose of 'flu, ran a temperature and saw visions.
Rabbi Lionel Blue *A Backdoor to Heaven*

8 When I was in sin the sight of lepers nauseated me beyond measure; then God himself led me into their company, and I had a pity on them; what had previously nauseated me became a source of spiritual and physical consolation. After that I did not wait long before leaving the world.
St Francis of Assisi *Testament of St Francis*

1   If the truth of religious doctrines is dependent on an inner
    experience that bears witness to the truth, what is one to make
    of the many people who do not have that experience?
    Sigmund Freud *The Future of an Illusion*

2   People who think that once they are converted all will be
    happy, have forgotten Satan.
    Martin Lloyd-Jones Quoted Christopher Catherwood *Five
    Evangelical Leaders*

3   I think I am the only person who was actually converted at his
    own confirmation service.
    Robert Runcie, Archbishop of Canterbury Quoted John
    Mortimer *In Character*

CONVICTION

4   Convictions are more dangerous enemies of youth than lies.
    Frederick Nietzsche *Human, All Too Human*

5   Of what worth are convictions that bring not suffering?
    Antoine de Saint-Exupéry *Flight to Arras*

CORRECTION

6   He who is fretted by his own failings will not correct them; all
    profitable correction comes from a calm, peaceful mind.
    St Francis de Sales

COURAGE

7   It is a brave act of valour to despise death, but where life is
    more terrifying than death it is then the truest valour to dare
    to stay alive.
    Sir Thomas Browne *Religio Medici*

8   Courage is almost a contradiction in terms. It means a strong
    desire to live taking the form of a readiness to die.
    G.K. Chesterton *Orthodoxy*

9   Healthy children will not fear life if their elders have integrity
    enough not to fear death.
    Erik M. Erikson *Children and Society*

10 The people I respect most behave as if they were immortal and
    as if society was eternal.
    E.M. Forster *Two Cheers for Democracy*

1   Be strong and of a good courage; be not afraid, neither be
    thou dismayed; for the Lord thy God is with thee,
    whithersoever thou goest.
        Holy Bible Joshua Chap. 1 v. 9

2   Courage faces fear and thereby masters it. Cowardice
    represses fear and is thereby mastered by it.
        Martin Luther King *The Words of Martin Luther King*

3   If the creator had a purpose in equipping us with a neck, he
    surely meant us to stick it out.
        Arthur Koestler *Encounter*

4   Perfect valour consists in doing without witnesses that which
    we would be capable of doing before everyone.
        François, Duc de la Rochefoucauld *Maxims*

5   Courage is not simply *one* of the virtues, but the form of every
    virtue at the testing point, which means at the point of highest
    reality.
        C.S. Lewis Quoted Cyril Connolly *The Unquiet Grave*

6   Life shrinks or expands in proportion to one's courage.
        Anais Nin *Diary*

7   Courage is the price that life exacts for granting peace.
    The soul that knows it not, knows no release
    From little things,
    Knows not the livid loneliness of fear
    Nor mountain heights where bitter joy can hear
    The sound of wings.
        Amelia Earhart Putnam (who disappeared on a solo flight to
        Australia in 1936) 'Courage'

8   Life without the courage for death is slavery.
        Seneca *Letters to Lucilius*

COVETOUSNESS

9   The man who covets is always poor.
        Claudian *In Rufinum*

10 Riches have made more covetous men than covetousness hath
    made rich men.
        Thomas Fuller *Gnomologia*

11 To avoid covetousness is to conquer a kingdom.
        Publilius Syrus

CREATION

1 The spacious firmament on high
With all the blue ethereal sky,
And spangled heavens, a shining frame,
Their great original proclaim:
The unwearied sun, from day to day,
Does his Creator's power display,
And publishes to every land
The work of an almighty hand.
    Joseph Addison 'The Wondrous Tale'

2 Had I been present at the creation I would have given some
useful hints for the ordering of the universe.
    Attributed to Alfonso X of Castile (Alfonso the Wise)

3 The hands of man touch the hands of the Creator in all that he
has made.
    Anon

4 Thou hast made us for Thyself, and the heart of man is restless
until it finds rest in thee.
    St Augustine of Hippo *Confessions*

5 Men are like trees; each one must put forth the leaf that is
created in him.
    Henry Ward Beecher *Proverbs from a Plymouth Pulpit*

6 Under my watchful eye the laws of nature take their course.
Thus is the world set in motion; thus the animate and the
inanimate are created.
    Bhagavad Gita

7 The pride of the peacock is the glory of God.
The lust of the goat is the bounty of God.
The wrath of the lion is the wisdom of God.
The nakedness of woman is the work of God.
    William Blake *Marriage of Heaven and Hell*

8 The heavens declare the glory of God: and the firmament
sheweth his handywork.
    Book of Common Prayer Psalm 19 v. 1

9 He laid the foundations of the earth that it never should move
at any time.
    Book of Common Prayer Psalm 104 v. 5

1 The created world is but a small parenthesis in eternity.
  Sir Thomas Browne *Christian Morals*

2 Let us sing how the eternal God, the author of all marvels,
  first created the heavens for the sons of men as a roof to cover
  them, and how their almighty protector gave them the earth
  for their dwelling place.
  Caedmon Quoted Richard Harries *Prayers of Grief and Glory*

3 Light was first
  Through the Lord's word
  Named day:
  Beauteous, bright creation.
  Caedmon *Creation* 'The First Day'

4 All created things are living in the Hand of God. The senses
  see only the action of the creatures; but faith sees in
  everything the action of God.
  Jean-Pierre de Caussade SJ *Abandonment to Divine Providence*

5 Gabriel: How about cleanin' up de whole mess of 'em and
      startin' all over ag'n wid some new kind of animal?
  God: And admit I'm licked?
  Marc Connelly *Green Pastures*

6 God made the country and man made the town.
  William Cowper *The Task*

7 Man, do not exalt yourself above the animals, they are without
  sin, while you defile the earth by your appearance on it, and
  you leave your traces of defilement behind you.
  Feodor Dostoevsky *The Brothers Karamazov*

8 I want to know how God created the world. I am not
  interested in this or that phenomenon, I want to know his
  thoughts, the rest are details.
  Albert Einstein Quoted Ronald W. Clark *Einstein, His Life and
  Times*

9 What really interests me is whether God had any choice in the
  creation of the world.
  Albert Einstein Quoted 'Einstein's Universe' BBC TV
  5 March 1979

10 Nature is a rag merchant who works up every shred and ort
   and end into new creations.
   Ralph Waldo Emerson *The Conduct of Life*

1 The bio-chemist J.B.S. Haldane was engaged in discussion
with an eminent theologian. 'What inference', asked the latter,
'might one draw about the nature of God from a study of
his works?' Haldane replied, 'An inordinate fondness for
beetles.'
   Clifton Fadiman *Little Brown Book of Anecdotes*

2 The presence in Nature of so many phenomena requiring
intelligence for their appreciation implies a kindred
intelligence to produce them.
   Sir Ambrose Fleming Presidential Address to the Victoria
   Institute 18 March 1936

3 Long Island represents the American's idea of what God
would have done with Nature if he'd had the money.
   Peter Fleming, in a letter to his brother Rupert
   29 September 1929

4 God creates out of the absolute superabundance of his mercy
and love.
   Fr George Florovsky *Collected Works* Vol. 3

5 Man unites himself with the world in the process of creation.
   Erich Fromm *The Art of Loving*

6 The First Cause worked automatically like a somnambulist,
not reflectively like a sage.
   Thomas Hardy *Jude the Obscure*

7 God only opened his hand to give flight to a thought that he
had held imprisoned for eternity.
   Josiah Holland *Goldfoil*

8 In the beginning God created the heaven and the earth.

   And the earth was without form, and void; and darkness was
   upon the face of the deep. And the spirit of God moved upon
   the face of the waters.

   And God said, Let there be light: and there was light.

   And God saw the light, that it was good: and God divided the
   light from the darkness.

   And God called the light Day, and the darkness he called
   Night. And the evening and the morning were the first day.
   Holy Bible Genesis Chap. 1 vv. 1−5

1   So God created man in his own image, in the image of God
    created he him; male and female created he them.
    Holy Bible Genesis Chap. 1 v. 27

2   Consider the lilies of the field, how they grow; they toil not,
    neither do they spin.
    Holy Bible St Matthew Chap. 6 v. 28

3   I am Alpha and Omega, the beginning and the ending, saith
    the Lord.
    Holy Bible Revelation Chap. 1 v. 8

4   Man is Creation's masterpiece: but who says so? — Man.
    Elbert Hubbard

5   The universe seems to have been designed by a pure
    mathematician.
    Sir James Jeans *The Mysterious Universe*

6   And God stepped out on space
    And he looked around and said
    'I am lonely — I'll make me a world.'

7   With his head in his hands
    God thought and thought
    Till he thought 'I'll make me a man.'
    James Weldon Johnson *God's Trombones*

8   I saw three properties; the first is, that God made it. The
    second is, that God loveth it. The third is, that God keepeth
    it. But what beheld I therein? Verily the Maker, the Keeper,
    the Lover.
    Julian of Norwich *Revelations of Divine Love*

9   God made us, not because He knew what we would do, but to
    find out what we would do.
    Damon Knight *The Man in the Tree*

10 It is a sobering reflection that if the five-day week had been in
    force at the Creation, man would not have been created.
    Would the world have been a better place? Only God knows.
    Frank H. Knight Letter to *The Spectator*

11 The visible marks of extraordinary wisdom and power appear
    so plainly in all the works of creation that a rational creature
    who will but seriously reflect on them cannot miss the
    discovery of the deity.
    John Locke *An Essay Concerning Human Understanding*

1   In creating, the only hard thing's to begin;
    A grass-blade's no easier to make than an oak.
    James Russell Lowell 'A Fable for Critics'

2   The parent of the universe fixed for eternity the causes
    whereby he keeps all things in order.
    Lucan *De Bello Civili*

3   God writes the gospel not in the Bible alone, but on trees, and
    flowers and clouds and stars.

4   God creates out of nothing. Therefore, until a man is nothing
    God can make nothing out of him.
    Martin Luther

5   God, in the beginning, formed matter in solid, massy, hard,
    impenetrable, moveable particles, of such sizes and figures,
    and with such other properties and such proportion to space as
    most conduced to the end for which he formed them.
    Sir Isaac Newton *Optics*

6   It is He who makes the flower of the sloe grow through the
    bark of the blackthorn, and the nut-flower on the trees;
    besides this, what miracle is greater.
    Tadhg Og o Huiginn 'Poem'

7   We live at a time when man believes himself fabulously
    capable of creation but he does not know what to create.
    José Ortega y Gasset *The Revolt of the Masses*

8   The country life is to be preferred, for there we see the works
    of God, but in cities little else but the works of men.
    William Penn *Reflexions and Maxims* No. 220

9   God is really only another artist. He invented the elephant,
    the giraffe and the cat. He has no real style. He just goes on
    trying other things.
    Pablo Picasso Quoted Françoise Gilot and Carlton Lake *Life
    with Picasso*

10 Men, it is you who stand in need of Allah. He is all sufficient
    and glorious. He can destroy you if He will and replace you
    with a new creation; this is no impossible thing for Allah.

11 In the alternation of night and day and what God has created
    in the heavens and the earth — surely there are signs for a god-
    fearing people.
    The Quran

1   Allah created you from dust, then from a little germ. Into two sexes He divided you: No female conceives or is delivered without his knowledge. No man grows old or has his life cut short but in accordance with his decree. All this is easy for him.

    The Qur'an

2   God made the rivers to flow. They feel no weariness, they cease not from flowing. They fly swiftly like birds in the air.

    Rig-Veda

3   Man is God's creature, not the manager of evolution.

    Gilbert Shaw 'Homily No. 20'

4   God has not needed me for his mighty works. He did not need me to create the souls of good men or to bring the spring flowers to life again. God can, as a matter of fact, get on perfectly without us, though his home circle would never be complete unless we were in it.

    Rev. H.R.L. Sheppard Sermon 1929

5   Had God thought that sin would enter Eden, he would have created a parson also.

    Laurence Sterne

6   In order to create there must be a dynamic force, and what force is more potent than love?

    Igor Stravinsky *An Autobiography*

7   Such is the likeness of God, wholly given, spent and drained in that sublime self-giving which is the ground and source and origin of the universe.

    W.H. Vanstone *Love's Endeavour Love's Expense*

8   The splendid discontent of God
With chaos, made the world.

    Ella Wheeler Wilcox 'Discontent'

9   I sometimes think that God, in creating man, overestimated his ability.

    Oscar Wilde

CREDIBILITY

10   Credibility does not belong to men — only to God and to Christ.

    Carlo Carretto *The God Who Comes*

CREED

1 Vain are the thousand creeds
   That move men's hearts: unutterably vain.
       Emily Brontë *Last Lines*

2 Where I may see saint, savage, sage
   Fuse their respective creeds in one
   Before the general Father's Throne!
       Robert Browning 'Christmas Eve'

3 There lies at the back of every creed something terrible and
   hard for which the worshipper may one day be required to
   suffer.
       E.M. Forster *Two Cheers for Democracy* 'What I Believe'

4 God has no religion.
       Gandhi

5 I belong to the Great Church which holds the world within its
   starlit aisles; that claims the great and good of every race and
   clime; that finds with joy the grain of gold in every creed, and
   floods with light and love the germs of good in every soul.
       Robert G. Ingersoll Quoted Farrell *Life of Robert G. Ingersoll*

6 He knew
   Behind all creeds the Spirit that is one.
       Andrew Lang *Herodotus in Egypt*

7 If you have embraced a creed which appears to be free from
   the ordinary dirtiness of politics — a creed from which you
   yourself cannot expect to draw any material advantage —
   surely that proves you are right?
       George Orwell *Shooting an Elephant*

8 Creeds are devices to keep heretics out rather than draw
   people in.
       Gerald Priestland *Something Understood*

9 Creeds grow so thick along the way,
   Their boughs hide God; I cannot pray.
       Lizette Woodworth Reese 'Doubt'

10 Forgive me if, midst all Thy works,
   No hint I see of damning;
   And think there's faith among the Turks,
   And hope for e'en the Brahmin.
       William Makepeace Thackeray 'Jolly Jack'

CRICKET

1   It is not the mere presence of clergy at Lords that is impressive but rather the twin stamp of English and Anglican that they bear. You can be sure they are cricketers all, and because cricket is the very soul of England it is in England's Church that they have found their vocation.
    Church Times Quoted Michael Bateman *This England*

2   Cricket is the game which the English, not being a spiritual people, have invented to give themselves some concept of eternity.
    Lord Mancroft Quoted Leon Harris *The Fine Art of Political Wit*

3   The parson in a village where a friend of mine lives was perturbed at the persistent shortage of rain. Cattle and roots were suffering. The outlook was gloomy. He decided to pray for rain at the morning service next Sunday. Then a troublesome thought struck him. 'No,' he told my friend; 'not next Sunday. I shall put it off until the next Sunday. *I am not going to do anything to spoil the test match.*'
    Frank Muir Quoted *Sunday Times* 'Frank Muir Goes Into —' 1978

CROSS

4   Nearer, my God, to Thee,
Nearer to Thee;
E'en though it be a cross
That raiseth me.
    Sarah Adams Hymn

5   But God forbid that I should glory, save in the cross of our Lord Jesus Christ.
    Holy Bible Galatians Chap. 6 v. 14

6   One who does not seek the Cross of Jesus isn't seeking the glory of Christ.
    St John of the Cross *Sayings*

7   If thou bear thy cross cheerfully, it will bear thee.

8   In the Cross there is safety.

9   Jesus hath now many lovers of the heavenly kingdom, but few bearers of His Cross.
    Thomas à Kempis *The Imitation of Christ*

1 I have lived with the conviction that unearned suffering is redemptive. There are some who still find the cross a stumbling block, others consider it foolishness. But I am more convinced than ever that it is the power of God to social and individual salvation.

   Martin Luther King *Strength to Love*

2 The cross preceded the resurrection; but the Resurrection has not abolished the cross. Suffering, sin, betrayal, cruelty of every kind, continued to exist after the crucifixion and they continue still. This is the failure of the cross. God made failure an instrument of victory.

   Una Kroll *Lawsuit for a Lost Enemy*

3 The Way of the Cross is the Way of Light.

   Mediaeval proverb

4 The Cross is where history and life, legend and reality, time and eternity, intersect. There, Jesus is nailed forever to show us how God would become a man and a man become God.

   Malcolm Muggeridge *Jesus Discovered*

5 O Saviour of the world, who by thy Cross and precious Blood has redeemed us: Save us and keep us, we humbly beseech Thee, O Lord.

   The Priest's Vade Mecum 'Antiphon'

6 Christianity without the Cross is nothing. The Cross is the fitting close of a life of rejection and scorn, and defeat. But in no true sense have these things ceased or changed, Jesus is still He whom men despised, and the rejected of men.

   James Thomson *The Greek Argument*

7 The Cross of Christ is the Jacob's ladder by which we ascend into the Highest Heaven.

   Thomas Traherne *Meditations*

8 The Cross is a picture of violence, yet the key to peace, a picture of suffering, yet the key to healing, a picture of death, yet the key to life.

   David Watson *Is Anyone There?*

9 When I survey the wondrous cross
   On which the Prince of Glory died,
   My richest gain I count but loss,
   And pour contempt on all my pride.

   Isaac Watts *Hymns and Spiritual Songs*

CRUCIFIXION

1 He knelt beneath the olives' shade
   And the trees bent over Him,
   And, though all light by Him was made,
   His soul in twilight dim
   Sought for the blessed will of God
   In agony and sweat of blood
   Till the Cross shone clear for Him.
   Then came He forth in strength again
   And went to die for sinful men.
   > Fr Andrew SDC *The Way of Victory* 'Gethsemane'

2 There He hangs, nailed to the Cross in the darkness and He
   loves us still.
   > Fr Andrew SDC *A Gift of Light*

3 The Son of David bowed to die,
   For man's transgression stricken;
   The Father's arm of power was nigh,
   The Son of God to quicken.
   Praise Him that He died for men;
   Praise Him that He rose again.
   > Joseph Anstice *Victor Funeris*

4 To guess from the insulted face
   Just what Appearances He saves
   By suffering in a public place
   A death reserved for slaves.
   > W.H. Auden 'Friday's Child'

5 No man took His life; He laid it down of Himself.
   > R.H. Benson *Spiritual Letters of Monsignor R. Hugh Benson to
   > One of His Converts*

6 The memory of Christ Jesus crucified was ever present in the
   depths of his [Francis'] heart like a bundle of myrrh.
   > St Bonaventure *The Life of St Francis* 'The Tree of Life'

7 In nailing Jesus' body to the cross his foes nailed his memory
   and teaching there.
   > Arthur Bryant *Makers of the Realm*

8 Where Life was slain and Truth was slandered
   On that one holier hill than Rome.
   > G.K. Chesterton

1   You can blame it on to Adam
You can blame it on to Eve
You can blame it on the apple
But that I can't believe.
It was God that made the Devil
And the woman and the man
And there wouldn't be an apple
If it wasn't in the plan.
It's God they ought to crucify
Instead of you and me
I said to the carpenter
A-hanging on the tree.
    Sydney Carter 'Friday Morning'

2   If it has to choose who is to be crucified the crowd will
always save Barabbas.
    Jean Cocteau *Le Rappel à l'Ordre*

3   Lovely was the death
Of him whose life was love.
    Samuel Taylor Coleridge

4   The gift which the good God gives His friends is the Cross.
    The Curé d'Ars (Jean-Baptiste Vianney) Quoted Fr Andrew
SDC *The Way of Victory*

5   The cross is the ladder to heaven.
    Thomas Draxe

6   O sacred head, sore wounded
With grief and shame bowed down
Now scornfully surrounded
With thorns, Thy only crown.
    Paul Gerhardt 'Passion Chorale' based on 12th-century Latin
hymn

7   The cry of thirst which Jesus gave on the Cross was a
statement of need. He spoke for a world in need; for the
myriads who would hunger and thirst down the ages of history.
    Norman Goodacre *Layman's Lent*

8   If we had not been taught how to interpret the story of the
Passion, would we have been able to say from their actions
alone whether it was the jealous Judas or the cowardly Peter
who loved Christ?
    Graham Greene *The End of the Affair*

1   God bought man here with his heart's blood expense,
    And man sold God here for base thirty pence.
    Robert Herrick 'God's Price and Man's Price'

2   He said, It is finished: and he bowed his head, and gave up the
    ghost.
    Holy Bible St John Chap. 19 v. 30

3   In those holy fields
    (over whose acres walked those blessed feet)
    Which fourteen hundred years ago were nailed
    For our advantage on the bitter cross.
    William Shakespeare *King Henry IV Part I* Act I Sc. 1

4   When Jesus came to Golgotha
    They hanged him on a tree
    They drove great nails through hands and feet
    And made a Calvary;
    They crowned him with a crown of thorns
    Red were his wounds and deep,
    For those were crude and cruel days
    And human flesh was cheap.
    G.A. Studdert-Kennedy 'Indifference'

5   Overheard in a Chiswick jeweller's shop, assistant to customer
    examining a collection of crucifix pendants: 'Are you looking
    for a plain one, or one with a little man on it?'
    The Times 'Diary' 3 February 1987

6   That cross is a tree set on fire with invisible flame, that
    illumineth all the world. The flame is love.
    Thomas Traherne *Centuries of Meditations*

7   He whose soul remains ever turned towards God though the
    nail pierces it finds himself nailed to the very centre of the
    universe. It is not the middle; it is beyond space and time; it is
    God.
    Simone Weil *The Love of God and Affliction*

8   All ye that pass by,
    To Jesus draw nigh;
    To you is it nothing that Jesus should die?
    Your ransom and peace,
    Your surety He is;
    Come, see if there ever was sorrow like this?
    Charles Wesley

CRUELTY

1 Cruelty is perhaps the worst kind of sin. Intellectual cruelty is certainly the worst kind of cruelty.

G.K. Chesterton *All Things Considered* 'Concert and Caricature'

2 Men are the only animals who devote themselves assiduously to making one another unhappy.

H.L. Mencken *Notebook*

CULTS

3 I regard Scientology as a cult. One of the definitions of a cult would be an organisation not well integrated into society as a whole, that surrounds a charismatic figure. In the case of Scientology, the figure would be Mr Ron Hubbard.

Rosemary Harthill *In Perspective*

CUSTOM

4 When I am in Rome I fast as the Romans do; when I am at Milan I do not fast: so, likewise you, whatever church you come to, observe the custom of the place.

St Ambrose to St Augustine, on Sabbath-keeping

DARKNESS

1   For this reason this darkness which is between you and your
    God, I do not call a cloud of the air, but a cloud of
    unknowing.

2   Reconcile yourself to wait in this darkness as long as is
    necessary, but still go on longing after him whom you love.
    For if you are to feel him in this life, it must always be in this
    cloud in this darkness.
        The Cloud of Unknowing

3   The light shineth in darkness; and the darkness
    comprehended it not.
        Holy Bible St John Chap. 1 v. 5

4   Darkness is looking back and saying: 'I have been deluded
    from the start; it has all been a mistake.' Darkness is looking
    forward and saying: 'I do not know what to do next; I have
    lost my way and it is too late to find it now.'
        Hubert van Zeller *The Inner Search*

DAWN

5   When he hears the cock crowing he should say, 'Blessed is He
    who has given to the cock understanding to distinguish
    between day and night.'
        Berakoth Quoted *Oxford Book of Prayer* 'Jewish Reform
        Prayers'

DEATH

6   See in what peace a Christian can die.
        Joseph Addison Last words

7   To die quickly is a privilege: I shall die by inches.
        H.F. Amiel *Journal*

1   The descent to Hades is much the same from whatever place
    we start.
    Anaxagoras

2   Think not disdainfully of death, but look upon it with favour:
    for even death is one of the things that Nature wills.
    Marcus Aurelius *Meditations*

3   Spend your brief moment according to nature's law, and
    serenely greet the journey's end as an olive falls when it is
    ripe, blessing the branch that bore it, and giving thanks to the
    tree that gave it life.
    Marcus Aurelius Quoted *A Little Book of Life and Death*

4   Men fear death as children fear to go in the dark; and as
    that natural fear in children is increased with tales, so is the
    other.
    Francis Bacon *Essays* 'Of Death'

5   Death borders upon our birth and our cradle stands in the
    grave.
    Richard Barnfield *Epistles*

6   I shall hear in Heaven.
    Beethoven, referring to his deafness

7   He who remembereth Me at the time of the end, being freed
    from the body, he, going forth, entereth into My being; there
    is no doubt of that.
    Bhagavad Gita

8   Death is the supreme festival on the road to freedom.
    Dietrich Bonhoeffer *Letters from Prison*

9   In the midst of life we are in death.
    Book of Common Prayer At the Burial of the Dead

10 If it were not for death there would be no urgency about
    religion.
    Gerald Brenan *Thoughts in a Dry Season*

11 I remember, in Middlesex Hospital, waiting guiltily for last
    words from Brendan Behan for a newspaper. 'Brendan,' I
    whispered, 'do you ever think about death?' He sat up, like an
    enormous Pooh bear, in a sheet like a toga. 'Think about
    death?' he shouted. 'Bigod I'd rather be dead than think about
    death.'
    Alan Brien Quoted E.H. Mikhail *Brendan Behan*

1 War knows no power; safe shall be my going,
Secretly armed against all death's endeavours;
Safe, though all safety's lost, safe where men fall;
And if these poor limbs die, safest of all.
    Rupert Brooke 'Safety'

2 We shall go down with unreluctant tread
Rose-crowned into the darkness.
    Rupert Brooke 'The Hill'

3 If I should die, think only this of me;
That there's some corner of a foreign field
That is for ever England.
    Rupert Brooke 'The Soldier'

4 The long habit of living indisposeth us to dying.
    Sir Thomas Browne *Urn Burial*

5 Could the Devil work my belief to imagine I could never die,
I would not outlive that very thought.
    Sir Thomas Browne *Religio Medici*

6 O Death! the poor man's dearest friend —
The kindest and the best.
    Robert Burns 'Man was made to Mourn'

7 If life must not be taken too seriously — then neither must
death.

8 To die is to leave off dying and do the thing once and for all.
    Samuel Butler *Notebooks*

9 While other people's deaths are deeply sad, one's own is
surely a bit of a joke.
    James Cameron *Observer* 'Sayings of the Week' 17 January 1982

10 The dead are all holy, even they that were base and wicked
while alive. Their baseness and wickedness was not they, was
but the heavy unmanageable environment that lay around
them.
    Thomas Carlyle *Biography*

11 There is a remedy for everything but death, which will be sure
to lay us out flat some time or other.
    Cervantes *Don Quixote*

12 For the unhappy man death is the commutation of a sentence
of life imprisonment.
    Alexander Chase *Perspectives*

1   I am ready to meet my Maker. Whether my Maker is
prepared for the ordeal of meeting me is another matter.
> Winston Churchill, on his 75th birthday

2   Death be not proud, though some have called thee
Mighty and dreadful, for, thou are not so,
For those, whom thou think'st, thou dost overthrow,
Die not, poor death, nor yet canst thou kill me.

3   One short sleep past, we wake eternally,
And Death shall be no more: Death, thou shalt die!
> John Donne *Holy Sonnets*

4   Any man's death diminishes me because I am involved in
mankind, and therefore never send to hear for whom the bell
tolls: it tolls for thee.
> John Donne *Devotions*

5   What is so intricate, so entangling as death? Whoever got out
of a winding sheet?
> John Donne Sermon preached to the King at Whitehall

6   Why, do you not know, then, that the origin of all human
evils, and of all baseness, and of cowardice, is not death, but
rather the fear of death?
> Epictetus *Discourses*

7   It is possible to provide security against other ills, but so far as
death is concerned we men all live in a city without walls.
> Epicurus

8   Death is a debt we all must pay.
> Euripides *Alcestis*

9   What good can come of meeting death with tears? If a man is
sorry for himself he doubles death.
> Euripides *Iphigenia in Tauris*

10   It hath often been said that it is not death, but dying, which is
terrible.
> Henry Fielding *Amelia*

11   I am afraid to think about my death,
When it shall be and whether, in great pain
I shall rise up and fight the air for breath
Or calmly wait the bursting of my brain.
> James Elroy Flecker *Hassan*

1 Our final experience, like our first, is conjectural. We move
   between two darknesses.
   > E.M. Forster *Aspects of the Novel*

poets

2 And thou, most kind and gentle death
   Waiting to hush our latest breath
   O Praise Him — Alleluia
   Thou leadest home the child of God
   And Christ our Lord the way hath trod.
   > St Francis of Assisi 'The Canticle of the Creatures'

+ Saints

3 Why fear death? It is the most beautiful adventure in life.
   > Charles Frohman Last words before going down on the
   > *Lusitania* 7 May 1915

4 If you would behold the spirit of death, open your heart wide
   unto the body of life. For life and death are one, even as the
   river and sea are one.
   > Kahlil Gibran *The Prophet*

poets

5 Death, that final curb on freedom, has itself suffered a death
   blow through the resurrection of Jesus.
   > Michael Green *Jesus Spells Freedom*

6 In the last analysis it is our conception of death which decides
   the answers to all the questions that life puts to us.
   > Dag Hammarskjöld *Diaries*

7 If even dying is to be made a social function, then, please,
   grant me the favour of sneaking out on tip-toe without
   disturbing the party.
   > Dag Hammarskjöld *Markings*

8 There was a time when we were not. This gives us no concern
   — why then should it trouble us that a time will come when we
   shall cease to be?
   > William Hazlitt *Table Talk* 'The Fear of Death'

Philos

9 To die is to go into the Collective Unconscious, to lose oneself
   in order to be transformed into form, pure form.
   > Hermann Hesse Quoted Miguel Serrano *C.G. Jung and
   > Hermann Hesse*

10 Dust thou art, and unto dust thou shalt return.
   > *Holy Bible* Genesis Chap. 3 v. 19

11 We must needs die, and are as water spilt on the ground,
   which cannot be gathered up again.
   > *Holy Bible* 2 Samuel Chap. 14 v. 14

1 Now the days of David drew nigh that he should die; and he charged Solomon his son, saying, I go the way of all the earth.
   Holy Bible 1 Kings Chap. 2 vv. 1–2

2 The Lord gave, and the Lord hath taken away; blessed be the name of the Lord.
   Holy Bible Job Chap. 1 v. 21

3 There the wicked cease from troubling; and there the weary be at rest.
   Holy Bible Job Chap. 3 v. 17

4 Let us eat and drink; for tomorrow we shall die.
   Holy Bible Isaiah Chap. 22 v. 13

5 We have made a covenant with death, and with hell are we at agreement.
   Holy Bible Isaiah Chap. 28 v. 15

6 The last enemy that shall be destroyed is death.
   Holy Bible 1 Corinthians Chap. 15 v. 26

7 For we brought nothing into this world, and it is certain we can carry nothing out.
   Holy Bible 1 Timothy Chap. 6 v. 7

8 And I looked, and behold a pale horse: and his name that sat on him was Death.
   Holy Bible Revelation Chap. 6 v. 8

9 Death o'ertakes the man who flees.
   Horace *Odes*

10 Amid the gloom of Churchill's farewell cabinet the secretary, Norman Brook, to cheer up Winston, told him, 'By the way, did you know that General X, the last survivor of Omdurman except for yourself, died this morning?' Winston replied, 'How very *civil* of him.'
    Alistair Horne *Sunday Times* 4 January 1987

11 It does not worry me that I did not exist in 1905, so why should I worry that I shall not exist in 1995.
    David Howarth *Pursued By a Bear*

12 Death is the only thing we haven't succeeded in completely vulgarising.
    Aldous Huxley *Eyeless in Gaza*

1 Teach me to live, that I may dread
The grave as little as my bed.
Bishop Thomas Ken Hymn 'Glory to Thee, My God, This
Night'

2 Strange, is it not? that of the myriads who
Before us passed the door of Darkness through,
Not one returns to tell us of the Road,
Which to discover we must travel too.
Omar Khayyam *Rubaiyat* Trans. Edward Fitzgerald

3 A man who won't die for something is not fit to live.
Martin Luther King *The Words of Martin Luther King*

4 Death is the only pure, beautiful conclusion of a great passion.
D.H. Lawrence *Fantasia of the Unconscious*

5 The only religious way to think of death is as a part and parcel
of life.

6 A man's dying is more the survivor's affair than his own.
Thomas Mann *The Magic Mountain*

7 Death opens unknown doors. It is most grand to die.
John Masefield *Pompey the Great*

8 When Death makes his arrest we have to go.
John Masefield 'The Widow in the Bye Street'

9 And may we find when ended is the page
Death but a tavern on our pilgrimage.
John Masefield 'The Word'

10 Whom the gods love dies young.
Menander *Dis Exapaton*

11 Not death is dreadful, but a shameful death.
Menander *Monostikoi*

12 In the attempt to defeat death man has been inevitably obliged
to defeat life, for the two are inextricably related. Life moved
on to death, and to deny one is to deny the other.
Henry Miller *The Wisdom of the Heart* 'Creative Death'

13 And to the faithful, death the gate of life.
John Milton *Paradise Lost*

14 We die only once, and for such a long time.
Molière *Le Dépit Amoureux*

1 Live holily, and you shall die happily:
  Live as though there were no gospel,
  But die as though there were no law.
> Henry Montague, Earl of Manchester Quoted *A Little Book of Life and Death*

2 Live as long as you please, you will strike nothing off the time you will have to spend dead.
> Montaigne *Essays*

3 See me safe up: for my coming down I can shift for myself.
> Sir Thomas More, on the scaffold

Poets

4 Life is a great surprise. I do not see why death should not be an even greater one.
> Vladimir Nabokov *Pale Fire*

5 All victory ends in the defeat of death. That's sure. But does defeat end the victory of death? That's what I wonder.
> Eugene O'Neill *Mourning Becomes Electra*

6 Christianity has made of death a terror that was unknown to the gay calmness of Pagans.
> Ouida *The Failure of Christianity*

7 Death's but a path that would be trod,
  If man would ever pass to God.
> Thomas Parnell 'A Night Piece on Death'

8 Death is but crossing the world, as friends do the sea; they live in one another still.
> William Penn *Some Fruits of Solitude*

9 A good death does honour to a whole life.
> Petrarch 'To Laura in Death'

10 The people who pretend that dying is rather like strolling into the next room always leave me unconvinced. Death, like birth, must be a tremendous event.
> J.B. Priestley *Outcries and Asides*

11 If thou expect death as a friend, prepare to entertain it; if thou expect death as an enemy, prepare to overcome it; death has no advantage, except when it comes as a stranger.
> Francis Quarles *Enchiridion*

12 We perish, we disappear, but the march of time goes on forever.
> Ernest Renan

1 Death is always, under all circumstances, a tragedy, for if it is
   not then it means that life has become one.
   > Theodore Roosevelt *Letter to Cecil Spring-Rice* 12 March 1900

2 The dark background which death supplies brings out the
   tender colours of life in all their purity.
   > George Santayana *Soliloquies in England*

3 Death is sometimes a punishment, often a gift; to many it has
   been a favour.
   > Seneca *Hercules Oetaeus*

4 Death either destroys us or unmasks us. If it means liberation,
   better things await us when our burden is gone; if destruction,
   nothing at all awaits us, blessings and curses are abolished.
   > Seneca *Letters to Lucilius*

5 This fell sergeant, death,
   Is strict in his arrest.
   > William Shakespeare *Hamlet* Act V Sc. 2

6 Men must endure
   Their going hence, even as their coming hither:
   Ripeness is all.
   > William Shakespeare *King Lear* Act V Sc. 2

7 The worst is death, and death will have his day.
   > William Shakespeare *King Richard II* Act III Sc. 2

8 Life levels all men; death reveals the eminent.
   > George Bernard Shaw *Man and Superman*

9 If there wasn't death I think you couldn't go on.
   > Stevie Smith *Observer* 9 November 1969

10 Nobody knows what death is, nor whether to man it is
   perchance the greatest of blessings, yet people fear it as if they
   surely knew it to be the worst of evils.
   > Socrates

11 A single death is a tragedy: a million deaths is a statistic.
   > Joseph Stalin

12 It is impossible that anything so natural, so necessary, and so
   universal as death should ever have been designed by
   Providence as an evil to mankind.
   > Jonathan Swift

poet

1 Death's stamp gives value to the coin of life, making it possible to buy with life what is truly precious.
   Rabindranath Tagore *Stray Birds*

2 No life that breathes with human breath
   Has ever truly longed for death.
   Alfred, Lord Tennyson

3 A beautiful death is for people who have lived like animals to die like angels.
   Mother Teresa of Calcutta Quoted Kathryn Spinks *For the Brotherhood of Man Under the Fatherhood of God*

4 After the first death, there is no other.
   Dylan Thomas 'A Refusal to Mourn the Death of a Child'

Theol

5 In the depth of the anxiety of having to die is the anxiety of being eternally forgotten.
   Paul Tillich *The Eternal Now*

6 Death is the flowering of life, the consummation of union with God.

7 When you think you are going to die say to yourself, 'So much the better! I am about to behold the Adorable!'
   Abbé de Tourville *Letters of Direction*

8 Death, the only immortal who treats us all alike, whose peace and whose refuge are for us all. The soiled and the pure, the rich and the poor, the loved and the unloved.
   Mark Twain, on his deathbed

9 Death hides, but it does not divide,
   They are but on Christ's other side.
   Thou art with Christ and Christ with me,
   In Him I still am close to thee.
   Elizabeth Urch *Ladders Up to Heaven* 'Friendship'

10 As a well-spent day brings happy sleep, so life well used brings happy death.
    Leonardo da Vinci *Notebooks*

11 Comes the supreme day and the inevitable hour.
    Virgil *Aeneid*

12 Death helps us to see what is worth trusting and loving and what is a waste of time.
    J. Neville Ward *Five for Sorrow Ten for Joy*

1   'We welcome news of old Boys particularly those who have
    died.'
    From school magazine Quoted David Watson *Is Anyone There?*

2   We are secretly more terrified of death now than in medieval
    times. It is the one aspect of life, so to speak, that civilisation
    has not improved.
    Peter Watson *The Times* 6 July 1981

3   Man has given a false importance to death. Any animal, plant
    or man who dies adds to Nature's compost heap, becomes the
    manure without which nothing could grow, nothing could be
    created. Death is simply part of the process.
    Peter Weiss *Marat/Sade*

4   The experiment will be over, the rinsed beaker returned to its
    shelf, the crystals gone dissolving down the wastepipe; the
    duster wipes the bench.
    H.G. Wells *First and Last Things*

5   Death is an angel with two faces —
    To us he turns
    A face of terrors, blighting all things fair.
    The other burns
    With glory of the stars, a love is there.
    T.C. Williams 'A Thanatopsis'

DEBT

6   If a man owes you money and he is unable to pay, do not pass
    before him.
    The Talmud

DECEIT

7   I have met many that would deceive; who would be deceived,
    no one.
    St Augustine of Hippo *Confessions*

8   Bread of deceit is sweet to a man; but afterwards his mouth
    shall be filled with gravel.
    Holy Bible Proverbs Chap. 20 v. 17

9   If we say that we have no sin, we deceive ourselves, and the
    truth is not in us.
    Holy Bible 1 John Chap. 1 v. 8

DECISION

1   How long halt ye between two opinions?
   Holy Bible 1 Kings Chap. 18 v. 21

2   All heaven's glory is within
   And so is hell's fierce burning.
   You must yourself decide
   In which direction
   You are turning.
   Angelus Silesius *The Book of Angelus Silesius*

DEDICATION

3   Lord, take my lips and speak through them, take my mind and
   think through it; take my heart and set it on fire.
   W.H.H. Aitken Quoted *Oxford Book of Prayer*

4   I wish the state of enthusiasm I am now in may last, for today
   I FELT there is a God. I have been devotional and my mind
   has been led away from the follies that it is mostly wrapped up
   in.
   Elizabeth Fry *Spiritual Experiences of Friends*

5   If any thing delight me for to print
   My book, 'tis this; that Thou, my God, art in't.
   Robert Herrick 'To God'

6   Father, into Thy hands I give the heart which left Thee but to
   learn how good Thou art.
   George MacDonald

7   May I become an unfailing store for the wretched, and be first
   to supply them with their needs.

8   May I become a medicine for the sick and their physician,
   their support until sickness come again.
   Santideva Quoted *The Path of Light*

9   Drop thy still dews of quietness,
   Till all our strivings cease;
   Take from our souls the strain and stress,
   And let our ordered lives confess
   The beauty of thy peace.
   John Greenleaf Whittier *Hymns Ancient and Modern* 'Dear
   Lord and Father of Mankind'

DEEDS

1 Who doeth right deeds is twice born, and who doeth ill deeds vile.
   Sir Edwin Arnold *The Light of Asia*

2 Our deeds still travel with us from afar,
   And what we have been makes us what we are.
   George Eliot *Middlemarch* Epigraph

3 Every thought I have imprisoned in expression I must free by my deeds.
   Kahlil Gibran *Sand and Foam*

4 For as one star another far exceeds,
   So souls in heaven are placed by their deeds.
   Robert Greene 'A Maiden's Dream'

5 I count this thing to be grandly true,
   That a noble deed is a step towards God.
   Josiah Gilbert Holland 'Gradatim'

6 The deeds of men never deceive the Gods.
   Ovid *Tristia*

DEIFICATION

7 Our Lord says to every living soul, 'I became man for you. If you do not become God for me, you do me wrong.'
   Meister Eckhart

DELIGHT

8 To give delight is hallowed — perhaps the toil of angels, whose avocations are concealed.
   Emily Dickinson *Selected Poems and Letters of Emily Dickinson*

DELIVERANCE

9 Our God whom we serve is able to deliver us from the burning fiery furnace.
   Holy Bible Daniel Chap. 3 v. 17

10 Deliver me from my own shadows, my Lord, from the wrecks and confusion of my days.
   Rabindranath Tagore Quoted *Holy Waters* Indian Psalm
   Meditations Text by Martin Kämpchen

DEMOCRACY

1   The voice of the people is the voice of God.
    Alcuin Letter to Charlemagne

2   The Church cannot exercise democracy. The Church does not
    belong to its members nor is it dependent on its members for
    its life or existence. It belongs to Christ.
    Rev. David J. Howson Quoted *Daily Telegraph* 3 January 1979

3   It is the evil in man that makes democracy necessary, and
    man's belief in justice that makes democracy possible.
    Reinhold Niebuhr

DENOMINATION

4   The account of religious terms towards the end of the book
    has been rearranged so that dissenters and nonconformists are
    no longer grouped with idolaters, fire-worshippers, and other
    heathens.
    D.C. Browning Introduction to Everyman edition of Roget's
    Thesaurus

5   Almost every sect of Christianity is a perversion of its essence,
    to accommodate it to the prejudices of the world.
    William Hazlitt *The Round Table* 'On the Causes of Methodism'

DEPRAVITY

6   A corrupt tree bringeth forth evil fruit.
    Holy Bible St Matthew Chap. 7 v. 17

DESERT

7   The wilderness and the solitary place shall be glad for them;
    and the desert shall rejoice, and blossom as the rose.
    Holy Bible Isaiah Chap. 35 v. 1

8   The desert was also the country of madness ... the sterile
    paradise of emptiness and rage.
    Thomas Merton *Thoughts in Solitude*

9   The desert bears the sign of man's complete helplessness as he
    can do nothing to subsist alone and by himself, and he thus
    discovers his weakness and the necessity of seeking help and
    strength in God.
    René Voillaume *Jesus Caritas*

DESIRE

1   O Lord our God, grant us grace to desire thee with our whole
    heart; that so desiring, we may seek, and seeking, find thee;
    and so finding thee, may love thee; and loving thee, may hate
    those sins from which thou hast redeemed us. Amen.
       St Anselm

2   A person who is not disturbed by the incessant flow of desires
    — that enter like rivers into the ocean which is ever being
    filled but is always still — can alone achieve peace, and not the
    man who strives to satisfy such desires.

3   Selfish desire is found in the senses, mind and intellect,
    misleading them and burying the understanding in delusion.
       Bhagavad Gita

4   It is by that which he longs for, that every man knows and
    apprehends the quality with which he has to serve God.
       Martin Buber *Hasidism*

5   As the hart panteth after the water brooks, so panteth my soul
    after thee, O God.
       Holy Bible Psalm 42 v. 1

6   The desire of love, Joy;
    The desire of life, Peace;
    The desire of the soul, Heaven;
    The desire of God — a flame-white secret for ever.
       William Sharp 'Desire'

7   If we do go down into ourselves we find that we possess
    exactly what we desire.
       Simone Weil *Gravity and Grace*

DESOLATION

8   Let him who is in consolation think how it will be with him in
    the desolation that will follow, laying up fresh strength for that
    time.
       St Ignatius Loyola *The Spiritual Exercises*

DESPAIR

9   To live without hope is to cease to live.
       Feodor Dostoevsky

1   There is no despair so absolute as that which comes with the
first moments of our first great sorrow, when we have not yet
known what it is to have suffered and be healed, to have
despaired and recovered hope.
     George Eliot *Adam Bede*

2   In a really dark night of the soul it is always three in the
morning, day after day.
     F. Scott Fitzgerald *The Crack-Up*

3   I turned to speak to God
About the world's despair;
But to make bad matters worse
I found God wasn't there.
     Robert Frost 'Not All There'

4   Utter despair, impossible to pull myself together; only when I
have become satisfied with my sufferings can I stop.
     Franz Kafka *The Diaries of Franz Kafka*

5   Despair is vinegar from the wine of hope.
     Austin O'Malley *Keystones of Thought*

DESPISER

6   I love the great despisers, because they are the great adorers,
and arrows of longing for the other shore.
     Friedrich Nietzsche *Thus Spake Zarathustra*

DESTINY

7   Nor sitting by his hearth at home
Does man escape his appointed doom.
     Aeschylus

8   Destiny has two ways of crushing us. By refusing our wishes
and by fulfilling them.
     H.F. Amiel *Journal*

9   We can in our own little lives be utterly certain that God
always has an alternative, in which the one purpose for which
we are here may be fulfilled, if other ways fail.
     Fr Andrew SDC *The Way of Victory*

10 Consider your origin: you were not born to live like brutes,
but to follow virtue and knowledge.
     Dante *Divine Comedy* 'Inferno'

1 If thou follow thy star, thou canst not fail of glorious heaven.
>Dante *Divine Comedy* 'Purgatory'

2 A consistent man believes in destiny, a capricious man in chance.
>Benjamin Disraeli *Vivian Grey*

3 We are not permitted to choose the frame of our destiny. But what we put into it is ours.
>Dag Hammarskjöld *Markings*

4 We are called to be a great living cloth of gold with not only the woof going from God to man and from man to God, but also the warp going from man to man.
>Baron Friedrich von Hügel *The Mystical Element in Religion*

5 When it is time for sleep and you approach your bed, say 'Bed, perhaps this night you will become my grave, I do not know.'
>St Isaac the Syrian *Mystic Treatises*

6 On the face of it, one would think that we must needs all complete our destinies, merely by the simple process of living out our lives to the end.
>Rose Macaulay *A Casual Commentary*

7 We are but as the instrument of Heaven:
Our work is not design, but destiny.
>Owen Meredith *Clytemnestra*

8 Your destiny is that of a man, your vows those of a god.
>Voltaire *La Liberté*

DETACHMENT

9 He who is without affection either for good or evil is firmly fixed in perfect knowledge.

10 One who restrains his senses and fixes his consciousness upon Me is known as a man of steady intelligence.
>*Bhagavad Gita*

DETERMINATION

11 Each day you must say to yourself, 'Today I am going to begin.'
>Jean-Pierre de Caussade SJ *Abandonment to Divine Providence*

1 He that shall endure unto the end, the same shall be saved.
Holy Bible St Mark Chap. 13 v. 13

2 It is still one of the tragedies of human history that the 'children of darkness' are frequently more determined and zealous than the 'children of light'.
Martin Luther King *The Words of Martin Luther King*

DEVIL

3 If evil is caused by the flesh, how explain the wickedness of the Devil who has no flesh?
St Augustine of Hippo *The City of God*

4 Dost thou, in the name of this child, renounce the devil and all his works?
Book of Common Prayer Order of Baptism

5 An apology for the Devil: it must be remembered we have only heard one side of the case. God has written all the books.

6 God without the devil is dead, being alone.
Samuel Butler *Notebooks*

7 The fiend with all his comrades
Fell then from heaven above
Through as long as three nights and three days
The angels from heaven into hell;
And them all the Lord transformed into devils
Because they his deed and word would not revere.
Caedmon *Creation* 'The Fall of the Rebel Angels'

8 Therefore behoveth him a full long spoon
That shall eat with a fiend, thus heard I say.
Geoffrey Chaucer *Canterbury Tales* 'The Squire's Tale'

9 The snake, it is known, is the animal monkeys most dread. Hence when men give their devil a definite form, they make him a snake. A race of super-chickens would have pictured their devil a hawk.
Clarence Day *This Simian World*

10 Every devil has not a cloven hoof.
Daniel Defoe *History of the Devil*

11 A religion can no more afford to degrade its Devil than to degrade its God.
Havelock Ellis *Impressions and Comments*

1 I do perceive that this devil is passing crafty, forasmuch as not being able to do a hurt unto my soul, he is fain to hinder a necessity of my body in such sort that I cannot sleep, and by this means to hinder the cheerfulness of my heart.
   St Francis of Assisi

2 One is always wrong to open a conversation with the Devil, for, however he goes about it, he always insists on having the last word.
   André Gide *Journals*

3 I called the devil, and he came;
   With wonder his form did I closely scan;
   He is not ugly and is not lame,
   But really a handsome and charming man.
   Heinrich Heine *Travel* 'Sketches'

4 Why should the devil have all the good tunes?
   Rev. Rowland Hill *Sermons*

5 And Satan came also among them to present himself before the Lord.
   Holy Bible Job Chap. 2 v. 1

6 And he shewed me Joshua the high priest standing before the angel of the Lord, and Satan standing at his right hand to resist him.
   Holy Bible Zechariah Chap. 3 v. 1

7 Be sober, be vigilant; because your adversary the devil, as a roaring lion, walketh about, seeking whom he may devour.
   Holy Bible 1 Peter Chap. 5 v. 8

8 Few people now believe in the Devil; but many enjoy behaving as their ancestors behaved when the Fiend was a reality as unquestionable as his opposite number.
   Aldous Huxley *The Devils of Loudon*

9 The Devil usually speaks a language called Bellsybabble which he makes up himself as he goes along but when he is very angry he can speak bad French very well though some who have heard him say that he has a strong Dublin accent.
   James Joyce *The Cat and the Devil*

10 It is so stupid of modern civilisation to have given up belief in the devil when he is the only explanation of it.
   Ronald Knox *Let Dons Delight*

1   Who is the most diligent bishop and prelate in England? I will tell you. It is the devil. He is never out of his diocese. The devil is diligent at his plough.

      Hugh Latimer *Sermon on Ploughers*

2   It is no use casting out devils. They belong to us, we must accept them and be at peace with them.

      D.H. Lawrence *Phoenix*

3   The devil is merely a fallen angel, and when God lost Satan he lost one of his best lieutenants.

      Walter Lippmann *A Preface to Politics* 'The Red Herring'

4   It is Lucifer,
The son of mystery;
And since God suffers him to be,
He, too, is God's minister,
And labours for some good
By us not understood!

      Henry Wadsworth Longfellow *The Golden Legend*

5   For where God built a church, there the devil would also build a chapel. Thus is the Devil ever God's ape.

      Martin Luther *Table Talk*

6   Would you see the devil? Look in the mirror.

      A.R. Orage *Essays and Aphorisms*

7   The spirit that I have seen
May be a devil; and the devil hath power
To assume a pleasing shape.

      William Shakespeare *Hamlet* Act II Sc. 2

8   The devil can cite scripture for his purpose.

      William Shakespeare *The Merchant of Venice* Act I Sc. 3

9   Sometimes the Devil is a gentleman.

      Percy Bysshe Shelley 'Peter Bell the Third'

10   When the devil was sick, the devil a saint would be;
When the devil was well, the devil a saint was he.

      Samuel Smiles *Thrift* (Various versions of this traditional saying can be traced back to the Middle Ages)

11   God seeks comrades and claims love:
The Devil seeks slaves and claims obedience.

      Rabindranath Tagore *Fireflies*

1   The Devil, even if he is a fact, has been an indulgence. We
    have relieved our own sense of moral submission to God by
    contemplating, even disapprovingly, something which was
    neither moral nor submissive. While the devil exists there is
    always something to which we can be superior.
        Charles Williams *He Came Down from Heaven*

DEVOTION

2   A state of temperance, sobriety and justice without devotion is
    a cold, lifeless, insipid condition of virtue, and is rather to be
    styled philosophy than religion.
        Joseph Addison *The Spectator*

3   Who loves me, no word of mine shall e'er betray,
    Though for faith unstained my life must forfeit pay.
        Emily Brontë

4   If workmen spent as much time in church as religious, if
    religious were exposed to the same pastoral calls as a bishop,
    such devotion would be ridiculous and cause intolerable
    disorder.
        St Francis de Sales *Introduction to a Devout Life*

5   The Knights [of St John of Jerusalem] neglected to live, were
    prepared to die, in the service of Christ.
        Edward Gibbon *Decline and Fall of the Roman Empire*

6   My spirit has become dry because it forgets to feed on you.
        St John of the Cross

7   The need for devotion to something outside ourselves is even
    more profound than the need for companionship.
        Ross Parmenter *The Plant in My Window*

DIPLOMACY

8   A soft answer turneth away wrath: but grievous words stir up
    anger.
        Holy Bible Proverbs Chap. 15 v. 1

DISAGREEMENT

9   Discords make the sweetest airs.
        Samuel Butler *Hudibras*

10 A disagreement may be the shortest cut between two minds.
        Kahlil Gibran *Sand and Foam*

DISASTER

1 The earth shall reel to and fro like a drunkard ... and it shall fall, and not rise again.
   Holy Bible Isaiah Chap. 24 v. 20

2 The living Church, though never neat, keeps God's world from complete disaster.
   George Macleod *Only One Way Left*

DISCIPLE

3 When Christ calls a man he bids him come and die.
   Dietrich Bonhoeffer *The Cost of Discipleship*

4 If we were willing to learn the meaning of real discipleship and actually to become disciples, the Church in the West would be transformed, and the resultant impact on society would be staggering.
   David Watson *Is Anyone There?*

DISCONTENT

5 The eye is not satisfied with seeing, nor the ear filled with hearing.
   Holy Bible Ecclesiastes Chap. 1 v. 8

6 To be discontented with the divine discontent, and to be ashamed with the noble shame, is the very germ and first upgrowth of all virtue.
   Charles Kingsley *Health and Education*

DISCRETION

7 He who knows does not talk; he who talks does not know.
   Lao-Tze

DISOBEDIENCE

8 And he shall go before him ... to turn the hearts of ... the disobedient to the wisdom of the just.
   Holy Bible St Luke Chap. 1 v. 17

9 Of man's first disobedience, and the fruit
   Of that forbidden tree, whose mortal taste
   Brought death into our world, and all our woe.
   John Milton *Paradise Lost*

1   God has established Government but he has not made it
autonomous. Thus if the office bearer commands that which is
contrary to God's Law his authority is abrogated. At this point
it is the Christian's duty to disobey.
> Francis Schaeffer Quoted Christopher Catherwood *Five
> Evangelical Leaders*

DISPUTE

2   The tree of knowledge blasted by dispute
Produces sapless leaves instead of fruit.
> Sir John Denham 'Progress of Learning'

DISSENT

3   All protestantism, even the most cold and passive, is a sort of
dissent. But [this] is a refinement of the principle of resistance:
it is the dissidence of dissent, and the protestantism of the
Protestant religion.
> Edmund Burke Speech on Conciliation with America 1775

4   Dissent stands by the freedom to divide and to differ.
> Rosemary Harthill *In Perspective*

5   The truth of dissent is in what it *asserts* rather than what it
denies. The only two seeds of dissent which have ever taken
root are love of the Gospel and freedom.
> Dr Howard Williams Quoted Rosemary Harthill *In Perspective*

DISTRACTION

6   I neglect God and his angels for the noise of a fly, for the
rattling of a coach, for the whining of a door.
> John Donne *Sermons*

7   When desire blinds the mind with delusion and dust, O thou
holy one, thou wakeful one, come with thy light and thunder.
> Rabindranath Tagore

DIVINE LIFE

8   In our earthly experience the Divine Life is not one, but
many. But to apprehend the one in the many constitutes the
special character of love.
> Ernst Troeltsch Quoted *Christianity and Other Religions* Ed.
> Hick and Hebblethwaite

DIVINITY

1 In divine things there is never hurry, and hurry is not a divine thing.
>Fr Andrew SDC *Letters of Fr Andrew SDC*

2 There is surely a piece of divinity in us, something that was before the elements, and owes no homage unto the sun.
>Sir Thomas Browne *Religio Medici*

3 Earth's crammed with heaven,
And every common bush afire with God.
>Elizabeth Barrett Browning *Aurora Leigh*

4 The mystery of a person, indeed, is ever divine to him that has a sense for the Godlike.
>Thomas Carlyle *Sartor Resartus*

5 If we meet no gods, it is because we harbour none. If there is grandeur in you, you will find grandeur in porters and sweeps.
>Ralph Waldo Emerson *The Conduct of Life* 'Worship'

6 Man is God by his faculty for thought.
>Alphonse de Lamartine *Les Premières Méditations*

7 I found Him in the shining of the stars,
I marked Him in the flowering of his fields
But in His ways with men I find Him not.
>Alfred, Lord Tennyson 'The Passing of Arthur'

DIVORCE

8 I should like to add an eighth Sacrament to those of the Roman Church — the sacrament of divorce.
>Samuel Butler *Notebooks*

9 What therefore God hath joined together, let not man put asunder.
>*Holy Bible* St Matthew Chap. 19 v. 6

10 There are four minds in the bed of a divorced man who marries a divorced woman.
>*The Talmud*

DOCTRINE

11 Doctrine is nothing but the skin of truth, set up and stuffed.
>Henry Ward Beecher *Life Thoughts*

1 Even a bad doctrine is better than none at all. You can test it, differ from it, your mind has something to bite on. You need the rock to plan the lighthouse.
  Joyce Cary *Art and Reality*

2 Any doctrine that will not bear investigation is not a fit tenant for the mind of an honest man.
  Robert G. Ingersoll *Intellectual Development*

3 A doctrine of black supremacy is as evil as a doctrine of white supremacy.
  Martin Luther King *The Words of Martin Luther King*

4 He who receives
  Light from above, from the Fountain of Light,
  No other doctrine needs, though granted true.
  John Milton *Paradise Regained*

5 Live to explain thy doctrine by thy life.
  Matthew Prior 'To Dr Sherlock'

6 No doctrine, however high, however true, can make men happy until it is translated into life.
  Henry Van Dyke *Joy and Power*

DOGMA

7 It is in the uncompromisingness with which dogma is held and not in the dogma, or want of dogma, that the danger lies.
  Samuel Butler *The Way of All Flesh*

8 Truths turn into dogmas the moment they are disputed.
  G.K. Chesterton

9 He who steadily observes those moral precepts in which all religions concur will never be questioned at the gates of heaven as to the dogma in which they all differ.
  Thomas Jefferson Letter to William Cauby 18 September 1813

10 A religion without dogma is like a parcel tied up without string.
  Christine Longford *Making Conversation*

11 All the formulas, all the precautions of orthodoxy, all the scruples of literal conformity, all barriers, in a word, are powerless to safeguard the purity of the faith. If the spirit should be lacking, dogma becomes no more than a myth and the Church no more than a party.
  Henri de Lubac *Paradoxes*

1   From the age of fifteen, dogma has been the fundamental
principle of my religion. I know of no other religion; I cannot
enter into the idea of any other sort of religion; religion, as a
mere sentiment, is to me a dream and a mockery.
  John Henry, Cardinal Newman *Apologia Pro Vita Sua*

2   I resent with all my soul that the orthodox have so complicated
the perfectly straightforward teaching of Christ that common
people neither hear him gladly, nor with understanding.
  Rev. H.R.L. Sheppard *The Impatience of a Parson*

3   We do much better to praise God together than to argue about
which set of defining words is the less grotesquely inadequate
and misleading.
  Philip Toynbee Quoted Richard Harries *Prayers of Grief and
Glory*

DOGMATISM

4   There are two kinds of people in this world, the conscious
dogmatists and the unconscious dogmatists. I have always
found myself that the unconscious dogmatists were by far the
most dogmatic.
  G.K. Chesterton *Generally Speaking*

5   No man should dogmatise except on the subject of theology.
Here he can take his stand and by throwing the burden of
proof on the opposition, he is invincible. We have to die to
find out whether he is right.
  Elbert Hubbard *The Note Book*

6   Profound ignorance makes a man dogmatic. The man who
knows nothing thinks he is teaching others what he has just
learned himself; the man who knows a great deal can't imagine
that what he is saying is not common knowledge, and speaks
indifferently.
  Jean de la Bruyère *Characters*

DOUBT

7   For I kept my heart from assenting to anything, fearing to fall
headlong; but by hanging in suspense I was the worse killed.
  St Augustine of Hippo *Confessions*

8   The more of doubt, the stronger faith, I say,
If faith o'ercomes doubt.
  Robert Browning 'Bishop Blougram's Apology'

1   A man was meant to be doubting about himself but
    undoubting about the truth. This has been exactly reversed.
    Nowadays the part of a man that a man does assert is exactly
    the part he ought not to assert — himself. The part he doubts
    is exactly the part he ought not to doubt — the Divine
    Reason.
       G.K. Chesterton *Orthodoxy*

2   Doubt is the vestibule which all must pass, before they can
    enter into the temple of truth.
       Charles Caleb Colton *Lacon*

3   Man may doubt here and there, but mankind does not doubt.
    The universal conscience is larger than the individual
    conscience, and that constantly comes in to check our own
    infidelity.
       Hugh Reginald Haweis *Speech in Season*

4   Wilt Thou not take the doubt of Thy children whom the time
    commands to try all things, in the place of the unquestioning
    faith of earlier generations?
       Oliver Wendell Holmes *The Poet at the Breakfast Table*

5   He that doubteth is damned.
       Holy Bible Romans Chap. 14 v. 23

6   Question with boldness even the existence of a God, because,
    if there be one, he must more approve of a homage of reason,
    than that of blindfold fear.
       Thomas Jefferson Letter to Peter Carr 10 August 1787

7   The man that feareth, Lord, to doubt,
    In that fear doubteth thee.
       George MacDonald *Disciple*

8   An honest man can never surrender an honest doubt.
       Walter Malone *The Agnostic's Creed*

9   Ten thousand difficulties do not make one doubt.
       John Henry, Cardinal Newman *Apologia Pro Vita Sua*

10 O Lord, if there is a Lord, save my soul, if I have a soul.
       Ernest Renan 'Prayer of a Sceptic'

11 I am afraid I shall not find God, but I shall still look for Him,
    if He exists. He will be appreciative of my efforts.
       Jules Renard *Journal*

1 William James used to preach 'the will to believe'. For my part, I should wish to preach 'the will to doubt'. What is wanted is not the will to believe, but the wish to find out, which is the exact opposite.
   Bertrand Russell *Sceptical Essays*

2 If we are sensible we will not doubt God, we will doubt our world and we will doubt ourselves.
   Agnes Sandford *The Healing Light*

3 Doubt is part of all religion. All the religious thinkers were doubters.
   Isaac Bashevis Singer Quoted Richard Burgen *New York Times Magazine* 3 December 1978

4 'There comes a time in every man's life,' he said in one sermon, 'when he must wonder what the hell it is all about.'
   G.A. Studdert-Kennedy (Padre Woodbine-Willie)

5 Doubt is faith in the main: but faith, on the whole, is doubt: We cannot believe by proof: but could we believe without?
   Algernon Charles Swinburne *The Heptalogia* 'The Higher Pantheism in a Nutshell'

6 There lives more faith in honest doubt,
   Believe me, than in half the creeds.
   Alfred, Lord Tennyson *In Memoriam*

7 A faith which does not doubt is a dead faith.
   Miguel de Unamuno *The Agony of Christianity*

DOVE

8 And the dove came in to him in the evening; and lo, in her mouth was an olive leaf pluckt off: so Noah knew that the waters were abated from the earth.
   Holy Bible Genesis Chap. 8 v. 11

DREAMS

9 Your old men shall dream dreams, your young men shall see visions.
   Holy Bible Joel Chap. 2 v. 28

10 Real are the dreams of Gods, and smoothly pass
   Their pleasures in a long immortal dream.
   John Keats *Lamia*

1 Shattered dreams are a hallmark of our mortal life.
   Martin Luther King *The Words of Martin Luther King*

2 Hope is but the dream of those who wake.
   Matthew Prior *Solomon*

3 Why does no one confess his sins? Because he is yet in them.
   It is for a man who has awoke from sleep to tell his dreams.
   Seneca *Epistles*

4 We are such stuff
   As dreams are made on; and our little life
   Is rounded with a sleep.
   William Shakespeare *The Tempest* Act IV Sc. 1

DUTY

5 In doing what we ought we deserve no praise, it is our duty.
   St Augustine of Hippo *Confessions*

6 It is better to perform one's own duties imperfectly than to
   master the duties of another.
   Bhagavad Gita

7 Duty does not have to be dull. Love can make it beautiful and
   fill it with life.
   Thomas Merton *The Sign of Jonas*

8 God obliges no man to more than he has given him ability to
   perform.
   The Qur'an

9 God never imposes a duty without giving time to do it.
   John Ruskin *Lectures on Architecture and Painting*

EARTH

1 Earth, my mother, set me securely with bliss in full accord with heaven. O Wise one, uphold me in grace and splendour!

2 Pleasant be thy hills, O Earth, thy snow-clad mountains and thy woods! O Earth brown, black, red and multi-coloured, the firm Earth protected by Indra. On this Earth may I stand unvanquished, unhurt, unstained.
   Atharva Veda Indian spirituality

3 One generation passeth away, and another generation cometh: but the earth abideth for ever.
   Holy Bible Ecclesiastes Chap. 1 v. 4

4 The earth is the Lord's, and the fulness thereof.
   Holy Bible 1 Corinthians Chap. 10 v. 26

5 Every part of this earth is sacred to my people. Every shining pine needle, every sandy shore, every mist in the dark woods, every clearing and humming insect is holy in the memory and experience of my people.
   Chief Seathl Letter to the President of the United States 1885

EASTER

6 Christ being raised from the dead dieth no more: death hath no more dominion over him.
   Book of Common Prayer Sentence for Easter Day Romans Chap. 6 v. 9

7 Christ our passover is sacrificed for us: therefore let us keep the feast.
   Book of Common Prayer Sentence for Easter Day 1 Corinthians Chap. 5 v. 7

1   Tomb, thou shalt not hold Him longer;
Death is strong, but life is stronger;
Stronger than the dark, the light;
Stronger than the wrong, the right;
Faith and Hope triumphant say
Christ will rise on Easter Day.
        Phillips Brooks 'An Easter Carol'

2   'Welcome happy morning' age to age shall say;
Hell today is vanquished, heaven is won today.
        St Fortunatus of Poitiers 'Welcome Happy Morning'

3   Thou art the Sun of other days,
They shine by giving back thy rays.
        John Keble *The Christian Year* 'Easter'

4   'Twas Easter Sunday. The full-blossomed trees
Filled all the air with fragrance and with joy.
        Henry Wadsworth Longfellow *The Spanish Student*

5   The fasts are done; the Aves said;
The moon has filled her horn,
And in the solemn night I watch
Before the Easter morn.
        Edna Dean Proctor 'Easter Morn'

6   Spring bursts today,
For Christ is risen and all the earth's at play.
        Christina Rossetti 'Easter Carol'

7   Didst thou not fall out with a tailor for wearing his new
doublet before Easter?
        William Shakespeare *Romeo and Juliet* Act III Sc. 1

8   God expects from men that their Easter devotions would in
some measure come up to their Easter clothes.
        Robert South *Sermons*

ECSTASY

9   Art and Religion are two roads by which men escape from
circumstance to ecstasy.
        Clive Bell *Art*

10   The ecstasy of religion, the ecstasy of art, and the ecstasy of
love are the only things worth thinking about or experiencing.
        Don Marquis *The Almost Perfect State*

ECUMENISM

1 The real ecumenical crisis today is not between Catholics and Protestants but between traditional and experimental forms of Church Life.

Harvey Cox *The Secular City*

2 When the doctrinal barriers between the churches are broken, and the bonds of peace are cemented by spiritual understanding and Love, there will be unity of spirit, and the healing power of Christ will prevail.

Mary Baker Eddy *Pulpit and Press*

3 It is as well that the stately synagogue should lift its walls by the side of the aspiring cathedral, a perpetual reminder that there are many mansions in the Father's earthly house as well as in the heavenly one.

Oliver Wendell Holmes *Over the Teacups*

4 Unity should exhibit and contain diversity. The Body of Christ has many differing members simply deriving from the fact that God by nature and by grace has given different gifts to his different children, and he desires his Church to conserve and exploit the rich variety of abilities contained within it.

James Packer, Colin Buchanan, Eric Mascall and Graham Leonard *Growing Into Union*

EFFORT

5 Anybody can do their best, but we are helped by the spirit of God to do better than our best.

Commissioner Catherine Bramwell-Booth *My Faith* Ed. Mary E. Callan

EGOISM

6 No egoism is so insufferable as that of the Christian with regard to his soul.

W. Somerset Maugham *A Writer's Notebook*

EMOTION

7 In the very nature of things emotions are more or less variable, while convictions, where they are really convictions, and are not purely notions or ideas, are permanent ... I learned therefore not to seek emotions, but to seek only for convictions.

Hannah Whithall Smith *Spiritual Experiences of Friends*

ENEMIES

1 There is only one true way of conquering enemies in this
   warring world, and that is to make your enemy your friend.
       Fr Andrew SDC *The Way of Victory*

2 He who has a thousand friends has not a friend to spare;
   And he who has one enemy will meet him everywhere.
       Ralph Waldo Emerson *Translations*

3 It is easy enough to be friendly to one's friends. But to
   befriend the one who regards himself as your enemy is the
   quintessence of true religion. The other is mere business.
       Gandhi *Non-Violence in Peace and War*

4 If thine enemy be hungry, give him bread to eat; and if he be
   thirsty, give him water to drink: For thou shalt heap coals of
   fire upon his head, and the Lord shall reward thee.
       Holy Bible Proverbs Chap. 25 vv. 21–22

5 Never yet
   Was noble man but made ignoble talk.
   He makes no friend who never made a foe.
       Alfred, Lord Tennyson 'Lancelot and Elaine'

6 A man can't be too careful in the choice of his enemies.
       Oscar Wilde *The Picture of Dorian Gray*

ENJOYMENT

7 Never ending, still beginning,
   Fighting still, and still destroying,
   If all the world be worth the winning,
   Think, oh think, it worth enjoying.
       John Dryden 'Alexander's Feast'

8 Let us start a new religion with one commandment 'Enjoy
   thyself'.
       Israel Zangwill *Children of the Ghetto*

ENVY

9 He who goes unenvied shall not be admired.
       Aeschylus *Agamemnon*

10 As iron is eaten away by rust, so the envious are consumed by
   their own passion.
       Antisthenes

1   Envy is the most stupid of vices, for there is no single
    advantage to be gained from it.
    Honoré de Balzac

2   If envy was not such a tearing thing to feel it would be the
    most comic of sins. It is usually, if not always, based on a
    complete misunderstanding of another person's situation.
    Monica Furlong *Christian Uncertainties*

3   Wrath killeth the foolish man, and envy slayeth the silly one.
    Holy Bible Job Chap. 5 v. 2

4   A sound heart is the life of the flesh: but envy the rottenness
    of the bones.
    Holy Bible Proverbs Chap. 14 v. 30

5   Charity envieth not.
    Holy Bible 1 Corinthians Chap. 13 v. 4

6   A little grit in the eye destroyeth the sight of the very
    Heavens; and a little Malice or Envy, a World of Joy.
    Thomas Traherne *Centuries of Meditations*

EPITAPH

7   If I am so quickly done for
    What on earth was I begun for?
    Anon Words on a gravestone of a little child

8   I was taking my daughter Jan, age six, through the local
    graveyard. At a tombstone which carried an epitaph ending
    with the words 'Well done', she asked, 'Does that mean she
    was cremated?'
    Michael Aspel *Child's Play*

9   When I am dead, I hope it may be said:
    'His sins were scarlet, but his books were read.'
    Hilaire Belloc *Epigrams* 'On his Books'

10 Here lies a Doctor of Divinity,
    He was a fellow of Trinity;
    He knew as much about Divinity
    As other fellows do of Trinity.
    Richard Porson *Penguin Book of Comic and Curious Verse*

11 Of this blest man, let his just praise be given:
    Heaven was in him, before he was in heaven.
    Izaak Walton

EQUALITY

1 Kneeling ne'er spoil'd silk stocking; quit thy state;
All equal are within the Church's gate.
George Herbert *The Temple* 'The Church Porch'

2 Abolish God in your thinking and you will have abolished true
equality, too.
Philip Pare *God Made the Devil*

ERROR

3 The best may err.
Joseph Addison *Cato* Act V

4 To err is human, to persist in error is devilish.
St Augustine of Hippo *Sermons*

5 They defend their errors as if they were defending their
inheritance.
Edmund Burke Speech on Economic Reform

6 The error of one moment becomes the sorrow of a whole life.
Chinese proverb

7 Error is just as important a condition of life as truth.
Carl Gustav Jung *Psychological Reflections*

8 There is no anguish like an error of which we feel ashamed.
Edward George Bulwer-Lytton *Ernest Maltravers*

9 A life spent making mistakes is not only more honourable but
more useful than a life spent doing nothing.
George Bernard Shaw *The Doctor's Dilemma*

ESCAPE

10 With the help of my God I shall leap over the wall.
Book of Common Prayer Psalm 18 v. 29

11 I am escaped with the skin of my teeth.
Holy Bible Job Chap. 19 v. 20

12 God is faithful, who will not suffer you to be tempted above
that ye are able; but will with the temptation also make a way
to escape, that ye may be able to bear it.
Holy Bible 1 Corinthians Chap. 10 v. 13

ETERNITY

1 Eternity! Thou pleasing, dreadful thought!
Through what variety of untried being,
Through what new scenes and changes must we pass!
The wide, the unbounded prospect lies before me,
But shadows, clouds, and darkness rest upon it.
   Joseph Addison *Cato*

2 Anyone who, at the end of life, quits his body remembering
ME, attains immediately to MY nature and there is no doubt
of this.

3 Only the material body of the indestructible, immeasurable
and eternal living entity is subject to destruction.
   Bhagavad Gita

4 'Tis very puzzling on the brink
Of what is called Eternity, to stare
And know no more of what is *here*, than *there*.
   Lord Byron *Don Juan*

5 Eternity! How know we but we stand
On the precipitous and crumbling verge
Of time e'en now, Eternity below.
   Abraham Coles 'Eternity'

6 Bring us, O Lord, at our last awakening to the house and gate
of heaven, to enter into that gate and dwell in that house
where there shall be no darkness nor dazzling but one equal
light, no noise nor silence but one equal music.
   John Donne

7 Today's today
Tomorrow we may be
Ourselves gone down the drain of Eternity.
   Euripides *Alcestis*

8 We do not know what to do with this short life, yet we want
another which will be eternal.
   Anatole France

9 Our theories of the eternal are as valuable as are those which a
chick which had not broken its way through its shell might
form of the outside world.
   Gautama, the Buddha

1 Eternity is not something that begins after you are dead. It is going on all the time. We are in it now.
   Charlotte Gilman *The Forerunner*

2 In the presence of eternity the mountains are as transient as the clouds.
   Robert G. Ingersoll *The Christian Religion*

3 It is eternity now. I am in the midst of it. It is about me in the sunshine; I am in it, as the butterfly in the light-laden air. Nothing has to come, it is now. Now is eternity, now is immortal life.
   Richard Jeffries *The Story of My Heart*

4 Let those who thoughtfully consider the brevity of life remember the length of eternity.
   Bishop Thomas Ken

5 But at my back I always hear
   Time's winged chariot hurrying near.
   And yonder all before us lie
   Deserts of vast eternity.
   Andrew Marvell 'To His Coy Mistress'

6 To have a sense of the eternal in life is a short flight for the soul. To have had it, is the soul's vitality.
   George Meredith *Diana of the Crossways*

7 Then shall be shown that but in name
   Time and eternity were both the same:
   A point which neither life nor death can sever,
   A moment standing still for ever.
   James Montgomery 'Time, A Rhapsody'

8 I can't believe, when I see the promise of Christ expressed in a particular person, that that's all coming to an end. But as for the geography and climate of an after-life — well, I'm an agnostic about that.
   Robert Runcie, Archbishop of Canterbury Quoted John Mortimer *In Character*

9 What man is capable of the insane self-conceit of believing that an eternity of himself would be tolerable even to himself.
   George Bernard Shaw

10 Eternity is a terrible thought. I mean, where is it going to end?
   Tom Stoppard *Rosencrantz and Guildenstern Are Dead*

1 If there is God and there is a future life, then there is truth
and there is goodness; and the highest happiness of man
consists in striving for their attainment.
   Leo Tolstoy *War and Peace*

2 I saw Eternity the other night,
   Like a great ring of pure and endless light,
   All calm, as it was bright;
   And round beneath it, Time in hours, days, years,
   Driv'n by the spheres
   Like a vast shadow moved; in which the world
   And all her train were hurled.
   Henry Vaughan *Silex Scintillans* 'The World'

3 O Sabbath rest by Galilee!
   O calm of hills above,
   Where Jesus knelt to share with thee
   The silence of eternity,
   Interpreted by love!
   John Greenleaf Whittier *Hymns Ancient and Modern* 'Dear
   Lord and Father of Mankind'

EUCHARIST

4 Breaking one bread, which is the medicine of immortality, the
antidote against death which gives eternal life in Jesus Christ.
   St Irenaeus

5 The Eucharist is the consummation of lovers.
   Fr Peter Ball CGA Clergy Conference at Swanwick 1985

6 Thou art thyself both he who offers and he who is offered, he
who receives and he who is distributed.
   Liturgy of St John Chrysostom *Liturgies Eastern and Western*

7 The great eucharistic prayer is a proclamation of the
fundamental fact: Christ is dead, Christ is risen.
   Jean-François Six *Prayer and Hope*

EVANGELISM

8 Christ beats his drum, but he does not press men; Christ is
served with volunteers.
   John Donne *Sermons*

9 I just want to lobby for God.
   Billy Graham *My Faith* Ed. Mary E. Callan

1 If he have faith, the believer cannot be restrained. He betrays himself. He breaks out. He confesses and teaches this gospel to the people at the risk of life itself.
   Martin Luther Preface to his translation of the New Testament

2 Ultimately, evangelism is not a technique. It is the Lord of the Church who reserves to Himself His sovereign right to add to His Church.
   John Stott Quoted Christopher Catherwood *Five Evangelical Leaders*

3 It is certainly no part of religion to compel religion.
   Tertullian *Ad Scapulam*

4 I look upon all the world as my parish.
   John Wesley *Journal*

EVIL

5 I inquired into the nature of Evil and found no substance there.
   St Augustine of Hippo *Confessions*

6 There would be no virtue in being good if it were not possible to be evil.
   St Augustine of Hippo

7 Must I do all the evil I can before I learn to shun it? Is it not enough to know the evil to shun it? If not we should be sincere enough to admit that we love evil too well to give it up.
   Gandhi *Non-Violence in Peace and War*

8 The resolution to avoid all evil is seldom framed till the evil is so advanced as to make avoidance impossible.
   Thomas Hardy

9 Evil is a fact, not to be explained away, but to be accepted; and accepted, not to be endured, but to be conquered. It is a challenge neither to our reason nor to our patience, but to our courage.
   John Haynes Holmes *My Idea of God*

10 Sufficient unto the day is the evil thereof.
   Holy Bible St Matthew Chap. 6 v. 34

11 For the good that I would I do not: but the evil which I would not, that I do.
   Holy Bible Romans Chap. 7 v. 19

1   Recompense to no man evil for evil.
    Holy Bible Romans Chap. 12 v. 17

2   Of two evils we should always choose the less.
    Thomas à Kempis *The Imitation of Christ*

3   He who passively accepts evil is as much involved in it as he
    who helps to perpetuate it.
    Martin Luther King *Strides Towards Freedom*

4   Theologists are always bothering about the origin of evil, but
    evil is just natural behaviour; it's the origin of human goodness
    that is really so extraordinary and inexplicable.
    Kingsley Martin Letter to Dorothy Collins

5   There is no explanation for evil. It must be looked upon as a
    necessary part of the order of the universe. To ignore it is
    childish, to bewail it, senseless.
    W. Somerset Maugham *The Summing Up*

6   Evil urges us to the selfish, envious or idle choice, but it is only
    when that choice is made that sins begin.
    Philip Pare *God Made the Devil*

7   Men never do evil so completely and cheerfully as when they
    do it from religious conviction.
    Blaise Pascal *Pensées*

8   I think the devil will not have me damned, lest the oil that's
    in me should set hell on fire; he would never else cross me
    thus.
    William Shakespeare *The Merry Wives of Windsor* Act V Sc. 5

9   Only among people who think no evil can evil flourish without
    fear.
    Logan Pearsall Smith *All Trivia* 'Afterthoughts'

EVOLUTION

10 The question is this: is man an ape or an angel? I, my Lord,
    am on the side of the angels.
    Benjamin Disraeli Speech to the Oxford Diocesan Conference
    1864

11 It's more comfortable that we're a slight improvement on a
    monkey than such a falling off from the angels.
    Finley Peter Dunne *Mr Dooley on Making a Will*

1 Evolution means an opening up of communication and contact. Attempts to cut ourselves off are against the meaning of the universe. Unloving separation, whatever form it takes, is a sin.

    Lev Gillet *Encounter at the Well*

2 We are descended not only from monkeys, but from monks.

    Elbert Hubbard

3 The Lord let the house of a brute to the soul of a man,
And the man said 'Am I your debtor?'
And the Lord — 'Not yet; but make it as clean as you can,
And then I will let you a better.'

    Alfred, Lord Tennyson 'By an Evolutionist'

4 I believe that our Heavenly Father invented man because he was disappointed in the monkey.

    Mark Twain *Mark Twain in Eruption*

EXAMPLE

5 If you are looking for an example of humility, look at the cross.

    St Thomas Aquinas

6 Shew some token upon me for good, that they who hate me may see it and be ashamed.

    Book of Common Prayer Psalm 86 v. 17

7 When one of you falls down he falls for those behind him, a caution against the stumbling stone.

    Kahlil Gibran *The Prophet*

8 Example moves the world more than doctrine.

    Henry Miller *The Cosmological Eye*

EXILE

9 By the waters of Babylon we sat down and wept: when we remembered thee, O Sion.

    Book of Common Prayer Psalm 137 v. 1

10 I have been a stranger in a strange land.

    Holy Bible Exodus Chap. 2 v. 22

11 O unexpected stroke, worse than of death!
Must I thus leave thee, Paradise? thus leave
Thee, native soil?

    John Milton *Paradise Lost*

EXISTENCE

1 Common sense tells us that our existence is but a brief crack of
   light between two eternities of darkness.
   > Vladimir Nabokov

2 Be humble and you will remain entire
   Be bent and you will remain straight
   Be vacant and you will remain full
   Be worn and you will remain new.

3 Existence is the mother of all things. From eternal non-
   existence, therefore, we serenely observe the mysterious
   beginning of the Universe.
   > Tao Te Ching Chinese spirituality

EXORCISM

4 The louder we shout at the devil, the louder he shouts back.
   The quieter we speak to him, the quieter he goes.

5 An Anglican vicar called on a Pentecostal pastor to exorcise
   his vestry. The pastor opened the door and said, 'In the name
   of Jesus, scram! That will be all right now,' and left.
   > Fr John Harper 'Sermons: St John-in-the-Fields, St Ives'

6 If I cast out devils by the Spirit of God, then the kingdom of
   God is come unto you.
   > *Holy Bible* St Matthew Chap. 12 v. 28

EXPECTATION

7 What we are doing here, *that* is the question. And ... in this
   immense confusion one thing alone is clear. We are waiting for
   Godot to come.
   > Samuel Beckett *Waiting for Godot*

8 Expect great things from God
   Attempt great things for God.
   > William Carey Quoted *Christian Classics*

EXPERIENCE

9 Whatever you may possess, and however fruitful your
   activities, regard them all as worthless without the inward
   certainty and experience of Jesus' love.
   > *The Cloud of Unknowing*

1   I could not say I believe, I know! I have had the experience of
    being gripped by something that is stronger than myself,
    something that people call God.
       Carl Gustav Jung *My Faith*

2   Solitude is a good school, but the world is the best theatre.
       Jeremy Taylor

3   Discontent, unhappiness, suffering, are the common
    experience of all. Sometimes we feel them acutely. More often
    we are able to smother them. They hover in the wings of our
    personality because we don't like to see them strutting upon
    the stage.

4   Christian experience is not so much a matter of imitating a
    leader as accepting and receiving a new quality of life, a life
    infinitely more profound and dynamic and meaningful than
    human life without Christ.
       H.A. Williams *The True Wilderness*

FAILURE

1 A man may fulfill the object of his existence by asking a question he cannot answer, and attempting a task he cannot achieve.
    Oliver Wendell Holmes *Life and Letters*

2 We have toiled all the night, and have taken nothing.
    Holy Bible St Luke Chap. 5 v. 5

3 The man who loses his opportunity loses himself.
    George Moore *Bending the Bough*

4 We learn wisdom from failure much more than success. We often discover what WILL do, by finding out what will NOT do.
    Samuel Smiles *Self Help*

5 Failure is as much a part of life as success is and by no means something in front of which one sits down and howls as though it is a scandal and a shame.
    J. Neville Ward *Five for Sorrow Ten for Joy*

FAITH

6 Lord I am not worthy to receive you but only say the word, and I shall be healed.
    Alternative Service Book Communion Service Rite A

7 Great faith is not the faith that walks always in the light and knows no darkness, but the faith that perseveres in spite of God's seeming silences, and that faith will most certainly and surely get its reward.
    Fr Andrew SDC *Meditations for Every Day*

8 I do not pretend to see light, but I do see gleams, and I know I am right to follow those gleams.
    Fr Andrew SDC *Life and Letters*

1   The first mark of the gift of faith is the love of truth.
     Fr Andrew SDC *The Way of Victory*

2   It takes faith to believe that God actually wants us to take part in His ongoing Spiritual warfare and to participate in the accomplishment of His purpose.
     George Appleton

3   Faith is to believe what you do not yet see: the reward for this faith is to see what you believe.
     St Augustine of Hippo *Sermons*

4   I am one of those who would rather sink with faith than swim without it.
     Stanley Baldwin Speech at Leeds 12 October 1923

5   A man consists of the faith that is in him. Whatever he is, his faith is.
     Bhagavad Gita

6   Religious faith is vital just in so far as it dares to listen to an atheist.
     H.N. Brailsford *Property or Peace*

7   It has been said that faith can move mountains but no one has ever seen it done, save by the faith that man has in himself, in the steam shovels and the dynamite he has invented in the face of a hostile Nature.
     Louis Bromfield *The Strange Case of Miss Annie Spragg*

8   One may not doubt that, somehow, good
    Shall come of water and of mud;
    And, sure, the reverent eye must see
    A purpose in liquidity.
     Rupert Brooke 'Heaven'

9   To believe only possibilities, is not faith, but mere Philosophy.
     Sir Thomas Browne *Religio Medici*

10   The act of faith is more than a bare statement of belief, it is a turning to the face of the living God.
     Christopher Bryant SSJE *The Bible and Meditation*

11   You can do very little with faith, but you can do nothing without it.
     Samuel Butler *Note Books*

1   The Christian has greatly the advantage of the unbeliever, having everything to gain and nothing to lose.
>Lord Byron

2   We derive our inspiration from God, but we are grateful to *The Times* for strengthening our convictions.
>A Bishop of Carlisle, addressing a Diocesan Conference
>Quoted Michael Bateman *This England*

3   The well-meaning person who, by merely studying the logical side of things, has decided that 'faith is nonsense' does not know how truly he speaks; later it may come back to him in the form that nonsense is faith.
>G.K. Chesterton *In Defence of Nonsense*

4   Faith is a voluntary anticipation.
>St Clement of Alexandria *Stromateis*

5   And therefore I would leave all that thing that I can think, and choose to my love that thing that I cannot think.
>*The Cloud of Unknowing*

6   I never saw a Moor —
I never saw the Sea —
Yet know I how the Heather looks
And what a Billow be.
I never spoke with God
Nor visited in Heaven —
Yet certain am I of the spot
As if the Checks were given.
>Emily Dickinson 'I Never Saw A Moor'

7   The world was never conquered by intrigue; it was conquered by faith.
>Benjamin Disraeli *Tancred*

8   No faith is our own that we have not arduously won.
>Havelock Ellis *The Dance of Life*

9   God cannot be grasped by the mind. If he could be grasped he would not be God.
>Evagrius of Pontus *Texts on Prayers*

10   Faith, to my mind, is a stiffening process, a sort of mental starch, which ought to be applied as sparingly as possible . . . I do not believe in it for its own sake at all.
>E.M. Forster *Two Cheers for Democracy* 'What I Believe'

1   The man of Faith may face death as Columbus faced his first
    voyage from the shores of Spain. What lies beyond the seas he
    cannot tell; all his special expectations may be mistaken, but
    his insight into the clear meaning of present facts may
    persuade him beyond doubt that the sea has another shore.
        Henry Emerson Fosdick Quoted Giles and Melville Harcourt
        Short Prayers for a Long Day

2   Although I am out of the King's protection, I am not out of
    the protection of Almighty God.
        Margaret Fox *Spiritual Experiences of Friends* 'From Prison'

3   Faith fills a man with love for the beauty of its truth, with faith
    in the truth of its beauty.
        St Francis de Sales *The Love of God*

4   Faith is much better than belief. Belief is when someone else
    does the thinking.
        Buckminster Fuller *Playboy* magazine 1972

5   The contradictions of the Old Testament mean that with a
    little effort anyone can find a faith that accords with his
    preferences and a moral code that is agreeable to his tastes,
    even if fairly depraved.
        John Kenneth Galbraith *Economics, Peace and Laughter*

6   I believe in God and in nature and in the triumph of good over
    evil.
        Goethe *My Faith* Ed. Mary E. Callan

7   If you have abandoned one faith, do not abandon all faith.
    There is always an alternative to the faith we lose. Or is it the
    same faith under another mask?
        Graham Greene *The Comedians*

8   Faith has no merit where human reason supplies the truth.
        St Gregory the Great *Homilies*

9   One of the mysteries of faith is that, although it constitutes our
    deepest response to God for what he has done for us in Jesus
    Christ, yet it is, at the same time, a gift from him when we lift
    our eyes beyond ourselves. He meets us with faith when we
    want to have faith.
        John Gunstone *The Lord is Our Healer*

10 To abandon religion for science is merely to fly from one
    region of faith to another.
        Giles and Melville Harcourt *Short Prayers for a Long Day*

1 A faith that sets bounds in itself, that will believe so much and no more, that will trust thus far and no further, is none.
  J.C. and A.W. Hare *Guesses at Truth*

2 Almighty God, bestow upon us the meaning of words, the light of understanding, the nobility of diction and the faith of the true nature. And grant that what we believe we may also speak.
  St Hilary of Poitiers

3 Faith in a holy cause is to a considerable extent a substitute for the lost faith in ourselves.
  Eric Hoffer *The True Believer*

4 The basic faith of Christianity is that the hidden God revealed himself in his world and in history in a very particular way. God became man. Jesus Christ is accepted in faith by Christians as both divine and human. Christ therefore is THE sacrament par excellence.
  Michael Hollings *Signs of Faith, Hope and Love* 'Sacrament is Now'

5 The great act of faith is when a man decides he is not God.
  Oliver Wendell Holmes Jnr *The Mind and Faith of Justice Holmes*

6 Be not faithless, but believing.
  Holy Bible St John Chap. 20 v. 27

7 The just shall live by faith.
  Holy Bible Romans Chap. 1 v. 17

8 We walk by faith, not by sight.
  Holy Bible 2 Corinthians Chap. 5 v. 7

9 Fight the good fight of faith.
  Holy Bible 1 Timothy Chap. 6 v. 12

10 I have fought a good fight, I have finished my course, I have kept the faith.
  Holy Bible 2 Timothy Chap. 4 v. 7

11 Faith is the substance of things hoped for, the evidence of things not seen.
  Holy Bible Hebrews Chap. 11 v. 1

12 Faith without words is dead.
  Holy Bible James Chap. 2 v. 26

1 Faith tells us of things we have never seen, and cannot come to know by our natural senses.
   St John of the Cross *The Ascent of Mount Carmel*

2 Our life is grounded in faith, with hope and love besides.
   Julian of Norwich *Revelations of Divine Love*

3 Faith is required of thee, and a sincere life, not loftiness of intellect, nor deepness in the mysteries of God.
   Thomas à Kempis *The Imitation of Christ*

4 Faith is the assent to any proposition not made out by the deduction of reason but upon the credit of the proposer.
   John Locke

5 Frankly, hard though it is to say so, it is lack of faith not to be able to bear the thought of anything which God allows.
   Leslie D. Weatherhead *The Will of God*

6 Faith is a living and unshakeable confidence, a belief in the grace of God so assured that a man would die a thousand deaths for its sake.
   Martin Luther Preface to his translation of St Paul's *Epistle to the Romans*

7 A faith cannot be a faith against, but *for*.
   Archibald MacLeish *Sunday Graphic* February 1941

8 'Tis faith alone that vividly and certainly comprehends the deep mysteries of our religion.
   Montaigne *Essays*

9 Faith, fantastic Faith, once wedded fast
   To some dear falsehood, hugs it to the last.
   Thomas Moore *Lallah Rookh* 'The Veiled Prophet of Khorassan'

10 Lead, kindly light, amid th'encircling gloom; lead thou me on.
   The night is dark, and I am far from home; lead thou me on.
   Keep thou my fear; I do not ask to see
   The distant scene — one step enough for me.
   John Henry, Cardinal Newman Hymn

11 The ascendency of faith may be impracticable but the reign of knowledge is impossible. The problem for statesmen of this age is how to educate the masses, and literature and science cannot give the solution.
   John Henry, Cardinal Newman *Tamworth Reading Room*

1 Nothing true or beautiful or good makes complete sense in any immediate context of history; therefore we must be saved by faith.
> Reinhold Niebuhr *The Irony of American History*

2 Console thyself, thou wouldst not seek Me, if thou hadst not found me.
> Blaise Pascal *Pensées*

3 Great is his faith who does believe his eyes.
> Coventry Patmore *The Rod, the Root and the Flower*

4 Faith is a permanent and vital endowment of the human mind — a part of reason itself. The insane alone are without it.
> Eden Phillpotts *A Shadow Passes*

5 Faith is a quality which the scientist cannot dispense with.
> Max Planck *Where is Science Going?*

6 God the Father of our Lord Jesus Christ increase us in faith and truth and gentleness, and grant us part and lot among His Saints.
> St Polycarp

7 It is at night that faith in light is admirable.
> Edmond Rostand *Chanticler* Act II Sc. 3

8 Proofs are the last thing looked for by a truly religious mind which feels the imaginative fitness of its faith.
> George Santayana *Interpretations of Poetry and Religion*

9 Faith, even when profound, is never complete.
> Jean-Paul Sartre *Words*

10 I do not believe I know anything about faith. Jesus is my God. I don't think I have any faith but that. But I have a love for men; somewhere in me I have love. I hang on to that.
> Rev. H.R.L. Sheppard *The Impatience of a Parson*

11 Faith is nothing at all tangible. It is simply believing God; and, like sight, it is nothing apart from its object. You might as well shut your eyes and look inside to see whether you have sight, as to look inside to discover if you have faith.
> Hannah Whithall Smith *The Christian's Secret of a Happy Life*

12 Onward in faith — and leave the rest to Heaven.
> Robert Southey *The Retrospect*

13 Your faith is what you believe, not what you know.
> John Lancaster Spalding *Means and Ends of Education*

1 Faith speaks when hope dissembles:
Faith lives when hope lies dead.
> Algernon Charles Swinburne *Astrophel and Other Poems*
> 'Jacobite Song'

2 Faith has need of the whole truth.
> Pierre Teilhard de Chardin *The Appearance of Man*

3 How sweet to have a common faith!
To hold a common scorn of death!
> Alfred, Lord Tennyson 'Supposed Confessions'

4 Strong Son of God, immortal Love,
Whom we, that have not seen thy face,
By faith, and faith alone, embrace,
Believing where we cannot prove.

5 We have but faith; we cannot know,
For knowledge is of things we see;
And yet we trust it comes from Thee,
A beam in darkness: let it grow.
> Alfred, Lord Tennyson *In Memoriam*

6 Faith which does not doubt is a dead faith.
> Miguel de Unamuno *The Agony of Christianity*

7 Faith consists in believing not what seems true, but what
seems false to our understanding.
> Voltaire *Philosophical Dictionary*

8 Faith builds a bridge across the gulf of death,
To break the shock blind nature cannot shun,
And lands thought smoothly on the farther shore.
> Edward Young *Night Thoughts*

9 Faith convinces us of the reality not only of the things which
we cannot see but also of those which we cannot feel.
> Hubert van Zeller *We Work While the Light Lasts*

FAITHFULNESS

10 Our prayer will be most like the prayer of Christ if we do not
ask God to show us what is going to be, or to make any
particular thing happen, but only pray that we may be faithful
in whatever happens.
> Fr Andrew SDC *Meditations for Every Day*

1 It is, however, only by fidelity in little things that a true and
   constant love of God can be distinguished from a passing
   fervour of spirit.
   François de la Mothe Fénelon *Letters and Reflections*

2 Only the person who has faith in himself is able to be faithful
   to others.
   Erich Fromm *The Art of Loving*

3 Whither thou goest, I will go; and where thou lodgest, I will
   lodge: thy people shall be my people, and thy God, my God.
   Where thou diest, will I die, and there will I be buried; the
   Lord do so to me, and more also, if aught but death part thee
   and me.
   Holy Bible Ruth Chap. 1 vv. 16−17

4 Be thou faithful unto death, and I will give thee a crown of
   life.
   Holy Bible Revelation Chap. 2 v. 10

FAITHLESSNESS

5 Curse God, and die.
   Holy Bible Job Chap. 2 v. 9

6 Be not faithless, but believing.
   Holy Bible St John Chap. 20 v. 27

FALL

7 The desire of power in excess caused the angels to fall; the
   desire of knowledge in excess caused man to fall.
   Francis Bacon *Essays* 'Of Goodness and Goodness of Nature'

8 How are the mighty fallen! Tell it not in Gath, publish it not in
   the streets of Askelon.
   Holy Bible 2 Samuel Chap. 1 vv. 19−20

9 As Chesterton pointed out, the Fall of Man is only the
   banana-skin joke carried to cosmic proportions.
   Malcolm Muggeridge *Jesus Rediscovered*

10 Like quicksilver the scales slip down,
   Upon the air the spirit flies,
   And so I build me Heaven and Hell
   To buy my bartered Paradise.
   Edwin Muir 'The Fall'

FALLIBILITY

1 The man who makes no mistakes does not normally make anything.
>   Edward John Phelps Speech at Mansion House, London
>   24 January 1899

2 A man should never be ashamed to own he has been in the wrong, which is but saying, in other words, that he is wiser today than he was yesterday.
>   Jonathan Swift

FAMILY

3 Each of us will have our own different ways of expressing love and care for the family. But unless that is a high priority, we will find that we may gain the whole world and lose our own children.
>   Michael Green *The Work of an Evangelist*

4 Every large family has its angel and its demon.
>   Joseph Roux *Meditations of a Parish Priest*

5 The family is one of nature's masterpieces.
>   George Santayana *The Life of Reason*

6 All happy families resemble one another; every unhappy family is unhappy in its own way.
>   Leo Tolstoy *Anna Karenina*

FANATICISM

7 What keeps me from talking about religion is the fact that in me there lies a fanatic dozing ever so lightly whom I particularly do not wish to rouse.
>   Julian Green *Diaries*

8 All fanaticism is a strategy to prevent doubt from becoming conscious.
>   H.A. Williams *The True Wilderness*

FASTING

9 Whoso will pray, he must fast and be clean,
  And fat his soul and make his body lean.
>   Geoffrey Chaucer *Canterbury Tales* 'The Summoner's Tale'

1 To fast is to learn to love and appreciate food, and one's own
good fortune in having it.
Monica Furlong *Church Times* 4 March 1983

2 Noah the first was (as Tradition says)
That did ordain the fast of forty days.
Robert Herrick 'The Fast, or Lent'

3 When the stomach is full it is easy to talk of fasting.
St Jerome *Letters* No. 58

FATE

4 Whatever befalls thee was preordained for thee from eternity.
Marcus Aurelius *Meditations*

5 I do not believe in a fate that falls on men however they act:
but I do believe in a fate that falls on them unless they act.
G.K. Chesterton *Generally Speaking*.

6 Events will take their course, it is no good
Our being angry at them; he is happiest
Who wisely turns them to the best account.
Euripides *Bellerophon*

7 God's mill grinds slow, but sure.
George Herbert *Jacula Prudentum*

8 Even-handed fate
Hath but one law for small and great:
That ample urn holds all men's names.
Horace *Odes*

9 The Moving Finger writes; and having writ
Moves on; not all thy Piety nor Wit
Shall lure it back to cancel half a Line,
Nor all thy Tears wash out a Word of it.
Omar Khayyam *Rubaiyat* Trans. Edward Fitzgerald

10 Human reason needs only to will more strongly than fate and
she *is* fate.
Thomas Mann *The Magic Mountain*

11 It is a great soul that surrenders itself to fate, but a puny
degenerate thing that struggles.
Seneca *Letters to Lucilius*

FATHER

1 A wise son maketh a glad father.
   Holy Bible Proverbs Chap. 10 v. 1

2 Whoso curseth his father or his mother, his lamp shall be put
   out in obscure darkness.
   Holy Bible Proverbs Chap. 20 v. 20

3 It is easier for a father to have children than for children to
   have a real father.
   Pope John XXIII *Reader's Digest* November 1960

FAULT

4 The business of finding fault is very easy, and that of doing
   better very difficult.
   St Francis de Sales *Spiritual Maxims*

5 Gladly we desire to make other men perfect but we will not
   amend our own fault.
   Thomas à Kempis *The Imitation of Christ*

FAVOURITISM

6 As the apple tree among the trees of the wood, so is my
   beloved among the sons.
   Holy Bible Song of Solomon Chap. 2 v. 3

7 Hail, thou that art highly favoured, the Lord is with thee:
   blessed art thou among women.
   Holy Bible St Luke Chap. 1 v. 28

FEAR

8 There are times when fear is good
   It must keep its watchful place
   At the heart's controls. There is
   Advantage in the wisdom won from pain.
   Aeschylus *The Eumenides*

9 Fear has a smell, as love does.
   Margaret Atwood *Surfacing*

10 Fear is never a good counsellor and victory over fear is the
   first spiritual duty of man.
   Nicolas Berdyaev *Towards a New Epoch*

1   I have seen the moment of my greatness flicker,
And I have seen the eternal Footman hold my coat, and
    snicker,
And in short, I was afraid.
     T.S. Eliot 'The Love Song of J. Alfred Prufrock'

2   The wise man in the storm prays God, not for safety from
danger, but for deliverance from fear.
     Ralph Waldo Emerson *Journals*

3   For it is not death and pain that is a fearful thing, but the fear
of death and pain.
     Epictetus *Discourses*

4   If it is fear you would dispel, the seat of that fear is in your
heart and not in the hand of the feared.
     Kahlil Gibran *The Prophet*

5   The best answer to fear is to have a firm grasp of what it
means to be accepted by God.
     John Gunstone *The Lord is Our Healer*

6   There is no fear in love; but perfect love casteth out fear:
because fear hath torment. He that feareth is not made perfect
in love.
     Holy Bible 1 John Chap. 4 vv. 18–19

7   God is good. There is no devil but fear.
     Elbert Hubbard *The Note Book*

8   'Twas only fear first in the world made gods.
     Ben Jonson *Sejanus* Act II Sc. 2

9   Pain is pain. Man is man. There is only one FEAR of Death,
only one Black Night of the soul: and when that comes,
wherever you are, you are on the Road that Leads to the Sea.
     Gerald Kersh *Clean, Bright and Slightly Oiled*

10   Of all the passions, fear weakens judgement most.
     Cardinal de Retz *Memoirs*

11   Fear is the main source of superstition and one of the main
sources of cruelty. To conquer fear is the beginning of
wisdom.
     Bertrand Russell *An Outline of Intellectual Rubbish*

12   Were the diver to think of the jaws of the shark he would
never lay hands on the precious pearl.
     Sa'di *Gulistan*

1 The love that dare not look at life's dark potentiality is not love at all, it is fear.
   J. Neville Ward *The Use of Praying*

2 He who fears aught else but God is in fear of all things.
   The Wisdom of the Sufis Compiled by Kenneth Cragg

FELLOWSHIP

3 Envy and hatred try to pierce our neighbour with a sword. But the blade cannot reach him unless it first pass through our own body.
   St Augustine of Hippo

4 We do weep with those who weep; we do not know enough of rejoicing with those who rejoice.
   A. Neave Brayshaw Society of Friends Rule Book
   'The Meeting as a Fellowship'

5 Try as hard as you like, but in the end only the language of the heart can ever reach another heart while mere words, as they slip from your tongue, don't get past your listener's ear.
   St Francis de Sales *Conferences*

6 Can two walk together, except they be agreed?
   Holy Bible Amos Chap. 3 v. 3

7 I stand at the door, and knock: if any man hear my voice, and open the door, I will come in to him, and will sup with him, and he with me.
   Holy Bible Revelation Chap. 3 v. 20

8 Fellowship is heaven, and lack of fellowship is hell: fellowship is life, and lack of fellowship is death; and the deeds that ye do upon earth, it is for fellowship's sake that ye do them.
   William Morris *A Dream of John Ball*

9 There is a fellowship more quiet even than solitude; and which, rightly understood, is solitude made perfect.
   Robert Louis Stevenson *Travels With a Donkey*

10 If Thy heart be as my heart, give me Thy hand.
   John Wesley

FEMINISM

11 When God made man she was only testing.
   Anon

1 The all-male religions have produced no religious imagery.
The great religious art of the world is deeply involved with the
female principle.
   Kenneth Clark *Civilisation*

2 Field-Marshal Montgomery: Lady Astor, I must tell you that I
   do not approve of female politicians.
Lady Astor: That's all right. The only General I approve of is
   Evangeline Booth.
   John Gregg *Nancy Astor: Portrait of a Pioneer*

3 The Catholic Church has never really come to terms with
women. What I object to is being treated either as Madonnas
or Mary Magdalenes.
   Shirley Williams *Observer* 22 March 1981

FIDELITY

4 Fidelity within marriage is the most profound of all because
the root it takes in love of each spouse cannot be pulled up. A
married couple may grow apart but they can no longer
UNMARRY.
   Michel Quoist *With Open Heart*

FINGERS

5 Why are the fingers tapered like pegs? So that if one hears
improper language he may insert them in his ears.
   The Talmud

FIRE

6 The bush burned with fire, and the bush was not consumed.
   Holy Bible Exodus Chap. 3 v. 2

7 There appeared a chariot of fire, and horses of fire, and parted
them both asunder; and Elijah went up by a whirlwind into
heaven.
   Holy Bible 2 Kings Chap. 2 v. 11

8 Christ, Who is the Ultimate Fire
Who will burn away the cold in the heart of Man.
   Edith Sitwell 'The Canticle of the Rose'

FLATTERY

9 A flattering mouth worketh ruin.
   Holy Bible Proverbs Chap. 26 v. 28

FLOOD

1 The only thing that stops God sending a second Flood is that the first one was useless.
   Nicolas Chamfort *Characters and Anecdotes*

FOLLY

2 Folly in youth is sin, in age 'tis madness.
   Samuel Daniel *The Tragedy of Cleopatra*

3 The common curse of mankind, folly and ignorance.
   William Shakespeare *Troilus and Cressida* Act II Sc. 3

4 Folly is the direct pursuit of Happiness and Beauty.
   George Bernard Shaw *Maxims for Revolutionists*

FOOD

5 Man doth not live by bread only, but by every word that proceedeth out of the mouth of the Lord.
   Holy Bible Deuteronomy Chap. 8 v. 3

6 Every man should eat and drink, and enjoy the good of all his labour, it is the gift of God.
   Holy Bible Ecclesiastes Chap. 3 v. 13

7 Strange to see how a good dinner and feasting reconciles everybody.
   Samuel Pepys *Diary*

8 Hunger and thirst are healthy drives unless you eat and drink solely for your own pleasure and in excess of what is reasonable. We must eat to live, and not live to eat.
   Michel Quoist *The Christian Response*

FOOLISHNESS

9 The fool hath said in his heart: there is no God.
   Book of Common Prayer Psalm 14 v. 1

10 Only the fool, fixed in his folly, may think
   He can turn the wheel on which he turns.
   T.S. Eliot *Murder In the Cathedral*

11 The foolishness of fools is folly.
   Holy Bible Proverbs Chap. 14 v. 24

12 Fools rush in where angels fear to tread.
   Alexander Pope *Essay on Criticism*

FORERUNNER

1 The voice of him that crieth in the wilderness, Prepare ye the
way of the Lord, make straight in the desert a highway for our
God.
Holy Bible Isaiah Chap. 40 v. 3

2 Behold, I will send my messenger, and he shall prepare the
way before me.
Holy Bible Malachi Chap. 3 v. 1

FORGIVENESS

3 You ought certainly to forgive them as a Christian, but never
to admit them in your sight, or allow their names to be
admitted in your hearing.
Jane Austen *Pride and Prejudice*

4 Cosmus, Duke of Florence, was wont to say of perfidious
friends, 'We read that we ought to forgive our enemies, but we
do not read that we ought to forgive our friends.'
Francis Bacon *Apophthegms*

5 The glory of Christianity is to conquer by forgiveness.
William Blake *Jerusalem*

6 Mutual Forgiveness of each Vice,
Such are the Gates of Paradise.

7 Without Forgiveness of Sin, Love is Itself Eternal Death.
William Blake *The Gates of Paradise*

8 Forgive us our trespasses as we forgive them that trespass
against us.
Book of Common Prayer The Lord's Prayer

9 We all like to forgive and we all love best not those who
offended us least, nor those who have done most for us, but
those who make it most easy for us to forgive them.
Samuel Butler *Notebooks* 'Reconciliation'

10 Forgiveness to the injured doth belong
But they ne'er pardon who have done the wrong.
John Dryden *The Conquest of Granada*

11 Forgive, O Lord, my little jokes on Thee
And I'll forgive Thy great big one on me.
Robert Frost *In the Clearing*

1 God will forgive me, that's His business.
   Heinrich Heine Dying words

2 If you forgive people enough you belong to them, and they to you, whether either person likes it or not — squatter's rights of the heart.
   James Hilton *Time and Time Again*

3 Whosoever shall smite thee on thy right cheek, turn to him the other also.
   Holy Bible St Matthew Chap. 5 v. 39

4 Forgive us our debts, as we forgive our debtors.
   Holy Bible St Matthew Chap. 6 v. 12

5 Her sins, which are many, are forgiven; for she loved much: but to whom little is forgiven, the same loveth little.
   Holy Bible St Luke Chap. 7 v. 47

6 Be ye kind one to another, tender-hearted, forgiving one another, even as God for Christ's sake hath forgiven you.
   Holy Bible Ephesians Chap. 4 v. 32

7 Forgiveness is not an occasional act, it is a permanent attitude.
   Martin Luther King *The Words of Martin Luther King*

8 Forgiveness needs to be accepted, as well as given, before it is complete.
   C.S. Lewis *The Problem of Pain*

9 To err is human, to forgive, divine.
   Alexander Pope *Essay on Criticism*

10 Forgive the trespasses that I may have committed. Many mornings remain to dawn upon us: lead us through them all.
   Rig-Veda

11 Only one petition in the Lord's Prayer has any condition attached to it: it is the petition for forgiveness.
   Archbishop William Temple *Personal Religion and the Life of Fellowship*

12 It is by forgiving that one is forgiven.
   Mother Teresa of Calcutta Quoted Kathryn Spink *For the Brotherhood of Man Under the Fatherhood of God*

13 God does not want to punish you; He has provided for your forgiveness.
   Colin Urquhart *Receive Your Healing*

1 There is so much for us all to forgive that we shall never get it done without putting in a lot of practice.
   J. Neville Ward *Five for Sorrow Ten for Joy*

2 I ask God's forgiveness for my lack of faithfulness in asking for his forgiveness.
   The Wisdom of the Sufis Compiled by Kenneth Cragg

FREEDOM

3 There is no question facing contemporary man which is more relevant and more clamant than this: how are we to use our freedom?
   Michael Green *Jesus Spells Freedom*

4 There can be no freedom without the freedom to fail.
   Eric Hoffer *The Ordeal of Change*

5 Christianity promises to make men free; it does not promise to make them independent.
   Dean W.R. Inge *The Philosophy of Plotinus*

6 Freedom has always been an expensive thing. History is fit testimony to the fact that freedom is rarely gained without sacrifice and self-denial.

7 Freedom is never voluntarily given by the oppressor; it must be demanded by the oppressed.

8 The hope of the world is still in dedicated minorities. The trail blazers in human, academic, scientific, and religious freedom have always been in the minority.
   Martin Luther King *The Words of Martin Luther King*

9 Freedom can be uncomfortable. Given choice, it is always possible to make the wrong decision.
   Observer Leading article 8 February 1982

10 Jesus Christ is the key which unlocks the door of the prison cell of our own making and sets us free to live in the wide world of God's love and purpose.
   Kenneth Pillar Letter to Margaret Pepper 1987

11 Be sure that if you offer your freedom to God — whether it is question of time or affection or place — or anything else, He will take it. But He will give you a far greater liberty instead.
   Hubert van Zeller *Praying While You Work*

FREE WILL

1 Only two possibilities exist: either one must believe in determinism and regard free-will as a subjective illusion, or one must become a mystic, and regard the discovery of natural laws as a meaningless illusion.

> Max Born (Nobel Prize Winner for Physics 1955) *Bulletin of the Atomic Scientists* June 1957

2 The greatest gift that God in His bounty made in creation, and the most conformable to His goodness, and that which He prizes the most, was the freedom of will, with which the creatures with intelligence, they all and they alone, were and are endowed.

> Dante *The Divine Comedy*

3 The human will is free *only* within the bounds of a determined cosmic system.

> Albert Einstein *The World As I See It*

4 God is not willing to do everything, and thus take away our free will and that share of glory that belongs to us.

> Niccolo Machiavelli *The Prince*

5 It is in the nature of all human experience to know that love demands free will on both sides. Whatever other freedoms are denied us the freedom to love or to hate cannot be taken from us.

> Philip Pare *God Made the Devil*

6 We have to believe in free will. We've got no choice.

> Isaac Bashevis Singer Quoted *The Times* 'Diary' 21 June 1982

FRIENDSHIP

7 No medicine is more valuable, none more efficacious, none better suited to the cure of all our temporal ills than a friend to whom we may turn for consolation in time of trouble — and with whom we may share our happiness in time of joy.

> St Aelred of Rievaulx *Christian Friendship*

8 The highest privilege there is, is the privilege of being allowed to share another's pain. You talk about your pleasures to your acquaintances; you talk about your troubles to your friends.

> Fr Andrew SDC *Seven Words from the Cross*

1 What is a friend? A single soul in two bodies.
> Aristotle Quoted Diogenes Laertius *Lives of Eminent Philosophers*

2 I was studying at theological college and the text said 'Go, get thyself a friend.' Another text said somewhat enigmatically that 'Thy friend has a friend.' You understand what it is all about on a public holiday when all the friends, the ones you know and the ones you have never heard of, pay a friendly call on you.
> Rabbi Lionel Blue *Kitchen Blues*

3 Friendship as the union of two selves lies beyond happiness or unhappiness. It is simply the other side of our life and thus free from all danger.
> Ladislaus Boros *Hidden God*

4 Let him have the key to thy heart who hath the lock to his own.
> Sir Thomas Browne *Christian Morals*

5 Don't walk in front of me
I may not follow
Don't walk behind me
I may not lead
Walk beside me
And just be my friend.
> Albert Camus

6 When a friend laughs, it is for him to disclose the subject of his joy; when he weeps, it is for me to discover the cause of his sorrow.
> Joseph François Desmahis Quoted Elizabeth Urch *Sorrow*

7 Saul and Jonathan were lovely and pleasant in their lives, and in their death they were not divided.
> *Holy Bible* 2 Samuel Chap. 1 v. 23

8 Faithful are the wounds of a friend; but the kisses of an enemy are deceitful.
> *Holy Bible* Proverbs Chap. 27 v. 6

9 Iron sharpeneth iron; so a man sharpeneth the countenance of his friend.
> *Holy Bible* Proverbs Chap. 27 v. 17

1 Greater love hath no man than this, that a man lay down his life for his friends.
    Holy Bible St John Chap. 15 v. 13

2 From acquaintances, we conceal our real selves. To our friends we reveal our weaknesses.
    Basil Hume OSB *Searching for God*

3 A friend is long sought, hardly found and with difficulty kept.

4 The friendship that can cease has never been real.
    St Jerome *Letters*

5 Friends are God's apology for relations.
    Hugh Kingsmill Quoted Michael Holroyd *The Best of Hugh Kingsmill*

6 A foe to God was ne'er true friend to man;
Some sinister intent taints all he does.
    Edward Young *Night Thoughts*

7 The reason why we allow our closest friendships to be broken up is because we cannot be content with simply having the other person, we want the other person's feelings as well.
    Hubert van Zeller *We Work While the Light Lasts*

FULFILMENT

8 He died in a good old age, full of days, riches, and honour.
    Holy Bible 1 Chronicles Chap. 29 v. 28

9 I am not come to destroy, but to fulfil. For verily I say unto you, Till heaven and earth pass, one jot or one tittle shall in no wise pass from the law, till all be fulfilled.
    Holy Bible St Matthew Chap. 5 vv. 17–18

10 The time is fulfilled, and the kingdom of God is at hand.
    Holy Bible St Mark Chap. 1 v. 15

FUNCTIONALISM

11 Functionalism had thrived in the 1950s, died in the 60s, the coffin had been nailed down in the 70s and it had been buried in the 80s. Now here was the Church of England trying to revive the corpse. We have something better to offer. We have the gospel of Jesus Christ which transforms society, not just glues all the bits together.
    Elaine Storkey Speech to the General Synod November 1987

FUNDAMENTALISM

1 Fundamentalists hold that the Bible in its entirety and in each
of its parts speaks the truth. The Bible cannot err.
Fundamentalist priests are nearly always seen clutching their
Bibles, their preaching is punctuated by the words 'the Bible
says'.

2 I suppose it is broadly time to say that all Fundamentalists are
Evangelicals but not all Evangelicals are Fundamentalists.
    Douglas Brown *Church Times* March 1988

FUNERAL

3 In the city a funeral is just an interruption of traffic. In the
country it is a form of entertainment.
    George Ade *Cosmopolitan* magazine 1928

4 The care of funeral, the manner of burial, the pomp of
obsequies, are rather a consolation to the living than of any
service to the dead.
    St Augustine of Hippo *Civitas Dei*

5 To those left behind memorial services serve as a sort of
surrogate encounter with death.
    Hugh Casson *Diary*

6 Friends make pretence of following to the grave,
But before one is in it, their minds are turned
And making the best of their way back to life
And living people, and things they understand.
    Robert Frost 'Home Burial'

7 And all along the path to the cemetery
The round dark heads of men crowded silently,
And black-scarved faces of women folk, wistfully
Watch at the banner of death, and the mystery.
    D.H. Lawrence 'Giorno dei Morti'

8 One of the crying needs of the time is for a suitable Burial
Service for the admittedly damned.
    H.L. Mencken *Prejudices*

9 I hate funerals and would not attend my own if it could be
avoided, but it is well for every man to stop once in a while
and think of what sort of mourners he is training for the event.
    Robert T. Morris *Fifty Years a Surgeon*

1 I cannot think of a more wonderful thanksgiving for the life I have lived than that everyone should be jolly at my funeral.

> Lord Mountbatten, in a recorded TV interview shown shortly after his death in 1979

FUTURE

2 Never let the future disturb you. You will meet it, if you have to, with the same weapons of reason which today arm you against the present.

> Marcus Aurelius *Meditations*

3 Men must pursue things which are just in present, and leave the future to divine Providence.

> Francis Bacon *Advancement of Learning*

4 You can never plan the future by the past.

> Edmund Burke Letter to a Member of the National Assembly

5 What we look for does not come to pass. God finds a way for what none foresaw.

> Euripides *Alcestis*

6 Trust no Future, howe'er pleasant!
Let the dead Past bury its dead!
Act, — act in the living Present!
Heart within, and God o'erhead!

> Henry Wadsworth Longfellow 'A Psalm of Life'

7 To most of us the future seems unsure; but then it always has been; and we who have seen great changes must have great hopes.

> John Masefield 'Grace Before Ploughing'

8 Order and certainty govern the art of nature, but in the life of any human being there is nothing finally predictable, for man, and man alone, can alter his environment and change his future.

> Norman Vincent Peale *Men, Morals and Maturity*

GAIN

1 Honour and profit lie not all in one sack.
   George Herbert *Jacula Prudentum*

2 In all labour there is profit.
   Holy Bible Proverbs Chap. 14 v. 23

3 For me to live is Christ, and to die is gain.
   Holy Bible Philippians Chap. 1 v. 21

4 Ill-gotten gains work evil.
   Sophocles *Antigone*

GENEROSITY

5 The hand that gives, gathers.
   English proverb

6 No one is so generous as he who has nothing to give.
   French proverb

7 All things come of thee, and of thine own have we given thee.
   Holy Bible 1 Chronicles Chap. 29 v. 14

8 Teach us, good Lord, to serve Thee as Thou deservest.
   To give and not to count the cost:
   To fight and not to heed the wounds:
   To toil and not to seek for rest:
   To labour and not to ask for any reward
   Save that of knowing that we do thy will.
   St Ignatius Loyola *Prayer for Generosity*

9 Whatever share of this world Thou dost bestow on me,
   bestow it on Thine enemies and whatever share of the next
   world Thou dost give me, give it to Thy friends. Thou art
   enough for me.
   Rabi'ah of Basra Muslim spirituality

GENTLENESS

1 Use a sweet tongue, courtesy, and gentleness, and thou mayest manage to guide an elephant by a hair.
   Sa'di *Gulistan*

GIFTS

2 God's gifts put man's best dreams to shame.
   Elizabeth Barrett Browning *Sonnets from the Portuguese*

3 That gift of his, from God descended:
   Ah friend, what gift of man's does not?
   Robert Browning 'Christmas Eve'

4 There are those who give little of the much they have — and they give it for recognition and their hidden desire makes their gifts unwholesome.
   Kahlil Gibran *The Prophet*

5 Thou shalt take no gift: for the gift blindeth the wise, and perverteth the words of the righteous.
   Holy Bible Exodus Chap. 23 v. 8

6 They presented unto him gifts; gold, and frankincense, and myrrh.
   Holy Bible St Matthew Chap. 2 v. 11

7 There are diversities of gifts, but the same Spirit.
   Holy Bible 1 Corinthians Chap. 12 v. 4

8 A cheerful giver does not count the cost of what he gives. His heart is set on pleasing and cheering him to whom the gift is given.
   Julian of Norwich *Revelations of Divine Love*

9 Nothing is small if God accepts it.
   St Teresa of Avila

GIVING

10 A man there was, though some did count him mad,
   The more he cast away, the more he had.
   John Bunyan *The Pilgrim's Progress*

11 It is well to give when asked, but it is better to give unasked, through understanding.
   Kahlil Gibran *The Prophet*

1   Giving much to the poor
    Doth enrich a man's store;
    It takes much from the account
    To which his sin doth amount.
        George Herbert *Jacula Prudentum*

2   Freely ye have received, freely give.
        Holy Bible St Matthew Chap. 10 v. 8

3   Go and sell that thou hast, and give to the poor, and thou
    shalt have treasure in heaven.
        Holy Bible St Matthew Chap. 19 v. 21

4   Give, and it shall be given unto you; good measure, pressed
    down, and shaken together, and running over.
        Holy Bible St Luke Chap. 6 v. 38

5   Silver and gold have I none; but such as I have give I thee.
        Holy Bible Acts Chap. 3 v. 6

6   It is more blessed to give than to receive.
        Holy Bible Acts Chap. 20 v. 35

7   God loveth a cheerful giver.
        Holy Bible 2 Corinthians Chap. 9 v. 7

8   By Jove the stranger and the poor are sent,
    And what to those is given, to Jove is lent.
        Homer *Odyssey*

9   The wise man does not lay up treasure. The more he gives to
    others, the more he has for his own.
        Lao-Tze *The Simple Way*

10 He gives nothing but worthless gold
    Who gives from a sense of duty.
        James Russell Lowell 'The Vision of Sir Launfal'

11 Whatever we hold to ourselves is loss.
    Whatever we give to God is gain.
        Gilbert Shaw *The Service of Love*

12 Man discovers his own wealth
    When God comes to ask gifts from him.
        Rabindranath Tagore *Fireflies*

13 He who gives alms in secret is greater than Moses.
        The Talmud

1 It is not always more blessed to give than to receive, though
many Christians have been persuaded by earnest mentors to
twist their reluctant minds into thinking it is.
J. Neville Ward *Five for Sorrow Ten for Joy*

2 Give all thou canst; high Heaven rejects the lore
Of nicely calculated less or more.
William Wordsworth 'King's College Chapel'

3 Better not to look at the gift, but look at the person you are
giving to.
Hubert van Zeller *The Inner Search*

GLORY

4 Seldom comes Glory till a man be dead.
Robert Herrick *Hesperides*

5 Who is this King of glory? The Lord of hosts, he is the King
of glory.
Holy Bible Psalm 24 v. 10

6 The glory of the Lord shone round about them.
Holy Bible St Luke Chap. 2 v. 9

7 How swiftly passes away the glory of the world.
Thomas à Kempis *The Imitation of Christ*

8 The glory of great men should always be measured by the
means they have used to acquire it.
François, Duc de la Rochefoucauld *Maxims*

GOD

9 God is that, the greater than which cannot be conceived.
St Anselm *Proslogion*

10 God is more truly imagined than expressed, and he exists
more truly than he is imagined.
St Augustine of Hippo *De Trinitate*

11 If the concept of God has any validity or use it can only be to
make us larger, freer, more loving. If God cannot do this, then
it is time we got rid of him.
James Baldwin *The Fire Next Time*

12 God is the poet, men are but the actors.
Honoré de Balzac *The Christian Socrates*

1 What is the prose for God?
    H. Granville Barker *Waste*

Rodo
1867-1931

2 To my mind the most poignant mystical exhortation ever
    written is 'Be still and know that I am God.'
    Arnold Bennett *Journals*

3 I am the father of the whole universe, the mother, the creator,
    the Lord, the friend.
    Bhagavad Gita

4 It is not the constant thought of their sins, but the vision of the
    holiness of God that makes the saints aware of their own
    sinfulness.
    Archbishop Anthony Bloom

5 A God who let us prove his existence would be an idol.
    Dietrich Bonhoeffer *No Rusty Swords*

6 Not three Gods, but one God.
    Book of Common Prayer Athanasian Creed

7 The Lord is gracious and merciful: long suffering and of great
    goodness.
    Book of Common Prayer Psalm 145 v. 8

8 Do not search for God by the discursive exercising of your
    mind; let him be, I say, as he is.
    The Book of Privy Counsel

9 God is the perfect poet,
    Who in his person acts his own creations.
    Robert Browning *Paracelsus*

10 God is the Thou which by its very nature cannot become it.

11 God is the Being ... that may properly only be addressed, not
    expressed.
    Martin Buber *I and Thou*

12 To the lexicographer 'God' is simply the word that comes next
    to 'go-cart'.
    Samuel Butler

13 God is sufficiently wise, and good and powerful and merciful
    to turn even the most, apparently, disastrous events to the
    advantage and profit of those who humbly adore and accept
    his will in all that he permits.
    Jean-Pierre de Caussade SJ

1 The celestial order and the beauty of the universe compel one
to admit that there is some excellent and eternal Being, who
deserves the respect and homage of men.
Cicero *De Divinatione*

2 God is for men and religion for women.
Joseph Conrad *Nostromo*

3 I took it for granted that God had never spoken anything but
the most dignified English.
Clarence Day *Life with Father*

4 I have never been able to conceive mankind without Him.
Feodor Dostoevsky

5 God can no more do without us than we can do without Him.

6 The eye with which I see God is the same with which God sees
me.
Meister Eckhart

7 God enters by a private door into every individual.

8 The only money of God is God. He pays never with anything
less, or anything else.
Ralph Waldo Emerson *Essays*

9 God is our name for the last generalization to which we can
arrive.
Ralph Waldo Emerson *Journals*

10 He was a wise man who originated the idea of God.
Euripides *Sisyphus*

11 The best way to find the heart of God is to trust our own best
affections whatever we are looking at.
Austin Farrer

12 The way to God is by ourselves.
Phineas Fletcher *The Purple Island*

13 No one has the capacity to judge God. We are drops in that
limitless ocean of mercy.
Gandhi *Non-Violence in Peace and War*

14 God is the expression of the intelligent universe.
Kahlil Gibran *Thoughts and Meditations*

15 God depends on us. It is through us that God is achieved.
André Gide *Journals*

1 God is in thy heart, yet thou searchest for him in the
  wilderness.

2 Where self exists God is not.
  Where God exists there is no self.
  The Granth Sikh spirituality

3 Teach me, my God and King
  In all things thee to see,
  And what I do in anything,
  To do it as for Thee.
  George Herbert *New English Hymnal* No. 456

4 God said unto Moses, I AM THAT I AM.
  Holy Bible Exodus Chap. 3 v. 14

5 God is our refuge and strength, a very present help in trouble.
  Holy Bible Psalm 46 v. 1

6 If this counsel or this work be of men, it will come to nought:
  but if it be of God, ye cannot overthrow it.
  Holy Bible Acts Chap. 5 vv. 38–39

7 For in him we live, and move, and have our being.
  Holy Bible Acts Chap. 17 v. 28

8 All things work together for good to them that love God.
  Holy Bible Romans Chap. 8 v. 28

9 If God be for us, who can be against us?
  Holy Bible Romans Chap. 8 v. 31

10 I am Alpha and Omega, the beginning and the end, the first
   and the last.
   Holy Bible Revelation Chap. 22 v. 13

11 I have never understood why it should be considered
   derogatory to the Creator to suppose that He has a sense of
   humour.
   Dean W.R. Inge Quoted William Merchant *The Wit and
   Wisdom of Dean Inge*

12 An honest God is the noblest work of man.
   Robert G. Ingersoll *The Gods*

13 I believe that God is in me as the sun is in the colour and
   fragrance of a flower — the light in my darkness, the Voice in
   my Silence.
   Helen Keller

1   Man proposes but God disposes.
       Thomas à Kempis *The Imitation of Christ*

2   God is what man finds divine in himself. God is the best way
    man can behave in the ordinary occasions of life, and the
    farthest point to which man can stretch himself.
       Max Lerner *The Unfinished Country* 'Seekers and Losers'

3   My great concern is not whether God is on our side, my great
    concern is to be on God's side.
       Abraham Lincoln

4   God is easy to please and hard to satisfy.
       George MacDonald Quoted Fr Andrew SDC *Letters of Fr
       Andrew SDC*

5   Only this I know,
    That one celestial Father gives to all.
       John Milton *Paradise Lost*

6   Sophia wished that Florence would not talk about the
    Almighty as if his real name was Godfrey, and God was just
    Florence's nickname for him.
       Nancy Mitford *Pigeon Pie*

7   He who leaveth home in search of knowledge walketh in the
    path of God.

8   He who knows his own self knows God.
       Mohammed Muslim spirituality

9   If triangles had a god it would have three sides.
       Charles, Baron de Montesquieu *Letters*

10 Let us weigh the gain and the loss, in wagering that God is.
    Consider these alternatives: if you win, you win all, if you lose
    you lose nothing. Do not hesitate, then, to wager that he is.
       Blaise Pascal *Pensées*

11 History, without God, is a chaos without design, or end, or
    aim. Political economy without God would be a selfish
    teaching about the acquisition of wealth. Physics without God
    would be but a dull enquiry into certain meaningless
    phenomena. All sciences may do good service, if those who
    cultivate them know their place. All things must speak of God,
    refer to God or they are atheistic.
       Edward B. Pusey *Collegiate and Professional Teaching*

1   When God shuts a door, He opens a window.
    John Ruskin

2   God is the indwelling and not the transient cause of all things.
    Spinoza *Ethics*

3   I looked at God and He looked at me, and we were one
    forever.
    Charles Haddon Spurgeon

4   We are, because God is.
    Emanuel Swedenborg *Divine Love and Wisdom*

5   Man is an organ of life, and God alone is life.
    Emanuel Swedenborg *True Christian Religion*

6   Though a sharp sword be laid to thy throat, still pray to God
    for mercy.
    The Talmud

7   It is a mistake to suppose that God is only, or even chiefly,
    concerned with religion.
    Archbishop William Temple Quoted R.V.C. Bodley *In Search
    of Serenity*

8   Rapture, being drawn out of oneself by God, is an experience
    in which one learns that God is stronger.
    St Teresa of Avila *The Complete Works of St Teresa*

9   If God were not a necessary Being of Himself, He might seem
    to be made for the use and benefit of men.
    John Tillotson *Sermons*

10 None but God can satisfy the longings of an immortal soul;
    that as the heart was made for Him, so He only can fill it.
    Richard Chenevix Trench *Notes on the Parables: The Prodigal
    Son*

11 We need God, not in order to understand the *why*, but in
    order to feel and sustain the ultimate wherefore, to give a
    meaning to the Universe.
    Miguel de Unamuno *The Tragic Sense of Life*

12 There is in God — some say —
    A deep, but dazzling darkness.
    Henry Vaughan *Silex Scintillans* 'The Night'

13 If God did not exist it would be necessary to invent him.
    Voltaire *Epîtres* 'A l'Auteur du Livre des Trois Imposteurs'

1   If cattle or horses, or lions, had hands, or were able to draw with their feet and produce the works which men do, horses would draw the forms of gods like horses, and cattle like cattle, and they would make the gods' bodies the same shape as their own.

    Xenophanes Quoted Diogenes Laertius *Lives of the Eminent Philosophers*

GOD — CREATOR

2   Grandfather Wakan-Tanka, you are the first and always have been. Everything belongs to you. It is you who have created all things. You are one and alone.

    Dakota-Sioux invocation Red Indian spirituality

3   They heard the voice of the Lord God walking in the garden.

    Holy Bible Genesis Chap. 3 v. 8

4   This is the day which the Lord hath made; we will rejoice and be glad in it.

    Holy Bible Psalm 118 v. 24

5   My help cometh from the Lord, which made heaven and earth.

    Holy Bible Psalm 121 v. 2

6   In the beginning was the Word, and the Word was with God, and the Word was God.

    Holy Bible St John Chap. 1 v. 1

GOD — FATHERHOOD OF

7   Call no man your father upon the earth: for one is your Father, which is in heaven.

    Holy Bible St Matthew Chap. 23 v. 9

GOD — GLORY OF

8   Set God apart from mortal men, and deem not that he, like them, is fashioned out of flesh. Thou knowest him not; now he appeareth as fire, now as water, now as gloom; and he is dimly seen in the likeness of wild beasts, of wind, of cloud, of lightning, thunder and of rain. All power hath he, lo, this is the glory of the Most High God.

    Aeschylus

1   And one cried unto another, and said, Holy, holy, holy, is the
    Lord of hosts: the whole earth is full of His glory.
        Holy Bible Isaiah Chap. 6 v. 3

2   The glory of God is man fully alive.
        St Irenaeus *Against Heresies*

3   You, O Lord, are mankind's bright sign
    Best, most beloved of the people, Awake!
    Give strength to the singer.
        Rig-Veda

GOD – GOODNESS OF

4   The earth is full of the goodness of the Lord.
        Holy Bible Psalm 33 v. 5

5   I will never leave thee, nor forsake thee.
        Holy Bible Hebrews Chap. 13 v. 5

6   In his love he clothes us, enfolds and embraces us; that tender
    love completely surrounds us, never to leave us. As I saw it he
    is everything that is good.
        Julian of Norwich *Revelations of Divine Love*

GOD – HOUSE OF

7   This is none other but the house of God, and this is the gate of
    heaven.
        Holy Bible Genesis Chap. 28 v. 17

8   My house shall be called the house of prayer; but ye have
    made it a den of thieves.
        Holy Bible St Matthew Chap. 21 v. 13

GOD – KINGDOM OF

9   The Kingdom of God is the outcome of a huge longing, a huge
    desire, born in the poor man's heart and transferred into the
    pierced heart of the Poor Man PAR EXCELLENCE –
    CHRIST.
        Carlo Carretto *The Desert in the City*

10 But with much trouble I was corrupted and made to learn the
    dirty devices of the world which I am now unlearning and
    becoming as it were a little child again, so that I may enter
    into the Kingdom of God.
        Thomas Traherne 'On His Childhood'

GOD – LIFE IN HIM

1   I beg you to come into my heart, for by inspiring it to long for
you, you make it ready to receive you.
St Augustine of Hippo *Soliloquies*

2   Just as there is an evil bitter zeal which cuts us off from God,
and leads to hell, so there is a good zeal which shields us from
vice and leads to God and eternal life.
St Benedict *The Rule of St Benedict*

3   I know that my redeemer liveth, and that he shall stand at the
latter day upon earth: And though ... worms destroy this
body, yet in my flesh shall I see God.
Holy Bible Job Chap. 19 vv. 25–26

4   Because you love the burning grounds, I have made one of my
heart, that you may dance therein your eternal dance.
Ramprasad Quoted *Holy Waters* Indian Psalm Meditations
Text by Martin Kämpchen

GOD – LOVE OF

5   God's richness is such that he can totally give himself to
everyman, can be there only for him – and likewise for a
second and third, for millions and thousands of millions. That
is the mystery of his infinity and inexhaustible richness.
Ladislaus Boros *Hidden God*

6   And so, don't talk too much about God, but live in the
certainty that He has written your name on the palm of His
hand.

7   Live your human task in the liberating certainty that nothing
in the world can separate you from God's love for you.
Brakkenstein Community of Blessed Sacrament Fathers,
Holland *Rule for a New Brother*

8   God makes of *all* things mysteries and sacraments of love, why
should not every moment of our lives be a sort of communion
with the divine love?
Jean-Pierre de Caussade SJ *Self-Abandonment to the Divine
Providence*

9   God so loved the world, that he gave his only begotten Son,
that whosoever believeth on him should not perish, but have
everlasting life.
Holy Bible St John Chap. 3 v. 16

1   What is the fitting love of God? It should be as if he were
     lovesick, unable to get the woman he loves out of his mind,
     pining for her constantly when he is at rest and in motion,
     when he eats and drinks. Even more than this should be the
     love of God in the heart of those who love him and yearn
     constantly for him, as he commanded us: 'With all your heart
     and with all your soul.'
     Maimonides

2   Let us make God the beginning and end of our love, for he is
     the fountain from which all good things flow and into him
     alone they flow back. Let him therefore be the beginning of
     our love.
     Richard Rolle Quoted *The Wisdom of the English Mystics*

GOD – NATURE OF

3   Never judge God by suffering, but judge suffering by the
     Cross.
     Fr Andrew SDC *The Gift of Light*

4   The nature of God is a circle of which the centre is everywhere
     and the circumference is nowhere.
     Anon Quoted *Oxford Dictionary of Quotations*

5   You are the garment which covers every nakedness. You feed
     the hungry in your sweetness.
     St Catherine of Siena *On Divine Revelation*

6   Dear God,
     What is your money like? Has it got your head on it?
     Love from Anna Light
     Children's Prayers and Letters to God Ed. Maggie Durran

7   By love can God be gotten and holden, by thought and
     understanding never.

8   Even if a man is deeply versed in the understanding and
     knowledge of all spiritual things ever created, he can never by
     such understanding come to know an uncreated spiritual thing
     ... which is none else than God.

9   For silence is not God, nor speaking; fasting is not God, nor
     eating; solitude is not God nor company; nor any other pairs
     of opposites. He is hidden between them and cannot be found
     by anything your soul does, but only by the love of your heart.
     The Cloud of Unknowing

1 The knower and the known are one. Simple people imagine that they should see God, as if He stood there and they here. This is not so. God and I, we are one in knowledge.

2 The more God is in all things, the more He is outside them. The more He is within, the more without.
    Meister Eckhart

3 Our minds act like a beam of a lighthouse, picking up one object after another. God's mind is like the sun radiating simultaneously on all things at once.
    Richard Harries *Turning to Prayer*

4 God is a sea of infinite substance.
    St John of Damascus *De Fide Orthodoxa*

5 All are but parts of one stupendous whole,
Whose body Nature is, and God the soul.
    Alexander Pope *An Essay on Man*

6 Thou my mother, and my father thou
Thou my friend, and my teacher thou
Thou my wisdom, and my riches thou
Thou art all to me, O God of all Gods.
    Ramanuja *Indian spirituality*

7 God in the depths of us receives God who comes to us; it is God contemplating God.
    Jan van Ruysbroeck Quoted F.C. Happold *Religious Faith and Twentieth-Century Man*

8 He is the core of the heart of love, and He, beyond labouring seas, Our ultimate shore.
    Edith Sitwell

9 It is with God Himself as it is with a great mountain. The important thing is to come to Him not with fear, but with love.
    Sherpa Tensing *Man of Everest – An Autobiography*

10 This is the sum and substance of it all – God is, God loveth thee, God beareth all thy care.
    Tukaram *Indian spirituality*

11 My life, which is not my own,
Has no asset except its sense of wonder:
Thou art the King of the realm of beauty,
I am but a helpless beggar.
    The Wisdom of the Sufis Compiled by Kenneth Cragg

1 No reason can be given for the nature of God, because that nature is the ground of rationality.
> Alfred North Whitehead *Science and the Modern World*

GOD – OMNISCIENCE OF

2 Nothing is too little to be ordered by our Father; nothing too little in which to see His hand; nothing which touches our souls too little to accept from Him; nothing too little to be done to Him.
> Edward B. Pusey

3 Not so much as the weight of an ant in earth or heaven escapes from the Lord, neither is aught smaller than that, or greater, but is clearly written in God's book.
> *The Qur'an*

GOD – POWER OF

4 The Lord shall preserve thy going out, and thy coming in: from this time forth for evermore.
> *Book of Common Prayer* Psalm 121 v. 8

5 The Lord is a great God, and a great King above all gods.
> *Holy Bible* Psalm 95 v. 3

6 His banner over me was love.
> *Holy Bible* The Song of Solomon Chap. 2 v. 4

7 Thy thunderbolt rules over meadows, hills and sky! O God, Slayer of Time! Thou the Great Void, King of righteousness! Thou blessed one, redeem me.
> Ramakrishna Quoted *Holy Waters* Indian Psalm Meditations Text by Martin Kämpchen

GOD – PRESENCE OF

8 How distant you are from my sight while I am present to your sight! You are wholly present everywhere and I do not see you.
> St Anselm *Proslogion*

9 God is seated in the hearts of all.
> *Bhagavad Gita*

10 You need not cast a spell over me, for I am always with you, as I always choose to be with you.
> Martin Buber *Mamre*

1 Wherever I go – only Thou!
  Wherever I stand – only Thou!
  Just Thou; again Thou! always Thou!
  Thou, Thou, Thou! When things are good Thou!
  When things are bad – Thou! Thou! Thou.
  Hasidic song

2 God is as present as the air.
  Michael Hollings *Day by Day*

3 I am the Almighty God; walk before me, and be thou perfect.
  Holy Bible Genesis Chap. 17 v. 1

4 The eyes of the Lord are in every place, beholding the evil and
  the good.
  Holy Bible Proverbs Chap. 15 v. 3

5 Utterly at home, he lives in us for ever.
  Julian of Norwich *Revelations of Divine Love*

6 If then a man does not seek God where he is, there is no profit
  in seeking him where he is not. What is the good of sitting at
  home seeking him, when his presence is in the Holy Eucharist.
  John Henry, Cardinal Newman *Parochial and Plain Sermons*

7 If you find God, you find life: if you miss God you miss the
  whole point of living.
  Kenneth Pillar Letter to Margaret Pepper 1987

8 God in me, God without! Beyond compare! A Being wholly
  here and wholly there!
  Angelus Silesius Quoted F.C. Happold *Religious Faith and
  Twentieth-Century Man*

9 In every place where you find the imprint of men's feet there
  am I.
  The Talmud

10 Those who die in grace go no further from us than God – and
  God is very near.
  Pierre Teilhard de Chardin

11 Seek contact with Him now in the goodness and splendour
  which is in other people.
  Evelyn Underhill *The Letters of Evelyn Underhill*

12 Spiritual Hunger does not mean that a man will necessarily
  find God, but it does strongly suggest that God exists.
  David Watson *Is Anyone There?*

GOD – RELATIONSHIP WITH

1 In every relationship in which we stand we are regarding the hem of the garment of the eternal Thou; from each there reaches us a waft of His breath; in each Thou we address the eternal Thou.
   Martin Buber *I and Thou*

2 Keep thy heart in a soft and tractable state lest thou lose the impress of His hands and thy life.
   St Irenaeus

3 He whose treasure house is God, his Earth is paradise.
   Why then call those who make this earth a hell
   The worldly wise?
   Angelus Silesius *The Book of Angelus Silesius*

GOD – WILL OF

4 Give what Thou dost demand: and then demand what Thou wilt.
   St Augustine of Hippo *Confessions*

5 We must not come to God in order to go through a range of emotions ... we must just come to God in order to be in his presence, and, if he chooses to make us aware of it, blessed be God, but if he chooses to make us experience his real absence, blessed be God again, because he is free to come near or not.
   Archbishop Anthony Bloom *Living Prayer*

6 Seek in reading and thou shalt find in meditation; knock in prayer and it shall be opened to thee in contemplation.
   St John of the Cross *Maxims*

7 And do not say, regarding anything, 'I am going to do that tomorrow,' but only 'if God will.'
   The Qur'an

8 God gives when he will, as he will and to whom he will.
   St Teresa of Avila *Mansions*

GOD – WORD OF

9 The Word of God is not a sounding but a piercing word, not pronounceable by the tongue but efficacious in the mind, not sensible to the ear but fascinating to the affection.
   St Bernard of Clairvaux *Sermons on the Canticles*

1   We should always approach God knowing that we do not
     know him. We must approach the unsearchable, mysterious
     God who reveals himself as he chooses; whenever we come to
     him, we are before a God we do not yet know.
         Archbishop Anthony Bloom *Living Prayer*

GODS

2   What the gods are is a matter of dispute but that they are is
     denied by nobody.
         Cicero *On the Nature of the Gods*

3   The gods possess the form of man; yet their form is not
     corporeal, but only resembles bodily substance.
         Caius Velleius, expounding the doctrines of Epicurus Quoted
         Cicero *De Natura Deorum*

4   All men have need of Gods.
         Homer *Odyssey*

GOODNESS

5   Waste no more time arguing what a good man should be; be
     one.
         Marcus Aurelius *Meditations*

6   Goodness is achieved, not in a vacuum but in the company of
     other men, attended by love.
         Saul Bellow *Dangling Man*

7   They are only truly great who are truly good.
         George Chapman *Revenge for Honour*

8   Be good and leave the rest to Heaven.
         William Combe *Dr Syntax in Search of the Picturesque*

9   Goodness that preaches undoes itself.

10   It is very hard to be simple enough to be good.
         Ralph Waldo Emerson *Journals*

11   Seek not good from without; seek it within yourselves or you
     will never find it.
         Epictetus *Discourses*

12   Blessed is he who does good to others and desires not that
     others should do him good.
         Br Giles *Little Flowers of St Francis*

1   Goodness is uneventful. It does not flash, it glows.
    David Grayson *Adventure in Contentment*

2   All things work together for good to them that love God.
    Holy Bible Romans Chap. 8 v. 28

3   God, whose gifts in gracious flood
Unto all who seek are sent,
Only asks you to be good
And is content.
    Victor Hugo

4   God is all that is good, in my sight, and the goodness that
everything has is his.
    Julian of Norwich *Revelations of Divine Love*

5   Goodness does not more certainly make men happy than
happiness makes them good.
    Walter Savage Landor *Imaginary Conversations* 'Lord Brooke
and Sir Philip Sidney'

6   An act of goodness, the least act of true goodness, is indeed
the best proof of the existence of God.
    Jacques Maritain *Approaches to God*

7   Abash'd the devil stood,
And felt how awful goodness is, and saw
Virtue in her shape how lovely.

8   Good, the more
Communicated, more abundant grows.
    John Milton *Paradise Lost*

9   No evil can happen to a good man, either in life or after death.
    Plato *Dialogues*

10   Men always love what is good, or what they find good. It is in
judging what is good that they go wrong.
    Jean-Jacques Rousseau *The Social Contract*

11   In every good man a god doth dwell.
    Seneca *Letters to Lucilius*

12   The saints see men and women through the golden haze of
their own goodness, and too nice a discrimination of the
characters of others is a sign that you are not too nice a
character yourself.
    Logan Pearsall Smith *All Trivia* 'Afterthoughts'

1   It was only when I lay there on rotting prison straw that I
    sensed within myself the first stirring of the good. Gradually it
    was disclosed to me that the line separating good and evil
    passes, not through states, not between classes, not between
    political parties either, but right through every human heart
    and through all human hearts.
       Alexander Solzhenitsyn

2   Good is no good, but if it be spend:
    God giveth good for none other end.
       Edmund Spenser *The Shepherd's Calendar* 'May'

3   Goodness needeth not to enter into the soul, for it is there
    already, only it is unperceived.
       Theologica Germanica Trans. S. Winkworth

4   A good is never productive of evil but when it is carried to a
    culpable excess, in which case it completely ceases to be a good.
       Voltaire *Philosophical Dictionary* 'Property'

5   To be good, according to the vulgar standard of goodness, is
    obviously quite easy. It merely requires a certain amount of
    sordid terror, a certain lack of imaginative thought, and a
    certain low passion for middle class respectability.
       Oscar Wilde *The Critic as Artist*

GOOD AND EVIL

6   The Spirit is always willing, always yearning for righteousness
    and love, but its purpose is deceived and betrayed by the
    delusions of experience.
       Warner Allen *The Happy Issue*

7   Every evil is based on some good, for it is present in a subject
    which is good and having some sort of nature. Evil cannot
    exist but in good, sheer evil is impossible.
       St Thomas Aquinas *Summa Contra Gentiles*

8   Woe unto them that call evil good, and good evil.
       Holy Bible Isaiah Chap. 5 v. 20

9   Be not overcome of evil, but overcome evil with good.
       Holy Bible Romans Chap. 12 v. 21

10 Doth a fountain send forth at the same place sweet water and
    bitter?
       Holy Bible James Chap. 3 v. 11

1   The shadow belongs to the light as the evil belongs to the good, and vice versa.
>   Carl Gustav Jung *Modern Man in Search of a Soul*

GOSPEL

2   Thy word is a lantern unto my feet: and a light unto my paths.
>   *Book of Common Prayer* Psalm 119 v. 105

3   The words of the Gospels, repeated to a child, a workman or a peasant, do not surprise him in the least. Nothing is told with a view to effect. Not a word in the Gospels is intended to startle.
>   Ernest Hello *Life, Science and Art*

4   The Gospel is essentially a message of spiritual redemption, not of social reform.
>   Dean W.R. Inge *Freedom, Love and Truth*

5   Let holy reading be always at hand. Sleep may fall upon thee as thou lookest thereon, and the sacred page meet the drooping face.
>   St Jerome

6   The Gospel is open to all; the most respectable sinner has no more claim on it than the worst.
>   Martyn Lloyd-Jones Quoted Christopher Catherwood *Five Evangelical Leaders*

7   Were we to devote to their [the Gospels'] comprehension a little of the selfless enthusiasm that is now expended on the riddle of our physical surroundings, we should cease to say that Christianity is coming to an end. We might even feel that it had only just begun.
>   E.V. Rieu

8   Whenever you read the Gospel Christ Himself is speaking to you. And while you read you are praying and talking to him.
>   St Tikhon of Zadonsk Quoted Esther de Waal *Seeking God: The Way of St Benedict*

9   Every morning after I have cleaned my cell and polished my tins, I read a little of the gospels ... It is a delightful way of opening the day. Everyone, even in a turbulent, ill-disciplined life, should do the same.
>   Oscar Wilde Quoted Richard Harries *Prayers of Grief and Glory*

GRACE

1   Lord, it belongs not to my care
    Whether I die or live;
    To love and serve Thee is my share
    And this Thy grace must give.
        William Blake

2   Cheap grace is grace without discipleship, grace without the
    cross, grace without Jesus Christ, living and incarnate.

3   Cheap grace is the deadly enemy of our church. Cheap grace
    means grace sold on the market like cheapjack's wares. Cheap
    grace is the preaching of forgiveness without requiring
    repentance, without church discipline, communion without
    confession, absolution without personal confession.

4   Costly grace is the treasure hidden in the field; for the sake of
    it a man will gladly go and sell all that he has. It is costly
    because it costs a man his life, and it is grace because it gives a
    man the only true life.
        Dietrich Bonhoeffer *The Cost of Discipleship*

5   The grace of the Lord Jesus Christ, and the love of God, and
    the communion of the Holy Ghost, be with you all. Amen.
        Holy Bible 2 Corinthians Chap. 13 v. 14

6   Let your speech be alway with grace, seasoned with salt.
        Holy Bible Colossians Chap. 4 v. 6

7   These things, good Lord, that we pray for, give us Thy grace
    to labour for.
        Sir Thomas More

8   We receive more than we can ever give; we receive it from the
    past on which we draw with every breath, but also — and this
    is a point of faith — from the source of the mystery itself, by
    the means which religious people call GRACE.
        Edwin Muir

9   All men who live with any degree of serenity live by some
    assurance of grace.
        Reinhold Niebuhr *Reflections on the End of Our Era*

10 The grace of God is in my mind shaped like a key, that comes
    from time to time and unlocks the heavy doors.
        Donald Swan

1 Grace strikes us when we are in great pain and restlessness. It strikes us when we walk through the dark valley of a meaningless and empty life. It strikes us when we feel that our separation is deeper than usual.
  Paul Tillich *The Shaking of the Foundations*

2 I have germs of all possible crimes, or nearly all, within me. This natural disposition is dangerous and very painful, but, like every variety of natural disposition, it can be put to good purpose if one knows how to make the right use of it with the help of grace.
  Simone Weil *Waiting on God*

GRATITUDE

3 Next to ingratitude, the most painful thing to bear is gratitude.
  Henry Ward Beecher *Proverbs from a Plymouth Pulpit*

4 Gratitude is heaven itself.
  William Blake

5 If it were our lot to suffer deprivation, as it is the lot of many in the world, then gratitude for the little things of life and the big things of God would come more readily to our lips.
  Cardinal Basil Hume OSM *Searching for God*

GRAVE

6 The boast of heraldry, the pomp of power,
  And all that beauty, all that wealth e'er gave,
  Awaits alike the inevitable hour,
  The paths of glory lead but to the grave.
  Thomas Gray *Elegy Written in a Country Churchyard*

7 A piece of the Churchyard fits everybody.
  George Herbert *Jacula Prudentum*

8 The house appointed for all living.
  Holy Bible Job Chap. 30 v. 23

9 O death, where is thy sting? O grave, where is thy victory?
  Holy Bible 1 Corinthians Chap. 15 v. 55

10 He spake well who said that graves are the footprints of angels.
  Henry Wadsworth Longfellow *Hyperion*

1 The grave itself is but a covered bridge,
Leading from light to light, through a brief darkness.
   Henry Wadsworth Longfellow *The Golden Legend*

2 The grave's a fine and private place,
But none I think do there embrace.
   Andrew Marvell 'To His Coy Mistress'

3 For who's a prince or beggar in the grave?
   Thomas Otway *Windsor Castle*

4 The grave unites; where even the great find rest,
And blended lie the oppresser and the oppressed.
   Alexander Pope

5 Of all the pulpits from which human voice is ever sent forth
there is none from which it reaches so far as from the grave.
   John Ruskin *Seven Lamps of Architecture*

6 The grave is but the threshold of eternity.
   Robert Southey *Joan of Arc*

GREATNESS

7 Attention to little things is a great thing.
   St John Chrysostom

8 Great men cling to the truth as if their hearts had teeth.
   Louis Danz *Dynamic Dissonance*

9 We all go to our graves unknown, worlds of unsuspected
greatness.
   Frederick W. Faber *Spiritual Conferences*

10 We are always glad when a great man reassures us of his
humanity by possessing a few peculiarities.
   André Maurois *The Art of Living*

11 All greatness grows great by self-abasement, and not by
exalting itself.
   Nestorius *Bazaar of Heracleides*

12 If we are intended for great ends, we are called to great
hazards.
   John Henry, Cardinal Newman *Oxford University Sermons*

13 Be great in little things.
   St Francis Xavier

GREED

1 Greed is a bottomless pit which exhausts the person in an endless effort to satisfy the need without ever reaching satisfaction.
> Erich Fromm *Escape from Freedom*

2 He is not poor that hath not much, but he that craves much.
> Thomas Fuller *Gnomologia*

3 Woe unto them that join house to house, that lay field to field, till there be no place.
> *Holy Bible* Isaiah Chap. 5 v. 8

4 The covetous man is ever in want.
> Horace

GRIEF

5 Grief drives men into the habits of serious reflection, sharpens the understanding and softens the heart.
> John Adams Letter to Thomas Jefferson 6 May 1816

6 It is dangerous to abandon one's self to the luxury of grief: it deprives one of courage and even of the wish for recovery.
> H.F. Amiel *Journal*

7 Grief should be the Instructor of the wise.
Sorrow is Knowledge: they who know the most
Must mourn the deepest.
> Lord Byron *Manfred*

8 Grief is to man as certain as the grave:
Tempests and storms in life's whole progress rise,
And hope shines dimly through o'er-clouded skies;
Some drops of comfort on the favoured fall,
But showers of sorrow are the lot of all.
> George Crabbe 'The Library'

9 It is idle to grieve if you get no help from grief.
> Seneca *Letters to Lucilius*

10 I sometimes hold it half a sin
To put in words the grief I feel;
For words, like Nature, half reveal
And half conceal the Soul within.
> Alfred, Lord Tennyson *In Memoriam*

GROWTH

1 I have nothing to give another; but I have a duty to open him to his own life, to allow him to be himself — infinitely richer than he could ever be if I tried to enrich and to shape him only from the outside.
   Michel Quoist *With Open Mind*

GUIDANCE

2 God does not make theological statements — but he gives the answer which his creatures need and which profits them.
   Martin Buber *Mamre*

3 Now I am in this place tossed by such billows of this world that I am in no way able to steer into port the old and rotten ship over which, in the hidden dispensation of God, I have assumed the guidance.
   St Gregory the Great *Letters*

4 From the unreal lead me to the real!
   From darkness lead me to light!
   From death lead me to immortality!
   The Upanishads

GUILT

5 Guilt punishes the author of the crime.
   Juvenal *Satires*

6 He that knows no guilt knows no fear.
   Philip Massinger *The Great Duke of Florence* Act IV Sc. 2

7 Every man is guilty of all the good he didn't do.
   Voltaire

HALO

1   What, after all,
    Is a halo? It's only one more thing to keep clean.
    Christopher Fry *The Lady's Not for Burning*

HAPPINESS

2   Man still wishes to be happy even when he so lives as to make
    happiness impossible.
    St Augustine of Hippo *The City of God*

3   The greatest happiness of the greatest number is the
    foundation of morals and legislation.
    Jeremy Bentham *Commonplace Book*

4   All who joy would win
    Must share it, — happiness was born a twin.
    Lord Byron *Don Juan*

5   Happiness is a mystery, like religion, and should never be
    rationalised.
    G.K. Chesterton *Heretics*

6   Happiness lies in the fulfilment of the spirit through the body.
    Cyril Connolly *The Unquiet Grave*

7   Happiness makes up in height for what it lacks in length.
    Robert Frost Poem title

8   Christians are the only people in the world who have anything
    to be happy about.
    Billy Graham *The Secret of Happiness*

9   The search for happiness is one of the chief sources of
    unhappiness.
    Eric Hoffer *The Passionate State of Mind*

1   It is pretty hard to tell what does bring happiness; poverty and
    wealth have both failed.
        Kim Hubbard *Abe Martin*

2   The supreme happiness of life is the conviction of being loved
    for yourself, of more correctly, of being loved of yourself.
        Victor Hugo

3   Wherein lies happiness? In that which becks
    Our ready minds to fellowship divine,
    A fellowship with essence: 'til we shine,
    Full alchemized, and free of space. Behold
    The clear religion of heaven!
        John Keats *Endymion*

4   Many persons have a wrong idea of what constitutes real
    happiness. It is not obtained through self-gratification, but
    through fidelity to a worthy purpose.
        Helen Keller *Journal*

5   That thou art happy, owe to God;
    That thou continuest such, owe to thyself,
    That is, to thy obedience.
        John Milton *Paradise Lost*

6   The small share of happiness attainable by man exists only in
    so far as he is able to cease to think of himself.
        Theodor Reik *Of Love and Lust*

7   To be without some of the things you want is an indispensable
    part of happiness.
        Bertrand Russell *The Conquest of Happiness*

8   Happiness is the only sanction of life; where happiness fails,
    existence remains a mad and lamentable experiment.
        George Santayana *The Life of Reason*

9   We have no more right to consume happiness without
    producing it than we have to consume wealth without
    producing it.
        George Bernard Shaw *Candida*

10 Call no man happy till he dies.
        Solon Quoted Herodotus *Histories*

11 A man is happy so long as he chooses to be happy.
        Alexander Solzhenitsyn *Cancer Ward*

1 Happy the man to whom 'tis given
   To eat the bread of life in heaven;
   This happiness in Christ we prove,
   Who feed on His forgiving love.
       Charles Wesley Hymn

2 Who never knew the price of happiness will not be happy.
       Yevgeny Yevtushenko 'Babi Yar'

HARVEST FESTIVAL

3 ... it's strange to me
   How very full the church can be
   With people I don't see at all
   Except at Harvest Festival.
       John Betjeman *Poems in the Porch* 'Diary of a Church Mouse'

4 At the Harvest Festival in church the area behind the pulpit
   was piled high with IXL tins of fruit for the old-age
   pensioners. We had collected the tinned fruit from door to
   door. Most of it came from the old-age pensioners.
       Clive James *Unreliable Memoirs*

HATRED

5 One of the reasons people cling to their hates so stubbornly is
   because they seem to sense, once hate is gone, that they will
   be forced to deal with pain.
       James Baldwin *Notes of a Native Son*

6 Hatred rarely does any harm to its object. It is the hater who
   suffers. His soul is warped and his life poisoned by dwelling on
   past injuries or projecting schemes of revenge. Rancour in the
   bosom is the foe of personal happiness.
       Lord Beaverbrook *The Divine Propagandist*

7 From envy, hatred, and malice, and all uncharitableness,
   Good Lord, deliver us.
       Book of Common Prayer The Litany

8 I tell you there is such a thing as creative hate.
       Willa Cather *The Song of the Lark*

9 Love, friendship, respect, do not unite people as much as a
   common hatred for something.
       Anton Chekhov *Notebooks*

1 The price of hating other human beings is loving oneself less.
   Eldridge Cleaver

2 Hatred does not cease by hatred, but only by love; this is the eternal rule.
   Dhammapada Buddhist spirituality

3 The pleasure of hating, like a poisonous mineral, eats into the heart of religion and turns it to rankling spleen and bigotry; it makes patriotism an excuse for carrying fire, pestilence and famine into other lands; it leaves to virtue nothing but the spirit of censoriousness.
   William Hazlitt *The Plain Speaker* 'On the Pleasure of Hating'

4 Hatred and bitterness can never cure the disease of fear; only love can do that. Hatred paralyses life; love releases it. Hatred confuses life; love harmonises it. Hatred darkens life; love illumines it.
   Martin Luther King *The Words of Martin Luther King*

5 It is proper to hate a corrupt person only for his defects, but in so far as he is endowed with a divine image, it is in order to love him.
   Abraham Isaac Kook *The Lights of Penitence*

6 He sowed doubtful speeches, and reaped plain, unequivocal hatred.
   Charles Lamb *Last Essays of Elia*

7 Enemies are not those who hate us, but rather those whom we hate.
   Dagobert Runes *A Dictionary of Thought*

8 There are very few who would not rather be hated than laughed at.
   Sydney Smith *Moral Philosophy*

9 May it be thy will, O Lord, that no man foster hatred against us in his heart, that we foster no hatred in our hearts against any man.
   The Talmud

10 An intellectual hatred is the worst.
   W.B. Yeats 'A Prayer for my Daughter'

11 Hate is a kind of 'passive suffering', but indignation is a kind of joy.
   W.B. Yeats *Letters*

HEAD

1 He that hath a head of wax must not walk in the sun.
   George Herbert *Jacula Prudentum*

2 It shall bruise thy head, and thou shalt bruise his heel.
   Holy Bible Genesis Chap. 3 v. 15

3 The very hairs of your head are all numbered.
   Holy Bible St Matthew Chap. 10 v. 30

4 Two heads are better than one.
   Homer *Iliad*

HEALING

5 The whole point of this life is the healing of the heart's eye
   through which God is seen.
   St Augustine of Hippo

6 By the truthful arguments you employ, and especially by the
   spirit of Truth and Love which you entertain, you will heal the
   sick.
   Christian Science Practice

7 Healing is one of the most striking manifestations of the
   redemption of our bodies which salvation will bring, but it is
   an anticipation graciously and mysteriously vouchsafed to
   some and, equally graciously and mysteriously, withheld from
   others.
   John Gunstone *The Lord is Our Healer*

8 Sometimes the Lord disturbs the waters before sending His
   healing angel.
   Fr John Harper 'Sermons: St John-in-the-Fields, St Ives'

9 A merry heart doeth good like a medicine.
   Holy Bible Proverbs Chap. 17 v. 22

10 And whithersoever he entered, into villages, or cities, or
   country, they laid the sick in the streets, and besought Him
   that they might touch if it were but the border of his garment:
   and as many as touched Him were made whole.
   Holy Bible St Mark Chap. 6 v. 56

11 The healing of the sick in His name is as much a part of the
   proclamation of the Kingdom as the preaching of the Good
   News of Jesus Christ.
   Lambeth Conference 1978 Resolution 8

1   Inner healing is simply this: Jesus can take the memories of our past and heal them ... and fill with his love all these places in us that have been empty for so long, once they have been healed and drained of the poison of past hates and resentment.

      Francis MacNutt *Healing*

2   The refusal to forgive and be forgiven lies at the root of a great deal of sickness. Like a root it is as often as not hidden. For true health we have to forgive God, others and ourselves.

      Philip Pare *God Made the Devil*

3   Inner healing is concerned to bring to light the causes of the inner pain; to help the sufferer to interpret them correctly; and to release the person from the emotional grip of the past.

      John Townroe *Christian Spirituality and Healing*

4   What cannot be questioned is God's willingness to heal and the provision He has already made for that purpose to be fulfilled.

      Colin Urquhart *Receive Your Healing*

HEART

5   The same heart beats in every human breast.

      Matthew Arnold *The Buried Life*

6   To my God, a heart of flame; to my fellow men, a heart of love; to myself, a heart of steel.

      St Augustine of Hippo

7   You have made us for yourself and our hearts are restless until they rest in you.

      St Augustine of Hippo *Confessions*

8   The 'heart' in the biblical sense is not the inward life, but the whole man in relation to God.

      Dietrich Bonhoeffer *Letters and Papers from Prison*

9   That which cometh from the heart will go to the heart.

      Jeremiah Burroughs *In Hosea*

10   Keep a green tree in your heart and perhaps a singing bird will come.

      Chinese proverb

11   A man after his own heart.

      Holy Bible 1 Samuel Chap. 13 v. 14

1 For the Lord seeth not as man seeth; for man looketh on the
outward appearance, but the Lord looketh on the heart.
Holy Bible 1 Samuel Chap. 16 v. 7

2 He that is of a merry heart hath a continual feast.
Holy Bible Proverbs Chap. 15 v. 15

3 The heart has its reasons, which reason knows not, as we feel
in a thousand instances.
Blaise Pascal *Pensées*

4 How else but through a broken heart
May Lord Christ enter in?
Oscar Wilde *The Ballad of Reading Gaol*

HEATHEN

5 Heathen. A benighted creature who has the folly to worship
something he can see and feel.
Ambrose Bierce *The Devil's Dictionary*

HEAVEN

6 Where imperfection ceaseth, heaven begins.
P.J. Bailey *Festus* 'Wood and Water'

7 The gates of heaven are so easily found when we are little, and
they are always standing open to let children wander in.
J.M. Barrie *Sentimental Journey*

8 Jerusalem the golden, with milk and honey blest,
Beneath thy contemplation, sink heart and voice oppressed.
St Bernard of Cluny *De Contemptu Mundi* Trans. John Mason
Neale

9 O how amiable are thy dwellings: thou Lord of hosts! My soul
hath a desire and longing to enter the courts of the Lord: my
heart and my flesh rejoice in the living God.
Book of Common Prayer Psalm 84 vv. 1—2

10 And in that heaven of all their wish
There shall be no more land, say fish.
Rupert Brooke 'Heaven'

11 The New Jerusalem, when it comes, will probably be found so
far to resemble the old as to stone its prophets freely.
Samuel Butler *Notebooks*

1 Hell is paved with good intentions, but Heaven goes in for something more dependable. Solid gold.

Joyce Cary *The Horse's Mouth*

2 Heaven is like an egg, and the earth is like a yolk of an egg.

Chang Heng *Sayings of Chang Heng*

3 This world cannot explain its own difficulties without the existence of another.

Charles Caleb Colton *Lacon*

4 Heaven means to be one with God.

5 He who offends against Heaven has none to whom he can pray.

Confucius *Analects*

6 Son of St Louis, ascend to Heaven.

L'Abbé Edgeworth de Firmont to Louis XVI, as he went up the steps to the guillotine (probably apocryphal)

7 All shall be well and
All manner of thing shall be well
When the tongues of flame are in-folded
Into the crowned knot of fire
And the fire and the rose are one.

T.S. Eliot *Little Gidding*

8 Heaven always bears some proportion to earth. The god of the cannibal will be a cannibal, of the crusader, a crusader and of the merchants, a merchant.

Ralph Waldo Emerson *The Conduct of Life* 'Worship'

9 There the wicked cease from troubling: and there the weary be at rest.

Holy Bible Job Chap. 3 v. 17

10 I had rather be a doorkeeper in the house of my God, than to dwell in the tents of wickedness.

Holy Bible Psalm 84 v. 10

11 Lay up for yourselves treasures in heaven, where neither moth nor rust doth corrupt, and where thieves do not break through nor steal.

Holy Bible St Matthew Chap. 6 v. 20

12 In my Father's house are many mansions.

Holy Bible St John Chap. 14 v. 2

1   Eye hath not seen, nor ear heard, neither have entered into
the heart of man, the things which God hath prepared for
them that love Him.
Holy Bible 1 Corinthians Chap. 2 v. 9

2   And I saw a new heaven and a new earth: for the first heaven
and the first earth were passed away.
Holy Bible Revelation Chap. 21 v. 1

3   Olympus, the abode of the Gods, that stands fast for ever.
Neither is it shaken by winds nor ever wet with rain, nor does
snow fall upon it, but the air is outspread clear and cloudless,
and over it hovers a radiant whiteness.
Homer *Odyssey*

4   The Kingdom of Heaven did gather us and catch us all, as in a
net, and his heavenly power at one time drew many hundreds
to land.
Francis Howgill 'God and Man'

5   Heaven: the Coney Island of the Christian imagination.
Elbert Hubbard

6   We sent up Yuri Gagarin to see if he could find the Kingdom
of Heaven, and he couldn't see it. So we sent up Gherman
Titov to make sure and he couldn't find it either.
Nikita Khrushchev

7   Heaven's net is indeed vast. Though its meshes are wide, it
misses nothing.

8   The Way of Heaven has no favourites. It is always with the
good man.
Lao-Tze *The Way of Lao-Tze*

9   I would give part of my lifetime for the sake of knowing what
is the average barometer reading in paradise.
G.C. Lichtenberg Quoted W.H. Auden *A Certain World*

10   We see but dimly through the mists and vapours;
Amid these earthly damps
What seem to us but sad, funereal tapers
May be heaven's distant lamps.
Henry Wadsworth Longfellow 'Resignation'

11   Heaven to me's a fair blue stretch of sky,
Earth's jest a dusty road.
John Masefield 'Vagabond'

1 Let us cease to wonder what they, the great, the illustrious
   ones, are doing in the beyond. Know that they are still singing
   hymns of praise. Here on earth they may have been practising.
   There they are perfecting their song.
   Henry Miller *The Books in My Life*

2 Heaven is for thee too high
   To know what passes there; be lowly wise:
   Think only what concerns thee and thy being;
   Dream not of other worlds, what creatures there
   Live, in what state, condition, or degree,
   Contented that thus far hath been revealed
   Not of Earth only but of highest Heaven.

3 What if Earth
   Be but the shadow of Heaven, and things therein
   Each to other like, more than on Earth is thought?
   John Milton *Paradise Lost*

4 Earth has no sorrow that Heaven cannot heal.
   Thomas Moore 'Come, Ye Disconsolate'

5 Take all the pleasures of all the spheres,
   And multiply each through endless years —
   One minute of heaven is worth them all.
   Thomas Moore *Lallah Rookh*

6 I think, while zealots fast and frown
   And fight for two or seven,
   That there are fifty roads to Town,
   And rather more to Heaven.
   Winthrop Mackworth Praed *Poems*

7 A Yorkshireman reached the Pearly Gates and gave one of
   those sniffs they use in the Ridings as a form of social
   comment. 'From Yorkshire, eh?' said the Recording Angel,
   unlocking the gates wearily. 'Well, yer can come in, but yer
   won't like it.'
   John Sandilands *Radio Times* 28 October 1971

8 If you go to heaven without being naturally qualified for it you
   will not enjoy yourself there.
   George Bernard Shaw *Man and Superman*

9 There are no crown-wearers in heaven that were not cross-
   bearers here below.
   Charles Haddon Spurgeon

1   Heaven is such that all who have lived well of whatever
     religion, have a place there.
          Emanuel Swedenborg *Divine Providence*

2   O Thou who art at home
     Deep in my heart
     Enable me to join you
     Deep in my heart.
          The Talmud

3   Short arm needs man to reach to Heaven,
     So ready is Heaven to stoop to him.
          Francis Thompson 'Grace of the Way'

4   O world invisible, we view thee,
     O world intangible, we touch thee,
     O world unknowable, we know thee,
     Inapprehensible, we clutch thee!

5   Yea, in the night, my Soul, my daughter,
     Cry — clinging Heaven by the hems;
     And lo, Christ walking on the water
     Not of Gennesareth, but Thames!
          Francis Thompson 'The Kingdom of God'

6   My soul, there is a country
     Far beyond the stars,
     Where stands a winged sentry
     All skilful in the wars:
     There, above noise and danger,
     Sweet Peace sits crown'd with smiles
     And One born in a manger
     Commands the beauteous files.
          Henry Vaughan *Silex Scintillans* 'Peace'

7   'It is a curious thing,' he thought, 'that every creed promises a
     paradise which will be absolutely uninhabitable for anyone of
     civilised taste.'
          Evelyn Waugh *Put Out More Flags*

HEAVENLY FOOD

8   Saviour of my life, grant me the food of grace and forgiveness
     as I journey forth.
          Rabindranath Tagore Quoted *Holy Waters* Indian Psalm
          Meditations Text by Martin Kämpchen

HELL

1 That's what Hell must be like, small chat to the babbling of
Lethe about the good old days when we wished we were dead.
    Samuel Beckett *Embers*

2 Hell is full of good intentions and desires.
    St Bernard of Clairvaux Quoted St Francis de Sales *Letters*

3 Hell has three gates, lust, anger and greed.
    Bhagavad Gita

4 When I was young I was certain that I was going to hell. I
would comfort myself by thinking that if I one day found
myself there, I would go on preaching about Christ and it
wouldn't be hell anymore!
    Commissioner Catherine Bramwell-Booth *My Faith* Ed. Mary
    E. Callan

5 There is probably no hell for authors in the next world — they
suffer so much from critics and publishers in this.
    C.N. Bruce *Summaries of Thought*

6 Hell is paved with priests' skulls.
    St John Chrysostom *Letters*

7 What is hell? Hell is oneself,
Hell is alone, the other figures in it
Merely projections.
    T.S. Eliot *The Cocktail Party* Act I Sc. 3

8 Behold, I am alive ... and have the keys of hell and of death.
    Holy Bible Revelation Chap. 1 v. 18

9 If hell is paved with good intentions it is, among other reasons,
because of the impossibility of calculating consequences.
    Aldous Huxley *After Many a Summer*

10 Hell is nothing else but nature departed or excluded from the
beams of divine light.
    William Law Quoted *The Wisdom of the English Mystics*

11 There is wishful thinking in Hell as well as on earth.
    C.S. Lewis *The Screwtape Letters*

12 Hell hath no limits, nor is circumscribed
In one self place, but where we are is hell,
And where hell is, there must we ever be.
    Christopher Marlowe *Doctor Faustus*

1 The infliction of cruelty with a good conscience is a delight to
   moralists. That is why they invented hell.
   > Bertrand Russell *Sceptical Essays*

2 To work hard, to live hard, to die hard, and then to go to hell
   after all would be too damned hard.
   > Carl Sandburg *The People, Yes*

3 Hell is full of musical amateurs. Music is the brandy of the
   damned.

4 There is plenty of humbug in Hell.
   > George Bernard Shaw *Man and Superman*

5 Hell is full of noise, and is probably full of clocks, that
   emphasise the time that never passes.
   > Fulton J. Sheen

6 Hell is a city much like London. A populous and smoky city.
   > Percy Bysshe Shelley 'Peter Bell the Third'

7 It doesn't matter what they preach
   Of high or low degree,
   The old Hell of the Bible
   Is Hell enough for me.
   > Frank L. Stanton 'Hell'

8 There is a dreadful Hell,
   And everlasting pains;
   There sinners must with devils dwell
   In darkness, fire, and chains.
   > Isaac Watts *Divine Songs for Children*

9 Hell is given up reluctantly by those who don't expect to go
   there.
   > Henry Leon Wilson *The Spenders*

HELP

10 He [God] does not want you to be dissecting your conscience.
    He simply wants you to come to Him for help in order that He
    may help you.
    > Fr Andrew SDC *Letters of Fr Andrew SDC*

11 God is our hope and strength: a very present help in trouble.
    Therefore will we not fear, though the earth be moved: and
    though the hills be carried into the midst of the sea.
    > *Book of Common Prayer* Psalm 46 vv. 1−2

1 Try first thyself, and after call in God,
For to the worker God himself lends aid.
   Euripides *Hippolytus*

2 The trouble is, we won't let God help us.
   George MacDonald *The Marquis of Lossie*

3 God helps those who help themselves.
   Algernon Sidney *Discourse Concerning Government*

HERESY

4 All heretics generally deceive by the ostentatious promise of
science; and reprehend the simplicity of believers.
   St Augustine of Hippo Quoted *Butler's Lives of the Saints*

5 The essence of a heretic, that is of someone who has a
particular opinion, is that he clings to his own ideas.
   Jacques Bénigne Bossuet *Histoire de Variations*

6 I did try to find a heresy of my own; and when I put the last
touches to it I discovered it was orthodoxy.
   G.K. Chesterton *Orthodoxy*

7 False doctrine does not necessarily make a man a heretic, but
an evil heart can make any doctrine heretical.
   Samuel Taylor Coleridge

8 A young priest came to me and said, 'Your Excellency, I am
losing my faith.' I said to him, 'Meaning no disrespect to your
intellectual attainments, but you and I are too dumb to lose
our faith. The great heretics like Martin Luther lose their
faith. You and I just get bored.'
   Cardinal Cushing Quoted Harry Reasoner 'The Unforgettable
Cardinal' *Reader's Digest* December 1973

9 By identifying the new learning with heresy we make
orthodoxy synonymous with ignorance.
   Erasmus

10 As a Roman Catholic I thank God for the heretics. Heresy is
only another word for freedom of thought.
   Graham Greene

11 Heresy is but the bridge between two orthodoxies.
   Francis Hackett *Henry VIII*

12 Heresy may be easier kept out than shook off.
   George Herbert *Jacula Prudentum*

1 They that approve a private opinion call it opinion, but they
that mislike it, heresy, and yet heresy signifies no more than
private opinion.
Thomas Hobbes *Leviathan*

2 A heresy can spring only from a system that is in full vigour.
Eric Hoffer *The Ordeal of Change*

3 The heresy of one age becomes the orthodoxy of the next.
Helen Keller *Optimism*

4 Heresy is a spiritual thing, cut with no iron, burned with no
fuse, drowned with no water. Though we should burn by force
every Jew and heretic, yet neither would there, nor will there,
be one conquered or converted thereby.
Martin Luther *Of Worldly Power*

5 Collective wisdom is no adequate substitute for the
intelligence of individuals. Individuals who have opposed
received opinion have been the source of all progress.
Socrates, Christ and Galileo all equally incurred the censure of
the orthodox.
Bertrand Russell *American Mercury*

6 In a dead religion there are no more heresies.
André Suares *Péguy*

HISTORY

7 It is still one of the tragedies of human history that the
'children of darkness' are frequently more determined and
zealous than the 'children of light'.
Martin Luther King *The Words of Martin Luther King*

8 All history is incomprehensible without Christ.
Ernest Renan

HOLINESS

9 Real holiness has a fragrance about it which is its own
advertisement.
Fr Andrew SDC *The Way of Victory*

10 Any natural act, if hallowed, leads to God, and nature needs
man for what no angel can perform on it, namely, its
hallowing.
Martin Buber *The Particular Way*

1　There is no one in the world who cannot arrive without difficulty at the most eminent perfection by fulfilling with love obscure and common duties.
　　　Jean-Pierre de Caussade SJ *Self-Abandonment to Divine Providence*

2　A true love of God must begin with a delight in his holiness, and not with a delight in any other attribute; for no other attribute is truly lovely without this.
　　　Jonathan Edwards *A Treatise Concerning Religious Affections*

3　God requires a faithful fulfilment of the merest trifle given us to do, rather than the most ardent aspiration to things to which we are not called.
　　　St Francis de Sales Quoted Aldous Huxley *The Perennial Philosophy*

4　Things that are holy are revealed only to men who are holy.
　　　Hippocrates

5　Holiness includes what we call moral goodness but moral goodness is not the same as holiness. It is only a constituent part of it.
　　　Graham Leonard *Firmly I Believe and Truly*

6　Holiness consists of doing the will of God with a smile.
　　　Mother Teresa of Calcutta Quoted Billy Graham *The Secret of Happiness*

HOLY COMMUNION

7　Almighty God, unto whom all hearts be open, all desires known, and from whom no secrets are hid: cleanse the thoughts of our hearts by the inspiration of thy Holy Spirit, that we may perfectly love thee, and worthily magnify thy holy name; through Christ our Lord. Amen.
　　　Book of Common Prayer Opening Collect

8　The Body of our Lord Jesus Christ which was given for thee, preserve thy body and soul unto everlasting life.

9　The Blood of our Lord Jesus Christ, which was shed for thee, preserve thy body and soul unto everlasting life.
　　　Book of Common Prayer At the Administration of Holy Communion

10　O now well work that sealing sacred ointment!
　　　Gerard Manley Hopkins 'The Bugler's First Communion'

1　Churchgoers attending Holy Communion in a Devon parish have been asked to be a little more abstemious when they approach the altar. 'Take only a small sip of the wine in the chalice,' the vicar urged. 'You do not get any more of God by taking a large gulp.'

　　The Revd David Niblett *Daily Telegraph* 14 April 1987

HOLY SPIRIT

2　The Holy Spirit Himself, which also operates in the prophets, we assert to be an effluence of God, flowing from Him and returning back again like a beam of the sun.

　　Athenagoras

3　We are all strings in the concert of his joy; the spirit from his mouth strikes the note and the tune of our strings.

　　Jakob Boehme *The Threefold Life of Man*

4　Come, Holy Ghost, our souls inspire,
　And lighten with celestial fire.
　Thou the anointing Spirit art,
　Who dost thy seven-fold gifts impart.

　　Book of Common Prayer The Ordering of Priests 'Veni, Creator Spiritus'

5　O God, forasmuch as without Thee we are not able to please Thee; mercifully grant, that thy Holy Spirit may in all things direct and rule our hearts.

　　Book of Common Prayer Collect for Nineteenth Sunday after Trinity

6　All the actions, all the movements of the saints, make up the gospel of the Holy Spirit. Their holy souls are the paper, their sufferings and their actions are the ink.

7　The Holy Spirit . . . writes his own gospel and he writes it in the hearts of the faithful.

　　Jean-Pierre de Caussade SJ *Self-Abandonment to Divine Providence*

8　Creator Spirit, by whose aid
　The world's foundations first were laid,
　Come visit every pious mind;
　Come pour thy joys on human kind;
　From sin and sorrow set us free,
　And make thy temples worthy thee.

　　John Dryden *Works*

1 It is good if man can bring about that God sings within him. *Theol*
     Rabbi Elimelekh of Lizhensk Hasidic spirituality

2 The gift of the Holy Spirit closes the gap between the life of *Theol*
    God and ours. When we allow the love of God to move in us
    we can no longer distinguish ours and his; he becomes us, he
    lives us. It is the first fruits of the Spirit, the beginning of our
    being made divine.
     Austin Farrer

3 I sincerely believe that any man preaching a simple Gospel
    message in the power of the Spirit can expect results if he is
    speaking to unconverted people.
     Billy Graham *Christian Life*

4 God is a Spirit: and they that worship him must worship him in
    spirit and in truth.
     Holy Bible St John Chap. 4 v. 24

5 But the fruit of the Spirit is love, joy, peace, long-suffering,
    gentleness, goodness, faith, meekness, temperance.
     Holy Bible Galatians Chap. 5 vv. 22–23

6 The inward stirring and touching of God makes us hungry and
    yearning; for the Spirit of God hurts our spirit; and the more
    he touches it, the greater our hunger and craving.
     Jan van Ruysbroeck *The Mirror of Eternal Salvation*

7 Only Jesus Christ by His Holy Spirit can open blind eyes, give
    life to the dead and rescue slaves from Satanic bondage.
     John Stott Quoted Christopher Calderwood *Five Evangelical*
     Leaders

8 No generation can claim to have plumbed to the depths the
    unfathomable riches of Christ. The Holy Spirit has promised
    to lead us step by step into the fullness of truth.
     Cardinal Suenens

HOME

9 The strength of a nation is derived from the integrity of its
    home.
     Confucius

10 The foxes have holes, and the birds of the air have nests; but
    the Son of man hath not where to lay his head.
     Holy Bible St Matthew Chap. 8 v. 20

HONESTY

1 Every man takes care that his neighbour shall not cheat him.
But a day comes when he begins to care that he does not cheat
his neighbour. Then all goes well.
   Ralph Waldo Emerson *The Conduct of Life*

2 A good name is rather to be chosen than great riches.
   Holy Bible Proverbs Chap. 22 v. 1

3 One little boy more honest than most said, 'Everybody loves
baby Jesus, but I don't. I love the three wise men because they
brought presents.'
   Laughter Lines Compiled by James A. Simpson

4 An honest man is the noblest work of God.
   Alexander Pope *An Essay on Man*

5 God looks at the clean hands, not the full ones.
   Publilius Syrus *Moral Sayings*

HOPE

6 Entertaining hope,
Means recognising fear.
   Robert Browning 'The Two Poets of Croisic'

7 Optimism means faith in men, in the human potential; hope
means faith in God and in His omnipotence.
   Carlo Carretto *The Desert in the City*

8 Hope means expectancy when things are otherwise hopeless.
   G.K. Chesterton *Heretics*

9 If you do not hope, you will not find what is beyond your
hopes.
   St Clement of Alexandria *Stromateis*

10 Hope deferred maketh the heart sick.
   Holy Bible Proverbs Chap. 13 v. 12

11 Forgetting those things which are behind, and reaching forth
unto those things which are before, I press toward the mark.
   Holy Bible Philippians Chap. 3 vv. 13—14

12 We must accept finite disappointment, but we must never lose
infinite hope.
   Martin Luther King *The Words of Martin Luther King*

1 The setting of a great hope is like the setting of the sun.
The brightness of our life is gone.
  Henry Wadsworth Longfellow *Hyperion*

2 I am full of hope, but the end lies in God.
  Pindar *Odes*

3 Hope springs eternal in the human breast:
Man never is, but always to be, blest.
The soul, uneasy and confin'd from home,
Rests and expatiates in a life to come.
  Alexander Pope *An Essay on Man*

4 I am a man of hope, not for human reasons, nor from any
natural optimism, but because I believe the Holy Spirit is at
work in the Church and in the world even when His name
remains unheard.
  Cardinal Suenens

5 Where there is life there is hope.
  Terence *The Self-Tormentor*

6 The virtue of hope is an orientation of the soul towards a
transformation after which it will be wholly and exclusively
love.
  Simone Weil *Letter to a Priest*

HOUSE

7 God planteth in mortal man the cause of sin whensoever he
wills utterly to destroy a house.
  Aeschylus *Niobe*

8 And the rain descended, and the floods came, and the winds
blew, and beat upon that house; and it fell not: for it was
founded upon a rock.
  Holy Bible St Matthew Chap. 7 v. 25

HUMANISM

9 I have, in common with yourself, a desire to leave the world a
little more human than if I had not lived; for a true humanity
is, I believe, our nearest approach to Divinity.
  Oliver Wendell Holmes *Life and Letters*

10 If you can't believe in God, Humanism is the next best thing.
  Lord Longford *Diary of the Year*

HUMILIATION

1 Humiliation is a violent condition of the whole corporal being,
which longs to surge up under the outrage but is forced by
impotence or fear, to hold itself in check.
Simone Weil 'The Love of God and Affliction'

HUMILITY

2 True humility is contentment.
H.F. Amiel *Journal*

3 If you should ask me concerning the precepts of the Christian
religion, I should answer you, Nothing but humility.
St Augustine of Hippo Quoted *Butler's Lives of the Saints*

4 Too humble is half proud.
Hanan J. Ayalti *Yiddish Proverbs*

5 Lowliness is the base of every virtue.
P.J. Bailey *Festus*

6 Humility is a voluntary abdication of power, wherever one's
own advantage and one's own self-assertion is involved.
Ladislaus Boros

7 He hath put down the mighty from their seat: and hath exalted
the humble and meek.
Book of Common Prayer Order of Evening Prayer
The Magnificat

8 See what you lack and not what you have, for that is the
quickest path to humility.
The Cloud of Unknowing

9 I am well aware that I am the 'umblest person going . . .
'umble we are, 'umble we have been, 'umble we ever shall be.
Charles Dickens *David Copperfield*

10 I am no link of Thy great chain,
But all my company is a weed.
Lord, place me in Thy consort; give one strain
To my poor reed.
George Herbert *The Temple* 'Employment'

11 For whosoever exalteth himself shall be abased; and he that
humbleth himself shall be exalted.
Holy Bible St Luke Chap. 14 v. 11

1   Humble yourselves therefore under the mighty hand of God,
    that he may exalt you in due time.
    Holy Bible 1 Peter Chap. 5 vv. 6–7

2   Make me pure, Lord: Thou art holy:
    Make me meek, Lord: Thou wert lowly.
    Gerard Manley Hopkins 'Moonless Darkness'

3   I would be subdued before my friends, and thank them for
    subduing me; but among multitudes of men I have no feel of
    stooping; I hate the idea of humility to them.
    John Keats *Letters*

4   God hath sworn to lift on high
    Who sinks himself by true humility.
    John Keble 'At Hooker's Tomb'

5   Humble thyself in all things.
    Thomas à Kempis *The Imitation of Christ*

6   Plenty of people wish to become devout, but no one wishes to
    be humble.
    François, Duc de la Rochefoucauld *Maxims*

7   I shall recommend humility to you as highly proper to be made
    the constant subject of your devotions, earnestly desiring you
    to think no day safe, or likely to end well, in which you have
    not called upon God to carry you through the day, in the
    exercise of a meek and lowly spirit.
    William Law *A Serious Call to a Devout and Holy Life*

8   A man who has humility will have acquired in the last reaches
    of his beliefs the saving doubt of his own certainty.
    Walter Lippmann *The Public Philosophy*

9   Spread abroad the name of Jesus in humility and with a meek
    heart; show him your feebleness, and he will become your
    strength.
    Thomas Merton *The Sayings of the Desert Fathers*

10 One of the Elders was asked, what was humility and he said –
    if you forgive a brother who has injured you before he himself
    asks pardon.
    Thomas Merton *The Wisdom of the Desert*

11 To the truly humble man the ordinary ways and customs and
    habits of men are not a matter of conflict.
    Thomas Merton *Seeds of Contemplation*

1   O God, make me live lowly and die lowly and rise from the dead among the lowly.
>   Muslim prayer *Said to be a prayer of Mohammed*

2   Who builds a church to God and not to fame
Will never mark the marble with his name.
>   Alexander Pope *Moral Essays*

3   The first test of a really great man is his humility.
>   John Ruskin *Modern Painters*

4   The sons of Adam are formed from dust; if not humble as the dust, they fall short of being men.
>   Sa'di *Gulistan*

5   Religion in its humility restores man to his only dignity, the courage to live by grace.
>   George Santayana *Dialogue in Limbo*

6   In peace there's nothing so becomes a man
As modest stillness and humility.
>   William Shakespeare *Henry V* Act III Sc. 1

7   The Church must learn humility, as well as teach it.
>   George Bernard Shaw *St Joan* Preface

8   Humility is to make a right estimate of one's self.
>   Charles Haddon Spurgeon *Gleanings Among the Sheaves*

9   We come nearest to the great when we are great in humility.
>   Rabindranath Tagore *Stray Birds*

10   Man was created on the sixth day so that he could not be boastful since he came after the flea in the order of creation.
>   *The Talmud*

11   I will try to find a lift by which I may be raised to God, for I am too small to climb the steep stairway to perfection.
>   St Thérèse of Lisieux Quoted *By Love Alone* Ed. Michael Hollings

12   I detest the humility I should have, and am angry when I am humble. I appreciate the social arrogance I have in the face of my humility.
>   Dylan Thomas Quoted Andrew Sinclair *Dylan Thomas, Poet of the People*

13   Humility, like darkness, reveals the heavenly lights.
>   Henry David Thoreau *Walden*

1 Perfection never exists apart from imperfection, just as good
health cannot exist without our feeling effort, fatigue, hunger
or thirst, heat or cold; yet none of those prevent the
enjoyment of good health.
    Abbé de Tourville *Letters of Direction*

2 Let the remembrance of all the glory wherein I was created
make me more serious and humble, more deep and penitent,
more pure and holy before Thee.
    Thomas Traherne

3 A small boy at my son's school was had up before the Head
for being a cocky little beast and urged to adopt humility. So
he did, for a bit; then he lapsed into his old self. 'So how
about the humility then?' demanded the Head. 'I *was* humble
for a fortnight,' he said. 'But nobody noticed.'
    Katherine Whitehorn *View from a Column*

HYMN

4 Were I a nightingale I would sing like a nightingale; were I a
swan, like a swan. But, as it is, I am a rational being, therefore
I must sing hymns of praise to God.
    Epictetus *Discourses*

HYPOCRISY

5 We are always making God our accomplice, that we may
legalize our own iniquities. Every successful massacre is
consecrated by a Te Deum, and the clergy have never been
wanting in benedictions for any victorious enormity.
    H.F. Amiel *Journal*

6 Hypocrisy will serve as well
To propagate a church as zeal,
As persecution and promotion
Do equally advance devotion: So
Round white stones will serve, they say,
As well as eggs to make hens lay.
    Samuel Butler *The Penguin Book of Comic and Curious Verse*

7 It is easier to pretend to be what you are not than to hide what
you really are, but he that can accomplish both has little to
learn from hypocrisy.
    Charles Caleb Colton *Lacon*

1 The only vice that cannot be forgiven is hypocrisy. The repentance of a hypocrite is itself hypocrisy.
   William Hazlitt *Characteristics*

2 A man may cry 'Church! Church!' at every word,
   With no more piety than other people —
   A crow's not reckoned a religious bird
   Because it keeps a-cawing from a steeple.
   Thomas Hood 'Ode to Rae Wilson, Esq.'

3 It is no fault of Christianity that a hypocrite falls into sin.
   St Jerome *Letters* No. 125

4 For neither man nor angel can discern
   Hypocrisy, the only evil that walks
   Invisible, except to God alone.
   John Milton *Paradise Lost*

5 There are people who laugh to show their fine teeth; and there are those who cry to show their good hearts.
   Joseph Roux *Meditations of a Parish Priest*

J

I AM

1 And God said unto Moses, I AM THAT I AM: and he said,
Thus shalt thou say unto the Children of Israel, I AM hath
sent me unto you.
Holy Bible Exodus Chap. 3 v. 14

IDEALS

2 An ideal is often but a flaming vision of reality.
Joseph Conrad *Chance*

3 Even a rich man is sad if he has no ideals. He may try to hide
his sadness from himself and others, but his efforts only make
him sadder still.
Yevgeny Yevtushenko *A Precious Autobiography*

IDEAS

4 The purpose of words is to convey ideas. When the ideas
are grasped, the words are forgotten. Where can I find a
man who has forgotten words? He is the one I would like to
talk to.
Chuang Tzu *The Way of Chuang Tzu* Taoist spirituality

5 To die for an idea: it is unquestionably noble. But how much
nobler it would be if men died for ideas that were true!
H.L. Mencken *Prejudices*

IDLENESS

6 The hardest work is to go idle.
Hanan J. Ayalti *Yiddish Proverbs*

7 To do nothing is very good, but to have nothing to do is very
bad.
Gonville ffrench-Beytagh *A Glimpse of Glory*

1 Consider the lilies of the field, how they grow; they toil not, neither do they spin. And yet I say unto you, that even Solomon in all his glory was not arrayed like one of these.
    Holy Bible St Matthew Chap. 6 vv. 28–29

2 Why stand you here all the day idle.
    Holy Bible St Matthew Chap. 20 v. 6

3 If any would not work, neither should he eat.
    Holy Bible 2 Thessalonians Chap. 3 v. 10

4 Find some work for your hands to do, so that Satan may never find you idle.
    St Jerome *Letters*

5 The devil tempts all other men, but idle men tempt the devil.
    Turkish proverb

IDOLATRY

6 'Tis mad idolatry
To make the service greater than the god.
    William Shakespeare *Troilus and Cressida* Act II Sc. 2

7 He who slays a king and he who dies for him are alike idolaters.

8 The savage bows down to idols of wood and stone; the civilised man to idols of flesh and blood.
    George Bernard Shaw *Man and Superman*

9 Your idol is shattered in the dust to prove that God's dust is greater than your idol.
    Rabindranath Tagore *Stray Birds*

IGNORANCE

10 Let the wise beware, lest they bewilder the minds of the ignorant.

11 Wisdom is prevented by ignorance, and delusion is the result.
    Bhagavad Gita

12 Ignorance is not innocence but sin.
    Robert Browning *The Inn Album*

13 If the blind lead the blind, both shall fall into the ditch.
    Holy Bible St Matthew Chap. 15 v. 14

1 It is worse still to be ignorant of your ignorance.
   St Jerome *Letters* No. 53

2 I count religion but a childish toy,
   And hold there is no sin but ignorance.
   Christopher Marlowe *The Jew of Malta* Prologue

3 Nothing is so good for an ignorant man as silence, and if he
   knew this he would no longer be ignorant.
   Sa'di *Gulistan*

4 Better to be ignorant of a matter than half know it.
   Publilius Syrus *Moral Sayings*

ILLNESS

5 Before all things and above all things, care must be taken of
   the sick, so that they may be served in very deed as Christ
   himself ... But let the sick on their part consider that they are
   being served for the honour of God, and not provoke their
   brethren who are serving them by their unreasonable
   demands.
   St Benedict *The Rule of St Benedict*

ILLUMINATION

6 Just as a reservoir is of little use when the whole countryside is
   flooded, scriptures are of little use to the illumined man or
   woman who sees the Lord everywhere.
   Bhagavad Gita

IMAGERY

7 The imagery of the heavens as being two thousand million
   light-years in diameter is awesome when compared to the tiny
   earth, but trivial when compared to the imagery of the 'hand
   that measured the heavens'.
   Fulton J. Sheen *Old Errors and New Labels*

IMAGINATION

8 For God hath made you able to create worlds in your own
   mind which are more precious to Him than those which He
   created.
   Thomas Traherne *Centuries of Meditations*

1 There is no power on earth like imagination, and the worst,
the most obstinate grievances, are imagined ones.
  Laurens van der Post *Venture to the Interior*

IMMACULATE CONCEPTION

2 This doctrine was revealed by God and therefore is to be
firmly and steadfastly believed by all the faithful.
  Pius IX Bull *Ineffabilis Deus* 1854

3 The virginal conception was understood from the very
beginning as a statement about God and about Jesus, and only
secondarily about Mary.
  Bishop Graham Leonard *Firmly I Believe and Truly*

IMMORTALITY

4 We are not made to rest in this world. It is not our true native
land.
  Fr Andrew SDC *In the Silence*

5 Immortality is the bravest gesture of our humanity towards the
unknown. It is always a faith, never a demonstration.
  Caius Glenn Atkins *Greatest Thoughts on Immortality*

6 Death is another life. We bow our heads
At going out, we think, and enter straight
Another golden chamber of the King's,
Larger than this we leave, and lovelier.
  P.J. Bailey *Festus*

7 To die
Is to begin to live. It is to end
An old, stale, weary work and to commence
A newer and a better. 'Tis to leave
Deceitful knaves for the society
Of gods and goddesses.
  Francis Beaumont and John Fletcher *Four Plays in One*

8 One cannot live for ever by ignoring the price of coffins.
  Ernest Bramah *Kai Lung Unrolls His Mat*

9 The belief in immortality rests not very much on the hope of
going on. Few of us want to do that, but we would like very
much to begin again.
  Heywood Broun *Pieces of Hate*

1 Death, with the might of his sunbeam,
Touches the flesh and the soul awakes.
   Robert Browning 'The Flight of the Duchess'

2 When the day that he [Valiant-for-Truth] must go hence was
come, many accompanied him to the riverside, into which as he
went he said, 'Death, where is thy sting?' And as he went down
deeper, he said, 'Grave, where is thy victory?' So he passed
over, and all the trumpets sounded for him on the other side.
   John Bunyan *The Pilgrim's Progress*

3 The last day does not bring extinction, but a change of place.
   Cicero *Tusculanae Disputationes*

4 Death be not proud, though some have called thee
Mighty and dreadful, for thou art not so,
For those whom thou thinkest thou dost overthrow
Die not, poor death, nor yet canst thou kill me.
   John Donne *Holy Sonnets* 'Annunciation'

5 There is adventure in eternal life. There is none in eternal
death. I am all for adventure.
   J.W. Dunne *The Serial Universe.*

6 Millions long for immortality who do not know what to do
with themselves on a rainy Sunday afternoon.
   Susan Ertz *Anger in the Sky*

7 Our Creator would never have made such lovely days and
have given us the deep hearts to enjoy them, unless we were
meant to be immortal.
   Nathaniel Hawthorne *Mosses from an Old Manse*

8 Man is the only animal that contemplates death, and also the
only animal that shows any sign of doubt of its finality.
   William Ernest Hocking *The Meaning of Immortality in Human
   Experience*

9 But whosoever drinketh of the water that I shall give him shall
never thirst; but the water that I shall give him shall be in him
a well of water springing up into everlasting life.
   Holy Bible St John Chap. 4 v. 14

10 He that heareth my word, and believeth on him that sent me,
hath everlasting life, and shall not come into condemnation;
but is passed from death unto life.
   Holy Bible St John Chap. 5 v. 24

1 In a moment, in the twinkling of an eye, at the last trump: for the trumpet shall sound, and the dead shall be raised incorruptible, and we shall be changed. For this corruptible must put on incorruption, and this mortal must put on immortality.
    Holy Bible 1 Corinthians Chap. 15 vv. 52—53

2 So when this corruptible shall have put on incorruption, and this mortal shall have put on immortality, then shall be brought to pass the saying that is written, Death is swallowed up in victory.
    Holy Bible 1 Corinthians Chap. 15 v. 54

3 The idea of immortality will continue to ebb and flow beneath the mists and clouds of doubt and darkness as long as love kisses the lips of death. It is the rainbow — hope, shining upon the tears of grief.
    Robert G. Ingersoll *Ghosts*

4 Once in my imagination I was taken down to the bed of the sea, and saw there green hills and dales that seemed to be clothed with moss, seaweed and stones. And I understood that if a person firmly believes that God is always with man, then even if he is thrown into the depths of the sea, he will be preserved in body and soul, and will enjoy greater solace and comfort than all this world can offer.
    Julian of Norwich *Revelations of Divine Love*

5 The dead don't die. They look on and help.
    D.H. Lawrence *Selected Essays of D.H. Lawrence*

6 There is no Death! What seems so is transition;
    This life of mortal breath
    Is but a suburb of the life elysian,
    Whose portal we call Death.
    Henry Wadsworth Longfellow 'Resignation'

7 We call this life, that is life's preparation;
    We call this life, a little time of tears;
    But think you God for this designed creation,
    A few short years?
    Douglas Malloch 'We Call This Life'

8 God needs immortality to vindicate his ways to man.
    W. Somerset Maugham *The Summing Up*

1 Either the soul is immortal and we shall not die, or it perishes with the flesh and we shall not know that we are dead. Live, then, as if you were immortal.
   André Maurois Quoted W. Durant *On the Meaning of Life*

2 Who can imagine by a stretch of fancy the feelings of those who, having died in faith, wake up to enjoyment!
   John Henry, Cardinal Newman *Sermons*

3 This day, which thou fearest as thy last, is the birthday of eternity.
   Seneca *Letters to Lucilius*

4 The immortal Gods alone have neither age nor death. All other things almighty Time disquiets.
   Sophocles *Oedipus at Colonus*

5 We feel and know that we are immortal.
   Spinoza *Ethics*

6 If there is a Universal and Supreme Conscience I am an idea in it. After I have died God will go on remembering me, and to be remembered by God, to have my consciousness sustained by the Supreme Conscience, is not that, perhaps, to be immortal.
   Miguel de Unamuno *The Tragic Sense of Life*

7 From the unreal lead me to the real
   From darkness lead me to light
   From death lead me to immortality.
   The Upanishads

8 The cry of a human for a life beyond the grave comes from that which is noblest in the soul of man.
   Henry Van Dyke *Greatest Thoughts on Immortality*

IMPERFECTION

9 No one should abandon duties because he sees defects in them. Every action, every activity, is surrounded by defects as a fire is surrounded by smoke.
   Bhagavad Gita

10 All things are literally better, lovelier, and more beloved for the imperfections which have been divinely appointed, that the law of human life may be Effort, and the law of human judgement — Mercy.
   John Ruskin *The Stones of Venice*

INCARNATION

1 I think that the purpose and cause of the Incarnation was that God might illuminate the world by his wisdom and excite it to the love of Himself.
    Peter Abelard

2 By His divine nature, Christ is simple,
  By His human nature, He is complex.
    St Thomas Aquinas

3 He built himself a temple, a body that is, in the Virgin, and so made himself an instrument in which to dwell.
    St Athanasius *The Discourse of St Athanasius* 'On the Incarnation of the Word'

4 As Man alone, Jesus could not have saved us; as God alone he would not. Incarnate, he could and did.
    Malcolm Muggeridge *Jesus*

INDIGNATION

5 Righteous indignation is your own wrath, as opposed to the shocking bad temper of others.
    Elbert Hubbard *The Philistine*

6 Indignation is the seducer of thought. No man can think clearly when his fists are clenched.
    George Jean Nathan *The World in Falseface*

INDOLENCE

7 I look upon indolence as a sort of suicide; for the man is effectively destroyed, though the appetites of the brute may survive.
    Lord Chesterfield *Letters*

INEVITABILITY

8 For certain is death for the born
  And certain is birth for the dead;
  Therefore over the inevitable
  Thou shalt not grieve.
    Bhagavad Gita

9 What might have been and what has been
  Point to one end, which is always present.
    T.S. Eliot 'Burnt Norton'

INFALLIBILITY

1 I'm sorry we're late, we misread the timetables. But there — nobody's infallible.

> Geoffrey Fisher to Pope John XXIII, December 1960, at the first meeting for 500 years between a Pope and an Archbishop of Canterbury

2 When a pope's theoretically infallible, doctrinal opinions are treated as infallible; authoritarian abuse of power begins.

> Hans Küng *Infallible?*

3 The basic infallibility of the Church consists in the persistence of the Church in the truth of Jesus Christ, despite all errors of individuals, or professors of theology, of lay people; but also of priests, bishops and, indeed, even the Pope.

> Hans Küng Address — St Patrick's Cathedral Dublin 1977

4 Human beings are perhaps never more frightening than when they are convinced beyond doubt that they are right.

> Laurens van der Post *The Lost World of the Kalahari*

INFANT

5 An empty book is like an infant's soul in which anything may be written. It is capable of all things, but containeth nothing.

> Thomas Traherne *Centuries of Meditations*

INFINITE

6 He who sees the Infinite in all things, sees God.

> William Blake *Poetry and Prose*

INGRATITUDE

7 Neither cast ye your pearls before swine, lest they trample them under their feet, and turn again and rend you.

> *Holy Bible* St Matthew Chap. 7 v. 6

8 How sharper than a serpent's tooth it is
To have a thankless child!

> William Shakespeare *King Lear* Act I Sc. 4

INHERITANCE

9 We are the children of God: And if children, then heirs; heirs of God, and joint heirs with Christ.

> *Holy Bible* Romans Chap. 8 vv. 16–17

INNOCENCE

1 Mother to 6 year old:
  'Jane, what are you doing?'
  'I'm drawing God.'
  'But, darling, nobody knows what God looks like.'
  'No, mummy, they don't YET, but they will when they've
  seen my drawing.'
      Robert Llewelyn *Love Bade Me Welcome*

2 Innocence comes in contact with evil and doesn't know it; it
  baffles temptation; it is protected where no one else is.
      Basil W. Maturin Quoted Maisie Ward *Father Maturin*

3 Adam in Paradise had not more sweet and curious
  apprehensions of the world than I when I was a child.
      Thomas Traherne *Centuries of Meditations*

JEALOUSY

1 The ear of jealousy heareth all things.
   Apocrypha The Wisdom of Solomon Chap. 1 v. 5

2 It is not love that is blind, but jealousy.
   Laurence Durrell *Justine*

3 Jealousy is the dragon in paradise; the hell of heaven; and the
   most bitter of the emotions because associated with the
   sweetest.
   A.R. Orage *Essays and Aphorisms*

4 But jealous souls will not be answered so;
   They are not ever jealous for the cause,
   But jealous for they are jealous.
   William Shakespeare *Othello* Act III Sc. 4

5 Moral indignation is jealousy with a halo.
   H.G. Wells *The Wife of Sir Isaac Harman*

JEHOVAH'S WITNESSES

6 The Witnesses are committed to the curious belief that before
   his incarnation Jesus was the Archangel Michael.
   Gilbert Kirby *Jehovah's Witnesses*

7 Jehovah's Witnesses, awaiting the Last Day with the quiet
   kind of satisfaction that a man gets in a dry season when he
   knows his neighbour's house is not insured for fire.
   Bernard Levin *The Pendulum Years*

8 If there is one thing that Jehovah's Witnesses are never tired
   of saying, it is that Religion is against God and that Religion is
   a racket. So they are not Religionists.

9 Jehovah's Witnesses suppose that when a man dies, his soul
   dies as well as his body.
   Kenneth N. Ross *Jehovah's Witnesses*

JEW

1 To be a Jew is a destiny.
   Vicki Baum *And Life Goes On*

2 Like many Jews I am inclined to believe too much and too
   often, which, I suppose, is why we Jews are still here.
   Rabbi Lionel Blue *A Backdoor to Heaven*

3 Have mercy upon all Jews, Turks, Infidels, and Hereticks.
   Book of Common Prayer Good Friday Third Collect

4 To the Christian the Jew is the incomprehensibly obdurate
   man, who declines to see what has happened, and to the Jew
   the Christian is the incomprehensibly daring man, who affirms
   in an unredeemed world that its redemption has been
   accomplished.
   Martin Buber *Paths in Utopia*

5 Who can deny that Jesus of Nazareth, the incarnate Son of the
   most High God, is the eternal glory of the Jewish race.
   Benjamin Disraeli

6 The pursuit of knowledge for its own sake, an almost fanatical
   love of justice and the desire for personal independence —
   these are the features of the Jewish tradition which make me
   thank my stars I belong to it.
   Albert Einstein *The World As I See It*

7 The race of the Hebrews is not new but is honoured among all
   men for its antiquity and is itself well known to all.
   Eusebius of Caesarea

8 What one Christian does is his own responsibility. What one
   Jew does is thrown back at all Jews.
   Anne Frank *Diary of a Young Girl*

9 When people talk about a wealthy man of my creed they call
   him an Israelite; but if he is poor, they call him a Jew.
   Heinrich Heine Quoted A. Marks *I've Taken a Page in the Bible*

10 The Jew's home has rarely been his 'castle'; throughout the
   ages it has been something far higher — his sanctuary.
   Joseph H. Hertz

11 If Christians were christian there would be no anti-Semitism.
   Jesus was a Jew. There is nothing the ordinary Christian so
   dislikes to remember as this awkward historical fact.
   John Haynes Holmes *The Sensible Man's View of Religion*

1 I don't think our main objective ought to be to fight off anti-Semitism and to prevent our destruction in another holocaust. I don't think such uncreative purposes can justify Jewish survival. We still have a role of moral pioneering to fulfil. I think this is the ultimate *raison d'être*. We have something durable and unique to contribute.

   Immanuel Jakobovits, Chief Rabbi *The Times* 12 March 1987

2 No intellectual society can flourish where a Jew feels even slightly uneasy.

   Paul Johnson *Sunday Times Magazine* 6 February 1977

3 If you ever forget you're a Jew, a gentile will remind you.

   Bernard Malamud

4 Pessimism is a luxury that a Jew can never allow himself.

   Golda Meir Quoted *Observer* 24 December 1974

5 If a Jew is fascinated by Christians, it is not because of their virtues, which he values little, but because they represent anonymity, humanity without race.

   Jean-Paul Sartre *Anti-Semite and Jew*

6 I am a Jew. Hath not a Jew eyes? Hath not a Jew hands, organs, dimensions, senses, affections, passions, fed with the same food, hurt with the same weapons, subject to the same diseases, healed by the same means? ... If you prick us, do we not bleed? If you tickle us do we not laugh? If you poison us, do we not die? And if you wrong us, shall we not revenge?

   William Shakespeare *The Merchant of Venice* Act III Sc. 1

7 I am a Jew who is an American. I was a Jew before I was an American. I have been an American all my life — 64 years, but I've been a Jew for 4,000 years.

   Stephen Samuel Wise *Time* magazine 'A Jew in America'
   20 June 1938

JOURNEY

8 The longest journey is the journey within.

   Dag Hammarskjöld

JOY

9 Sheer joy is His [God's] and this demands companionship.

   St Thomas Aquinas *Theological Texts*

1   In this world, full often, our joys are only the tender shadows which our sorrows cast.
> Henry Ward Beecher *Proverbs from a Plymouth Pulpit*

2   He who binds to himself a joy
Doth the winged life destroy;
But he who kisses the joy as it flies
Lives in Eternity's sun rise.
> William Blake

3   The joy that comes from not having harmed one's brother far surpasses the joy given by some object that has been obtained at the cost of a mountain of corpses.
> Carlo Carretto *In Search of the Beyond*

4   True joy is the earnest wish we have of heaven, it is a treasure of the soul, and therefore should be laid in a safe place, and nothing in this world is safe to place it in.
> John Donne *Sermons*

5   There is no such thing as the pursuit of happiness, there is only the discovery of joy.
> Joyce Grenfell

6   Joy untouched by thankfulness is always suspect.
> Theodor Haecker *Journal in the Night*

7   All worldly joys go less
To the one joy of doing kindnesses.
> George Herbert Quoted *A Little Book of Life and Death*

8   Joy is the serious business of heaven.
> C.S. Lewis Quoted Billy Graham *The Seed of Happiness*

9   The Kingdom of God is simply God's power enthroned in our hearts. Faith in the Kingdom of God is what makes us light of heart and what Christian joy is all about.
> John Main *Moment of Christ*

10   Christian joy is a gift of God flowing from a good conscience.
> St Philip Neri

11   The more joy we have, the more nearly perfect we are.
> Spinoza *Ethics*

12   The joy which a man finds in his work and which transforms the tears and sweat of it into happiness and delight — that joy is God.
> H.A. Williams *True Wilderness*

1   A sprinkling note of mirth
    Cascades from heaven to earth:
    O weary hearts be gay,
    This is your day today.
       The Wisdom of the Sufis Compiled by Kenneth Cragg

JUDAS

2   So Judas did to Christ; but he, in twelve,
    Found truth in all but one.
       William Shakespeare *King Richard II* Act IV Sc. 1

JUDGEMENT

3   Enter not into judgement with thy servant: for in thy sight
    shall no man living be justified.
       Holy Bible Psalm 143 v. 2

4   Judge not, that ye be not judged.
       Holy Bible St Matthew Chap. 7 v. 1 St Luke Chap. 6 v. 37

5   God does not care
    What good you did
    But why you did it. He does not grade the fruit
    But probes the core and tests the root.
       Angelus Silesius *The Book of Angelus Silesius*

JUDGEMENT DAY

6   Kill not the moth nor butterfly,
    For the Last Judgement draweth nigh.
       William Blake 'Auguries of Innocence'

7   Don't wait for the Last Judgement. It takes place every day.
       Albert Camus *The Fall*

8   I know that my Redeemer liveth, and that he shall stand at the
    latter day upon the earth. And though after my skin worms
    destroy this body, yet in my flesh shall I see God: whom I shall
    see for myself, and mine eyes shall behold, and not another.
       Holy Bible Job Chap. 19 vv. 25–27

9   Only our concept of time makes it possible for us to speak of
    the Day of Judgement by that name; in reality it is a summary
    court in perpetual session.
       Franz Kafka

1 Truly at the day of judgement we shall not be examined on what we have read, but what we have done; not how well we have spoken, but how religiously we have lived.

Thomas à Kempis *The Imitation of Christ*

2 And on that day no soul shall be wronged at all, nor shall you be rewarded for aught but that which ye have done.

The Qur'an

3 Nothing keeps people together like the exalted conviction that they alone are to be spared that eternal anguish of hell fire to which everyone else will be condemned at a rapidly approaching Day of Judgement.

Philip Toynbee *Observer* 25 March 1979

JUSTICE

4 True peace is not merely the absence of tension; it is the presence of justice.

Martin Luther King *The Words of Martin Luther King*

5 Words cannot express the exultation felt by the individual as he finds himself, with hundreds of his fellows, behind prison bars for a cause he knows is just.

Martin Luther King *The Words of Martin Luther King*

6 Before we loose the word
That bids new worlds to birth,
Needs must we loosen first the sword
Of Justice upon earth.

Rudyard Kipling 'Justice'

7 Justice is what we get when the decision is in our favour.

John W. Raper *What This World Needs*

8 Though justice be thy plea, consider this,
That in the course of justice none of us
Should see salvation.

William Shakespeare *The Merchant of Venice* Act IV Sc. 1

9 Men are always invoking justice; and it is justice which should make them tremble.

Madame Swetchine *The Writings of Madame Swetchine*

10 One must always be ready to change sides with justice, that fugitive from the winning camp.

Simone Weil Quoted Peter Viereck *The Unadjusted Man*

JUSTIFICATION BY FAITH

1 The whole doctrine of justification by faith hinges, for me, on my painfully reluctant realisation that my Father is not going to be more pleased with me when I am good than when I am bad. He accepts me and delights in me as I am. It is ridiculous of him, but that is how it is between us.

　　Bishop John V. Taylor *The Go-Between God*

2 The courage to be is the courage to accept oneself as accepted in spite of being unacceptable...this is the genuine meaning of the Paulinian-Lutheran doctrine of justification by faith.

　　Paul Tillich *The Courage to Be*

KINDNESS

1 The heart benevolent and kind
   The most resembles God.
      Robert Burns 'A Winter Night'

2 Kindness has converted more sinners than zeal, eloquence and
   learning.

3 There is a grace of kind listening as well as a grace of kind
   speaking.

4 Nobody is kind to only one person at once, but to many
   persons in one.
      Frederick W. Faber

5 Getting money is not all a man's business: to cultivate
   kindness is a valuable part of the business of life.
      Samuel Johnson Boswell's *Life of Johnson*

6 Kindness which is bestowed on the good is never lost.
      Plato

7 That best portion of a good man's life,
   His little, nameless, unremembered acts
   Of kindness and of love.
      William Wordsworth 'Lines Composed above Tintern Abbey'

KINGDOM

8 A miracle is not the breaking of the laws of the fallen world, it
   is the re-establishment of the laws of the kingdom.
      Archbishop Anthony Bloom *Living Prayer*

9 Thy kingdom come, Thy will be done, in earth as it is in heaven.
      Book of Common Prayer The Lord's Prayer

10 The kingdom of God is within you.
      Holy Bible St Luke Chap. 17 v. 21

KNOWLEDGE

1 Knowledge is the rich storehouse for the glory of the Creator and the relief of man's estate.
    Francis Bacon *The Advancement of Learning*

2 There is no purifier like knowledge in this world. Time makes man find himself in his heart.

3 The raft of knowledge ferries the worst sinner to safety.
    Bhagavad Gita

4 The fruit of the tree of knowledge always drives men from some paradise or other, and even the paradise of fools is not an unpleasant abode while it is habitable.
    Dean W.R. Inge *Outspoken Essays* 'The Idea of Progress'

5 He who knows others is wise: he who knows himself is enlightened.

6 When the people of the earth all know beauty as beauty,
There arises the recognition of ugliness.
When they all know the good as good
There arises the recognition of evil.
    Lao-Tze *The Way of Lao-Tze*

7 Sin, guilt, neurosis — they are one and the same, the fruit of the tree of knowledge.
    Henry Miller *The Wisdom of the Heart*

8 The ink of the scholar is more sacred than the blood of a martyr.
    Mohammed

9 Know then thyself; presume not God to scan:
The proper study of mankind is man.
    Alexander Pope *An Essay on Man*

10 Some don't know *better* as they grow older; they merely know *more*.
    Saki (H.H. Munro)

11 I knew a mathematician who said, 'I do not know as much as God, but I know as much as God did at my age.'
    Milton Shulman 'Stop the Week' BBC Radio 4 March 1979

LABOUR

1 Thou, O God, dost sell us all good things at the price of labour.
    Leonardo da Vinci

LANGUAGE

2 The English language is the richest in the world for monosyllables. There are four words of one syllable each — words of salvation for the country and the whole world. They are Faith, Hope, Love and Work.
    Stanley Baldwin Speech in the House of Commons
    16 February 1923

3 Language can easily be a barrier rather than a bridge, whereas in every language the smile, the gentle touch, the embrace are the same — and in every century, too.
    Philip Pare *God Made the Devil*

LAST WORDS

4 I bless you, Father of my Lord Jesus Christ.
    St Agnes Last words at the stake Quoted *Calendar of Saints*

5 Tell my Priests, when I am gone,
O'er me shed no tears,
For I shall be no deader then
Than they have been for years.
    A Bishop's last directions Quoted *The Penguin Book of Comic and Curious Verse*

LAUGHTER

6 Laughter is a property in man essential to his reason.
    Lewis Carroll

1 We are in the world to laugh. In purgatory or hell we shall no longer be able to do so. And in heaven it would not be proper.
   Jules Renard *Journal*

2 The world loved man when he smiled. The world became afraid of him when he laughed.
   Rabindranath Tagore *Stray Birds*

3 It is a humiliating fact that without laughter most of us cannot take life seriously.
   Hubert van Zeller *Praying While You Work*

LAW

4 Where there is no vision, the people perish; but he that keepeth the law, happy is he.
   Holy Bible Proverbs Chap. 29 v. 18

5 When the Gentiles, which have not the law, do by nature the things contained in the law, these, having not the law, are a law unto themselves.
   Holy Bible Romans Chap. 2 v. 14

LEARNING

6 God often works more by the illiterate seeking the things that are God's than by the learned seeking the things that are their own.
   St Anselm

7 See how the unlearned start up and take heaven by storm whilst we with all our learning grovel upon the earth.
   St Augustine of Hippo *Confessions*

LEISURE

8 All too often modern man becomes the plaything of his circumstances because he no longer has any leisure time; he doesn't know how to provide himself with the leisure he needs to stop to take a good look at himself.
   Michel Quoist *The Christian Response*

LIBERAL

9 The fallacy of the liberal mind is to see good in everything. This has been of great assistance to the devil.
   Malcolm Muggeridge Quoted John Mortimer *In Character*

LIBERATION THEOLOGY

1   The God we know through the Bible is a liberating God, a
God who destroys myths and alienations, a God who
intervenes in history to break down the structures of injustice
and who raises up prophets to point the way to justice and
mercy. He is the God who frees slaves (Exodus), who makes
empires fall and lifts up the oppressed (Magnificat).
    Address in Methodist Evangelical Church in Bolivia 1970

2   Whereas when liberation theology is good, it is very, very
good, when it is bad, unless it is corrected, it might very soon
become horrid.
    Rosemary Harthill *In Perspective*

3   I have never agreed with those who say ... the churches
should not comment on political and social problems. But
politicians have an equal right to comment on the role the
Churches play and there is little point in either side shouting
'foul' when they do not like what is being said.
    Douglas Hurd, Home Secretary Address to the General Synod
    1988

LIBERTY

4   Liberty is the way, and the only way, of perfectibility. Without
liberty heavy industry can be perfected, but not justice or
truth.
    Albert Camus *Resistance, Rebellion and Death*

5   Our reliance is in the love of liberty which God has planted in
us. Our defence is in the spirit which prizes liberty as the
heritage of men, in all lands, everywhere.
    Abraham Lincoln Speech 1858

6   O Liberty! what crimes are committed in thy name!
    Madame Roland Quoted Alphonse de Lamartine *Histoire des
    Girondins*

7   Liberty means responsibility. That is why most men dread it.
    George Bernard Shaw *Maxims for Revolutionists*

LIE

8   Sin has many tools, but a lie is the handle that fits all of
them.
    Oliver Wendell Holmes *The Autocrat of the Breakfast Table*

1 A lie is an abomination unto the Lord and a very present help in trouble.

    Adlai Stevenson *Speech*

2 The cruellest lies are often told in silence.

    Robert Louis Stevenson

3 A statesman is an easy man,
He tells his lies by rote;
A journalist makes up his lies
And takes you by the throat;
So stay at home and drink your beer
And let the neighbours vote.

    W.B. Yeats 'The Old Stone Cross'

LIFE

4 Remember that no man loses other life than that which he lives, nor lives other than that which he loses.

    Marcus Aurelius *Meditations*

5 Man must know that in this theatre of man's life it is reserved only for God and angels to be lookers on.

    Francis Bacon *The Advancement of Learning*

6 Life is rather like a tin of sardines — we are all looking for the key.

    Alan Bennett 'Beyond the Fringe' BBC TV 1960

7 Some great spiritual teachers thought life was rather like a waiting-room. It's certainly not your eternal home, but there is no reason why you shouldn't make yourself as comfortable as you can before you get there.

    Rabbi Lionel Blue *Kitchen Blues*

8 Human beings are designed for paradise. How is it our lives are such hell?

    Edward Bond *Restoration*

9 In the morning it is green, and groweth up: but in the evening it is cut down, dried up, and withered.

    Book of Common Prayer Psalm 90 v. 6

10 The days of our age are threescore years and ten; and though men be so strong that they come to fourscore years: yet is their strength then but labour and sorrow; so soon passeth it away, and we are gone.

    Book of Common Prayer Psalm 90 v. 10

1 Your life unfolds in a continuous succession of experience and
expectations ... Every day has enough trouble of its own.
When you go to sleep, bury all that has happened in the mercy
of God. It will be safe there. Stand back from what has
happened and be grateful for it all.
> Brakkenstein Community of Blessed Sacrament Fathers, Holland
> *Rule for a New Brother*

2 How can we understand life, when it is the will of God, and as
such, far grander in design than we could ever imagine?
> Commissioner Catherine Bramwell-Booth *My Faith* Ed. Mary
> E. Callan

3 God give me work
Till my life shall end
And life
Till my work is done.
> Winifred Holtby Written on her grave

4 As for man, his days are as grass: as a flower of the field, so he
flourisheth.
> *Holy Bible* Psalm 103 v. 15

5 A living dog is better than a dead lion.
> *Holy Bible* Ecclesiastes Chap. 9 v. 4

6 He that findeth his life shall lose it: and he that loseth his life
for my sake shall find it.
> *Holy Bible* St Matthew Chap. 10 v. 39

7 For me to live is Christ, and to die is gain.
> *Holy Bible* Philippians Chap. 1 v. 21

8 The glory of God is a living man; and the life of man consists
in beholding God.
> St Irenaeus *Against Heresies*

9 It matters not how a man dies, but how he lives.
> Samuel Johnson Boswell's *Life of Johnson*

10 Teach me to live, that I may dread
The grave as little as my bed.
> Bishop Thomas Ken 'Glory to Thee, My God, This Night'

11 Life is something to do when you can't get to sleep.
> Fran Lebowitz Quoted John Heilpern *Observer*
> 21 January 1979

1   No conceivable life can be so interesting, so stimulating, as
    that which we live in Christ.
        William Little *Spiritual Experiences of Friends*

2   Whenever your life ends, it is all there. The advantage of
    living is not measured by length, but by use: some men have
    lived long, and lived little: attend to it while you are in it. It
    lies in your will, not in the number of years, for you to have
    lived enough.
        Montaigne *Essays*

3   It is now clear that science is incapable of ordering life. A life
    is ordered by values.
        Jawaharlal Nehru

4   Life is perhaps best regarded as a bad dream between two
    awakenings.
        Eugene O'Neill *Marco Millions*

5   Our life is love, and peace, and tenderness; and bearing one
    with another, and forgiving one another, and not laying
    accusations one against another.
        Isaac Penington *The Art of Living*

6   And what is life? a weary pilgrimage
    Whose glory in one day doth fill the stage
    With childhood, manhood and decrepit age.
        Francis Quarles 'What is Life'

7   There is no cure for birth and death save to enjoy the interval.
        George Santayana *Soliloquies in England*

8   Not a soul takes thought how well he may live — only how
    long; yet a good life might be everybody's, a long one can be
    nobody's.
        Seneca *Letters to Lucilius*

9   Would that life were like the shadow cast on a wall by a tree,
    but it is like the shadow of a bird in flight.
        The Talmud

10 Life can be worth the energy it takes to live it only if it is
    governed by something that is stronger than death.
        J. Neville Ward *Five for Sorrow Ten for Joy*

11 Take care of your life; and the Lord will take care of your
    death.
        George Whitefield

1   Life is an unanswered question, but let's still believe in the
    dignity and importance of the question.
        Tennessee Williams *Camino Real*

LIGHT

2   It is the business of the Church to be the candlestick in which
    that Light ever shines, the holy lamp wherein that flame ever
    burns.
        Fr Andrew SDC *Meditations for Every Day*

3   What does light give me compared with what your [Christ's]
    love gives? The light is useful to me in my present life, but
    your love weaves for me a crown in the future.
        St John Chrysostom

4   If we walk in the light, as He is in the light, we have fellowship
    one with another.
        Holy Bible 1 John Chap. 1 v. 7

5   Into my heart's night
    Along a narrow way
    I groped; and lo! the light,
    An infinite land of day.
        Rumi Trans. Reynold Nicholson

LISTENING

6   Half an hour's listening is essential except when you are very
    busy. Then a full hour is needed.
        St Francis de Sales

7   Give every man thy ear, but few thy voice.
        William Shakespeare *Hamlet* Act I Sc. 3

LITURGY

8   Christianity is a liturgical religion. The Church is first of all a
    worshipping community. Worship comes first, doctrine and
    discipline second.
        George Florovsky *The Elements of Liturgy in the Orthodox
        Catholic Church*

9   Liturgy is an outward and visible sign of the Holy Spirit
    working in the community.
        Carolyn Legg Quoted *Land's Ender* November 1987

LIVING

1 We can make up our minds whether our lives in this world shall wound like thorns and nettles, or be beautiful and fragrant like the lilies of the field.
     Fr Andrew SDC *Meditations for Every Day*

2 If we are not full grown men and Christians, the fault is not in Quakerism, but in ourselves.
     John Greenleaf Whittier *The Art of Living*

LONGING

3 Thou awakest us to delight in Thy praises; for Thou madest us for Thyself and our heart is restless, until it reposes in Thee.
     St Augustine of Hippo Quoted *Oxford Book of Prayer*

4 I thirst for Thee, O God; when shall I meet with Thee? Is there a Friend, a Saint; a God's own who'll take me to the Lord? Without Him I'm comforted not.
     The Granth Sikh spirituality

5 Lord, enfold me in the depths of your heart; and there, hold me, refine, purge, and set me on fire, raise me aloft, until my own self knows utter annihilation.
     Pierre Teilhard de Chardin

LOVE

6 In a kiss, two spirits meet, mingle and become one; and as a result there arises in the mind a wonderful feeling of delight that awakens and binds together the love of them that kiss.
     St Aelred of Rievaulx *Treatise on Spiritual Friendship*

7 The highest love of all finds its fulfilment not in what it keeps, but in what it gives.
     Fr Andrew SDC *Seven Words from the Cross*

8 Space is the Whom our loves are needed by,
   Time is our choice of How to love and Why.
     W.H. Auden *For the Time Being*

9 He who is filled with love is filled with God himself.
     St Augustine of Hippo *On the Trinity*

10 You can love a person deeply and sincerely whom you do not like. You can like a person passionately whom you do not love.
     R.H. Benson *Spiritual Letters of Monsignor R. Hugh Benson*

1 Love is self sufficient; it is pleasing to itself and on its own account. Love is its own payment, its own reward.

> St Bernard of Clairvaux *Sermons of St Bernard* 'Song of Songs'

2 Love seeketh not itself to please,
Nor for itself hath any care,
But for another gives its ease,
And builds a Heaven in Hell's despair.

> William Blake *Songs of Experience* 'The Clod and the Pebble'

3 Love may be a fool's paradise, but it is the only paradise we know on this troubled planet.

> Robert Blatchford *My Eighty Years*

4 God created the world out of pure love, since he can do nothing other than love ... God can't force us to meet him in love, He stands there defenceless, full of goodness and understanding.

> Ladislaus Boros *In Time of Temptation*

5 Courage, stoic endurance, the search for wisdom, intellectual integrity, strength, detachment — these are the virtues normally worshipped by mankind and preached by his many religions. And Love is a contradiction of many of them.

> Antony Budge

6 The voice said: 'Come with me into the desert. There is something much greater than human action — prayer. And it has a power much stronger than the words of men: LOVE.' And I went into the Desert.

> Carlo Carretto *Letters from the Desert*

7 We only deliberately waste time with those we love — it is the purest sign that we love someone if we choose to spend time idly in their presence when we could be doing something more constructive.

> Sheila Cassidy *Prayer for Pilgrims*

8 To love a thing means wanting it to live.

> Confucius *Analects*

9 Love for God is ecstatic, making us go out from ourselves: it does not allow the lover to belong any more to himself, but he belongs only to the Beloved.

> St Dionysius the Areopagite

1   Paul's description of love in 1 Corinthians 13 and 14, 3 is a
    portrait, for which Christ Himself has sat.
        C.H. Dodd Quoted Elizabeth Urch *Friendship*

2   If mountains can be moved by faith, is there less power in love?
        Frederick W. Faber *Sermons*

3   What must come first in all prayers, however varied they may
    be, and what gives them real value is the love with which they
    are made.
        Charles de Foucauld Letter to his cousin

4   Love is the child of freedom, never that of domination.
        Erich Fromm *The Art of Loving*

5   Love gives naught but itself and takes naught but from itself.
    Love possesses not nor would it be possessed,
    For love is sufficient unto love.
        Kahlil Gibran *The Prophet*

6   The spirituality of Love knows how to set aside, when
    necessary, the search for the most theoretical solution, in
    favour of a search for that which is best for the soul
    concerned. It is in love that salvation can be found.
        Lev Gillet *Encounter at the Well*

7   The love of God, with arms extended on a cross, bars the way
    to hell. But if that love is ignored, rejected and finally refused,
    there comes a time when love can only weep while man pushes
    past into the self-chosen alienation which Christ went to the
    cross to avert.
        Michael Green *The Empty Cross of Jesus*

8   Love is that liquor sweet and most divine,
    Which my God feels as blood; but I as wine.
        George Herbert 'The Agonie'

9   The God of love my Shepherd is,
    And he that doth me feed:
    While he is mine, and I am his,
    What can I want or need?
        George Herbert *The Temple* '23rd Psalm'

10 I am distressed for thee, my brother Jonathan: very pleasant
    hast thou been unto me: thy love to me was wonderful,
    passing the love of women.
        Holy Bible 2 Samuel Chap. 1 v. 26

1 Better is a dinner of herbs where love is, than a stalled ox and hatred therewith.
>   *Holy Bible* Proverbs Chap. 15 v. 17

2 Set me as a seal upon thine heart, as a seal upon thine arm: for love is strong as death; jealousy is cruel as the grave.
>   *Holy Bible* The Song of Solomon Chap. 8 v. 6

3 Many waters cannot quench love, neither can floods drown it.
>   *Holy Bible* The Song of Solomon Chap. 8 v. 7

4 Greater love hath no man than this, that a man lay down his life for his friends.
>   *Holy Bible* St John Chap. 15 v. 13

5 Love worketh no ill to his neighbour: therefore love is the fulfilling of the law.
>   *Holy Bible* Romans Chap. 13 v. 10

6 Let brotherly love continue. Be not forgetful to entertain strangers: for thereby some have entertained angels unawares.
>   *Holy Bible* Hebrews Chap. 13 vv. 1–2

7 There is no fear in love; but perfect love casteth out fear.
>   *Holy Bible* 1 John Chap. 4 v. 18

8 Love is not to be purchased and affection has no price.
>   St Jerome *Letters*

9 An instant of pure love is more precious to God and the soul, and more profitable to the Church, than all other good works together, though it may seem as if nothing were done.
>   St John of the Cross

10 Love of God and love of created things are contrary the one to the other; two contraries cannot coexist in one and the same person.
>   St John of the Cross *Ascent I*

11 If there be anywhere on earth a lover of God who is always kept safe from falling, I know nothing of it — for it was not shown me. But this was shown — that in falling and rising again we are always held close in one love.

12 Peace and love are always alive in us, but we are not always alive to peace and love.
>   Julian of Norwich *Revelations of Divine Love*

1 Love is swift, sincere, pious, pleasant, gentle, strong, patient, faithful, prudent, long-suffering, manly and never seeking her own: for wheresoever a man seeketh his own, there he falleth from love.

Thomas à Kempis *The Imitation of Christ*

2 Love is the most durable power in the world. This creative force, so beautifully exemplified in the life of our Christ, is the most potent instrument available in mankind's quest for peace and security.

3 Love is the only force capable of transforming an enemy into a friend.

Martin Luther King *The Words of Martin Luther King*

4 To love and to be loved the wise would give
All that for which alone the unwise live.

Walter Savage Landor

5 It is His long-term policy, I fear, to restore to them a new kind of self-love — a charity and gratitude for all selves including their own; when they have really learned to love their neighbours as themselves, they will be allowed to love themselves as their neighbours.

C.S. Lewis *The Screwtape Letters*

6 Far above love is the Beloved; far beneath it is the lover; and Love, which lies between these two, makes the Beloved to descend to the Lover and the Lover to rise toward the Beloved. And this ascending and descending is the being and the life to Love.

Ramón Lull *The Book of the Lover and the Beloved*

7 The first step in personhood is to allow ourselves to be loved. To know ourselves loved is to have the depths of our own capacity to love opened up.

John Main *The Present Choice*

8 The great tragedy of life is not that men perish but that they cease to love.

W. Somerset Maugham *The Summing Up*

9 If the Church makes outcasts of people with Aids then it has no right to exist for that particular community. Love is the only answer and for the Christian anything less will simply not do.

Fr John Michael OFM *Sunday Times* 13 March 1988

1 If Jesus, the Messiah of the Kingdom, came to the poor, the
wretched and the sick, he made plain by his action that
poverty, hunger and sickness rob a man of all dignity and that
the kingdom of God will fill him bodily with riches.
  Jürgen Moltmann *Towards a Political Hermeneutic of the Gospel*

2 Very often, when people first turn towards God and realise
that God loves them and that everything about them matters
to Him, a wave of joyful emotion overwhelms them. But
actual faith is mostly the realisation that, even though we don't
in the least deserve it, God believes in us and finds us lovable.
This is astonishing.
  Philip Pare *God Made the Devil*

3 To be able to say how much love, is to love but little.
  Petrarch 'To Laura in Death'

4 Only love enables humanity to grow, because love engenders
life and it is the only form of energy that lasts forever.
  Michel Quoist *With Open Heart*

5 When a man sees that his neighbour hates him, then he must
love him more than he did before to fill up the gap.
  Rabbi Rafael Quoted Martin Buber *Mamre*

6 Love begets love and kindness begets kindness. This is the law
which knows no exception. People dislike us because we have
no more love for them.
  Swami Ramdas Indian spirituality

7 Only through Love can we attain communion with God.
  Albert Schweitzer *My Faith* Ed. Mary E. Callan

8 Love is the only weapon we need.
  Rev. H.R.L. Sheppard *The Human Parson*

9 God is love, ind a three times divorced cinema actor is the
perfect lover, and heaven gets mixed up with hell.
  G.A. Studdert-Kennedy *The New Man in Christ*

10 Essentially man is not a slave either of himself or of the world;
but he is a lover. His freedom and fulfilment is in love, which
is another name for perfect comprehension.

11 Wherever there is a bit of colour, a note of song, a grace of
form, then comes the call of our love.
  Rabindranath Tagore *Sadhana*

1 Love of God is the root, love of our neighbour the fruit of the Tree of Life. Neither can exist without the other, but the one is cause and the other effect.
>   Archbishop William Temple *Readings of St John's Gospel*

2 It is not a matter of thinking a great deal but of loving a great deal, so do whatever arouses you most to love.
>   St Teresa of Avila *Mansions of the Interior Castle*

3 I have found the paradox that if I love until it hurts, then there is no hurt, but only more love.
>   Mother Teresa of Calcutta Quoted Daphne Rae *Love Until it Hurts*

4 There is a net of love by which you can catch souls.
>   Mother Teresa of Calcutta Quoted Kathryn Spink *For the Brotherhood of Man Under the Fatherhood of God*

5 By love alone is God enjoyed; by love alone delighted in, by love alone approached and admired. His nature requires love. The law of nature commands thee to love him: the law of his nature, and the law of thine.
>   Thomas Traherne *The First Century*

6 Show love to all creatures and thou wilt be happy; for when thou lovest all things, thou lovest the Lord, for he is all in all.
>   Tulsi Das Hindu spirituality

7 Of all man's inborn dispositions there is none more heroic than the love in him. Everything else accepts defeat and dies, but love will fight no-love every inch of the way.
>   Laurens van der Post *The Lost World of the Kalahari*

8 When we love we hand ourselves over to receive from another our own triumph and our own tragedy.
>   W.H. Vanstone *The Stature of Waiting*

9 To love as Jesus loves; that is not only the Lord's precept, it is our vocation. When all is said and done it is the one thing we have to learn, for it is perfection.
>   René Voillaume *Seeds of the Desert*

10 Were the whole realm of nature mine,
That were an offering far too small;
Love so amazing, so Divine,
Demands my soul, my life, my all.
>   Isaac Watts *Hymns and Spiritual Songs* 'When I Survey the Wondrous Cross'

1   Each time we have some pain to go through, we can say to
ourselves quite truly that it is the universe, the order and the
beauty of the world and the obedience of creation to God that
are entering our body. After that how can we fail to bless with
tenderest gratitude the Love that sends us this gift?

      Simone Weil

2   Love divine, all loves excelling,
Joy of Heaven, to earth come down,
Fix in us Thy humble dwelling,
All Thy faithful mercies crown.
Jesus, Thou art all compassion,
Pure, unbounded love Thou art;
Visit us with Thy salvation,
Enter every trembling heart.

      Charles Wesley Hymn

3   His Love enableth me to call every country my country, and
every man my brother.

      Daniel Wheeler *Spiritual Experiences of Friends* 'Memoirs'

4   My God I love thee not because
I hope for Heaven thereby,
Or because they that love thee not
Must burn eternally.

      St Francis Xavier Quoted *The Wisdom of the English Mystics*

LOW CHURCH

5   Of course Low Churches are very holy but they do so treat
God like their first cousin.

      Nancy Mitford Quoting her grandmother in a letter to Mark
      Ogilvie Grant 30 December 1929

LOYALTY

6   No man can serve two masters: for either he will hate the one
and love the other; or else he will hold to the one and despise
the other. Ye cannot serve God and mammon.

      Holy Bible St Matthew Chap. 6 v. 24

LUCK

7   Shallow men believe in luck. Strong men believe in cause and
effect.

      Ralph Waldo Emerson *The Conduct of Life* 'Worship'

LUST

1 When lust hath conceived, it bringeth forth sin: and sin, when it is finished, bringeth forth death.
   Holy Bible James Chap. 1 v. 15

2. Abstain from fleshly lusts, which war against the soul.
   Holy Bible 1 Peter Chap. 2 v. 11

3 The expense of spirit in a waste of shame
   Is lust in action.
   William Shakespeare *Sonnets*

4 For the crown of our life as it closes
   Is darkness, the fruit thereof dust;
   No thorns go as deep as a rose's,
   And love is more cruel than lust.
   Algernon Swinburne *Dolores*

MAN

1 The significance of man is that he is that part of the universe that asks the question — what is the significance of man?
    Cal Lotus Becker *Progress and Power*

2 Man's inhumanity to man
Makes countless thousands mourn.
    Robert Burns 'Man Was Made to Mourn'

3 Man is an exception, whatever else he is. If it is not true that a divine being fell, then we can only say that one of the animals went entirely off its head.
    G.K. Chesterton *All Things Considered*

4 Man is not only a contributory creature, but a total creature; he does not only make one, but he is all; he is not a piece of the world, but the world itself, and next to the glory of God, the reason why there is a world.
    John Donne *Sermons*

5 Man's greatest problem is man himself.
    Billy Graham Amsterdam Conference 1983

6 If all hearts were open and all desires known — as they would be if people showed their souls — how many gapings, sighings, clenched fists, knotted brows, broad grins and red eyes would we see in the market place?
    Thomas Hardy *Diary*

7 Thou art the man.
    Holy Bible 2 Samuel Chap. 12 v. 7

8 Man as we know him is a poor creature; but he is half way between an ape and a god, and he is travelling in the right direction.
    Dean W.R. Inge *Outspoken Essays*

1 We must not reject man in favour of God, nor reject God in favour of man, for the glory of God is man alive, supremely in Christ.

    Cardinal Suenens

2 If this is God's world, there are no unimportant people.

    Rt Hon. George Thomas, Speaker of the House of Commons, to Richard Baker BBC TV 2 August 1981

MARRIAGE

3 Holy matrimony . . . is an honourable estate, instituted of God in the time of man's innocency, signifying to us the mystical union that is betwixt Christ and His Church.

    Book of Common Prayer Solemnisation of Matrimony

4 Marriage is distinctly and repeatedly excluded from heaven. Is this because it is thought likely to mar the general felicity?

    Samuel Butler *Notebooks*

5 Whoso findeth a wife findeth a good thing.

    Holy Bible Proverbs Chap. 18 v. 22

6 There is no more lovely, friendly or charming relationship, communion or company, than a good marriage.

    Martin Luther *Table Talk*

7 Since marriage is designed by Providence as a life, the worst possible way of embarking upon that life is by the premature exercise of what is meant to be its final consummation.

    Hubert van Zeller *We Work While the Light Lasts*

MARTYRDOM

8 Lucky are soldiers who strive in a just war, for them it is an easy entry into heaven.

    Bhagavad Gita

9 To die for a religion is easier than to live it absolutely.

    Jorge Luis Borges *Labyrinths*

10 A Christian martyrdom is never an accident, for saints are not made by accident. Still less is a Christian martyrdom the effect of a man's will to become a Saint . . . for the true martyr is he who has become the instrument of God, who has lost his will in the will of God.

    T.S. Eliot *Murder in the Cathedral*

1 He that will not live a saint cannot die a martyr.
    Thomas Fuller *Gnomologia*

2 The few of understanding, vision rare,
  Who veiled not from the herd their hearts but tried,
  Poor generous fools, to lay their feelings bare,
  Them have men always burnt and crucified.
    Goethe *Faust*

3 Perhaps there is no happiness in life so perfect as the martyr's.
    O. Henry *The Trimmed Lamp*

4 Our admiration is so given to dead martyrs that we have little
  time for living heroes.
    Elbert Hubbard *The Note Book*

5 To die in agony upon a cross
  Does not create a martyr, he must first
  Will his own execution.
    Henrik Ibsen *Brand*

6 It is not the least of a martyr's scourges to be canonised by the
  persons who burnt him.
    Murray Kempton *Part of Our Time*

7 The tyrant dies and his rule is over, the martyr dies and his
  rule begins.
    Søren Kierkegaard

8 There were no heroes, were there no martyrs.
    Edward George Bulwer-Lytton

9 It is the cause, not the death, that makes the martyr.
    Napoleon *Maxims*

10 Must then a Christ perish in torment in every age to save those
   that have no imagination?
    George Bernard Shaw *St Joan* Epilogue

11 The blood of the martyrs is the seed of the Church.
    Tertullian *Apologeticus*

12 It is truer to say that martyrs make faith than that faith makes
   martyrs.
    Miguel de Unamuno *The Tragic Sense of Life*

13 Love makes the whole difference between an execution and
   martyrdom.
    Evelyn Underhill

MASS

1 The Mass is the greatest blasphemy of God and the highest idolatry upon earth; an abomination the like of which has never been in Christendom since the time of the Apostles.
    Martin Luther *Table Talk*

MATERIALISM

2 From anger, delusion arises, and from delusion bewilderment of memory. When memory is bewildered intelligence is lost, and when intelligence is lost one falls down again into the material pool.
    Bhagavad Gita

3 High thinking is inconsistent with complicated material life based on high speed imposed on us by mammon worship.
    Gandhi *Non-Violence in Peace and War*

MATURITY

4 Four stages of growth in Christian maturity
    Love of self for self's sake
    Love of God for self's sake
    Love of God for God's sake
    Love of self for God's sake.
    St Bernard of Clairvaux

5 When I was a child, I spake as a child, I understood as a child, I thought as a child: but when I became a man, I put away childish things.
    Holy Bible 1 Corinthians Chap. 13 v. 11

MEDITATION

6 One who is able to withdraw his senses from sense objects, as the tortoise draws his limbs within the shell, is to be understood as truly situated in knowledge.
    Bhagavad Gita

7 God enlightens the soul, making it see not only its misery and meanness, but also his grandeur and majesty.
    St John of the Cross Quoted *Lamps of Fire*

8 My son has taken up meditation — at least it's better than sitting doing nothing.
    Max Kauffman

1 Meditation is not the means to an end. It is both the means
and the end.
Krishnamurti *The Penguin Krishnamurti Reader*

2 A man will be effective to the degree that he is able to
concentrate. Concentration is not a mode of doing, but above
all a mode of being.
Michel Quoist *The Christian Response*

3 Meditation and action:
He who knows these two together
Through action leaves death behind
And through meditation gains immortality.
The Upanishads

MEEKNESS

4 He giveth his cheek to him that smiteth him.
Holy Bible Lamentations Chap. 3 v. 30

5 If thou have any good things believe better things of others,
that thou may keep thy meekness.
Thomas à Kempis *Imitation of Christ*

6 Turning the other cheek is a kind of moral ju-jitsu.
Gerald Stanley Lee *Crowds*

MERCY

7 Two works of mercy set a man free: forgive and you will be
forgiven, and give and you will receive.
St Augustine of Hippo *Sermons*

8 Yea, like as a father pitieth his own children: even so is the
Lord merciful unto them that fear him.
Book of Common Prayer Psalm 103 v. 13

9 His mercy endureth for ever.
Book of Common Prayer Psalm 136 v. 1

10 Mercies should not be temptations; yet we too often make
them so.
Oliver Cromwell

11 Animals lack cruelty, but they also lack mercy.
Rosemary Dunnage *Observer* 'The Animal Factor' 25 April 1979

12 We hand folks over to God's mercy, and show none ourselves.
George Eliot *Adam Bede*

1 God tempers the cold to the shorn lamb.
   Henri Estienne *Prémices*

2 The mercy of the Lord is from everlasting to everlasting upon
   them that fear him.
   Holy Bible Psalm 103 v. 17

3 And the publican, standing afar off, would not lift up so much
   as his eyes to heaven, but smote upon his breast, saying, God
   be merciful to me, a sinner.
   Holy Bible St Luke Chap. 18 v. 3

4 The corn that makes the holy bread
   By which the soul of man is fed,
   The holy bread, the food unpriced,
   Thy everlasting mercy, Christ.
   John Masefield 'The Everlasting Mercy'

5 Teach me to feel another's woe,
   To hide the fault I see;
   That mercy I to others show,
   That mercy show to me.
   Alexander Pope 'The Universal Prayer'

6 It is an attribute of God himself,
   And earthly power doth then show likest God's
   When mercy seasons justice.
   William Shakespeare *The Merchant of Venice* Act IV Sc. 1

7 Who will not mercy unto others show,
   How can he mercy ever hope to have?
   Edmund Spenser *The Faerie Queene* Book VI

8 A God all mercy is a God unjust.
   Edward Young *Night Thoughts*

MESSIAH

9 For unto us a child is born, unto us a son is given: and the
   government shall be upon his shoulder: and his name shall be
   called Wonderful, Counsellor, The mighty God, The
   everlasting Father, The Prince of Peace.
   Holy Bible Isaiah Chap. 9 v. 6

10 But whom say ye that I am? And Peter answereth and saith
   unto him, Thou art the Christ.
   Holy Bible St Mark Chap. 8 v. 29

MIDDLE AGE

1   The long, dull, monotonous years of middle-aged prosperity or middle-aged adversity are excellent campaigning weather for the Devil.
>   C.S. Lewis *The Screwtape Letters*

MIND

2   The mind is its own place, and in itself
Can make a heaven of hell, a hell of heaven.
>   John Milton *Paradise Lost*

MIRACLE

3   In Israel in order to be a realist, you must believe in miracles.
>   David Ben-Gurion Quoted A. Marks *I've Taken a Page in the Bible*

4   The most serious doubt that has been thrown on the authenticity of the miracles is the fact that most of the witnesses in regard to them were fishermen.
>   Arthur Brinstead *Pitcher's Proverbs*

5   There is in every miracle a silent chiding of the world, and a tacit reprehension of them who require, or who need miracles.
>   John Donne *Sermons*

6   The Christian religion not only was first attended by miracle, but even at this day cannot be believed by any reasonable person without one.
>   David Hume *On Miracles*

7   Magic is usually a labour-saving device which spares the magician or his client time and trouble, and quite often magic is irrational. Miracle on the other hand tends to mean not less but more work for its beneficiaries.
>   Philip Pare *God Made the Devil*

8   Miracles enable us to judge of doctrine, and doctrine enables us to judge of miracles.
>   Blaise Pascal *Pensées*

9   Everything is miraculous. It is a miracle that one does not melt in one's bath.
>   Pablo Picasso

1 Seen in a butcher's shop in Ireland: 'This bacon was cured in Lourdes'!

    Quoted Plympton St Maurice parish paper 2 August 1987

2 Miracles are propitious accidents, the natural causes of which are too complicated to be readily understood.

    George Santayana *The Ethics of Spinoza*

3 A miracle is an event which creates faith. Frauds deceive. An event which creates faith does not deceive; therefore it is not a fraud, but a miracle.

    George Bernard Shaw *St Joan*

4 Religion seems to have grown an infant with age, and requires miracles to nurse it, as it had in its infancy.

    Jonathan Swift *Thoughts on Various Subjects*

5 Why, who makes much of a miracle?
As to me I know nothing else but miracles —
To me every hour of night and day is a miracle,
Every cubic inch of space a miracle.

    Walt Whitman

MISERY

6 Man that is born of a woman hath but a short time to live, and is full of misery.

    Book of Common Prayer The Burial of the Dead

7 Who going through the vale of misery use it for a well: and the pools are filled with water. They will go from strength to strength.

    Book of Common Prayer Psalm 84 vv. 6–7

8 Human misery must somewhere have a stop:
There is no wind that always blows a storm.

    Euripides *Heracles*

MISFORTUNE

9 I never knew any man in my life who could not bear another's misfortune perfectly like a Christian.

    Alexander Pope *Thoughts on Various Subjects*

10 To be brave in misfortune is to be worthy of manhood; to be wise in misfortune is to conquer fate.

    Agnes Repplier *Under Dispute, Strayed Sympathies*

MISSIONARY

1 Be patterns, be examples in all countries, places, islands, nations, wherever you come, that your carriage and life may preach among all sorts of people, and to them; then you will come to walk cheerfully over the world, answering that of God in every one.
George Fox

2 My father was an educational missionary padre in India. He always said he'd been wrong to try to convert Bengalis to Christianity when they had a perfectly satisfactory religion of their own.
E.P. Thompson Quoted John Mortimer *In Character*

MODERATION

3 Moderation is the silken string running through the pearl chain of all virtues.
Joseph Hall *Christian Moderation*

MODESTY

4 He who speaks without modesty will find it difficult to make his words good.
Confucius *Analects*

5 In some remote regions of Islam, it is said a woman caught unveiled by a stranger will raise her skirt to cover her face.
Raymond Mortimer *Colette*

MONASTICISM

6 The secluded God-pursuing life is bigger than Catholicism, bigger even than Christianity; Buddhist monks have more in common with Benedictines and Franciscans than with the oriental villagers who begot them.
Anthony Burgess *Observer* 5 April 1987

7 Monks are the lightning conductors of society.
J.K. Huysmans Quoted Euan Cameron *Independent* 9 April 1987

8 I envy them, those monks of old:
Their books they read, and their beads they told.
G.P.R. James 'The Monks of Old

1 Monasteries are houses of the soul, and their deepest language comes from the depths of silence.
>   Peter Levi *The Frontiers of Paradise*

2 A certain brother went to the Abbot and asked him for a good word. The elder said, 'Go and sit in your cell, your cell will tell you everything.'
>   Thomas Merton *The Wisdom of the Desert*

3 A monk was asked, 'What do you do there in the monastery?' He replied, 'We fall and get up, we fall and get up, fall and get up again.'
>   Esther de Waal *Seeking God: The Way of St Benedict*

MONEY

4 If you would know what the Lord God thinks of money you have only to look at those He gives it to.
>   Maurice Baring Quoted *Writers at Work*

5 The love of money is the root of all evil.
>   *Holy Bible* 1 Timothy Chap. 6 v. 10

6 The most grievous kind of destitution is to want money in the midst of wealth.
>   Seneca

7 But the financiers will ask
> in that day: Is it not better
> to leave broken bank balances
> behind us than broken heads?
> And Christ recognising the
> new warriors will feel breaching
> his healed side their terrible
> pencil and the haemorrhage of its figures.
>   R.S. Thomas 'The Interrogation'

MORALITY

8 No morality can be founded on authority, even if the authority were divine.
>   A.J. Ayer 'Essay on Humanism'

9 Morality's not practical, morality's a gesture. A complicated gesture learned from books.
>   Robert Bolt *A Man for All Seasons*

1 He who wears his morality but as his best garment were better
naked.
   Kahlil Gibran *The Prophet* 'On Religion'

2 What is moral is what you feel good after, and what is immoral
is what you feel bad after.
   Ernest Hemingway *Death in the Afternoon*

3 Half, at least, of all morality is negative and consists in
keeping out of mischief.
   Aldous Huxley *The Doors of Perception*

4 If there is to be peace on earth and good will toward men, we
must finally believe in the ultimate morality of the universe,
and believe that all really hinges on moral foundations.
   Martin Luther King *The Words of Martin Luther King*

5 Morality which is based on ideas or on an ideal, is an
unmitigated evil.
   D.H. Lawrence *Fantasia of the Unconscious*

6 The whole speculation about morality is an effort to find a way
of living which men who live it will instinctively feel is good.
   Walter Lippmann *A Preface to Politics*

7 The difference between a moral man and a man of honour is
that the latter regrets a discreditable act even when it has
worked.
   H.L. Mencken *Prejudices*

8 The essence of morality is the subjugation of nature in
obedience to social needs.
   John Morley *Critical Miscellanies* 'Carlyle'

9 The ultimate foundation for morality is that immorality
doesn't work. It doesn't lighten the burden of living, but
increases it.
   Norman Vincent Peale *Man, Morals and Maturity*

10 Without civic morality communities perish, without personal
morality their survival has no value.
   Bertrand Russell *Authority and the Individual*

11 The people who are regarded as moral luminaries are those
who forego ordinary pleasures themselves and find
compensation in interfering with the pleasures of others.
   Bertrand Russell *Autobiography*

1 Morality consists of suspecting other people of not being
married.
George Bernard Shaw *The Doctor's Dilemma*

2 The so-called new morality is too often the old immorality
condoned.
Lord Shawcross *Observer* 17 November 1963

3 Morals are an acquirement — like music, like a foreign
language, like piety, paralysis — no man is born with them.
Mark Twain *Seventieth Birthday*

4 All sects differ, because they come from men; morality is
everywhere the same because it comes from God.
Voltaire *Philosophical Dictionary*

5 As society is now constituted, a literal adherence to the moral
precepts scattered throughout the Gospels would mean sudden
death.
A.N. Whitehead *Adventures in Ideas*

6 What is morality in any given time or place? It is what the
majority then and there happen to like and immorality is what
they dislike.
A.N. Whitehead *Dialogues*

MORMON

7 A Mormon challenged Mark Twain to cite any passage of
scripture forbidding polygamy. 'Nothing easier,' replied
Twain. 'No man can serve two masters.'
Edmund Fuller *Thesaurus of Anecdotes*

8 When our father Adam came into the Garden of Eden he
came into it with a celestial body and brought Eve, one of his
wives, with him. He is our father and our God and the only
God with whom we have to do.
Brigham Young *Journal of Discourses*

MOTHER

9 And Adam called his wife's name Eve; because she was the
mother of all living.
Holy Bible Genesis Chap. 3 v. 20

10 God could not be everywhere and therefore he made mothers.
Jewish proverb

1 As we know, our own mother bore us only into pain and dying. But our true mother, Jesus, who is all love, bears us into joy and endless living. Blessed may he be.
   Julian of Norwich *Revelations of Divine Love*

2 Every mother is a working mother.
   Laughter Lines Compiled by James A. Simpson

MOURNING

3 'Mourning is not forgetting,' he said gently. 'It is an undoing. Every minute tie has to be untied and something permanent and valuable recovered and assimilated from the dust.'
   Margery Allingham *Tiger in the Smoke*

4 The capacity for grief is as much from God as the capacity for love — and we have not really lived until we have sounded them both.
   Anon 'For Those Who Mourn' SPCK

5 We who are left how shall we look again
   Happily on the sun or feel the rain
   Without remembering how they who went
   Ungrudgingly and spent
   Their lives for us loved, too, the sun and rain.
   Wilfred Wilson Gibson 'Lament'

6 When we lose one we love our bitterest tears are called forth by the memory of hours when we loved not enough.
   Maurice Maeterlinck *Wisdom and Destiny*

MURDER

7 No actions are bad in themselves, even murder can be justified.
   Dietrich Bonhoeffer *No Rusty Swords*

MUSIC

8 Music, the greatest good that mortals know
   And all of heaven we have below.

9 Music religious hearts inspires;
   It wakes the soul, and lifts it high,
   And wings it with sublime desires,
   And fits it to bespeak the Deity.
   Joseph Addison 'A Song for St Cecilia's Day'

1 Whether the angels play only Bach praising God I am not quite sure. I am sure however that *en famille* they play Mozart.

> Karl Barth Quoted *New York Times* 'Obituary'
> 11 December 1968

2 Of all earthly music that which reaches farthest into heaven is the beating of a truly loving heart.

> Henry Ward Beecher

3 Music strikes in me a deep fit of devotion, and a profound contemplation of the First Composer. There is something in it of Divinity more than the ear discovers.

> Sir Thomas Browne *Religio Medici*

4 Music is edifying, for from time to time it sets the soul in operation.

> John Cage *Forerunner of Modern Music*

5 When music sounds, gone is the earth I know,
And all her lovely things even lovelier grow.

> Walter de la Mare 'Farewell'

6 When the morning stars sang together, and all the sons of God shouted for joy.

> *Holy Bible* Job Chap. 38 v. 7

7 After silence, that which comes nearest to expressing the inexpressible is music.

> Aldous Huxley *Music at Night*

8 Music is given us with our existence. Above other arts it can be possessed without knowledge.

> Yehudi Menuhin *Unfinished Journey*

9 All art constantly aspires towards the condition of music.

> Walter Pater *The Renaissance*

10 Light quirks of music, broken and unev'n,
Make the soul dance upon a jig to Heaven.

> Alexander Pope *Moral Essays*

11 As some to church repair,
Not for the doctrine, but the music there.

> Alexander Pope *Essay on Criticism*

12 I touch by the edge of the far-spreading wing of my song thy feet which I could never aspire to reach.

> Rabindranath Tagore *Gitanjali*

MYSTERY

1 Protestants say there is no mystery, Roman Catholics explain all mysteries, Orthodoxy says all is Mystery.
  Archimandrite Barnabas *Strange Pilgrimage*

2 God keeps His holy mysteries
  Just on the outside of man's dream.
  Elizabeth Barrett Browning 'Human Life's Mystery'

3 Mysteries are not dark shadows, before which we must shut our eyes and be silent. On the contrary, they are dazzling splendours, with which we ought to sate our gaze.
  A Carthusian *They Speak in Silences*

4 The most beautiful experience we can have is the mysterious. It is the fundamental notion that stands at the cradle of true art and true science.
  Albert Einstein *Ideas and Opinions*

5 To pray is to take notice of the wonder, to regain a sense of the mystery that animates all beings, the divine margin in all our attainments.
  Abraham Joshua Heschel *The Sigh*

MYSTICISM

6 What is night for all beings is the time of awakening for the self-controlled; and the time of awakening for all beings is night for the introspective sage.
  Bhagavad Gita

7 God is an unutterable sigh in the Human Heart, said the German mystic. And thereby said the last word.
  Havelock Ellis *Impressions and Comments*

8 I have found a perfect description of mysticism, it is the attempt to get rid of mystery.
  Roger Fry Quoted Virginia Woolf

9 Without mysticism man can achieve nothing great.
  André Gide *The Counterfeiters*

10 In order to arrive at that which thou knowest not,
   Thou must go by a way that thou knowest not.
   In order to arrive at that which thou possesseth not
   Thou must go by a way that thou possesseth not.
   St John of the Cross

1 The incommunicableness of the transport is the keynote of all mysticism. Mystical truth exists for the individual who had the transport, but for no one else.
    William James *The Varieties of Religious Experience*

2 The simplicity of the gospels makes false mysticism impossible. Christ has delivered us forever from the esoteric and the strange. He has brought the light of God to our own level to transfigure our ordinary existence.
    Thomas Merton Quoted Robert Llewelyn *Prayer and Contemplation*

3 The ultimate gift of a conscious life is the sense of the mystery that encompasses it.
    Lewis Mumford *The Conduct of Life*

4 Mystics always hope that one day science will overtake them.
    Booth Tarkington *Looking Forward to the Great Adventure*

5 Mysticism is the name of that organic process which involves the perfect consummation of the love of God.
    Evelyn Underhill *The Love of God*

6 He who is in the Fire, and He who is in the Heart, and He who is in the Sun, are all One and the Same, and he who knows this becomes one with the One.
    The Upanishads

7 That the world *is*, is the mystical.
    Ludwig Wittgenstein

NAME

1 Naught but the name of Jesus can restrain the impulse of anger, repress the swelling of pride, cure the wound of envy, bridle the onslaught of luxury, extinguish the flame of carnal desire — can temper avarice, and put to flight impure and ignoble thoughts.
   St Bernard of Clairvaux 'On the Name of Jesus'

2 Flog your enemies with the Name of Jesus, for there is no weapon more powerful in heaven or on earth.
   St John Climacus *Ladder of Divine Ascent*

3 Do not concern yourself with anxiety for the show of a great name.
   Thomas à Kempis *The Imitation of Christ*

4 The medieval Saints would scarcely have been pleased if they could have foreseen that their names would be associated nowadays chiefly with racehorses and the cheaper clarets.
   Saki (H.H. Munro) 'Reginald at the Carlton'

NATIONALISM

5 War springs from the love and loyalty being offered to God being applied to some God-substitute, one of the most dangerous being nationalism.
   Robert Runcie, Archbishop of Canterbury *Prayers for Peace* 'Visions of Unity'

NATIONS

6 Nations are the wealth of mankind, its collective personalities; the very least of them wears its own special colours and bears within itself a special facet of divine intention.
   Alexander Solzhenitsyn *Solzhenitsyn: A Documentary Record*

NATIVITY

1 The manger is Heaven, yes greater than Heaven. Heaven is
  the handiwork of this child.

2 Trumpets! Lightnings! The earth trembles
  But into the Virgin's womb thou didst descend with noiseless
      tread.
        Agathias 'On the Birth of Christ'

3 The Angels in their orison
  Looked down from their Eternity
  Unto the time they once had sped
  To worship at a lowly shed.
  'Is it to-night', they whispered,
  'Or was it long, long, long ago,
  Or is it on some future morn
  That unto Earth her Peace is born?'
        D.M. Rowena Cade *Minack Sonnets*

4 I saw a stable, low and very bare,
  A little child in a manger.
  The oxen knew Him, had Him in their care,
  To men He was a stranger.
  The safety of the world was lying there,
  And the world's danger.
        Mary Coleridge Quoted *Christian Poetry*

5 Poor World (said I) what wilt thou do
  To entertain this starry Stranger?
  Is this the best thou canst bestow,
  A cold, and not too cleanly manger?
  Contend, ye powers of heaven and earth,
  To fit a bed for this huge birth.

6 Great little one! whose all-embracing birth
  Lifts Earth to Heaven, stoops Heaven to Earth.
        Richard Crashaw 'An Hymn of the Nativity'

7 Behold, a virgin shall conceive, and bear a son, and shall call
  his name Immanuel.
        Holy Bible Isaiah Chap. 7 v. 14

8 And she brought forth her firstborn son, and wrapped him in
  swaddling clothes, and laid him in a manger; because there
  was no room for them in the inn.
        Holy Bible St Luke Chap. 2 v. 7

1 I sing the birth was born tonight,
   The author both of life and light.
       Ben Jonson 'A Hymn on the Nativity'

2 This is the month, and this the happy morn,
   Wherein the Son of Heav'n's Eternal King,
   Of wedded maid and virgin mother born,
   Our great redemption from above did bring;
   For so the holy sages once did sing,
   That He our deadly forfeit should release,
   And with His Father work us a perpetual peace.
       John Milton 'On the Morning of Christ's Nativity'

3 A virgin shall conceive, a virgin bear a son?
   From Jesse's root behold a branch arise,
   Whose sacred flower with fragrance fills the skies.

4 The Saviour comes, by ancient bards foretold!
   Hear him, ye deaf, and all ye blind, behold!
       Alexander Pope 'Messiah'

5 Little Jesus, wast thou shy
   Once, and just so small as I?
   And what did it feel to be
   Out of Heaven and just like me?
       Francis Thompson 'Ex Ore Infantum'

NATURE

6 In all things of nature there is something of the marvellous.
       Aristotle *Historia Animalium*

7 Nature, with equal mind,
   Sees all her sons at play;
   Sees man control the wind,
   The wind sweep man away.
       Matthew Arnold *Empedocles on Etna*

8 By reason of the frailty of our nature we cannot always stand
   upright.
       Book of Common Prayer Collect, Fourth Sunday after Epiphany

9 Nature, the vicaire of the almyghty lorde.
       Geoffrey Chaucer *The Parliament of Fowls*

10 The whole of Nature, as has been said, is a conjugation of the
   verb to eat, in the active and passive.
       Dean W.R. Inge *Outspoken Essays*

1   Rain, rock, broken to wine and bread
    Are formed now into the blessed Body;
    The baptismal river floods to the will of God,
    And tallow burns to His glory.
        Norman Nicholson *The Holy Mountain in Five Rivers*

2   Nature has some perfections to show that she is the image of
    God, and some defects to show that she is only His image.
        Blaise Pascal *Pensées*

NEIGHBOUR

3   He alone loves the Creator perfectly who manifests a pure
    love for his neighbour.
        The Venerable Bede

4   We make our friends; we make our enemies; but God sends
    our next door neighbour.
        G.K. Chesterton

5   Love your neighbour, yet pull not down your hedge.
        George Herbert *Jacula Prudentum*

6   This is the sum of all true righteousness: do nothing to your
    neighbour which you would not have him do to you after.
        Hindu spirituality Quoted *Prayers for Peace* 'The Way of
        Empathy'

7   The good neighbour looks beyond the external accidents and
    discerns those inner qualities that make all men human and
    therefore brothers.
        Martin Luther King *Strength to Love*

8   When a man realises that he is a beloved child of the Creator
    of all, then he is ready to see his neighbours in the world as
    brothers and sisters.
        Robert Runcie, Archbishop of Canterbury Quoted *Prayers for
        Peace* 'Visions of Unity'

9   Regard your neighbour's gain as your own gain, and your
    neighbour's loss as your loss.
        Taoist spirituality Quoted *Prayers for Peace* 'The Way of
        Empathy'

10 Love of God is the root, love of our neighbour the fruit of the
    Tree of Life. Neither can exist without the other, but the one
    is cause and the other effect.
        Archbishop William Temple *Readings from St John's Gospel*

NEW CREATION

1 We are members of that body which was nailed to the cross, laid in a tomb and raised to life on the third day. There is only one organism of the new creation, and we are members of that organism which is Christ.

   Lionel Thornton CR *The Common Life of the Body of Christ*

NEW JERUSALEM

2 I, John, saw the holy city, new Jerusalem, coming down from God out of heaven, prepared as a bride adorned for her husband.

3 And God shall wipe away all tears from their eyes; and there shall be no more death, neither sorrow, nor crying, neither shall there be any more pain: for the former things are passed away.

4 And he that sat upon the throne said, Behold, I make all things new.

   Holy Bible Revelation Chap. 21 vv. 2, 4 & 5

NIGHT

5 Lighten our darkness, we beseech Thee, O Lord; and by Thy great mercy defend us from all perils and dangers of this night.

   Book of Common Prayer Order of Evening Prayer

6 To see God only, I go out of sight:
   And to scape stormy days, I choose
   An everlasting night.

   John Donne 'A Hymn to Christ'

7 You shouldn't go far in the daylight, cos it stops where you can't see. The night time is better. It stretches your soul right out to the stars.

   'Fynn' *Mister God, This is Anna*

8 O God, my God, the night has values that the day never dreamed of.

   Thomas Merton *The Sign of Jonas*

9 Night, you are for a man more nourishing than bread and wine.

   Charles Péguy *God Speaks*

10 We must welcome the night. It's the only time that the stars shine.

   Michel Quoist *With Open Heart*

NOAH

1 And Noah he often said to his wife when he sat down to dine,
'I don't care where the water goes if it doesn't get into the
wine.'
> G.K. Chesterton 'Wine and Water'

NONCONFORMIST

2 The Nonconformist conscience makes cowards of us all.
> Max Beerbohm *King George IV*

3 The children of dogmatic atheists tend to become Wesleyan
missionaries.
> Gerald Brenan *Thoughts in a Dry Season*

NOSTALGIA

4 Looking back is fatal — the truest thing in scripture is what
happened to Lot's wife.
> William J. Locke *Septimus*

NOURISHMENT

5 The Lord is my shepherd: therefore can I lack nothing. He
shall feed me in a green pasture: and lead me forth beside the
waters of comfort.
> *Book of Common Prayer* Psalm 23 vv. 1–2

6 He bringeth forth ... food out of the earth, and wine that
maketh glad the heart of man: and oil to make him a cheerful
countenance, and bread to strengthen man's heart.
> *Book of Common Prayer* Psalm 104 v. 15

OBEDIENCE

1   Holy obedience puts to shame all natural and selfish desires. It mortifies our lower nature and makes it obey the spirit and our fellow men.

     St Francis of Assisi *The Writings of St Francis* Trans. Benen Fahy

2   O let thy sacred will
All thy delight in me fulfil!
Let me not think an action mine own way,
But as thy love shall sway,
Refining up the rudder to thy skill.

     George Herbert *The Temple* 'Obedience'

3   All religions have based morality on obedience, that is to say, on voluntary slavery. That is why they have always been more pernicious than any political organisation. For the latter makes use of violence, the former, of corruption of the will.

     Alexander Herzen *From the Other Shore*

4   Lord, make me according to thy heart.

     Br Lawrence *The Practice and Presence of God*

5   I find the doing of the will of God leaves me no time for disputing about His plans.

     George MacDonald *The Marquis of Lossie*

6   That thou art happy, owe to God;
That thou continuest such, owe to thyself,
That is, to thy obedience.

     John Milton *Paradise Lost*

7   Obedience is not slavery: but ordered liberty.

     Gilbert Shaw *Perfection*

8   It is a bitter dose to be taught obedience after you have learned to rule.

     Publilius Syrus *Moral Sayings*

1   Every revelation of God is a demand, and the way to
    knowledge of God is by obedience.
        Archbishop William Temple

2   What we did today was not the negative thing of saying we
    disobeyed. It was the positive thing of saying we obeyed God.
        Archbishop Desmond Tutu 29 February 1988

OLD AGE

3   My deafness I endure
    To dentures I'm resigned
    Bifocals I can manage
    But God, how I miss my mind.
        Anon

4   When I became ninety I had been passed over as a speaker at
    a Salvation Army gathering, and this depressed me. So, to
    comfort myself, I said 'Lord, help me to be reconciled to old
    age.' Well, the next day, the telephone rang and it was the
    BBC asking if they could interview me.
        Commissioner Catherine Bramwell-Booth *My Faith* Ed.
        Mary E. Callan

5   The arrogance of age must submit to be taught by youth.
        Edmund Burke

6   With the approach of death I care less and less about religion
    and truth. One hasn't long to wait for revelation and darkness.
        Graham Greene *A Sort of Life*

7   And he died in a good old age, full of days, riches, and honour.
        Holy Bible 1 Chronicles Chap. 29 v. 28

8   With the ancient is wisdom; and in length of days
    understanding.
        Holy Bible Job Chap. 12 v. 12

9   Great men are not always wise: neither do the aged
    understand judgement.
        Holy Bible Job Chap. 32 v. 9

10 If only, when one heard
    That Old-Age was coming
    One could bolt the door
    Answer 'Not at home'
    And refuse to meet him.
        Kokinshu *Anthology of Japanese Literature*

1   It ought to be lovely to be old,
    To be full of the peace that comes from experience
    And wrinkled ripe fulfilment.
    D.H. Lawrence *Selected Poems*

2   The older I grow the more I distrust the familiar doctrine that
    age brings wisdom.
    H.L. Mencken

3   One of the many pleasures of old age is giving things up.
    Malcolm Muggeridge

4   King David and King Solomon
    Led merry, merry lives,
    With many, many lady friends
    And many, many wives;
    But when old age crept over them,
    With many, many qualms,
    King Solomon wrote the Proverbs
    And King David wrote the Psalms.
    James Ball Naylor *David and Solomon*

5   Religion often gets credit for curing radicals when old age is
    the real medicine.
    Austin O'Malley *Keystones of Thought*

6   Old age comes from God, old age leads on to God, old age
    will not touch me only so far as He wills.
    Pierre Teilhard de Chardin

OMNIPOTENCE

7   The will of God is the measure of things.

8   What is impossible to God? Not that which is difficult to His
    power, but that which is contrary to His nature.
    St Ambrose

9   God exists not in any single mode, but embraces and
    prepossesses all beings within Himself, absolutely and without
    limit.
    St Dionysius the Areopagite

10 So it is written in your Torah: 'The Lord shall rule forever and
    ever.'
    Jewish Daily Service

1   Blessed are they who do not their own will on earth, for God will do it in heaven above.
   St Francis de Sales

2   To be omnipotent but friendless is to reign.
   Percy Bysshe Shelley *Prometheus Unbound*

ORATORY

3   Let us have reason for beginning, and let our end be within due limits. For a speech that is wearisome only stirs up anger.
   St Ambrose *Select Works and Letters*

ORDER

4   The rich man in his castle,
   The poor man at his gate,
   God made them, high or lowly,
   And ordered their estate.
   C.F. Alexander Hymn 'All Things Bright and Beautiful'

5   The eternal fitness of things.
   Samuel Clarke *Being and Attributes of God*

6   Order is Heaven's first law.
   Alexander Pope *An Essay on Man*

ORDINAND

7   A Catholic seminary's pamphlet has all the details a would-be priest needs: 'If God is calling you, God will see you through. His address is: Allen Hall, 28 Beaufort Street, London SW3.' Don't tell the neighbours.
   The Times 'Diary' 22 February 1987

PACIFISM

1 Would it not be a blasphemous frivolity to think that the devil could be exorcised with the cry 'No more war' and with a new organisation?
   Dietrich Bonhoeffer *No Rusty Swords*

2 My pacifism is not based on any intellectual theory, but on a deep antipathy to every form of cruelty and hatred.
   Albert Einstein, on the outbreak of World War I

3 Mental violence has no potency and injures only the person whose thoughts are violent. It is otherwise with mental non-violence, it has a potency which the world does not yet know.

4 Non-violence is not a garment to be put off and on at will. Its seat is in the heart, and it must be an inseparable part of our very being.
   Gandhi *Non-Violence in Peace and War*

5 We who advocate peace are becoming an irrelevance when we speak peace. The government speaks rubber bullets, live bullets, tear gas, police dogs, detention and death.
   Archbishop Desmond Tutu Quoted Peter Godwin *Sunday Times Magazine* 8 June 1986

PAIN

6 Our pains are real things, but all our pleasures, but fantastical.
   Samuel Butler *Satire on the Weakness of Man*

7 Much of your pain is self-chosen. It is the bitter potion by which the physician within you heals your sick self.

8 Your pain is the breaking of the shell that encloses your passion.
   Kahlil Gibran *The Prophet*

1 Pain is the price God putteth upon all things.
      James Howell *Proverbs*

2 Pain makes men think,
   Thinking gives man wisdom;
   And wisdom confers peace.
      Boris Pasternak

3 No pain, no palm; no thorn, no throne.
      William Penn *No Cross, No Crown*

4 Pain past is pleasure, and experience comes by it.
      Charles Spurgeon *John Ploughman*

5 Behind joy and laughter there may be a temperament coarse,
   hard and callous. But, behind sorrow, there is always sorrow.
   Pain, unlike pleasure, wears no mask.
      Oscar Wilde *De Profundis*

PARABLE

6 'What parable do you like best?' the Sunday School teacher
   asked her class. One pupil replied, 'The one about the
   multitude what loafs and fishes.'
      Reader's Digest September 1981

7 Without their fictions, the truths of religion would for the
   multitude be neither intelligible nor even apprehensible, and
   the prophets would prophesy and the teachers teach in vain.
      George Bernard Shaw *Back to Methuselah*

PARADISE

8 He that will enter Paradise must have a good key.
      George Herbert *Jacula Prudentum*

9 Paradise is a centre whither the souls of all men are
   proceeding, each sect in its particular road.
      Napoleon *Maxims*

10 The loves that meet in Paradise shall cast out fear,
    And Paradise hath room for you and me and all.
      Christina Rossetti 'Saints and Angels'

11 All we know
    Of what they do above,
    Is that they happy are, and that they love.
      Edmund Waller 'Upon the Death of My Lady Rich'

1 There is a land of pure delight
Where saints immortal reign;
Infinite day excludes the night
And pleasures banish pain.
  Isaac Watts *Hymns and Spiritual Songs*

PARDON

2 He pardoneth and absolveth all them that truly repent, and unfeignedly believe His Holy Gospel.
  Book of Common Prayer The Absolution

3 We pardon as long as we love.
  François, Duc de la Rochefoucauld *Maxims*

4 Pardon, not wrath, is God's best attribute.
  Bayard Taylor *The Temptation of Hassan Ben Khaled*

PARENT

5 You are the bows from which your children as living arrows are sent forth.
  Kahlil Gibran *The Prophet*

6 I was ever of opinion, that the honest man who married and brought up a large family, did more service than he who continued single and only talked of population.
  Oliver Goldsmith *The Vicar of Wakefield*

PARTING

7 Parting is all we know of Heaven,
And all we need of hell.
  Emily Dickinson 'Parting'

8 When you part from your friend, you grieve not; for that which you love most in him may be clearer in his absence, as the mountain to the climber is clearer from the plain.
  Kahlil Gibran *The Prophet*

PASSION

9 The way to avoid evil is not by bemoaning our passions, but by compelling them to yield their vigour to our moral nature.
  Henry Ward Beecher *Proverbs from a Plymouth Pulpit*

10 Only great passions can elevate the soul to great things.
  Denis Diderot *Philosophical Thoughts*

1   Passions destroy more prejudices than philosophy does.
     Denis Diderot *Discourses*

2   Passion, though a bad regulator, is a powerful spring.
     Ralph Waldo Emerson *The Conduct of Life*

3   Passions are spiritual rebels and raise sedition against
   understanding.
     Ben Jonson *Timber*

4   If we resist our passions, it is more because of their weakness
   than our strength.
     François, Duc de la Rochefoucauld *Maxims*

5   Take heed lest passion sway
   Thy judgement to do aught which else free will
   Would not admit.
     John Milton *Paradise Lost*

6   If the truth of God is disclosed and the glory of God is
   manifest in Jesus, then the truth of God must be this, and the
   glory of God must appear in this — that God so initiates and
   acts that he destines himself to enter into passion, to wait and
   to receive.
     W.A. Vanstone *The Stature of Waiting*

PATIENCE

7   The man of perfect knowledge should not unsettle the foolish
   whose knowledge is imperfect.
     Bhagavad Gita

8   Though God take the sun out of heaven, yet we must have
   patience.
     George Herbert *Jacula Prudentum*

9   At the least bear patiently, if thou canst not joyfully.
     Thomas à Kempis *The Imitation of Christ*

10   Patience may be defined as that quality of life which makes
   suffering creative; and impatience as that whereby suffering
   becomes a destructive force.
     Robert Llewelyn *A Doorway to Silence*

11   They also serve who only stand and wait.
     John Milton 'On His Blindness'

12   Patience and diligence, like faith remove mountains.
     William Penn *Some Fruits of Solitude*

PATRIOTISM

1 If you love freedom, you must hate slavery; if you love your people, you cannot but hate the enemies that compass their destruction; if you love your country, you cannot but hate those who seek to annexe it.

    Menachem Begin, on signing the Egyptian-Israeli Treaty 1979

PAYMENT

2 To pray and pay, too, is the devil.

    Daniel Defoe *Everybody's Business*

3 He that cannot pay, let him pray.

    Thomas Fuller *Gnomologia*

PEACE

4 There is no peace but in the will of God. God's will is our peace and there is no other peace. God's service is perfect freedom and there is no other freedom.

    Fr Andrew SDC *Letters of Fr Andrew SDC*

5 Peace be to the Earth and to the Air!
Peace be to Heaven, peace to the Waters!
By this invocation of peace may peace bring peace.

    Atharva Veda

6 He knows peace who has forgotten desire.

    Bhagavad Gita

7 Give peace in our time, O Lord. Because there is none other that fighteth for us, but only Thou, O God.

    Book of Common Prayer Order of Morning Prayer

8 O God, make us children of quietness, and heirs of peace.

    St Clement of Rome

9 Acquire inner peace and a multitude will find their salvation near you.

    Catherine de Hueck Doherty *Poustinia*

10 Go placidly amid the noise and haste, and remember what peace there may be in silence.

    Max Ehrmann *Desiderata*

11 Thou wilt keep him in perfect peace, whose mind is stayed on thee.

    Holy Bible Isaiah Chap. 26 v. 3

1 Peace I leave with you, my peace I give unto you.
   Holy Bible St John Chap. 14 v. 27

2 The peace of God, which passeth all understanding.
   Holy Bible Philippians Chap. 4 v. 7

3 We should have much peace if we would not busy ourselves
   with the sayings and doings of others.
   Thomas à Kempis *The Imitation of Christ*

4 Peace is more important than all justice: and peace was not
   made for the sake of justice, but justice for the sake of peace.
   Martin Luther 'On Marriage'

5 Where people are praying for peace the cause of peace is
   being strengthened by their very act of prayer, for they are
   themselves becoming immersed in the spirit of peace.
   John Macquarrie *The Concept of Peace*

6 Peace does not mean the end of all our striving,
   Joy does not mean the drying of our tears;
   Peace is the power that comes to souls arriving
   Up into the light where God himself appears.
   G.A. Studdert-Kennedy *The Suffering God*

7 Let nothing disturb thee, nothing afright thee;
   All things are passing; God never changeth;
   Patient endurance
   Attaineth to all things;
   Who God possesseth
   In nothing is wanting;
   Alone God sufficeth.
   St Teresa of Avila

8 Peace comes not by establishing a calm outward setting so
   much as by inwardly surrendering to whatever the setting.
   Hubert van Zeller *Leave Your Life Alone*

PENANCE

9 A precious jewel I will give thee,
   Called penance, wise voider of adversity.
   Everyman Morality play

10 I will that you wisely know your penance and you shall see in
   truth that all your living is penance profitable.
   Julian of Norwich *Revelations of Divine Love*

PENITENCE

1 The underside of the splendours of the saint's robes is the sackcloth of his penitence.

2 Where there is no penitence there can be no progress.
   Fr Andrew SDC *Meditations for Every Day*

3 Thou shalt purge me with hyssop, and I shall be clean: thou shalt wash me, and I shall be whiter than snow.
   Book of Common Prayer Psalm 51 v.7

4 Rend your heart, and not your garments, and turn unto the Lord your God: for he is gracious and merciful, slow to anger, and of great kindness, and repenteth him of the evil.
   Holy Bible Joel Chap. 2 v. 13

5 Bad I am, but yet thy child.
   Father, be thou reconciled,
   Spare thou me, since I see
   With thy might that thou art mild.
   Gerard Manley Hopkins

6 And so by coaches to church — where a pretty good sermon — and a declaration of penitence of a man that had undergone the Church censure for his wicked life.
   Samuel Pepys *Diary*

PEOPLE

7 The voice of the people is the voice of God.
   Alcuin *Epistles* Letter to Charlemagne

8 The Lord prefers common-looking people. That is the reason He makes so many of them.
   Abraham Lincoln Quoted James Morgan *Our Presidents*

PERFECTION

9 If thou shouldst say 'It is enough, I have reached perfection' all is lost, since it is the function of perfection to make one know one's imperfections.
   St Augustine of Hippo

10 All mankind is born for perfection, and each shall attain it, will he but follow his nature's duty.
   Bhagavad Gita

1 The greatest politeness
Is free of all formality
Perfect conduct
Is free from concern.
Perfect wisdom
Is unplanned
Perfect love is without demonstrations
Perfect sincerity offers
No guarantee.
Chuang Tzu *The Way of Chuang Tzu*

2 Be ye therefore perfect, even as your Father which is in heaven is perfect.
Holy Bible St Matthew Chap. 5 v. 48

3 Elected Silence, sing to me
And beat upon my whorled ear,
Pipe me to pastures still and be
The music that I long to hear.
Gerard Manley Hopkins 'The Habit of Perfection'

4 Rightfulness has two qualities: it is right, and it is full. Such are all the works of God. They lack neither mercy nor grace, for they are altogether right, and nothing is lacking in them.
Julian of Norwich *Revelations of Divine Love*

5 I shall seek to develop the perfection of generosity, virtue, doing without, wisdom, energy, forbearance, truthfulness, resolution, love, serenity.
The Ten Perfections Buddhist spirituality

6 Counsels of perfection.
Theological term — source unknown

PERSECUTION

7 Christians have burnt each other, quite persuaded
That all the Apostles would have done as they did.
Lord Byron *Don Juan*

8 Christian leaders from the fourth century onwards told the Jews, 'You have no right to live among us as Jews.' Succeeding secular rulers told them, 'You have no right to live among us.' Hitler told them, 'You have no right to live.'
Iain Mackenzie Review of *Approaches to Auschwitz* in *Church Times*

1 What mean and cruel things men do for the love of God.
   W. Somerset Maugham *A Writer's Notebook*

2 To persecute
   Makes a faith hated, and is furthermore
   No perfect witness of a perfect faith
   In him who persecutes.
   Alfred, Lord Tennyson *Queen Mary*

3 If the Tiber reaches the walls, if the Nile does not rise, if the
   sky does not move or if the earth does, if there is a famine or a
   plague, the cry is 'The Christians to the lions!'
   Tertullian *Apologeticus*

PERSEVERANCE

4 Attempt the end, and never stand to doubt;
   Nothing's so hard, but search will find it out.
   Robert Herrick *Hesperides*

5 God is with those who persevere.
   The Qur'an

6 By perseverance the snail reached the Ark.
   Charles Haddon Spurgeon

PETITION

7 God of all goodness, grant us to desire ardently, to seek
   wisely, to know surely and to accomplish perfectly Thy holy
   will, for the glory of Thy name.
   St Thomas Aquinas

8 O Lord, Thou knowest how busy I must be this day. If I forget
   Thee, do not forget me.
   Jacob Astley, before the battle of Edgehill

9 Most high, glorious God, enlighten the darkness of my heart
   and give me, Lord, a correct faith, a certain hope, a perfect
   charity, sense and knowledge, so that I may carry out Your
   holy and true command.
   St Francis of Assisi 'Prayer Before the Crucifix'

10 And I say unto you, Ask, and it shall be given you; seek, and
   ye shall find; knock, and it shall be opened unto you. For
   every one that asketh receiveth; and he that seeketh findeth;
   and to him that knocketh it shall be opened.
   Holy Bible St Luke Chap. 11 vv. 9-10

1 When the thought of thee wakes in our hearts let it not
awaken like a frightened bird that flies about in dismay, but
like a child waking from its sleep with a heavenly smile.
   Søren Kierkegaard

2 May God Almighty give us success over these fellows and
enable us to get a Peace.
   Horatio, Viscount Nelson, two days before Trafalgar

3 God, give us grace to accept with serenity the things that
cannot be changed, courage to change the things that should
be changed, and the wisdom to distinguish the one from the
other.
   Reinhold Niebuhr

4 I want to want to want to want you God.
   Michael Ramsey, Archbishop of Canterbury Address to students
   Quoted Richard Harries *Turning to Prayer*

5 Father of storms, may your favour flash upon us!
Do not deprive us of the sight of the sun.
   Rig-Veda

PHILANTHROPY

6 Do not give, as many rich men do, like a hen that lays an egg,
and then cackle.
   Henry Ward Beecher *Proverbs from a Plymouth Pulpit*

7 Philanthropy is commendable, but it must not cause the
philanthropist to overlook the circumstances of economic
injustice which make philanthropy necessary.
   Martin Luther King *Strength to Love*

8 The dignity of the individual demands that he be not reduced
to vassalage by the largesse of others.
   Antoine de Saint-Exupéry *Flight to Arras*

9 Philanthropy is almost the only virtue which is sufficiently
appreciated by mankind.
   Henry David Thoreau *Walden*

PHILOSOPHY

10 A little philosophy inclineth man's mind to atheism, but depth
in philosophy bringeth men's minds about to religion.
   Francis Bacon *Essays* 'Of Atheism'

1   All good moral philosophy is but an handmaid to religion.
    Francis Bacon *The Advancement of Learning*

2   The philosopher is Nature's pilot. And there you have our
    difference; to be in hell is to drift; to be in heaven is to steer.
    George Bernard Shaw *Man and Superman*

PIETY

3   Bernard always had a few prayers in the hall and some
    whiskey afterwards as he was rather pious.
    Daisy Ashford *The Young Visiters*

4   Faith is never identical with Piety.
    Karl Barth

5   The strength of a man consists in finding out which way God is
    going, and going that way too.
    Henry Ward Beecher *Proverbs from a Plymouth Pulpit*

6   Let them learn first to shew piety at home.
    Holy Bible 1 Timothy Chap. 5 v. 4

7   The Moving Finger writes; and having writ,
    Moves on: nor all thy Piety nor Wit
    Shall lure it back to cancel half a Line,
    Nor all thy Tears wash out a Word of it.
    Omar Khayyam *Rubaiyat* Trans. Edward Fitzgerald

8   Men always try to make virtues of their weaknesses. Fear of
    death and fear of life both become piety.
    H.L. Mencken *Notebooks*

9   I remain suspicious of piety in the young — eleven to twenty-
    one is probably a decade which is better left spiritually alone.
    Gerald Priestland *Something Understood*

10 It is rash to intrude upon the piety of others; both the depth
    and grace of it elude the stranger.
    George Santayana *Dialogues in Limbo*

PILGRIM

11 Man! The pilgrim of a day.
    Thomas Campbell *The Pleasures of Hope*

12 All of us are pilgrims on this earth. I have even heard it said
    that the earth itself is a pilgrim in the heavens.
    Maxim Gorky *The Lower Depths*

1 We should be low and lovelike and lean each man to the
other
And patient as pilgrims, for pilgrims are we all.
William Langland *The Vision of Piers the Plowman*

2 Give me my scallop shell of quiet,
My staff of faith to walk upon,
My scrip of joy, immortal diet,
My bottle of salvation,
My gown of glory, hope's true gage,
And thus I'll take my pilgrimage.
Sir Walter Raleigh *Diaphantus* 'The Passionate Man's
Pilgrimage'

PITY

3 When a man suffers himself, it is called misery; when he
suffers in the suffering of another, it is called pity.
St Augustine of Hippo

4 Pity melts the Mind to Love.
John Dryden 'Alexander's Feast'

5 More helpful than all wisdom is one draught of simple human
pity that will not forsake us.
George Eliot *The Mill on the Floss*

PLEASURE

6 Every quest for pleasure is fundamentally a striving for the
infinite.

7 No pleasure ever becomes our permanent possession until it
has passed through a moment of pain.
Fulton J. Sheen *Lift Up Your Heart*

PLYMOUTH BRETHREN

8 The Brethren did not believe in celebrating any special days or
festivals. The Incarnation was to be borne in mind at all times,
but never one time.
Anne Arnott *The Brethren*

9 Never in all my early childhood did anyone address to me the
affectionate 'Once upon a time'. I was told about missionaries
but never about pirates. I had never heard of fairies.
Edmund Gosse *Father and Son*

POLITICS

1 The parson leaves the *Christian* in the lurch
Whene'er he brings his politics into Church.
John Byrom *Epigrams*

2 The introduction of religious passion into politics is the end of
honest politics, and the introduction of politics into religion is
the prostitution of true religion.
Lord Hailsham *The Conservative Case*

3 A clergyman with no politics is never made a bishop.
St John Hankin

4 I submit that Christians ought not to be scared of a moral issue
just because someone has stuck a political flag on it.
Gerald Priestland 'Yours Faithfully' BBC Radio 4 5 August 1978

5 The Church should no longer be satisfied to represent only the
Conservative Party at prayer.
Agnes Maud Royden Address, City Temple London 1917

6 No government can expect to be wholly at ease with the
church since the church serves the Kingdom which is not of
this world.
Bishop Mark Santer Speech to the Southwark Diocesan Synod
5 March 1988

7 There are three very good reasons for a cleric not to harbour
political ambition: Archbishop Makarios, Ayatollah Khomeini
and Bishop Musorewa.
Archbishop Desmond Tutu Quoted Peter Godwin *Sunday Times
Magazine* 8 June 1986

8 If there is a God, Richelieu will have much to answer for. If
not, he has done well.
Pope Urban VIII, on hearing of the death of Cardinal Richelieu

9 Organised religion is making Christianity political rather than
politics religious.
Laurens van der Post *Observer* 'Sayings of the Week'
9 November 1986

POPE

10 The Bishop of ROME hath no jurisdiction in this Realm of
ENGLAND.
Book of Common Prayer Article XXXVII 'Of the Bishop
of Rome'

1 Being a man I may come to be Pope.
>   Miguel de Cervantes *Don Quixote*

2 The Papacy is not other than the ghost of the deceased Roman Empire, sitting crowned upon the grave thereof.
>   Thomas Hobbes *Leviathan*

3 Anybody can be pope; the proof of this is that I have become one.
>   Pope John XXIII Letter to a boy who wanted to know whether to be a pope or a policeman

POSSESSIONS

4 It is our nature's law that makes a man set higher value on the things he has not got than upon those he has, so that he loathes his actual possessions in longing for the things that are not his.
>   St Bernard of Clairvaux Quoted *On the Love of God*

5 How could there be any question of acquiring or possessing, when the one thing needful for a man is to *become* — to *be* at last, and to die in the fullness of his being.
>   Antoine de Saint-Exupéry *The Wisdom of the Sands*

6 He who says, what is mine is yours and what is yours is yours, is a saint. He who says, what is yours is mine and what is mine is mine is a wicked man.
>   *The Talmud*

POVERTY

7 To stand poor beside the brother I love means being his equal in terms of cultural values, intelligence and human dignity far more than in terms of money.
>   Carlo Carretto *In Search of the Beyond*

8 Poverty is no sin.
>   George Herbert *Jacula Prudentum*

9 Go and sell that thou hast, and give to the poor, and thou shalt have treasure in heaven.
>   *Holy Bible* St Matthew Chap. 19 v. 21

10 The worst poverty today is the poverty of not having spiritual values in life.
>   Cardinal Basil Hume OSB *To Be a Pilgrim*

1 Poverty is to have nothing
  And desire nothing
  And yet to possess everything
  In the spirit of liberty.
      Jacopone of Todi

2 A decent provision for the poor is the true test of civilisation.
      Samuel Johnson Quoted Boswell's *Life of Johnson*

3 He is much to be dreaded who stands in dread of poverty.
      Pindar *Odes*

4 Poverty comes from God, but not dirt.
      The Talmud

POWER

5 It is not yet possible to call it a virtue to slaughter one's fellow
  citizens, to be without faith, pity, without religions; by such
  methods power can be gained but not glory.
      Niccolo Machiavelli *The Prince*

6 Religions which condemn the pleasures of sense, drive men to
  seek the pleasures of power. Throughout history power has
  been the vice of the ascetic.
      Bertrand Russell *New York Herald-Tribune Magazine*
      6 May 1938

7 Because they are part of God's sovereign rule, Christians have
  authority over every power that belongs to the enemy.
      Colin Urquhart *Receive Your Healing*

PRAISE

8 God's in his heaven —
  All's right with the world!
      Robert Browning *Pippa Passes*

9 God! sing ye meadow-streams with gladsome voice!
  Ye pine-groves, with your soft and soul-like sounds!
  And they, too, have a voice, yon piles of snow,
  And in their perilous fall shall thunder, God!
      Samuel Taylor Coleridge 'Hymn before Sunrise, in the Vale of
      Chamouni'

10 In the prison house I sung praises to my God, and esteemed
   the bolts and locks put upon me as jewels.
      William Dewsbury *Spiritual Experiences of Friends*

1 Holy, Holy, Holy! Merciful and Mighty!
Early in the morning our song shall rise to Thee.
   Reginald Heber *Hymns*

2 Let all the world in every corner sing
My God and King.
The heavens are not too high,
His praise may thither fly;
The earth is not too low,
His praises there may grow.
Let all the world in every corner sing
My God and King.
   George Herbert *The Temple* 'Antiphon'

3 My soul doth magnify the Lord, and my spirit hath rejoiced in
God my Saviour.
   Holy Bible St Luke Chap. 1 vv. 46–47

4 And suddenly there was with the angel a multitude of the
heavenly host praising God, and saying, Glory to God in the
highest, and on earth peace, good will toward men.
   Holy Bible St Luke Chap. 2 vv. 13–14

5 Whether therefore ye eat, or drink, or whatsoever ye do, do
all to the glory of God.
   Holy Bible 1 Corinthians Chap. 10 v. 31

6 Glory be to God for dappled things.

7 All things counter, original, spare, strange;
Whatever is fickle, freckled (who knows how?)
With swift, slow; sweet, sour; adazzle, dim;
He fathers-forth whose beauty is past change.
   Gerard Manley Hopkins 'Pied Beauty'

8 Far better in its place the lowliest bird
Should sing aright to Him the lowliest song,
Than that a seraph strayed should take the word
And sing His glory wrong.
   Jean Ingelow ' .onours'

9 Praise, my soul, the King of Heaven,
To His feet thy tribute bring.
   Henry Francis Lyte

10 A slowness to applaud betrays a cold temper or an envious
spirit.
   Hannah More

1 You O Lord are mankind's bright sign
   Best, most beloved of the people.
   Awake! Give strength to the singer.
   Rig-Veda

2 It is a sure sign of mediocrity to be niggardly with praise.
   Marquis de Vauvenargues *Reflections and Maxims*

3 My praise dispraises Thee, Almighty God,
   For praise is being and to be is sin.
   The Wisdom of the Sufis Compiled by Kenneth Cragg

PRAYER

4 Give rest to the weary, visit the sick, support the poor; for this
   also is prayer.
   Afrahat, the first Syriac Father

5 The best prayer is not that which feels most, but that which
   gives most.
   Fr Andrew SDC *A Gift of Light*

6 The God to whom little boys say their prayers has a face very
   like their mother.
   J.M. Barrie

Poet

7 To wish to pray is a prayer in itself.
   Georges Bernanos *The Diary of a Country Priest*

Poet

8 'Forgive me, aren't we talking rather loud?
   I think I see a woman praying there.'
   'Praying? The service is all over now
   And here's the verger waiting to turn out
   The lights and lock the church up. She cannot
   Be Loyal Church of England.'
   John Betjeman 'Bristol and Clifton'

Poet

9 Although dear Lord I am a sinner
   I have done no major crime;
   Now I'll come to Evening Service
   Whensoever I have the time.
   So, Lord, reserve for me a crown,
   And do not let my shares go down.
   John Betjeman 'In Westminster Abbey'

10 A prayer is not holy chewing gum and you don't have to see
   how far you can stretch it.
   Rabbi Lionel Blue *Kitchen Blues*

1 Is prayer your steering wheel or your spare tyre?
    Corrie Ten Boom

loretes 1972-1983

2 And all day, I sent prayer like incense up
To God the strong, God the beneficent,
God ever mindful in all strife and strait
Who, for our own good, makes the need extreme,
Till at the last He puts forth might and saves.
    Robert Browning

3 The best prayers have often more groans than words.

4 When thou prayest, rather let thy heart be without words
than thy words be without heart.
    John Bunyan

5 The truth of the Gospel, which is essentially and initially a
corporate possession, is personally appropriated by prayer in
the heart of the believer.
    John Byrom *Prayer of Passion and Love*

6 Be thou a bright flame before me,
Be thou a guiding star above me,
Be thou a smooth path below me,
And be a kindly Shepherd behind me,
Today, tonight and for ever.
    Alexander Carmichael *Carmina Gadelica*

7 Prayer takes place in the heart, not in the head.
    Carlo Carretto *The Desert in the City*

8 Prayer is the sum of our relationship with God. We are what
we pray. The degree of our faith is the degree of our prayer.
Our ability to love is our ability to pray.
    Carlo Carretto *Letters from a Desert*

9 The soul must be kept peaceful during prayer and end prayer
in peace.
    Jean-Pierre de Caussade SJ *Self-Abandonment to Divine
    Providence*

0 Prayer is more than meditation. In meditation the source of
strength is one's self. When one prays he goes to a source of
strength greater than his own.

1 When you pray don't insult God's intelligence by asking Him to
do something which would be unworthy of even you, a mortal.
    Mme Chiang Kai-shek *I Confess My Faith*

1 No one should give the answer that it is impossible for a man occupied with worldly cares to pray always. You can set up an altar to God in your mind by means of prayer. And so it is fitting to pray at your trade, on a journey, standing at a counter or sitting at your handicraft.

    St John Chrysostom

2 God wants us to pray and will tell us how to begin where we are.

    The Cloud of Unknowing

3 He prayeth well, who loveth well
Both man and bird and beast.
He prayeth best, who loveth best
All things both great and small;
For the dear God who loveth us,
He made and loveth all.

    Samuel Taylor Coleridge *The Ancient Mariner*

4 'Does God always answer prayer?' the cardinal was asked. 'Yes,' he said, 'and sometimes the answer is "No".'

    Alistair Cooke 'Letter from America' BBC Radio 4
    8 March 1981

5 Two went to pray? O rather say
One went to brag, the other to pray.

    Richard Crashaw *Steps to the Temple*

6 When we pray we should open our heart to God, like a fish when it sees a wave coming.

    The Curé d'Ars (Jean-Baptiste Vianney)

7 A prayer may chance to rise
From one whose heart lives in the Grace of God,
A prayer from any other is unheeded.

    Dante *Divine Comedy* 'Purgatory'

8 Prayer is the little implement
Through which men reach
Where presence is denied them.

    Emily Dickinson *Poems*

9 Caesarius of Heisterbach (c. 1180—1240), the Cistercian chronicler, tells of a lay brother who was heard to pray to Christ: 'Lord, if Thou free me not from this temptation I will complain of Thee to Thy Mother.'

    Will Durant *The Story of Civilisation*

1 Prayer can neither change God, nor bring His designs into mortal modes, but it can and does change our modes and our false sense of Life, Love, and Truth, uplifting us to Him.

2 True prayer is not asking God for love; it is learning to love, and to include all mankind in one affection.
   Mary Baker Eddy *No and Yes*

3 Prayer is the contemplation of the facts of life from the highest point of view.
   Ralph Waldo Emerson *Essays 'Self-Reliance'*

4 To pray ... is to desire; but it is to desire what God would have us desire. He who desires not from the bottom of his heart, offers a deceitful prayer.
   François de la Mothe Fénelon *Advice Concerning Prayer*

5 You are not drawn to God primarily for your own benefit but for his.
   Gonville ffrench-Beytagh *A Glimpse of Glory*

6 Some men will spin out a long prayer telling God who and what He is, or they pray out a whole system of divinity. Some people preach, others exhort the people, till everybody wishes they would stop and God wishes so, too, most undoubtedly.
   Charles Finney *Lectures on Revivals of Religion*

7 God is not a cosmic bell-boy for whom we can press a button to get things.
   Harry Emerson Fosdick *The Meaning of Prayer*

8 Every Christian needs an half hour of prayer each day, except when he is busy, then he needs an hour.
   St Francis de Sales

9 None can pray well but he that lives well.

10 Prayer should be the key of the day and the lock of the night.
    Thomas Fuller *Gnomologia*

11 Prayer is not an old woman's idle amusement. Properly understood and applied it is the most potent instrument of action.
    Gandhi *Non-Violence in Peace and War*

12 You pray in your distress and in your need, would that you might pray also in the fullness of your joy and your days of abundance.
    Kahlil Gibran *The Prophet*

1 Prayer is a *cri de coeur*, not an insipid platitude.
  Norman Goodacre *Layman's Lent*

2 The prayer of the heart is the source of all good, which
  refreshes the soul as if it were a garden.
  St Gregory of Sinai

3 Your cravings as a human animal do not become a prayer just
  because it is God you ask to attend to them.
  Dag Hammarskjöld

4 Prayer, the Church's banquet, Angel's age
  God's breath in man returning to his birth,
  The soul in paraphrase, heart in pilgrimage,
  The Christian plummet sounding heaven and earth.
  George Herbert 'Prayer'

5 Who goes to bed and does not pray
  Maketh two nights to every day.
  George Herbert *The Temple*

6 Here a little child I stand,
  Heaving up my either hand;
  Cold as paddocks though they be,
  Here I lift them up to Thee,
  For a benison to fall
  On our meat, and on us all.
  Robert Herrick 'A Child's Grace'

7 In prayer the lips ne'er act the winning part,
  Without the sweet concurrence of the heart.
  Robert Herrick 'The Heart'

8 Prayer takes the mind out of the narrowness of self-interest,
  and enables us to see the world in the mirror of the holy.
  Abraham Joshua Heschel *Modern Spirituality* 'The Essence of
  Spiritual Living'

9 Prayer is good, but while calling on the gods a man should
  himself lend a hand.
  Hippocrates *Regimen*

10 Whoever obeys the gods, to him they particularly listen.
  Homer *The Iliad*

11 Certain thoughts are prayers. There are moments when,
  whatever be the attitude of the body, the soul is on its knees.
  Victor Hugo *Les Misérables*

1 Prayer gives a man the opportunity of getting to know a gentleman he hardly ever meets. I do not mean his maker, but himself.
>   Dean W.R. Inge

2 God knows what is in me, I don't need to tell Him, so I recite prayers to impress a certain message on myself, my dependence on God. For I am the addressee; the form of the prayer is addressed to God, but I am not meant to change God, I'm meant to change myself.
>   Immanuel Jakobovits, Chief Rabbi *The Times* 12 March 1987

3 The exercise of prayer, in those who habitually exert it, must be regarded by us doctors as the most adequate and normal of all the pacifiers of the mind and calmers of the nerves.
>   William James *Essays on Faith and Morals* 'The Energies of Men'

4 Affliction teacheth a wicked person sometime to pray: prosperity never.
>   Ben Jonson *Timber*

5 Pray inwardly, even if you do not enjoy it. It does good though you feel nothing, even though you think you are doing nothing.
>   Julian of Norwich *Revelations of Divine Love*

6 Help us, this and every day,
  To live more nearly as we pray.
>   John Keble *The Christian Year*

7 Do not pray for easy lives. Pray to be stronger men.
>   John F. Kennedy Speech 7 February 1963

8 Hold yourself in prayer before God, like a dumb or paralytic beggar at a rich man's gate: let it be your business to keep your mind in the presence of God.
>   Br Lawrence *The Practice and Presence of God*

9 The world has been forced to its knees. Unhappily we seldom find our way there without being beaten to it by suffering.
>   Anne Morrow Lindbergh *The Wave of the Future*

10 Prayer is a strong wall and fortress of the church; it is a good Christian weapon.
>   Martin Luther *Table Talk*

1 God warms his hands at man's heart when he prays.
John Masefield 'The Widow in the Bye Street'

2 Who rises from his prayer a better man, his prayer is answered.
George Meredith *The Ordeal of Richard Feverel*

3 There are few men who dare publish to the world the prayers they make to Almighty God.
Montaigne *Essays* 'Of Prayer'

4 Even the gods are moved by the voice of entreaty.
Ovid *The Art of Love*

5 In his prayers he says 'Thy will be done' but means his own, at least acts so.
William Penn *Some Fruits of Solitude*

6 The people think that they pray before God. But it is not so. For the prayer itself is the essence of the Godhead.
Rabbi Pinhas of Korez *Hasidism*

7 Those who recite the Book of Allah and attend to their prayers and give alms in private and in public may hope for imperishable gain.
The Qur`an

8 Prayer can be like a slow interior bleeding, in which grief and sorrow make the heart's blood of the inner man trickle away silently into his own unfathomed depths.
Karl Rahner *Encounters with Silence*

9 The way through to the vision of the Son of Man and the knowledge of God, which is the heart of contemplative prayer, is by unconditional love of thy neighbour, of the nearest THOU to hand.
Bishop John Robinson *Honest to God*

10 My words fly up, my thoughts remain below.
Words without thoughts never to heaven go.
William Shakespeare *Hamlet* Act III Sc. 3

11 The world may doubt the power of prayer. But the saints know better.
Gilbert Shaw *Homily*

12 Prayer is neither word nor gesture,
Chant nor sound.
It is to be in still communication with our Ground.
Angelus Silesius *The Book of Angelus Silesius*

1 Walk you in remote places crying to Wakonda. Neither eat nor drink for four days. Even though you do not gain power, Wakonda will aid you. If you behave as poor men and pray as you cry, he will aid you.
   Sioux Instruction to a Novice Red Indian spirituality

2 Complaint is the largest tribute Heaven receives, and the sincerest part of our devotion.
   Jonathan Swift *Thoughts on Various Subjects*

3 If you talk to God you are praying; if God talks to you, you have schizophrenia.
   Thomas Szasz *The Second Sin*

4 Her eyes are homes of silent prayer.
   Alfred, Lord Tennyson *In Memoriam*

5 ... More things are wrought by prayer
   Than this world dreams of ...
   Alfred, Lord Tennyson 'The Passing of Arthur'

6 Pray as you can for prayer doesn't consist of thinking a great deal, but of loving a great deal.
   St Teresa of Avila *Mansions of the Interior Castle*

7 A family that prays together stays together.
   Mother Teresa of Calcutta Quoted Kathryn Spink *For the Brotherhood of Man Under the Fatherhood of God*

8 His safest haven was prayer; not of a single moment or idle, but prayer of long devotion ... walking, sitting, eating or drinking, he was always intent upon prayer.
   Thomas of Celano *Life of St Francis*

9 You can't pray a lie.
   Mark Twain *The Adventures of Huckleberry Finn*

10 We should spend as much time in thanking God for His benefits as we do in asking him for them.
   St Vincent de Paul Quoted J.A. Boudignan *St Vincent de Paul*

11 O Lord, thou knowest I have nine houses in the City of London, and have lately purchased an estate in Essex. I beseech thee to preserve the counties of Middlesex and Essex from earthquakes and fire.
   Joshua Ward

12 When the gods wish to punish they answer our prayers.
   Oscar Wilde *An Ideal Husband*

1   Prayer is the greatest of spells, the best healing of all remedies.
      The Yosht Zoroastrianism

2   If you do not pray, everything can disappoint you by going wrong. If you do pray, everything can still go wrong, but not in a way that will disappoint you.
      Hubert van Zeller *Praying While You Work*

PREACHING

3   The priest should preach as a dying man to dying men.
      Richard Baxter Quoted Giles Harcourt *Dawn on Our Darkness*

4   He preaches well that lives well.
      Miguel de Cervantes *Don Quixote*

5   Christ's lore, and His apostles twelve,
    He taught, and first he followed it himself.
      Geoffrey Chaucer *Canterbury Tales*

6   Go forth and preach impostures to the world, but give them truth to build on.
      Dante *The Divine Comedy*

7   People who know how to act are never preachers.
      Ralph Waldo Emerson *Journals*

8   It is no use walking anywhere to preach unless we preach as we walk.
      St Francis of Assisi

9   Truth from his lips prevail'd with double sway,
    And fools, who came to scoff, remained to pray.
      Oliver Goldsmith *The Deserted Village*

10   What do clergy lose by reading their sermons? They lose preaching, the preaching of the voice in many cases, the preaching of the eyes almost always.
      J.C. and A.W. Hare *Guesses at Truth*

11   The preacher's garment is cut according to the pattern of that of the hearers for the most part.
      Oliver Wendell Holmes *Over the Teacups*

12   For the preaching of the cross is to them that perish foolishness; but unto us which are saved it is the power of God.
      Holy Bible 1 Corinthians Chap. 1 v. 18

1   Do not let your deeds belie your words, lest when you speak
    in church someone may say to himself 'Why do you not
    practise what you preach?'
        St Jerome *Letters*

2   A woman's preaching is like a dog's walking on his hinder
    legs. It is not done well, but you are surprised to find it done
    at all.
        Samuel Johnson Quoted Boswell's *Life of Johnson*

3   In truth, sublime words make not a man holy and just, but a
    virtuous life maketh him dear to God.
        Thomas à Kempis *The Imitation of Christ*

4   An orator preaches to get a bishopric, an apostle to save souls;
    the latter deserves what the other aims at.
        Jean de la Bruyère *Characters*

5   He that has but one word of God before him, and out of that
    word cannot make a sermon, can never be a preacher.
        Martin Luther *Table Talk*

6   Only the sinner has the right to preach.
        Christopher Morley Quoted Jonathan Green *The Cynic's
        Lexicon*

7   Preaching should break a hard heart, and heal a broken heart.
        John Newton Quoted Christopher Catherwood *Five Evangelical
        Leaders*

8   An ounce of practice is worth a pound of preaching.
        John Ray *English Proverbs*

9   Preaching has become a by-word for a long and dull
    conversation of any kind, and whoever wishes to imply, in any
    piece of writing, the absence of everything agreeable and
    inviting, calls it a sermon.
        Sydney Smith Quoted Lady Holland *Memoirs*

10 The preaching of divines helps to preserve well-inclined men
    in the course of virtue, but seldom, or never, reclaims the
    vicious.
        Jonathan Swift *Thoughts on Various Subjects*

11 Preach not because you have to say something, but because
    you have something to say.
        Richard Whately *Apophthegms*

1 To preach more than half an hour, a man should be an angel
and have angels for hearers.
   G. Whitefield

PRIDE

2 He hath scattered the proud in the imagination of their hearts.
He hath put down the mighty from their seat: and hath exalted
the humble and meek.
   Book of Common Prayer Magnificat

3 He that is down need fear no fall,
He that is low no pride.
   John Bunyan *The Pilgrim's Progress*

4 Surely pride is harboured within, wherever such mock humility
is so plentifully displayed.
   The Cloud of Unknowing

5 Pride cannot see itself by mid-day light:
The peacock's tail is furthest from his sight!
   Barten Holyday

6 Pride, the never-failing vice of fools.
   Alexander Pope

7 He that fancies he is perfect, may lose that pride which he
attained by grace.
   Thomas Wilson *Maxims of Piety*

PRIESTHOOD

8 There is nothing in the world more easy or agreeable than the
office of a bishop, priest, or deacon if it be performed in a
slight, careless and complying manner; but nothing is more
miserable in itself, or more criminal and unjust in the sight of
God.
   St Augustine of Hippo Quoted *Butler's Lives of the Saints*

9 The Roman Catholic priests are always better or worse than
the Protestant clergy — either intensely devoted to God and
their neighbour, or sly, covetous and sensual.
   Caroline Fox *Journal*

PRINCIPLE

10 Here I stand. I can do no other. God help me. Amen.
   Martin Luther Speech at the Diet of Worms 1521

PROMISE

1 The more seriously we take the future promise of God's
Kingdom, the more unbearable will be the contradictions of
that promise which we meet in the present.
Jürgen Moltmann *The Theology of Hope*

2 Those who are quick to promise are generally slow to perform.
Charles Haddon Spurgeon *Ploughman's Pictures*

PROPHECY

3 In the best prophecies 60% is man, 40% is God. In the usual
prophecies 90% is man, 10% is God.
Fr John Harper 'Sermons: St John-in-the-Fields, St Ives'

4 The voice of one crying in the wilderness, Prepare ye the way
of the Lord, make his paths straight.
Holy Bible St Matthew Chap. 3 v. 3

5 Tell the faithful that Allah has bounteous blessings in store for
them. Do not yield to the unbelievers and hypocrites:
disregard their insolence. Put your trust in Allah; Allah is your
all-sufficient guardian.
The Qur'an

PROPHET

6 It is no use arguing with a prophet, you can only disbelieve him.
Winston Churchill Quoted John Colville *The Churchillians*

7 A prophet is not without honour, save in his own country.
Holy Bible St Matthew Chap. 13 v. 57

8 Saints and prophets are terms used to describe those who most
fully respond to God . . . The false prophet speaks out of the
self-centred conditioning of the world in which he lives.
Gilbert Shaw *Homily*

PROSPERITY

9 The folds shall be full of sheep: the valleys also shall stand so
thick with corn, that they shall laugh and sing.
Book of Common Prayer Psalm 65 v. 14

10 It is beyond our power to explain either the prosperity of the
wicked or the afflictions of the righteous.
The Talmud

PROTECTION

1   He shall defend thee under his wings, and thou shalt be safe under his feathers: his faithfulness and truth shall be thy shield and buckler.
>   *Book of Common Prayer* Psalm 91 v. 4

PROTESTANT

2   A real Protestant is a person who has examined the evidences of religion for himself and who accepts them because, after examination, he is satisfied of their genuineness and sufficiency.
>   J.A. Hammerton *Modern Frenchmen*

3   The Catholic must adopt the decision handed down to him; the Protestant must learn to decide for himself.
>   Jean-Jacques Rousseau *Confessions*

4   Ants are not only essentially Pelagian, but also exponents of the coarser aspects of the Protestant ethic; work hard for material success and the Lord will reward you.
>   Martin Thornton *The Joyous Heart*

PROVIDENCE

5   The Lord will provide, dear, but you must give Him some help.
>   Sir Hugh Casson Quoted Joyce Grenfell *Nanny Says*

6   There is nothing so small or apparently indifferent which God does not ordain or permit even to the fall of a leaf.
>   Jean-Pierre de Caussade SJ *Treatise*

7   There is nothing more agreeable than to find Providence dislikes the same people that we do. It adds to our good opinion of providence.
>   Frank Moore Colby *The Colby Essays*

8   Take therefore no thought for the morrow: for the morrow shall take thought for the things of itself. Sufficient unto the day is the evil thereof.
>   *Holy Bible* St Matthew Chap. 6 v. 34

9   The wisdom of providence is as much revealed in the rarity of genius, as in the circumstance that not everyone is deaf or blind.
>   Georg Christoph Lichtenberg *Aphorisms*

1 Men almost universally have acknowledged a Providence, but that fact has no force to destroy natural aversions and fears in the presence of events.

George Santayana *The Life of Reason* 'Reason in Religion'

2 Dear God, we pray not that wrecks shouldn't happen, but if it be Thy will that they do, we pray Thee let them be for the benefit of Thy poor people of Scilly.

Parson Troutbeck, Chaplain to the Scilly Isles Quoted F.E. Halliday *A History of Cornwall*

3 Trust in the providence of God is not a heaven-sent formula for the indolent, not a way of bypassing responsibility with regard to social and material concerns . . . you have to take on the affairs that come your way, knowing that they come from God and must be steered back again to him.

Hubert van Zeller *Leave Your Life Alone*

PSALMS

4 Shew ourselves glad in him with psalms.

Book of Common Prayer Psalm 95 v. 2

5 It is worth while to have a *storm* of abuse once in a while, for *one* reason to read the Psalms — they are a radiant field of glory that never shines unless the night shuts in.

Harriet Beecher Stowe Quoted Catherine Gilbertson *Harriet Beecher Stowe*

PUNISHMENT

6 A rod is for the back of him that is void of understanding.

Holy Bible Proverbs Chap. 10 v. 13

7 A whip for the horse, a bridle for the ass, and a rod for the fool's back.

Holy Bible Proverbs Chap. 26 v. 3

8 What can only be taught by the rod and with blows will not lead to much good: they will not remain pious any longer than the rod is behind them.

Martin Luther *The Great Catechism* 'Second Command'

PURITAN

9 A puritan is a person who pours righteous indignation into the wrong things.

G.K. Chesterton

1 To the puritan all things are impure.
    D.H. Lawrence *Etruscan Places*

2 The old Puritans took away the maypoles and the mince pies, but they did not bring in the millennium, they only brought in the Restoration.
    C.S. Lewis Lecture, University College of North Wales 1941

3 Puritanism is the haunting fear that someone, somewhere, may be happy.
    H.L. Mencken *A Book of Burlesques*

4 The objection to Puritans is not that they try to make us think as they do, but that they try to make us do as they think.
    H.L. Mencken *Prejudices*

5 Puritanism is an attitude of mind which singles out an essential quality and refuses to enrich it with subsidiary qualities.
    Eric Newton *European Painting and Sculpture*

6 The virtues of enterprise, diligence and thrift are the indispensable foundations of any complex and vigorous civilisation. It was Puritanism which, by investing them with a supernatural sanction, turned them from an unsocial eccentricity into a habit, a religion.
    R.H. Tawney *Religion and the Rise of Capitalism*

PURITY

7 When he has no lust, no hatred, a man walks safely among the things of lust and hatred.
    Bhagavad Gita

8 Unto the pure, all things are pure.
    Holy Bible Titus Chap. 1 v. 15

9 There cannot be perfect transformation without perfect pureness.
    St John of the Cross *The Ascent of Mount Carmel*

10 Our eyes may see some uncleanness, but let not our mind see things that are not clean. Our ears may hear some uncleanness, but let not our mind hear things that are not clean.
    Shinto prayer

11 Purity is the ability to contemplate defilement.
    Simone Weil *Gravity and Grace*

PURPOSE

1 The Almighty has his own purposes.
   Abraham Lincoln Second Inaugural Address 4 March 1865

2 If people want a sense of purpose they should get it from
  the archbishops and not from politicians.
   Harold Macmillan

QUAKERISM

1 This is the comfort of Friends, that though they may be said to Die, yet their Friendship and Society are, in the best sense, ever present because *Immortal*.
   William Penn *Some Fruits of Solitude*

2 I asked a Quaker friend to describe the essence of his faith. 'No pomp', he replied, 'under any circumstance.'
   Edward Stevenson *Reader's Digest* June 1982

3 The Catholic Church is a church of sinners in the sense that the Quaker Church is a church of saints.
   Shirley Williams *Observer* 22 March 1981

QUARRELLING

4 Most quarrels are inevitable at the time; incredible afterwards.
   E.M. Forster

5 For souls in growth, great quarrels are great emancipators.
   Logan Pearsall Smith *All Trivia* 'Afterthoughts'

QUIETNESS

6 If we have not quiet in our minds, outward comfort will do no more for us than a golden slipper on a gouty foot.
   John Bunyan

7 In quietness and in confidence shall be your strength.
   Holy Bible Isaiah Chap. 30 v. 15

8 Happiness is the harvest of a quiet eye.
   Austin O'Malley

9 Sometimes quiet is disquieting.
   Seneca Epistle 56

10 The holy time is quiet as a nun.
   William Wordsworth 'It is a Beauteous Evening'

RACISM

1 Whites must be made to realise that they are only human, not superior. Same with blacks. They must be made to realise that they are also human, not inferior.
   Steve Biko

2 Skin colour does not matter to God, for he is looking upon the heart ... When men are standing at the foot of the cross there are no racial barriers.
   Billy Graham

3 A doctrine of black supremacy is as evil as a doctrine of white supremacy.
   Martin Luther King *The Words of Martin Luther King*

4 We shall match your capacity to inflict suffering with our capacity to endure suffering. Do to us what you will and we shall continue to love you.
   Martin Luther King *Strength to Love*

5 I think God is silly because he should have painted everybody the same colour and then they wouldn't fight.
   Ricardo, aged 7 Quoted Nanette Newman *Lots of Love*

6 Thank God I am black. White people will have a lot to answer for at the last judgement.
   Archbishop Desmond Tutu

READING

7 Read not to contradict and confute, nor to believe and take for granted, nor to find talk and discourse, but to weigh and consider.
   Francis Bacon *Essays* 'Of Studies'

8 If thou wilt receive profit, read with humility, simplicity and faith; and seek not at any time the fame of being learned.
   Thomas à Kempis *The Imitation of Christ*

REASON

1 Reason in man is rather like God in the world.
   St Thomas Aquinas *Opuscule XI*

2 Let craft, ambition, spite,
   Be quenched in Reason's night,
   Till weakness turn to might,
   Till what is dark be light,
   Till what is wrong be right!
   Lewis Carroll 'The Warden's Charm'

3 Reason in itself is a matter of faith. It is an act of faith to
   assert that our thoughts have any relation to reality at all.
   G.K. Chesterton *Orthodoxy*

4 Reason is a God-given faculty, and is to be valued
   enormously, but you must put it in its right place. And the
   right place is certainly not when it says, like a blind man in a
   sunlit garden, 'Anything I can't see doesn't exist.'
   Michael Green *Jesus Spells Freedom*

5 The heart has its reasons of which reason knows nothing.
   Blaise Pascal *Pensées* 'Apology'

6 Reason is God's crowning gift to man.
   Sophocles *Antigone*

REASSURANCE

7 Do not think meanly of yourself and do not despair of
   perfection.
   Moses Maimonides Quoted Giles Harcourt *Dawn of Our
   Darkness*

REBELLION

8 Watch over your heart that you may not give way, in the very
   least to bitterness, spite, complaints or voluntary rebellion.
   Jean-Pierre de Caussade SJ *Self-Abandonment to Divine
   Providence*

REBUKE

9 Reprove not a scorner, lest he hate thee; rebuke a wise man,
   and he will love thee.
   Holy Bible Proverbs Chap. 9 v. 8

RECOMPENSE

1 How can we ever be sold short, or cheated, we who for every service have long ago been overpaid?
Meister Eckhart

RECONCILIATION

2 Whosoever shall smite thee on thy right cheek, turn to him the other also.
Holy Bible St Matthew Chap. 5 v. 39

3 When powers and institutions are reconciled to God, they become more modest, and take on their proper place in His purposes.
Bishop David Sheppard *Bias to the Poor* 'Human Hearts and Social Structures'

4 Some people think reconciliation is a soft option, that it means papering over the cracks. But the biblical meaning means looking facts in the face and it can be very costly; it cost God the death of his own son.
Archbishop Desmond Tutu Quoted Peter Godwin *Sunday Times Magazine* 8 June 1986

REDEMPTION

5 He became what we are that he might make us what he is.
St Athanasius of Alexandria *De Incarnatione*

6 The great Christian invitation is to be asked by Christ to share in his redemptive work — to enter into Jerusalem with him.
Fr Peter Ball CGA Conference at Swanwick 1985

7 No one can be redeemed by another. No God and no saint is able to shield a man from the consequence of his evil doings. Every one of us must become his own redeemer.
Subhadna Bhikshu Buddhist spirituality

8 Blessed be the Lord God of Israel: for He hath visited, and redeemed his people.
Book of Common Prayer Order of Morning Prayer 'Benedictus' St Luke Chap. 1 v. 68

9 I know that my Redeemer liveth, and that he shall stand at the latter day upon the earth.
Book of Common Prayer Order of the Burial of the Dead Job Chap. 19 v. 25

1   Never be misled by the thought that after failing and sinning
there can be no forgiveness. Look critically at your own
shortcomings, but be sure that, with the Lord, there is always
abundance of redemption.

> Brakkenstein Community of Blessed Sacrament Fathers, Holland
> *Rule for a New Brother*

2   If Christ offers us up with his own death in this sacrament, it is
that we may die a voluntary and daily death, and merit a daily
resurrection.

> Austin Farrer *The Crown of the Year*

3   Arise, shine; for thy light is come, and the glory of the Lord is
risen upon thee.

> *Holy Bible* Isaiah Chap. 60 v. 1

4   If you are cut down in a movement that is designed to save the
soul of a nation, then no other death could be more
redemptive.

> Martin Luther King *The Words of Martin Luther King*

5   I did not think, I did not strive,
The deep peace burnt my me alive:
The bolted door had broken in,
I knew that I had done with sin.
I knew that Christ had given me birth
To brother all the souls on earth,
And every bird and every beast
Should share the crumbs broke at the feast.

> John Masefield 'The Everlasting Mercy'

6   In prayer ... the perfections of God, and especially his
mercies in our redemption, should occupy our thoughts as
much as our sins; our obligation to him as much as our
departure from him.

> Hannah More *Practical Piety*

7   Sin is always loving badly, or not loving at all.
Redemption is Jesus Christ restoring to the world the full
weight of Love, of which man robbed it through his sin.

> Michel Quoist *With Open Mind*

8   What does being redeemed in Christ mean if you are a Jew
about to be gassed?

> Robert Runcie, Archbishop of Canterbury Quoted John
> Mortimer *In Character*

1   Oh, foolish Christians
Who think you can attain redemption
While with your bodies and your souls
Remain attached to worldly goals.
     Angelus Silesius *The Book of Angelus Silesius*

2   There is nothing in this world or the next which cannot, and
will not, be turned into the valid currency we need to buy the
one pearl of great price. That is what is meant when we say
that we are redeemed.
     H.A. Williams CR *The True Wilderness*

REFORM

3   It is very insulting to attempt to reform people. When you
behead a person you leave his soul as it is. But when you
reform him you change his soul, and it is a dangerous thing to
tamper with human souls.
     Don Marquis *The Almost Perfect State*

REFORMATION

4   The invention of printing and the Reformation are and remain
the two outstanding services of central Europe to the cause of
humanity.
     Thomas Mann *The Magic Mountain*

REFUGE

5   No devotee of mine is ever lost. Take refuge in Me and you
reach the highest goal.
     Bhagavad Gita

6   The eternal God is thy refuge, and underneath are the
everlasting arms.
     Holy Bible Deuteronomy Chap. 33 v. 27

REINCARNATION

7   I held that when a person dies
His soul returns again to earth;
Arrayed in some new flesh-disguise
Another mother gives him birth.
With sturdier limbs and brighter brain
The old soul takes the roads again.
     John Masefield 'A Creed'

1 I do not know whether I was then a man dreaming I was a
butterfly, or whether I am now a butterfly dreaming I am a
man.
Chuang Tzu *On Levelling All Things*

RELATIONSHIP

2 Relationship *is* life, and this relationship is a constant
movement, a constant change.
Krishnamurti *You Are the World*

3 You couldn't make everyone in the world love each other.
They don't even get on in blocks of flats.
Lois, aged 7 Quoted Nanette Newman *Lots of Love*

4 When a man realises that he is a beloved child of the Creator
of all, then he is ready to see his neighbours in the world as
brothers and sisters.
Robert Runcie, Archbishop of Canterbury Quoted *Prayers for
Peace*

5 Christianity is not a religion, it is a relationship.
Dr Thieme

RELIGION

6 We use religion like a 'bus — we ride on it only while it is
going our way.
Anon

7 God is much more beautiful than Religion. Trials enable
people to rise above Religion to God.
Fr Andrew SDC *Letters of Fr Andrew SDC*

8 Religion is not proficiency in the fine art of spiritual
knowledge, but just the love of God and our neighbour.
Fr Andrew SDC *Life and Letters*

9 Religion bestoweth upon man the most precious of all gifts,
offereth the cup of prosperity, imparteth eternal life, and
showereth imperishable benefits upon mankind.
Bahá'u'Uáh, founder of the Baha'i faith Quoted *Prayers for
Peace*

10 One's religion is whatever one is most interested in.
J.M. Barrie *The Twelve Pound Look*

11 Man is by his constitution a religious animal.
Edmund Burke Letter to William Smith 29 January 1795

1   Nothing is so fatal to religion as indifference.
     Edmund Burke *Ibid.*

2   One religion is as true as another.
     Robert Burton *The Anatomy of Melancholy*

3   It is the purpose of temporal rule ... to foster and support the
     external worship of God, to defend pure doctrine and the
     standing of the Church, to conform our lives to human society,
     to mould our conduct to civil justice, to harmonise us with
     each other and to preserve the common peace and tranquillity.
     John Calvin *Institutes of the Christian Religion*

4   Religion is by no means a proper subject of conversation in a
     mixed company.
     Lord Chesterfield Undated letter to his godson

5   The old religionist cried out for his God. The new religionist
     cries out for some god to be his.
     G.K. Chesterton *All Things Considered*

6   A cosmic philosophy is not constructed to fit a man, a cosmic
     philosophy is constructed to fit a cosmos. A man can no more
     possess a private religion than he can possess a private sun or
     moon.
     G.K. Chesterton *The Book of Job*

7   Man will wrangle for religion; write for it; fight for it; die for
     it; anything but live for it.
     Charles Caleb Colton

8   Where true religion has prevented a crime, false religions have
     provided a pretext for a thousand.
     Charles Caleb Colton *Lacon*

9   In my religion there would be no exclusive doctrine, all would
     be love, poetry and doubt.
     Cyril Connolly *The Unquiet Grave*

10   The cosmic religious experience is the strongest and the
     noblest driving force behind scientific research.
     Albert Einstein

11   God builds his temple in the heart of ruins of churches and
     religions.
     Ralph Waldo Emerson *The Conduct of Life* 'Worship'

12   Religious talk is a very feast to self-deceit.
     Frederick W. Faber *Spiritual Conferences*

1   Religion means binding together.
    Gonville ffrench-Beytagh *A Glimpse of Glory*

2   When I mention religion I mean the Christian religion, not
    only the Christian religion, but the Protestant religion; and not
    only the Protestant religion, but the Church of England.
    Henry Fielding *Tom Jones*

3   If men are so wicked with religion, what would they be
    without it?
    Benjamin Franklin

4   Nature teaches us to love our friends, but religion our
    enemies.
    Thomas Fuller *Gnomologia*

5   Religion is not what you will get after reading all the scriptures
    of the world. It is not really what is grasped by the brain. It is
    a heart grasp.
    Gandhi Quoted *News Chronicle* Obituary 31 January 1948

6   All sects seem to me to be right in what they assert, and wrong
    in what they deny.
    Goethe *Conversations with Goethe* Ed. J.P. Eckermann

7   Religion either makes men wise and virtuous, or it makes
    them set up false pretences to both.
    William Hazlitt *The Round Table* 'On Religious Hypocrisy'

8   Religion, credit and the eyes are not to be touched.
    George Herbert *Jacula Prudentum*

9   If any man among you seem to be religious, and bridleth not
    his tongue, but deceiveth his own heart, this man's religion is
    vain.
    Holy Bible James Chap. 1 v. 26

10 Pure religion and undefiled before God the Father is this, To
    visit the fatherless and widows in their affliction, and to keep
    himself unspotted from the world.
    Holy Bible James Chap. 1 v. 27

11 Religion is always a patron of the arts but its taste is by no
    means impeccable.
    Aldous Huxley *Tomorrow and Tomorrow and Tomorrow*

12 Religion is caught, not taught.
    Dean W.R. Inge

1 Religion has not civilised man, man has civilised religion.
   Robert Green Ingersoll

2 Religion's in the heart, not in the knee.
   Douglas Jerrold *The Devil's Ducat*

3 One man finds in religion his literature and his science;
   another finds in it his joy and his duty.
   Joseph Joubert *Pensées*

4 Science investigates; religion interprets. Science gives man
   knowledge; religion gives man wisdom which is control.
   Martin Luther King *The Words of Martin Luther King*

5 Do not call yourself Lutherans, call yourself Christians. Has
   Luther been crucified for the world?
   Martin Luther

6 Religion without mystery ceases to be religion.
   William Thomas Manning Sermon 2 February 1930

7 Man makes religion: religion does not make man. Religion is
   indeed man's self-consciousness and self-awareness so long as
   he has not found himself or has lost himself again.

8 Religion is the sigh of the oppressed creatures, the heart of a
   heartless world, just as it is the soul of soulless conditions. It is
   the opium of the people.
   Karl Marx *Critique of Hegel's Philosophy of Right*

9 We give people a dose of religion, when they are looking for
   an encounter with the Living God.
   F.D. Maurice Quoted Kenneth Pillar in letter to Margaret
   Pepper

10 Religion is always revolutionary, far more revolutionary than
   bread and butter philosophies.
   Henry Miller *The Air-Conditioned Nightmare*

11 Religion is an attempt, a noble attempt, to suggest in human
   terms more than human realities.
   Christopher Morley *Religio Journalistica*

12 Religion is a candle inside a multi-coloured lantern. Everyone
   looks through a particular colour but the candle is always
   there.
   Mohammed Neguib, Egyptian Head of State Speech
   31 December 1953

1 Religion indeed enlightens, terrifies, subdues, it gives faith, it inflicts remorse, it inspires resolutions, it draw tears, it inflames devotion, but only for the occasion.

2 True religion is slow in growth, and when once planted is difficult of dislodgement, but its intellectual counterfeit has no root in itself. It springs up suddenly, it suddenly withers.
   John Henry, Cardinal Newman *The Idea of a University*

3 Religion is a process of turning your skull into a tabernacle, not of going up to Jerusalem once a year.
   Austin O'Malley

4 Religion is so great a thing that it is right that those who will not take the trouble to seek it, if it be obscure, should be deprived of it.
   Blaise Pascal *Pensées*

5 To be furious in religion is to be unreligiously religious.
   William Penn *Some Fruits of Solitude*

6 Religions which have any strong hold over men's actions have generally some instinctive basis.
   Bertrand Russell *Marriage and Morals*

7 Religion is the love of life in the consciousness of impotence.
   George Santayana *Winds of Doctrine*

8 Religion should be disentangled as much as possible from history and authority and metaphysics, and made to rest honestly on one's finer feelings, on one's indomitable optimism and trust in life.
   George Santayana *Character and Opinion in the United States*

9 Men say they are of the same religion for quietness sake, but if the matter were well examined, you would scarce find those anywhere of the same religion in all points.
   John Selden *Table Talk* 'Religion'

10 There is only one religion, though there are a hundred versions of it.
   George Bernard Shaw

11 Religion pervades intensely the whole frame of society, and is according to the temper of the mind which it inhabits, a passion, a persuasion, an excuse, a refuge; never a check.
   Percy Bysshe Shelley *The Cenci* Preface

1 Extreme happiness invites religion almost as much as extreme
misery.
>Dodie Smith *I Capture the Castle*

2 Religion has nothing more to fear than not being sufficiently
understood.
>Stanislaus I of Poland *Maxims*

3 All religion relates to life, and the life of religion is to do good.
>Emanuel Swedenborg *Doctrine of Life*

4 We have just enough religion to make us hate, but not enough
to make us love one another.
>Jonathan Swift *Thoughts on Various Subjects*

5 In religion our exclusions are nearly always wrong, and our
inclusions, however inconsistent, nearly always right.
>Evelyn Underhill *The Letters of Evelyn Underhill*

6 What a travesty to think religion means saving my little soul
through my little good deeds and the rest of the world go
hang.
>Gerald Vann *The Heart of Man*

7 Educate men without religion and you make them but clever
devils.
>Duke of Wellington 'Remarks'

8 Some people have just enough religion to make them feel
uncomfortable.
>John Wesley

9 The fact of the religious vision, and its history of persistent
expansion, is our one ground of optimism. Apart from it,
human life is a flash of occasional enjoyments lighting up a
mess of pain and misery, a bagatelle of transient experience.
>Alfred North Whitehead *Science and the Modern World*

10 Religion is the fashionable substitute for belief.
>Oscar Wilde *The Portrait of Dorian Grey*

11 I would rather think of my religion as a gamble than think of it
as an insurance policy.
>Attributed to Stephen Samuel Wise

12 Of the one light of Truth teach us to see in every religion a
several ray.
>Zoroastrian spirituality

REMEMBRANCE

1 They shall grow not old, as we that are left grow old:
Age shall not weary them, nor the years condemn.
At the going down of the sun and in the morning
We will remember them.
   Laurence Binyon 'For the Fallen'

REMORSE

2 Remorse, the fatal egg by pleasure laid.
   William Cowper *The Progress of Error*

3 You cannot lay remorse upon the innocent nor lift it from the
heart of the guilty. Unbidden shall it call in the night, that men
may wake and gaze upon themselves.
   Kahlil Gibran *The Prophet*

4 Remorse does but add to the evil which bred it, when it
promotes not penitence, but despair.
   Arthur Helps *Friends in Council*

5 Chronic remorse is a most undesirable sentiment. Rolling in
the muck is no way of getting clean.
   Aldous Huxley *Brave New World*

6 Remorse is pride's *ersatz* for repentance.
   Aldous Huxley *Time Must Have a Stop*

7 Remorse is impotence, it will sin again. Only repentance is
strong, it can end everything.
   Henry Miller *The Wisdom of the Heart*

8 Remorse sleeps during prosperity, but awakes to bitter
consciousness during adversity.
   Jean-Jacques Rousseau *Confessions*

9 Remorse at feeling no remorse is a form of the holiest
contrition.
   Logan Pearsall Smith *All Trivia* 'Afterthoughts'

RENEWAL

10 One often has more delight finding refreshment anew than one
ever had grief in its loss.
   Jean-Pierre de Caussade SJ *Self-Abandonment to Divine
Providence*

1 Charismatic Renewal fostered loyalty to the Church, recourse
to the Sacraments, love of the Scriptures, a spirit of confidence
and hope, growth in prayer — especially spontaneous prayer of
praise and thanksgiving — and an awareness of God's
presence, in particular of the Holy Spirit.
>   Cardinal Suenens Quoted Elizabeth Hamilton *Cardinal
>   Suenens — A Portrait*

2 As water, lifted from the deep again,
Falls back in individual drops of rain
Then melts into the universal main.
All you have been, and seen, and done, and thought.
Not you, but I have seen and been and wrought.
>   *The Wisdom of the Sufis* Compiled by Kenneth Cragg

REPENTANCE

3 Repentance is good, but innocence better.
>   Anon

4 The sinning is the best part of repentance.
>   Arab proverb

5 The seeds of repentance are sown in youth by pleasure, but
the harvest is reaped in age by pain.
>   Charles Caleb Colton *Lacon*

6 Amendment is repentance.
>   Thomas Fuller *Gnomologia*

7 Who after his trangression doth repent,
Is half, or altogether, innocent.
>   Robert Herrick 'Penitence'

8 Set thine house in order: for thou shalt die, and not live.
>   *Holy Bible* Isaiah Chap. 38 v. 1

9 Repent ye; for the Kingdom of Heaven is at hand.
>   *Holy Bible* St Matthew Chap. 3 v. 2

10 I am not come to call the righteous, but sinners to repentance.
>   *Holy Bible* St Matthew Chap. 9 v. 13

11 The sun and every vassal star,
All space, beyond the soar of angel wings,
Wait on His word; and yet He stays His ear
For every sigh a contrite suppliant brings.
>   John Keble *The Christian Year* 'Ascension Day'

1 We shall have to repent in this generation, not so much for the evil deeds of the wicked people, but for the appalling silence of the good people.
  Martin Luther King

2 Our repentance is not so much regret for the evil we have done as a fear of what may happen to us because of it.
  François, Duc de la Rochefoucauld *Maxims*

3 Whatever is foolish, ridiculous, vain or earthly, or sensual, in the life of a Christian is something that ought not to be there. It is a spot and a defilement that must be washed away with tears of repentance.
  William Law *A Serious Call to a Devout and Holy Life*

4 The true physician does not preach repentance, he offers absolution.
  H.L. Mencken *Prejudices*

5 Confess yourself to heaven;
  Repent what's past; avoid what is to come.
  William Shakespeare *Hamlet* Act III Sc. 4

6 He punishes himself who repents of his deeds.
  Publilius Syrus *Moral Sayings*

7 The repentant say never a brave word. Their resolves should be mumbled in silence.
  Henry David Thoreau *Journal*

8 The repentance of man is accepted by God as a virtue.
  Voltaire *Philosophical Dictionary*

9 It can take less than a minute to commit a sin. It takes not as long to obtain God's forgiveness. Penitence and amendment should take a lifetime.
  Hubert van Zeller

REPUTATION

10 The invisible thing called 'GOOD NAME' is made up of the breath of numbers that speak well of you.
  Lord Halifax *Works*

11 The purest treasure mortal times afford
  Is spotless reputation.
  William Shakespeare *King Richard II* Act I Sc. 1

RESIGNATION

1 When the house in Washington of Thomas Hart Benton
(1782–1858), the American senator, was destroyed by fire he
was summoned from Congress to view the ruin. He gazed at it
for a while and then said: 'It makes dying easier. There is so
much less to leave.'
    Edmund Fuller *Anecdotes*

2 It's no use crying over spilt milk.
    W.S. Gilbert *Foggerty's Fairy*

3 It is hard for thee to kick against the pricks.
    Holy Bible Acts Chap. 9 v. 5

4 Be still, be still, my soul; it is but for a season:
Let us endure an hour and see injustice done.
    A.E. Housman *A Shropshire Lad*

5 My bags are packed and I am ready to go.
    Pope John XXIII

6 We cannot conquer fate and necessity, yet we can yield to
them in such a manner as to be greater than if we could.
    Walter Savage Landor *Imaginary Conversations* 'Marius Tullius
    and Quinctus Cicero'

7 I have changed my mind in this sense, that whereas yesterday I
intended being shaved before execution, I have now changed
my mind and intend that my beard shall go with my head.
    Sir Thomas More, at his execution

8 Give me, good Lord, a humble, lowly, quiet, peaceable,
patient, charitable, kind, tender and pitiful mind; with all my
works and all my words and all my thoughts to have a taste of
the holy blessed spirit.
    Sir Thomas More His own prayer for use whilst in the Tower

9 God's plans, like lilies, pure and white, unfold;
We must not tear the close-shut leaves apart;
Time will reveal the chalices of gold.
    Mary Louise Riley Smith 'Sometimes'

RESPECT

10 Without feelings of respect, what is there to distinguish men
from beasts?
    Confucius *Analects*

RESPONSIBILITY

1   A wrong decision can make me very miserable. But I have trust in God. If you have this trust you don't have to worry, as you don't have sole responsibility.
      Lord Denning, on retiring as a judge September 1982

2   Lay on us the burden of the world's suffering, and drive us forth with the apostolic fervour of the early Church.
      John Wilhelm Rowntree *International Responsibilities*

REST

3   You have made us for yourself, and our hearts are restless till they find their rest in you.
      St Augustine of Hippo

4   The end and the reward of toil is rest.
      James Beattie 'Ease of Life'

5   Absence of occupation is not rest,
      A mind quite vacant is a mind distress'd.
      William Cowper 'Retirement'

6   Rest comes at length, though life be long and dreary;
      The day must dawn, and darksome night be passed.
      Frederick W. Faber 'Hark, Hark My Soul'

7   And He rested on the seventh day from all his work.
      Holy Bible Genesis Chap. 2 v. 2

8   Come unto me, all ye that labour and are heavy laden, and I will give you rest.
      Holy Bible St Matthew Chap. 11 v. 28

9   No soul can have rest until it finds created things are empty. When the soul gives up all for love, so that it can have Him that is all, then it finds true rest.
      Julian of Norwich *Revelations of Divine Love*

10   We wish him health, he sighs for rest,
      And Heaven accepts the prayer.
      John Keble *The Christian Year* 'Restoration of the Royal Family'

11   Sleep after toil, port after stormy seas,
      Ease after war, death after life does greatly please.
      Edmund Spenser *The Faerie Queene* Book 1

RESURRECTION

1 Those coming out of church . . .
   . . . spread all over the churchyard. They scan
   The crowd, recognise, smile and shake hands.
   By each tombstone a well-dressed person stands.
   It looks just like the Resurrection.
       Patricia Beer 'Concert at Long Melford Church'

2 Jesus's resurrection makes it impossible for man's story to end
   in chaos — it has to move inexorably towards light, towards
   life, towards love.
       Carlo Carretto *The Desert in the City*

3 I danced on a Friday
   When the sky turned black;
   It's hard to dance
   With the devil on your back.
   They buried my body
   And they thought I'd gone
   But I am the dance and I still go on.
       Sydney Carter *100 Hymns Today*

4 Christ has turned all our sunsets into dawns.
       St Clement of Alexandria

5 The Resurrection is not a miracle like any other. It is a unique
   manifestation within this world of the transition God makes
   for us out of this way of being into another.
       Austin Farrer *Saving Belief*

6 Up, and away,
   Thy Saviour's gone before.
   Why dost thou stay,
   Dull soul?
       George Herbert 'The Resurrection'

7 I am the resurrection, and the life: he that believeth in me,
   though he were dead, yet shall he live: and whosoever liveth
   and believeth in me shall never die.
       Holy Bible St John Chap. 1 vv. 25–26

8 Now is Christ risen from the dead, and become the first fruits
   of them that slept. For since by man came death, by man came
   also the resurrection of the dead.
       Holy Bible 1 Corinthians Chap. 15 vv. 20–21

1   The day of resurrection. Earth tell it out abroad!
    The Passover of gladness, the Passover of God.
    From death to life eternal, from this world to the sky,
    Our Christ has brought us over, with hymns of victory.
    St John of Damascus 'The Day of Resurrection'

2   I accept the resurrection of Jesus not as an invention of the
    community of disciples, but as an historical event.
    Pinchas Lapide *The Resurrection of Jesus*

3   In the bonds of Death He lay,
    Who for our offence was slain;
    But the Lord is risen today,
    Christ hath brought us life again.
    Wherefore let us all rejoice,
    Singing loud, with cheerful voice, Hallelujah.
    Martin Luther 'In the Bonds of Death'

4   The strife is o'er, the battle done;
    Now is our Victor's triumph won;
    O let the song of praise be sung,
    'Alleluia!'
    G.P. da Palestrina Hymn

5   To renounce all is to gain all; to descend is to rise; to die is to
    live.
    Karl Rahner

6   Every parting gives a foretaste of death; every coming
    together again a foretaste of the Resurrection.
    Arthur Schopenhauer

7   Christianity is in its very essence a resurrection religion. The
    concept of resurrection lies at its heart. If you remove it,
    Christianity is destroyed.
    John R. Stott

8   I think the resurrection of the body, unless much improved in
    construction, a mistake.
    Evelyn Underhill *Letters*

9   When every argument has been considered and weighed, the
    only conclusion acceptable to the historian must be that the
    women who set out to pay their last respects to Jesus found to
    their consternation not a body, but an empty tomb.
    Geza Vermes *Jesus the Jew*

1   Lift your voices in triumph on high,
    For Jesus is risen and man cannot die.
        Henry Ware 'Lift Your Glad Voices'

2   This is our destiny in heaven — to be like Christ: not Christ
    limited, as he was on earth, to the confines of time and flesh,
    but Christ risen, the great, free, timeless Christ of the Easter
    morning.
        David Winter *Hereafter*

3   'Good to have you back, son,' the old man said.
        'Nice to be back.'
        'You've had a rough time.' The eyes clouded with guilt.
    'Hope you don't think I let you down.'
        The younger shook his head — 'You warned me, dad. But it
    wasn't the nails. It was the kiss.'
        Roger Woddis Quoted *The Book of Mini Sagas*

4   Without the resurrection, at the name of Jesus every knee
    would not bow; more likely, people would say, 'Jesus, who?'
        John Young *The Case Against Christ*

RETREAT

5   Churches are best for prayer that have least light:
    To see God only, I go out of sight.
        John Donne 'A Hymn to Christ'

6   Religion in this world needs the refurbishing which is provided
    by retreats. But a retreat is not merely the run back so as to
    spring forward: it is the sitting in prepared positions.
        Hubert van Zeller *Praying While You Work*

RETRIBUTION

7   Many of our most futile prayers are attempts to dodge the
    divinely established fact that we reap what we sow.
        David Head *He Sent Leanness*

8   Eye for eye, tooth for tooth, hand for hand, foot for foot,
    burning for burning, wound for wound, stripe for stripe.
        Holy Bible Exodus Chap. 21 vv. 24–25

9   Heap coals of fire upon his head.
        Holy Bible Proverbs Chap. 25 v. 22

10 They have sown the wind, and they shall reap the whirlwind.
        Holy Bible Hosea Chap. 8 v. 7

1   For the wrath of God is revealed from heaven against all
    ungodliness and unrighteousness of men, who hold the truth in
    unrighteousness.
    Holy Bible Romans Chap. 1 v. 18

REVELATION

2   The end of my labours is come. All that I have written
    appears to be as so much straw after the things that have been
    revealed to me.
    St Thomas Aquinas, on being urged to finish his Summa
    Theologica Quoted *Calendar of Saints*

3   To see a World in a Grain of Sand
    And a Heaven in a Wild Flower
    Hold Infinity in the palm of your hand
    An Eternity in an hour.
    William Blake 'Auguries of Innocence'

4   And the glory of the Lord shall be revealed, and all flesh shall
    see it together: for the mouth of the Lord hath spoken it.
    Holy Bible Isaiah Chap. 40 v. 5

5   The world is charged with the grandeur of God.
    Gerard Manley Hopkins 'God's Grandeur'

6   A dark night through which the soul passes in order to attain
    to the Divine light of the perfect union of the love of God.
    St John of the Cross *The Ascent of Mount Carmel*

7   My soul, sit thou a patient looker-on;
    Judge not the play before the play is done:
    Her plot hath many changes; every day
    Speaks a new scene; the last act crowns the play.
    Francis Quarles 'Respice Finem'

8   Biblical revelation has given the church the tools for
    understanding society, discerning justice from injustice,
    understanding conflict and meeting people where their need is
    People don't want superglue. Why are we wasting our time
    wandering round old grave-yards?
    Elaine Storkey Speech to the General Synod November 1987

9   We affirm, then, that unless all existence is a medium of
    Revelation, no particular revelation is possible.
    Archbishop William Temple *Nature, Man and God*

REVENGE

1 The best way of revenge is to avoid imitating the injury.
   Marcus Aurelius

2 Revenge is a kind of wild justice, which the more man's nature runs to, the more ought law to weed it out.
   Francis Bacon *Essays 'Of Revenge'*

3 Revenge, at first, though sweet —
   Bitter ere long, back on itself recoils.
   John Milton *Paradise Lost*

4 It is not right to return an injury or to do evil to any man, however one may have suffered from him.
   Plato *Crito*

5 If it will feed nothing else, it will feed my revenge.
   William Shakespeare *The Merchant of Venice* Act III Sc. 1

6 It costs more to revenge injuries than to bear them.
   Thomas Wilson *Maxims*

REVERENCE

7 When John Vianney, Curé d'Ars, was asked by a peasant what he said at his daily evening vigil, he said, 'I don't say anything, I look at Him and He looks at me.'
   Christopher Bryant SSJE 'Contemplation in the Christian Spiritual Tradition' Lecture October 1978

8 I ought to feel free, yet I cannot keep my hat on in church, even when no one is looking.
   E.M. Forster Quoted Raymond Mortimer *Try Anything Once*

REWARD

9 The 'wages' of every noble work do yet lie in Heaven or else nowhere.
   Thomas Carlyle *Past and Present*

10 Cast thy bread upon the waters: for thou shalt find it after many days.
   Holy Bible Ecclesiastes Chap. 11 v. 1

11 The reward of a thing rightly done is to have done it.
   Seneca *Letters to Lucilius*

12 Preferment goes by letter and affection.
   William Shakespeare *Othello* Act I Sc. 1

RICHES

1 Riches are a good handmaid, but the worst mistress.
   Francis Bacon *De Augmentis Scientiarium*

2 We are so very rich if we know just a few people in a way in which we know no others.
   Commissioner Catherine Bramwell-Booth *My Faith* Ed. Mary E. Callan

3 Riches are gotten with pain, kept with care and lost with grief.
   Thomas Fuller *Gnomologia*

4 He died in a good old age, full of days, riches, and honour.
   Holy Bible 1 Chronicles Chap. 29 v. 28

5 He heapeth up riches, and knoweth not who shall gather them.
   Holy Bible Psalm 39 v. 6

6 Lay not up for yourselves treasures upon earth, where moth and rust doth corrupt, and where thieves break through and steal.
   Holy Bible St Matthew Chap. 6 v. 19

7 It is easier for a camel to go through the eye of a needle, than for a rich man to enter into the kingdom of God.
   Holy Bible St Matthew Chap. 19 v. 24

8 It is better to live rich than to die rich.
   Samuel Johnson Boswell's *Life of Johnson*

9 The use of riches is better than their possession.
   Fernando de Rojas *La Celestina*

10 It is a wretchedness of being rich that you have to live with rich people.
   Logan Pearsall Smith *All Trivia* 'Afterthoughts'

RIDICULE

11 Mockery is often poverty of wit.
   Jean de la Bruyère *Characters*

RIDICULOUSNESS

12 From the sublime to the ridiculous is but a step.
   Napoleon Bonaparte to the Abbé du Pradt, referring to the retreat from Moscow

1 The sublime and the ridiculous are so close that they touch.
  Edward, Lord Oxford *Common-place Book*

RIGHT

2 Two blacks make no white
  Two wrongs do not make a right.
  H.G. Bohn *Proverbs*

3 Better, though difficult, the right way to go
  Than wrong, tho' easy, where the end is woe.
  John Bunyan *The Pilgrim's Progress*

4 For Right is right, since God is God,
  And Right the day must win;
  To doubt would be disloyalty,
  To falter would be sin.
  Frederick W. Faber Quoted *Old and True*

5 Lord, give us faith that right makes might.
  Abraham Lincoln *Speeches and Letters*

6 With malice toward none; with charity for all; with firmness in
  the right, as God gives us to see the right.
  Abraham Lincoln Second Inaugural Address

RIGHTEOUSNESS

7 Righteousness is one thing, self-righteousness is another. May
  God keep me from ever confusing them.
  Rabbi Lionel Blue *Kitchen Blues*

8 The path of the just is as the shining light, that shineth more
  and more unto the perfect day.
  Holy Bible Proverbs Chap. 4 v. 18

9 Better is a little with righteousness than great revenues
  without right.
  Holy Bible Proverbs Chap. 16 v. 8

10 Fear thou not; for I am with thee: be not dismayed; for I am
   thy God: I will strengthen thee; yea, I will help thee; yea, I
   will uphold thee with the right hand of my righteousness.
   Holy Bible Isaiah Chap. 41 v. 10

11 But seek ye first the Kingdom of God, and His righteousness;
   and all these things shall be added unto you.
   Holy Bible St Matthew Chap. 6 v. 33

1   [C.S.] Lewis possesses the rare gift of making righteousness readable.
>   C.E.M. Joad

RITUAL

2   Down in adoration falling
Lo! The sacred Host we hail;
Lo! o'er ancient forms departing,
Never rites of grace prevail:
Faith for all defects supplying,
Where the feeble senses fail.
>   St Thomas Aquinas

3   I realise that ritual will always mean throwing away something. *Destroying* our corn or wine upon the altar of our gods.
>   G.K. Chesterton *Tremendous Trifles*

4   But, whatsoe'er they do or say, I'll build a Christian hope
On incense and on altar-lights, on chasuble and cope.
>   Bret Harte 'The Ritualist'

RIVALRY

5   Nothing is ever done beautifully which is done in rivalship, nor nobly which is done in pride.
>   John Ruskin *Ethics of the Dust*

ROMAN CATHOLIC

6   It is the Mass that matters.
>   Augustine Birrell 'What, Then, Did Happen at the Reformation?'

7   Defoe says there were a hundred thousand stout country-fellows in his time ready to fight to the death against popery, without knowing whether popery was a man or a horse.
>   William Hazlitt *Sketches* 'On Prejudice'

8   Religion went to Rome, subduing those,
Who, that they might subdue, made all their foes.
>   George Herbert 'The Church Militant'

9   Why leave a serious, moral, pious home,
Scotland, renown'd for sanctity of old,
Far distant Catholics to rate and scold
For — doing as the Romans do at Rome?
>   Thomas Hood 'Ode to Rae Wilson, Esq.'

1   It is said of Evelyn Waugh that when reproached for behaving badly he replied, 'Think how much worse I would have been had I not been a Catholic.'

   Dom Edmund Jones Quoted *Yes, Lord, I Believe*

2   The [Catholic] church has three sorts of enemies: the Jews, who have never been of her body; the heretics who have withdrawn from it; the evil Christians who tear her from within.

   Blaise Pascal *Pensées*

3   All roads lead to Rome, and unless you place yourself there you will never be in the heart of the world or see it in the right perspective. To be a Protestant is to be cross-eyed.

   George Santayana *Letters*

RULE

4   If you are at Rome live in the Roman style; if you are elsewhere live as they live elsewhere.

   St Ambrose Quoted Jeremy Taylor *Ductor Dubitantium*

5   No rule is so general, which admits not some exception.

   Robert Burton *Anatomy of Melancholy*

6   He shall rule them with a rod of iron.

   Holy Bible Revelation Chap. 2 v. 27 Chap. 19 v. 15

7   What is hateful to thyself do not unto thy neighbour.

   The Talmud

8   He that only rules by terror
   Doeth grievous wrong.
   Deep as Hell I count his error.
   Let him hear my song.

   Alfred, Lord Tennyson 'The Captain'

SABBATH

1 O what their joy and their glory must be
   Those endless sabbaths the blessed ones see!
   Peter Abelard 'O Quanta Qualia' Trans. A. Neale

2 The Indian sees no need for setting apart one day in seven as a
   holy day, since to him all days are God's.
   Charles E. Eastman *The Soul of the Indian*

3 God blessed the seventh day, and sanctified it: because that in
   it he had rested from all his work which God created and made.
   Holy Bible Genesis Chap. 2 v. 3

4 You have made us the masters of your world, to tend it, to
   serve it, to enjoy it. For six days we measure and we build, we
   count and carry the real and imagined burdens of our task, the
   success we earn and the price we pay. On this, the Sabbath
   day, give us time.
   Jewish Daily Service

5 And the Sabbath bell
   That over wood and wild and mountain dell
   Wanders so far, chasing all thoughts unholy
   With sounds most musical, most melancholy.
   Samuel Rogers 'Human Life'

6 And the sabbath rang slowly
   In the pebbles of the holy streams.
   Dylan Thomas 'Fern Hill'

SACRAMENTS

7 The symbolic actions of former and present times, which
   because of their pertaining to divine things are called
   sacraments.
   St Augustine of Hippo *Letters*

1 Christ bore himself in his hands when he said 'This is my Body.'

2 If you have received well, you are what you have received.
   St Augustine of Hippo *Sermons*

3 Q: What meanest thou by this word Sacrament?
   A: I mean an outward and visible sign of an inward and spiritual grace.
   Book of Common Prayer Offices of Instruction

4 For you yourself both offer and are offered, you yourself both receive and are distributed, O Christ our God.
   Liturgy of St John Chrysostom

5 He was the Word that spake it;
   He took the bread and brake it;
   And what the Word do make it,
   That I believe and take it.
   John Donne 'On the Sacrament'

6 For English Catholics, sacraments are the psychological equivalent of traitors in Russia.
   Aldous Huxley *Eyeless in Gaza*

7 What was visible in Christ has now passed over into the sacraments of the Church.
   St Leo the Great *Sermons*

8 If we would serve Him in His sacrament we must serve Him also wherever He has declared Himself to be and especially in his poor.
   Edward Pusey

SACRIFICE

9 The Christian character is the flower of which sacrifice is the seed.
   Fr Andrew SDC *The Gift of Life*

10 Here we offer and present unto thee, O Lord, ourselves, our souls and bodies, to be a reasonable, holy, and lively sacrifice unto Thee.
   Book of Common Prayer Order of Holy Communion

11 It is a far, far better thing that I do, than I have ever done; it is a far, far better rest that I go to, than I have ever known.
   Charles Dickens *A Tale of Two Cities*

1 No sacrifice is worth the name unless it is a joy. Sacrifice and a long face go ill together.
   Gandhi

2 The very act of sacrifice magnifies the one who sacrifices himself to the point where his sacrifice is much more costly to humanity than would have been the loss of those for whom he is sacrificing himself. But in his abnegation lies the secret of his grandeur.
   André Gide *Journals*

3 We cannot be sure we have something worth living for unless we are ready to die for it.
   Eric Hoffer *The True Believer*

4 Would God I had died for thee, O Absalom, my son, my son!
   Holy Bible 2 Samuel Chap. 18 v. 33

5 I desired mercy, and not sacrifice; and the knowledge of God more than burnt offerings.
   Holy Bible Hosea Chap. 6 v. 6

6 The good shepherd giveth his life for the sheep.
   Holy Bible St John Chap. 10 v. 11

7 It is only through the mystery of self-sacrifice that a man may find himself anew.
   Carl Gustav Jung

8 Ultimately, on the cross Jesus gave all his blood, to the very last drop, not to revive one patient for the remainder of a waning life, but to revivify all mankind forever.
   Malcolm Muggeridge *Jesus: The Man Who Lives*

9 Pray, brethren: that my sacrifice and yours may be acceptable to God the Father almighty.

10 The Lord receive this sacrifice at thy hands, to the praise and glory of his name, to our benefit and that of all his holy Church.
   From the Order of Roman Mass

11 Nothing so much enhances a good as to make sacrifices for it.
   George Santayana *The Sense of Beauty*

12 My own self and my pleasures, my righteous past, present and future, may I sacrifice without regard, in order to achieve the welfare of other beings.
   Santideva Buddhist spirituality

1 We live by our Lord's own power. But we can only live by His power in proportion as we give ourselves to be in His crucifixion.

    Gilbert Shaw 'Homily'

2 Self-sacrificial love cannot be planted in someone's heart simply by bringing in a new economic order. Christianity is both about justice and about Christ changing people from inside out.

    David Sheppard *Bias to the Poor*

3 The principle of sacrifice is that we choose to do or to suffer what apart from our love we should not choose to do or to suffer.

    Archbishop William Temple

4 Buddha to King: 'If the sacrifice of a lamb helps you to go to heaven, sacrificing a man will help you better, so sacrifice me.'

    Vivekananda Indian spirituality

5 Too long a sacrifice can make a stone of the heart.

    W.B. Yeats

SAFETY

6 Safe shall be my going,
Secretly armed against all death's endeavour;
Safe though all safety's lost; safe where men fall;
And if these poor limbs die, safest of all.

    Rupert Brooke 'Safety'

7 A safe stronghold our God is still
A trusty shield and weapon.

    Martin Luther *Klug'sche Gesangbuch*

SAINTS

8 God lifted matter to manhood, He desires to lift manhood to Christhood. God made men that men might make themselves saints.

    Fr Andrew SDC

9 A poor man may go mad in a prison cell because he is shut up by himself, and a saint may be in rapture in a convent cell because he is alone with God.

    Fr Andrew SDC *The Way of Victory*

1 Saintliness is also a temptation.
   Jean Anouilh *Becket*

2 The Church made saints when it needed them and where it needed them. It was not an affair left to the Divine will of God. It was geography and politics.
   Louis Bromfield *The Strange Case of Miss Annie Sprigg*

3 A saint abroad, and a devil at home.
   John Bunyan *The Pilgrim's Progress*

4 Can one be a saint if God does not exist? That is the only concrete problem I know of today.
   Albert Camus *The Plague*

5 It is better to speak wisdom foolishly like the saints, than to speak folly wisely, like the deans.

6 The great painter boasted that he mixed all his colours with brains, and the great saint may be said to mix all his thoughts with thanks.
   G.K. Chesterton

7 And never a saint took pity on
   My soul in agony.
   Samuel Taylor Coleridge *The Ancient Mariner*

8 Some reputed saints that have been canonised ought to have been cannonaded.
   Charles Caleb Colton

9 There are more saints in Cornwall than in Heaven.
   Cornish proverb

10 I call saintliness not a state but the moral procedure leading to it.
   Jean Genet Quoted Jean-Paul Sartre *Saint Genet*

11 The tears of Saints more sweet by far
   Than all the songs of sinners are.
   Robert Herrick 'Tears'

12 Many of the insights of the saint stem from his experiences as a sinner.
   Eric Hoffer *The Passionate State of Mind*

13 Precious in the sight of the Lord is the death of his Saints.
   Holy Bible Psalm 116 v. 15

1 But of all prides, since Lucifer's attaint,
The proudest swells a self-elected Saint.
Thomas Hood 'Ode to Rae Wilson, Esq.'

2 Behind every saint stands another saint.
Baron Friedrich von Hügel *The Mystical Element in Religion*

3 Many people genuinely do not wish to be saints, and it is probable that some who achieve or aspire to sainthood have never felt much temptation to be human beings.
George Orwell *Shooting an Elephant*

4 Grace is indeed needed to turn a man into a saint, and he who doubts it does not know what a saint or a man is.
Blaise Pascal *Pensées*

5 It is easier to make a saint out of a libertine than out of a saint.
George Santayana *The Life of Reason and Religion*

6 Sanctity is as rebellious as vice.
George Santayana *Little Essays*

7 Such an injury would vex a very saint.
William Shakespeare *The Taming of the Shrew* Act III Sc. 2

8 During their lifetime saints are a nuisance.
George Bernard Shaw *St Joan*

9 It is the bad that's in the best of us
Leaves the saint so like the rest of us.
Arthur Stringer 'Humanity'

10 God deliver us from sullen saints.
St Teresa of Avila

11 To most, even good people, God is a belief. To the saints he is an embrace.
Francis Thompson *Works* Vol. III

12 The greatest Saints have always shown the perfect combination of nearness to our Lord on the one hand, and a deep sense of their own unworthiness and weakness on the other.

13 Every Saint is a pattern; but no Saint is a pattern of everything.
Abbé de Tourville *Letters of Direction*

1 A saint is a human creature devoured and transformed by love: a love that has dissolved and burnt out those instinctive passions, acquisitive and combative, proud and greedy, which commonly rule the lives of men.
Evelyn Underhill *The Love of God*

2 I don't believe in God, but I do believe in His Saints.
Edith Wharton Quoted Percy Lubbock *Portrait of Edith Wharton*

3 The only difference between the Saint and the Sinner is that every saint has a past and every sinner has a future.
Oscar Wilde *A Woman of No Importance*

4 St Paul was clearly the Wykehamist among the Apostles, since he knew everything.
Harold Wilson *Memoirs — The Making of a Prime Minister*

SALT

5 Thou hast put salt in our mouths that we may thirst for Thee.
St Augustine *Confessions*

6 Spilt salt is never all gathered.
W.G. Benham *Proverbs*

7 But his wife looked back from behind him, and she became a pillar of salt.
Holy Bible Genesis Chap. 19 v. 26

8 Ye are the salt of the earth: but if the salt have lost his savour, wherewith shall it be salted?
Holy Bible St Matthew Chap. 5 v. 13

SALVATION

9 Our salvation, thank God! depends much more on His love of us than on our love of Him.
Fr Andrew SDC *Meditations for Every Day*

10 Lord my God, you have formed and reformed me.
St Anselm

11 O saving Victim, opening wide
The gate of heaven to man below
Our foes press hard on every side
Thine aid supply, thy strength bestow.
St Thomas Aquinas 'Hymn for Corpus Christi'

1 Three things are necessary for the salvation of man: to know what he ought to believe; to know what he ought to desire; and to know what he ought to do.
   St Thomas Aquinas *Two Precepts of Charity*

2 He who helps in the saving of others, saves himself as well.
   Hartmann von Aue *Poor Henry*

3 There is no salvation outside the Church.
   St Augustine of Hippo *Confessions*

4 No devotee of mine is ever lost. Take refuge in me and you reach the highest goal.
   Bhagavad Gita

5 By His first work He gave me to myself; and by the next He gave Himself to me. And when He gave Himself, He gave me back myself that I had lost.
   St Bernard of Clairvaux *De Diligendo Deo*

6 The Lord is my light and my salvation; whom then shall I fear?
   Book of Common Prayer Psalm 27 v. 1

7 Holy Scripture containeth all things necessary to salvation.
   Book of Common Prayer Articles of Religion VI

8 O Rock of Israel, Rock of Salvation struck and cleft for me, let those two streams of blood and water which once gushed out of thy side bring down with them salvation and holiness into my soul.
   Daniel Brevint *Works*

9 Jesus was killed by a group of those 'respectable pharisees' because they were not waiting for salvation; they thought they were saved already.
   Carlo Carretto *In Search of the Beyond*

10 If God in his love for the human race had not given us tears, those being saved would be few indeed and hard to find.
   St John Climacus *The Ladder of Divine Ascent*

11 General William Booth was in full spate. Suddenly he stopped and stabbed a finger at a young man busily writing, and called out, 'Young man, are you saved?' To which the astonished individual replied, 'Me, sir? I'm a reporter.'
   Colin R. Coote *Memoirs*

1 Oh! for a closer walk with God,
A calm and heavenly frame;
A light to shine upon the road
That leads me to the Lamb!
William Cowper *Olney Hymns*

2 God both represents to us what we are to become and shows
us the way to become it.
Don Cupitt *Taking Leave of God*

3 Souls are not saved in bundles.
Ralph Waldo Emerson *The Conduct of Life* 'Worship'

4 Salvation is the receiving of Christ's body and blood, as
paupers existing on the dying charity of the Son of God. We
are not our own; we are bought with a price.
Austin Farrer *The Crown of the Year*

5 Man needs, above all else, salvation. He needs to turn round
and see that God is standing there with a rope ready to throw
to him if only he will catch it and attach it to himself.
Norman Goodacre *Layman's Lent*

6 Strait is the gate, and narrow is the way, which leadeth unto
life, and few there be that find it.
Holy Bible St Matthew Chap. 7 v. 14

7 Behold, now is the accepted time; behold, now is the day of
salvation.
Holy Bible 2 Corinthians Chap. 6 v. 2

8 Above all, taking the shield of faith, wherewith ye shall be
able to quench all the fiery darts of the wicked. And take the
helmet of salvation, and the sword of the Spirit, which is the
word of God.
Holy Bible Ephesians Chap. 6 vv. 16–17

9 Work out your own salvation with fear and trembling.
Holy Bible Philippians Chap. 3 v. 12

10 A Welsh revivalist preacher swept to his conclusion by asking
all the congregation who wished to go to heaven to hold up
their hands. They all did, except for Deacon Evans, sitting in
the front row. 'But Mr Evans,' the affronted shepherd said,
'surely you want to go to heaven?' 'Yes,' said Deacon Evans,
'but not by the excursion train.'
Roy Jenkins *Observer* 8 March 1987

1 There is nothing to save, now all is lost,
But a tiny core of stillness in the heart
Like the eye of a violet.
    D.H. Lawrence Quoted *Beyond All Pain*

2 What is most contrary to salvation is not sin but habit.
    Charles Péguy *Basic Virtues: Sinners and Saints*

3 God changes not what is in a people, until they change what is
in themselves.
    The Qur'an

4 I can't believe in a God who only saves people who live in
certain latitudes. If I had happened to be born in Delhi I'd
probably be a Hindu; or in Iran a Muslim.
    Robert Runcie, Archbishop of Canterbury Quoted John
    Mortimer *In Character*

5 Consider this, —
That in the course of justice none of us
Should see salvation; we do pray for mercy,
And that same prayer doth teach us all to render
The deeds of mercy.
    William Shakespeare *The Merchant of Venice* Act IV Sc. 1

6 Wot prawce Selvytion nah?
    George Bernard Shaw *Major Barbara*

7 Since God will be my end
Let Him be my beginning,
So that I may now fully live
Instead of falling, straying, sinning.
    Angelus Silesius *The Book of Angelus Silesius*

8 Deliver me from my own shadows, my Lord, from the wrecks
and confusion of my days.
    Rabindranath Tagore

9 There is no expeditious road
To pack and label men for God,
And save them by the barrel-load.
    Francis Thompson *A Judgement in Heaven* Epilogue

10 Lead me from the unreal to the real
Lead me from darkness to light
Lead me from death to immortality.
    The Upanishads

1   The Christian is saved not in isolation but as a member of the
     community; he is saved in and through others. We can only be
     saved when praying for the salvation of all and with the aid of
     the prayers of all.
         Timothy Ware *The Orthodox Ethos*

2   Mrs Ape, as was her invariable rule, took round the hat and
     collected nearly two pounds. 'Salvation doesn't do them the
     same good, if they think it's free,' was her favourite axiom.
         Evelyn Waugh *Vile Bodies*

3   Jesus, Lover of my soul,
     Let me to Thy bosom fly,
     While the nearer waters roll,
     While the tempest still is high:
     Hide me, O thou Saviour, hide
     Till the storm of life is past;
     Safe into the haven guide,
     O receive my soul at last.
         Charles Wesley *Hymns Ancient and Modern*

4   O Thou who camest from above
     The pure celestial fire to impart,
     Kindle a flame of sacred love
     On the mean altar of my heart.
         Charles Wesley Hymn

5   I felt my heart strangely warmed. I feel I did trust in Christ,
     Christ alone, for salvation; an assurance was given me that he
     had taken away my sins, even mine; and saved me from the
     bore of sin and death.
         John Wesley *Journal*

6   Being brought into his presence [Christ's] one becomes
     something. And everybody is predestined to his presence.
     Once at least in his life each man walks with Christ to
     Emmaus.
         Oscar Wilde Quoted *Morning Has Broken*

SALVATION ARMY

7   The Salvation Army is the bulldozer of Evangelism.

8   The Salvation Army is the merriest, maddest thing that ever
     struck the life of the world.
         Salvation Army General Albert Osborn Quoted *News Review*
         26 November 1946

SANCTITY

1 God attributes to place
No sanctity, if none be thither brought
By men who there frequent, or therein dwell.
John Milton *Paradise Lost*

SATAN

2 Get thee behind me, Satan.
Holy Bible St Matthew Chap. 16 v. 23

3 High on a throne of royal state, which far
Outshone the wealth of Ormus and of Ind,
Or where the gorgeous East with richest hand
Showers on her kings barbaric pearl and gold,
Satan exalted sat, by merit raised
To that bad eminence.
John Milton *Paradise Lost*

4 Satan finds some mischief still
For idle hands to do.
Isaac Watts *Divine Songs for Children*

SATISFACTION

5 Thou shalt ever joy at eventide if thou spend the day fruitfully.
Thomas à Kempis *The Imitation of Christ*

6 Be satisfied with life always, but never with oneself.
George Jean Nathan *Testament of a Critic*

SCANDAL

7 Gossips are frogs, they drink and talk.
George Herbert *Jacula Prudentum*

8 Tattlers and busybodies, speaking things which they ought not.
Holy Bible 1 Timothy Chap. 5 v. 13

SCEPTICISM

9 What has not been examined impartially has not been well
examined. Scepticism is therefore the first step towards truth.
Denis Diderot *Pensées Philosophiques*

10 The civilised man has a moral obligation to be sceptical, to
demand the credentials of all statements that claim to be facts.
Bergen Evans *The Natural History of Nonsense*

1 She believed in nothing: only her scepticism kept her from
   being an atheist.
   Jean-Paul Sartre *Words*

2 The sceptic does not mean him who doubts, but him who
   investigates or researches, as opposed to him who asserts and
   thinks he has found.
   Miguel de Unamuno *Essays and Soliloquies* 'My Religion'

SCIENCE

3 We have grasped the mystery of the atom and rejected the
   Sermon on the Mount.
   General Omar Bradley USA Speech 11 November 1948

4 Only scientists could be so absurd and so arrogant as to
   suggest that God does not understand his own universe.
   David Brooks Letter to *Daily Telegraph* on 'Reisenberg's
   Uncertainty Principle' 17 March 1979

5 Science and religion ... are two sides of the same glass,
   through which we can see darkly until these two, focusing
   together, reveal the truth.
   Pearl S. Buck *A Bridge for Passing*

6 If scientists are worthy of the name, they are indeed about
   God's path, and about his bed, spying out all his ways.
   Samuel Butler *Notebooks*

7 I find whenever science gets to the right answer it agrees with
   the Bible.
   Charles Duke, Astronaut BBC TV 11 October 1981

8 The cosmic religious experience is the strongest and noblest
   driving force behind scientific research.
   Albert Einstein Quoted in an obituary 19 April 1955

9 Science without religion is lame, religion without science is
   blind.
   Albert Einstein *The World as I See It*

10 Science finds out ingenious ways to kill
    Strong men, and keep alive the weak and ill,
    That these a sickly progeny may breed
    Too poor to tax, too numerous to feed.
    Colin Ellis

1 The religion that is afraid of science dishonours God and commits suicide.
   Ralph Waldo Emerson *Journals*

2 Science investigates, religion interprets. Science gives man knowledge, which is power. Religion gives man wisdom, which is control.
   Martin Luther King *Strength to Love*

3 The effort to reconcile science and religion is almost always made not by theologians, but by scientists unable to shake off altogether the piety absorbed with their mother's milk.
   H.L. Mencken *Minority Report*

4 Science is a methodology. As a belief system it's disastrous.
   Ed Mitchell, Astronaut BBC TV 11 October 1981

5 Those whom the gods wish to destroy they first blind with science.
   John Naughton *Observer* 'The Meaning of Expertise' 6 April 1979

6 Science brings man nearer to God.
   Louis Pasteur

7 Increasing knowledge of science without a corresponding growth of religious wisdom only increases our fear of death.
   Radhakrishnan *Philosophy*

8 Historically, religion came first and science grew out of religion. Science has never superseded religion, and it is my expectation that it never will.
   Arnold Toynbee

9 Religion will not regain its old power until it can face change in the same spirit as does science. Its principles may be eternal, but the expression of these principles requires continual development.
   Alfred North Whitehead *Science and the Western World*

SCRIPTURE

10 The Scripture moveth us in sundry places to acknowledge and confess our manifold sins and wickedness.
   Book of Common Prayer From the Order of Morning Prayer

11 Thy word is a lamp unto my feet, and a light unto my path.
   Holy Bible Psalm 119 v. 105

1   Everything must be decided by Scripture.
      Martin Lloyd-Jones Quoted Christopher Catherwood *Five Evangelical Leaders*

2   By the reading of Scripture I am so renewed that all nature seems renewed around me and with me. The sky seems to be a purer, a cooler blue, the trees a deeper green, light is sharper on the outlines of the forest and the hills and the whole world is charged with the glory of God.
      Thomas Merton *The Sign of Jonas*

3   The Scripture in time of disputes is like an open town in time of war − which serves indifferently the occasions of both parties.
      Alexander Pope *Thoughts on Various Subjects*

4   We pick out a text here and there to make it serve our turn; whereas if we take it all together, and considered what went before and what followed after, we should find it meant no such thing.
      John Selden *Table Talk* 'The Scriptures'

5   The devil can cite Scripture for his purpose.
      William Shakespeare *The Merchant of Venice* Act I Sc. 3

SEA

6   He that will learn to pray, let him go to sea.
      George Herbert *Jacula Prudentum*

7   He maketh the deep to boil like a pot: he maketh the sea like a pot of ointment.
      Holy Bible Job Chap. 41 v. 31

8   They that go down to the sea in ships, that do business in great waters; these see the works of the Lord, and his wonders in the deep.
      Holy Bible Psalm 107 vv. 23−24

9   The dim, dark sea, so like unto Death,
    That divides and yet unites mankind!
      Henry Wadsworth Longfellow 'The Building of the Ship'

10 Rocked in the cradle of the deep
    I lay me down in peace to sleep;
    Secure I rest upon the wave,
    For Thou, O Lord! hast power to save.
      Emma Hart Willard 'Rocked in the Cradle of the Deep'

SEARCH

1 To seek God means first of all to let yourself be found by Him.
   Brakkenstein Community of Blessed Sacrament Fathers, Holland
   Rule for a New Brother

2 And ye shall seek me, and find me, when ye shall search for
   me with all your heart.
   Holy Bible Jeremiah Chap. 29 v. 13

3 My only task is to be what I am, a man seeking God in silence
   and solitude, with respect for the demands and realities of his
   own vocation, and fully aware that others too are seeking the
   truth in their own way.
   Thomas Merton *Contemplation of a World in Action*

4 Whoso seeks God and takes the intellect for guide
   God drives him forth, in vain distraction to abide;
   With wild confusion He confounds his inmost heart
   So that, distraught, he cries: 'I know not if Thou art.'
   Sufi spirituality

SEASON

5 To every thing there is a season, and a time to every purpose
   under the heaven:

   A time to be born, and a time to die; a time to plant, and a
   time to pluck up that which is planted;

   A time to kill, and a time to heal; a time to break down, and a
   time to build up;

   A time to weep, and a time to laugh; a time to mourn, and a
   time to dance;

   A time to cast away stones, and a time to gather stones
   together; a time to embrace, and a time to refrain from
   embracing;

   A time to get, and a time to lose; a time to keep, and a time to
   cast away;

   A time to rend, and a time to sew; a time to keep silence, and
   a time to speak;

   A time to love, and a time to hate; a time of war, and a time
   of peace.
   Holy Bible Ecclesiastes Chap. 3 vv. 1–8

SECTS

1 No truly great man, from Jesus Christ down, ever founded a sect.
   Thomas Carlyle *Journal*

2 Sects tend to have doctrines that resemble some of the beliefs of mainstream religions, but skew them in certain directions. A colleague of mine once received three leaflets in the same week; one from Christadelphians, one from Christian Scientists and one from Jehovah's Witnesses. All three began with 'Christendom is astray'. All three thought they had the only solution.
   Rosemary Harthill *In Perspective*

3 The amazing capacity of human nature for credulity, folly, and self-deception has never been shown so conclusively as in the number of spasmodic sects and religious cults which sprang up in America during the last century.
   Ray Strachey *Religious Fanaticism*

SECURITY

4 The way to be safe is never to be secure.
   Thomas Fuller *Gnomologia*

5 From the contagion of the world's slow stain
   He is secure, and now can never mourn
   A heart grown cold.
   Percy Bysshe Shelley *Adonais*

6 Our safety lies in God and not in our feeling safe.
   Hubert van Zeller *We Work While the Light Lasts*

SELF

7 First learn to love yourself, then you can love me.
   St Bernard of Clairvaux *Letters*

8 To begin with oneself, but not to end with oneself;
   To start from oneself, but not to aim at oneself;
   To comprehend oneself, but not to be preoccupied with oneself.
   Martin Buber

9 Self-centredness of any kind is always a movement away from God and consequently a very serious form of disorder.
   Philip Pare *God Made the Devil*

1 This above all — to thine own self be true,
And it must follow, as the night the day,
Thou canst not then be false to any man.
    William Shakespeare *Hamlet* Act I Sc. 3

2 I, being self-confined, self did not merit
Till leaving self behind, did self inherit.
    Sufi spirituality

3 You never know yourself until you know more than your
body. The image of God is not sealed in the features of your
face, but in the lineaments of your soul.
    Thomas Traherne *Centuries of Meditations*

SELF-DISCIPLINE

4 What it lies in our power to do, it lies in our power not to do.
    Aristotle *Nicomachean Ethics*

5 Discipline puts back in its place that something in us which
should serve but wants to rule.
    A Carthusian *They Speak in Silences*

6 He that requires much from himself and little from others will
keep himself from being the object of resentment.
    Confucius *Analects*

7 Freedom is not procured by a full enjoyment of what is
desired, but by controlling the desire.
    Epictetus *Discourses*

8 Do not consider painful what is good for you.
    Euripides *Medea*

9 It is good for a man that he bear the yoke in his youth.
    Holy Bible Lamentations Chap. 3 v. 27

10 For better or worse, man is the tool-using animal, and as such
he has become the lord of creation. When he is lord also of
himself, he will deserve his self-chosen title of *homo sapiens*.
    Dean W.R. Inge *Outspoken Essays*

11 He who conquers others is strong.
He who conquers himself is mighty.
    Lao-Tze *The Character of Tao*

12 Man who man would be,
Must rule the empire of himself.
    Percy Bysshe Shelley *Political Greatness*

SELF-DENIAL

1   That you may have pleasure in everything
Seek your own pleasure in nothing.
That you may know everything
Seek to know nothing.
That you may possess all things
Seek to possess nothing.
That you may be everything
Seek to be nothing.
    St John of the Cross *The Ascent of Mount Carmel*

2   Self-discipline never means giving up everything, for giving up
is a loss. Our Lord did not ask us to give up the things of
earth, but to exchange them for better things.
    Fulton J. Sheen

SELF-INDULGENCE

3   It is a sober truth that people who live only to amuse
themselves work harder at the task than most people do in
earning their daily bread.
    Hannah More

SELFISHNESS

4   Selfish action imprisons the word. Act selflessly, without any
thought of personal profit.
    Bhagavad Gita

5   He who hates not in himself his self-love and that instinct
which leads him to make himself a God, is indeed blind.
    Blaise Pascal *Pensées*

6   He who lives only for himself is truly dead to others.
    Publilius Syrus *Moral Sayings*

SELF-KNOWLEDGE

7   A humble knowledge of thyself is a surer way to God than a
deep search after learning.
    Thomas à Kempis *The Imitation of Christ*

8   Beware of no man more than yourself; we carry our worst
enemies within us.
    Charles Haddon Spurgeon

SELFLESSNESS

1 Inwardness, mildness and self-renouncement do make for man's happiness.
   Matthew Arnold

2 Free from self-seeking, envy, low design,
  I have not found a whiter soul than thine.
   Charles Lamb 'To Martin Charles Burney'

3 The one true way of dying to self is most simple and plain ... if you ask what is this one true, simple, plain and immediate and unerring way? It is the way of patience, meekness, humility and resignation.
   William Law *A Serious Call to a Devout and Holy Life*

4 Where self exists, God is not;
  Where God exists, there is no self.
   Sikh morning prayer

5 The more thou thine own self
  Out of thy self dost throw
  The more will into thee
  God with his Godhead flow.
   Angelus Silesius *Rhymes of a German Mystic*

6 The most satisfactory thing in life is to have been able to give a large part of oneself to others.
   Pierre Teilhard de Chardin

SENSES

7 The senses are so strong and impetuous that they forcibly carry away the mind even of a man of discrimination who is endeavouring to control them.
   Bhagavad Gita

8 While contemplating the objects of the senses, a person develops attachment for them, and from such attachment lust develops and from lust anger arises.
   Bhagavad Gita

SEPARATION

9 Unloving separation, whatever form it takes, is a sin.
   Lev Gillet *Encounter at the Well*

1   If they are with Christ and Christ is with us, then they cannot be very far away.
>Pierre Teilhard de Chardin

SERMON

2   The glow of a good sermon always makes me regret that religion is not true.
>Augustine Birrell *Essays and Addresses*

3   It seems to me easier to give sermons than to sit through them.
>Rabbi Lionel Blue *Kitchen Blues*

4   Complaining that modern sermons tended to be too secular in tone, Margot Asquith remarked, 'It would be as surprising to hear God mentioned in one of them as to find a fox in a bus.'
>Lord David Cecil *Observer* 'Staying with Margot'
>20 December 1981

5   Having been forced to sit through an evangelical sermon on the consequences of sin, Lord Melbourne grumbled, 'Things have come to a pretty pass when religion is allowed to invade private life.'
>Lord David Cecil *Melbourne*

6   Sermons remain one of the last forms of public discourse where it is culturally forbidden to talk back.
>Harvey Cox *The Secular City*

7   Go into one of our cool churches, and count the words that might be spared, and in most places the entire sermon will go.

8   The sermon which I write inquisitive of truth is good year after year, but that which is written because a sermon must be writ is musty the next day.
>Ralph Waldo Emerson *Journals*

9   We set no time limit on sermons, but we feel no souls are saved after the first twenty minutes.
>Donald MacGregor, quoting advice to a new incumbent
>*Reader's Digest* November 1941

10   Man to wife: 'He preaches a remarkably good sermon. It is so hard to avoid offending people like us.'
>*New Yorker* cartoon Caption

11   The half-baked sermon causes spiritual indigestion.
>Austin O'Malley

1 Americans are so tensed and keyed up that it is impossible to put them to sleep even with a sermon.
   Norman Vincent Peale

2 The Bishop of Chichester preached before the King and made a great flattering sermon which I did not like, that clergy should meddle in matters of state.
   Samuel Pepys *Diary*

3 A visitor to a Cardiff church admired the altar flowers. Agreeing on their beauty, the verger added, 'On Sunday nights they are always given to those who are sick after the sermon.'
   Peterborough *Daily Telegraph*

4 I hate sermons. All our questions to God are absolutely ridiculous, so how can we expect answers.
   Muriel Spark Quoted Nicholas Shakespeare *The Times*
   21 November 1983

5 The Revd Tubby Clayton, preaching at a Royal Navy church parade at once captured the attention of the entire ship's company. 'This morning, lads,' he began, 'I am going to take my text out of my hat.' He held up his trilby and read aloud the makers' name: 'Hope Brothers'.
   Joseph Stansfield *Reader's Digest* May 1975

6 Once in seven years I burn all my sermons for it is a shame if I cannot write better sermons now than I did seven years ago.
   John Wesley

7 Three or four gentlemen in Durham put me in mind of the honest man at London, who was so gay and unconcerned, while Dr Sherlock was preaching concerning the day of judgement. One asked, 'Do you not hear what the doctor says?' He answered, 'Yes, but I am not of this parish!'
   John Wesley *Journal*

SERPENT

8 And the woman said, The serpent beguiled me and I did eat.
   Holy Bible Genesis Chap. 3 v. 13

9 The infernal serpent; he it was, whose guile
   Stirred up with envy and revenge, deceiv'd
   The mother of mankind.
   John Milton *Paradise Lost*

1 The serpent, subtlest beast of all the field,
  Of huge extent sometimes, with brazen eyes
  And hairy mane terrific.
  > John Milton *Paradise Lost*

SERVICE

2 Every day bring God sacrifices and be the priest in this
  reasonable service, offering thy body and the virtue of thy
  soul.
  > St John Chrysostom *A Little Book of Life and Death*

3 Great works do not always lie in our way, but every moment
  we may do little ones excellently, that is, with great love.
  > St Francis de Sales *On the Love of God*

4 If a man is called to be a street sweeper he should sweep
  streets even as Michelangelo painted, or Beethoven
  composed music. He should sweep streets so well that all the
  host of heaven and earth will pause and say, here lived a great
  street sweeper who did his job well.
  > Martin Luther King

5 O most merciful Redeemer, Friend and Brother
  May we know Thee more clearly,
  Love Thee more dearly,
  Follow Thee more nearly:
  For ever and ever.
  > St Richard of Chichester

6 For the fulfilment of his purpose God needs more than priests,
  bishops, pastors and missionaries. He needs mechanics and
  chemists, gardeners and street sweepers, dressmakers and
  cooks, tradesmen, physicians, philosophers, judges and
  shorthand typists.
  > Paul Tournier *Serving God in Everything*

7 Lord of all being, I give you my all;
  If e'er I disown you I stumble and fall.
  But, sworn in glad service your word to obey,
  I walk in your freedom to the end of the way.
  > Jack Winslow Quoted *100 Hymns for Today*

8 God said: O world, serve those who serve Me and render
  weary those who serve you.
  > *The Wisdom of the Sufis* Compiled by Kenneth Cragg

SEX

1 Christianity is unique in having hated and outlawed sex and in making people feel guilty because they are sexual beings.
    Karen Armstrong *The Gospel According to Woman*

2 Adam may have put the blame on Eve for the sin of disobedience, but it is nearly always Eve who puts the blame on Adam for the sins of sex.
    Hubert van Zeller *We Work While the Light Lasts*

SHEPHERD

3 The Church is like a great ship sailing the sea of the world and tossed by the waves of temptation in this life. But it is not to be abandoned — it must be brought under control.
    St Boniface *Letters of St Boniface*

4 He maketh me to lie down in green pastures: he leadeth me beside the still waters.
    Holy Bible Psalm 23 v. 2

5 He shall feed his flock like a shepherd: he shall gather the lambs with his arm, and carry them in his bosom, and shall gently lead those that are with young.
    Holy Bible Isaiah Chap. 40 v. 11

SICKNESS

6 It must be clear to you that sickness is no more the reality of being than is sin. This mortal dream of sickness, sin and death should cease through Christian Science.
    Christian Science Practice

7 Psychosomatic illnesses are illnesses of the soul transmitted to the body; a sick spirit and a healthy body inevitably come into conflict and finally break down.
    Michel Quoist *With Open Heart*

8 Many are sick because they have not the heart to be well.
    John Lancaster Spalding *Thoughts and Theories of Life and Education*

9 It was our Lord's desire not to be ill. He cured all the sick who were brought to Him. God eliminates illness through the growth of knowledge and of human wisdom.
    Abbé de Tourville *Letters of Direction*

SILENCE

1 Here rests in silent clay
   Miss Arabella Young
   Who on the 21st May
   Began to hold her tongue.
   > Anon

2 Silence is when the wholeness of God embraces the wholeness
   of man.
   > Fr Peter Ball CGA Clergy Conference at Swanwick 1985

3 We are silent at the beginning of the day because God should
   have the first word, and we are silent before going to sleep
   because the last word also belongs to God.
   > Dietrich Bonhoeffer *Life Together*

4 In silence man can most readily preserve his integrity.
   > Meister Eckhart *Directions for the Contemplative Life*

5 Words, after speech, reach
   Into the silence. Only by the form, the pattern,
   Can words or music reach
   The stillness.
   > T.S. Eliot *Four Quartets*

6 Silence is listening to the truth of things.
   > Heraclitus Quoted Hubert van Zeller *Leave Your Life Alone*

7 Elected Silence, sing to me
   And beat upon my whorlèd ear,
   Pipe me to pastures still and be
   The music that I care to hear.
   > Gerard Manley Hopkins 'The Habit of Perfection'

8 Speech is the organ of this present world. Silence is the
   mystery of the world to come.
   > St Isaac the Syrian

9 Silences are the only scrap of Christianity we still have left.
   > Søren Kierkegaard

10 It is better to keep silence and to be, than to talk and not to be.
   > St Ignatius Loyola

11 A Bishop is most like God when he is silent.
   > St Ignatius Loyola Quoted Fr Peter Ball CGA Clergy
   > Conference at Swanwick 1985

1 Silence isolates us from the crowds that love to pool their misery; an unhappy civilization is always gregarious.
   Fulton J. Sheen *Lift Up Your Heart*

2 When the heart is hard and parched up, come upon me with a shower of mercy.
   When grace is lost from life, come with a burst of song.
   When tumultuous work raises its din on all sides shutting me out from beyond, come to me, my lord of silence, with thy peace and rest.
   Rabindranath Tagore *Collected Poems*

3 God is the friend of silence. Trees, flowers, grass grow in silence. See the stars, moon and sun how they move in silence.
   Mother Teresa of Calcutta Quoted Kathryn Spink *For the Brotherhood of Man Under the Fatherhood of God*

4 Christ's life sets the pattern for silence: silence at the beginning in the cave; silence at the end in the tomb; long silences in between.

5 Silence is not much preached today, so it is for prayer to preach it. If we do not listen we do not come to the truth. If we do not pray we do not even get as far as listening. The four things go together: silence, listening, prayer, truth.
   Hubert van Zeller *Leave Your Life Alone*

SIMPLICITY

6 Be simple; take our Lord's hand and walk through things.
   Fr Andrew SDC

7 So long as one does not become simple like a child, one does not get divine illumination. Forget all the worldly knowledge that thou hast acquired and become as a child, and then will thou get the divine wisdom.
   Ramakrishna Hindu spirituality

8 Simplicity is found in the unfettered joy of a Brother who forsakes an obsession with his own progress or backslidings in order to fix his gaze on the light of Christ.
   The Taizé Rule

9 Hair-splitting can be left to theologians and legalists; simplicity is the aim in the life of prayer.
   Hubert van Zeller *Leave Your Life Alone*

SIN

1   There is nothing so dull as sin.
      Fr Andrew SDC *Seven Words from the Cross*

2   Sin is not a monster to be mused on, but an impotence to be
      got rid of.
      Matthew Arnold

3   A man does not sin by commission only, but often by
      omission.
      Marcus Aurelius *Meditations*

4   He [Christ] carried our sin, our captivity and our suffering,
      and he did not carry it in vain. He CARRIED IT AWAY.
      Karl Barth *Deliverance to the Captives*

5   When Jesus blessed sinners, they were real sinners, but Jesus
      did not make everyone a sinner first. He called them away
      from the sin, not into their sin.
      Dietrich Bonhoeffer *Letters and Papers from Prison*

6   O remember not the sins and offences of my youth.
      Book of Common Prayer Psalm 25 v. 6

7   Sin, that old dynamo, has lost much of its power since we
      ceased to believe in hell.
      Gerald Brenan *Thoughts in a Dry Season*

8   I rejoice indeed, as is right, for the growth of the fruits of your
      virtues, but I lament and am ashamed that I lie inert and
      torpid in the filth of my sins.
      St Bruno Letter to his Carthusian sons

9   For sin is just this, what man cannot by its very nature do with
      his whole being; it is possible to silence the conflict in the soul,
      but it is not possible to uproot it.
      Martin Buber *Hasidism*

10 One leak will sink a ship, and one sin will destroy a sinner.
      John Bunyan *The Pilgrim's Progress*

11 Pleasure's a sin, and sometimes sin's a pleasure.
      Lord Byron *Don Juan*

12 There are only three sins — causing pain, causing fear, causing
      anguish. The rest is window dressing.
      Roger Caras

1 Without the spice of guilt, sin cannot be fully savoured.
   Alexander Chase *Perspectives*

2 There are different kinds of wrong. The people sinned against
   are not always the best.
   Ivy Compton-Burnett *The Mighty and Their Fall*

3 Those of us who were brought up as Christians and have lost
   our faith have retained the sense of sin without the saving
   belief in redemption.
   Cyril Connolly *The Unquiet Grave*

4 Hark, my soul! it is the Lord;
   'Tis thy Saviour, hear his word;
   Jesus speaks, and speaks to thee:
   'Say, poor sinner, lov'st thou me?'
   William Cowper *Olney Hymns*

5 In best understandings, sin began:
   Angels sinned first, then Devils, then Man.
   John Donne *Letters to Sacred Persons* 'Sir Henry Wotton'

6 He that once sins, like him that slides on ice,
   Goes swiftly down the slippery way of vice:
   Though conscience checks him, yet those rubs gone o'er,
   He slides on smoothly and looks back no more.
   John Dryden *Journal*

7 The root of sin is indolence of heart.
   Alan Ecclestone *The Night Sky of the Lord*

8 It's harder to confess the sin that no one believes in
   Than the crime that everyone can appreciate.
   For the crime is in relation to the law
   And the sin is in relation to the sinner.
   T.S. Eliot *The Elder Statesman*

9 That which we call sin in others is experiment for us.
   Ralph Waldo Emerson

10 Hark! Hark! my soul, angelic songs are swelling,
   O'er earth's green fields and ocean's wave-beat shore;
   How sweet the truth those blessed strains are telling,
   Of that new life when sin shall be no more!
   F.W. Faber *Oratory Hymns* 'The Pilgrims of the Night'

11 Only the wages of sin have no deductions.
   Ellis C. Galt *Saturday Evening Post* 28 May 1955

1 The most scandalous charges were suppressed; the Vicar of Christ was only accused of piracy, rape, sodomy and incest.
> Edward Gibbon, on the condemnation of Pope John XXIII in 1415 *Decline and Fall of the Roman Empire*

2 The sins of the bedroom are not the only ones. The sins of the boardroom should be just as much a matter of concern.
> Bishop Richard Harries Address to Diocesan Synod, Oxford 27 February 1988

3 Be sure your sin will find you out.
> *Holy Bible* Numbers Chap. 32 v. 23

4 I will arise, and go to my father, and will say unto him, Father, I have sinned against heaven, and before thee, and am no more worthy to be called thy son.
> *Holy Bible* St Luke Chap. 15 vv. 18–19

5 If we say that we have no sin, we deceive ourselves, and the truth is not in us. If we confess our sins, he is faithful and just to forgive us our sins, and to cleanse us from all unrighteousness.
> *Holy Bible* 1 John Chap. 1 vv. 8–9

6 Through sin do men reach the light.
> Elbert Hubbard *Epigrams*

7 We are punished by our sins, not for them.
> Elbert Hubbard *The Note Book*

8 Really to sin you have to be serious about it.
> Henrik Ibsen *Peer Gynt*

9 There is but one thing more dangerous than sin — the murder of a man's sense of sin.
> Pope John Paul II Quoted *Observer* 8 April 1979

10 It is true that sin is the cause of all this pain; but all shall be well, and all shall be well, and all manner of things shall be well.
> Julian of Norwich *Revelations of Divine Love*

11 Perhaps there is only one cardinal sin: impatience. Because of impatience we were driven out of Paradise; because of impatience we cannot return.
> Franz Kafka

1   It does not matter how small the sins are provided that their
    cumulative effect is to edge the man away from the light and
    out into nothing. Murder is no better than cards, if cards can
    do the trick. Indeed, the safest road to hell is the gradual
    one — the gentle slope, soft under foot, without sudden
    turnings, without signposts.
        C.S. Lewis *The Screwtape Letters*

2   The mind sins, not the body. If there is no intention, there is
    no blame.
        Livy *History of Rome*

3   Sin has always been an ugly word, but it has been made so in a
    new sense over the past half-century. It has been made not
    only ugly, but passé. People are no longer sinful, they are
    only immature or underprivileged or frightened, or, more
    particularly, sick.
        Phyllis McGinley *The Province of the Heart in Defence of Sin*

4   Sin is a dangerous toy in the hands of the virtuous. It should
    be left to the congenitally sinful, who know when to play with
    it and when to leave it alone.
        H.L. Mencken *The American Mercury* 'A Good Man Gone
        Wrong' February 1929

5   Nobody comes so close to the heart of Christianity as the
    sinner. Nobody except perhaps the saint.
        Charles Péguy Quoted Philip Toynbee *Observer* 24 January 1968

6   Everything comes from our good Father, except our sins. They
    never do.
        Brother Roger CR *So Easy to Love*

7   Now there is an eighth Cardinal Sin.
        Cardinal Sin of the Philippines, on getting his hat

8   We don't call it sin today, we call it self-expression.
        Baroness Stocks Quoted Jonathan Green *The Cynic's Lexicon*

9   Sins cannot be undone, only forgiven.
        Igor Stravinsky *Conversations with Igor Stravinsky*

10 All Sins are attempts to fill voids.
        Simone Weil Quoted W.H. Auden *A Certain World*

11 It is only the great sinner who can do the two things of hating
    the sin and loving the sinner, the other sort only hate the sin.
        J.B. Yeats *Letters to His Son, W.B. Yeats — and Others*

SINCERITY

1 The kindling power of our words must not come from outward show but from within, not from oratory but straight from the heart.
St Francis de Sales *Conferences*

2 The Devil is sincere, but he is sincerely wrong.
Billy Graham

3 Sincerity is the way to Heaven.
Meng-Tze *The Book of Meng-Tze*

4 Be suspicious of your sincerity when you are the advocate of that upon which your livelihood depends.
John Lancaster Spalding *Thoughts and Theories of Life and Education*

SINGING

5 In Quires and Places where they sing here followeth the Anthem.
Book of Common Prayer Order of Morning Prayer Rubric after Third Collect

6 Singing in the Spirit doesn't mean at this Conference you will sing 'Majesty' at every opportunity.
Canon Peterkin Anglo Charismatic Congress 1986

SINGLEMINDEDNESS

7 He that loves God seeks neither gain nor reward but only to lose all, even himself.
St John of the Cross *The Spiritual Canticle*

SLANDER

8 My duty towards my neighbour is . . . to keep my tongue from evil-speaking, lying and slandering.
Book of Common Prayer The Catechism

9 The slanderous tongue kills three: the slandered, the slanderer, and him who listens to the slander.
The Talmud

SLOTH

10 Sloth is the tempter that beguiles and expels from paradise.
Amos Bronson Alcott *Table Talk* 'Pursuits'

1 Go to the ant, thou sluggard; consider her ways, and be wise.
   Holy Bible Proverbs Chap. 6 v. 6

2 No one has become immortal through sloth.
   Sallust *Jugurtha*

SOCIALISM

3 Christian socialism is but the holy water with which the priest consecrates the heart-burnings of the aristocrat.
   Friedrich Engels and Karl Marx *Manifesto of the Communist Party*

SOCIAL JUSTICE

4 The preaching of the Gospel and its acceptance imply a social revolution whereby the hungry are fed and justice becomes the right of all.
   Cardinal Suenens

SOLITUDE

5 The soul that is growing in holiness is the least lonely when it is most alone.
   Fr Andrew SDC Quoted in *Love is the Key*

6 The desert does not mean the absence of men, it means the presence of God.
   Carlo Carretto *The Desert in the City*

7 When you have shut your doors and darkened your room, remember never to say that you are alone: for you are not alone, but God is within, and your genius is within.
   Epictetus *Discourses*

8 Solitude is bearable only with God.
   André Gide *Journals*

9 The more powerful and original a mind, the more it will incline towards the religion of solitude.
   Aldous Huxley *Proper Studies*

10 Religion is what an individual does with his own solitude. If you are never solitary you are never religious.
   Dean W.R. Inge

11 A solitude is the audience chamber of God.
   Walter Savage Landor *Imaginary Conversations* 'Lord Brooke and Sir Philip Sidney'

1   Solitude sometimes is best society,
    And short retirement urges sweet return.
      John Milton *Paradise Lost*

2   Birth and death are solitary; thought and growth are solitary;
    every final reality of a man's life is incommunicable.
      Charles Morgan *The Fountain*

3   Solitude is the playfield of Satan.
      Vladimir Nabokov *Pale Fire*

4   Solitude is the profoundest fact of the human condition. Man
    is the only being who knows he is alone.
      Octavio Paz *The Labyrinth of Solitude*

5   Solitude vivifies: isolation kills.
      Joseph Roux *Meditations of a Parish Priest*

6   Settle yourself in solitude and you will come upon Him in
    yourself.

7   We need no wings to go in search of Him, but have only to
    find a place where we can be alone — and look upon Him
    present within us.
      St Teresa of Avila

SORROW

8   One cannot weep for the entire world, it is beyond human
    strength. One must choose.
      Jean Anouilh *Cécile*

9   No greater sorrow than to recall in our misery the time when
    we were happy.
      Dante *The Divine Comedy*

10 The deeper that sorrow carves into your being, the more joy
    you can contain. Joy and sorrow are inseparable.
      Kahlil Gibran

11 Sorrow is better than laughter: for by the sadness of the
    countenance the heart is made better.
      Holy Bible Ecclesiastes Chap. 7 v. 3

12 He who has occasion to kill many people has cause for deep
    sorrow and tears.
      Lao-Tze Taoist spirituality

1 The ground work of life is sorrow. But that once established,
one can start to build. And until that is established one can
build nothing; no life of any sort.
    D.H. Lawrence *Letters*

2 For gnarling sorrow hath less power to bite
The man that mocks at it and sets it light.
    William Shakespeare *King Richard II* Act I Sc. 3

3 The deeper the sorrow the less tongue it has.
    The Talmud

4 Pure and complete sorrow is as impossible as pure and
complete joy.
    Leo Tolstoy *War and Peace*

SOUL

5 The soul is that which denies the body. For example, that
which refuses to run when the body trembles, to strike when
the body is angry, to drink when the body is thirsty.
    'Alain' (Emile Chartier) *Definitions*

6 The souls of those who have known God seek after the
verdant pastures, the beautiful vistas, the fresh green gardens.
    Al-Junaid *Sufi spirituality*

7 Blessed is the soul which, at the hour of its separation from
the body, is sanctified from the vain imaginings of the peoples
of the world. Such a soul liveth and moveth in accordance with
the will of its Creator, and entereth the all-highest Paradise.
    Bahá'u'Uáh, founder of the Baha'i faith

8 Despise the flesh, for it passes away; be solicitous for your
soul, which will never die.
    St Basil

9 The soul is restless and furious, it wants to tear itself apart,
and cure itself of being human.
    Ugo Betti *Goat Island*

10 It is said that the soul is invisible, inconceivable, inimitable
and unchangeable. Knowing this you should not grieve for the
body.

11 That which pervades the entire body is indestructible. No one
is able to destroy the imperishable soul.
    Bhagavad Gita

1 The soul can never be cut into pieces by any weapon, nor can
he be burned nor dried. He is everlasting, all-pervading,
unchangeable, immovable and eternally the same.
    Bhagavad Gita

2 My mother bore me in the southern wild,
And I am black, but O! my soul is white.
    William Blake 'The Little Black Boy'

3 Interior disturbance renders the soul incapable of listening to
and following the voice of the divine Spirit, of receiving the
sweet and delightful impressions of His grace, and of applying
itself to devotional exercises and to exterior duties.
    Jean-Pierre de Caussade SJ *Self-Abandonment to Divine
    Providence*

4 If you put fine grapes into the wine-press there will come out a
delicious juice; our souls, in the winepress of the Cross, give
out juice which nourishes and strengthens.
    The Curé d'Ars (Jean-Baptiste Vianney)

5 Let man's Soul be a Sphere, and then, in this,
The intelligence that moves, devotion is.
    John Donne 'Good Friday, 1613'

6 Since, O my soul, thou art capable of God, woe to thee if thou
contentest thyself with anything less than God.
    St Francis de Sales Quoted *Love is the Key*

7 I've never met a healthy person who worried much about his
health or a good person who worried much about his soul.
    J.B.S. Haldane

8 Love bade me welcome; yet my soul drew back,
Guilty of dust and sin.
    George Herbert 'Love'

9 What is a man profited, if he shall gain the whole world, and
lose his own soul?
    Holy Bible St Matthew Chap. 16 v. 26

10 Love unites the soul with God: and the more love the soul has
the more powerfully it enters into God and is centred on him.
    St John of the Cross *The Living Flame of Love*

11 The soul that is united with God is feared by the devil as
though it were God himself.
    St John of the Cross

1 God never deserts the soul, but abides there in bliss for ever.
   Julian of Norwich *Revelations of Divine Love*

2 I do believe in the soul, but I don't believe that I've got one
   that bothers me all the time. I'd rather think of it as an object
   like the samovar, bubbling all the time.
   Peter Levi *The Frontiers of Paradise*

3 It is with the soul that we grasp the essence of another human
   being, not with the mind, nor even with the heart.
   Henry Miller *The Books in My Life*

4 The souls of emperors and cobblers are cast in the same
   mould.
   Montaigne *Essays*

5 Body am I entirely and nothing else; and soul is only a word
   for something about the body.
   Frederick Nietzsche *Thus Spake Zarathustra* 'On the Despisers
   of the Body'

6 Our soul is cast into a body, where it finds number, time,
   dimension. Thereupon it reasons, and calls this nature
   necessity and can believe nothing else.
   Blaise Pascal *Pensées*

7 The soul of man is immortal and imperishable.
   Plato *Dialogues*

8 The soul takes nothing with her to the other world but her
   education and her culture and these, it is said, are of the
   greatest service or the greatest injury to the dead man, at the
   very beginning of his journey thither.
   Plato *Dialogues*

9 All are but parts of one stupendous whole,
   Whose body Nature is, and God the soul.
   Alexander Pope *An Essay on Man*

10 They will question thee concerning the soul. Say 'The soul is
   the concern of my Lord and you have been given of
   knowledge but a little.'
   The Qur'an

11 We can now recognise that the fate of the soul is the fate of
   the social order; that if the spirit within us withers, so, too,
   will all the world we build about us.
   Theodore Roszak *Where the Wasteland Ends*

1 The soul is the captain and ruler of the life of mortals.
   Sallust *Jugurtha*

2 An Empty Book is like an Infants Soul, in which any Thing
   may be written.
   Thomas Traherne *Centuries of Meditations*

3 Four thousand volumes of metaphysics will not teach us what
   the soul is.
   Voltaire

4 For as to the spiritual direction of my soul, I think that God
   Himself has taken it in hand from the start and still looks
   after it.
   Simone Weil *Waiting for God*

SPIRIT

5 The spirit is the true self, not that physical figure which can be
   pointed out by your finger.
   Cicero *De Republica*

6 Who is the third who walks always beside you?
   When I count, there are only you and I together
   But when I look ahead up the white road
   There is always another one walking beside you ...
   T.S. Eliot *The Waste Land*

7 The Holy Spirit knocks us unconscious — so that God can do
   His work of love within us, which we resist when we are awake.
   Fr John Harper 'Sermons: St John-in-the-Fields, St Ives'

8 God is a Spirit: and they who worship him must worship him
   in spirit and in truth.
   Holy Bible St John Chap. 4 v. 24

9 Absent in body, but present in spirit.
   Holy Bible 1 Corinthians Chap. 5 v. 3

10 Dust as we are, the immortal spirit grows
   Like harmony in music.
   William Wordsworth *The Prelude* Book I

SPIRITUALISM

11 The Spiritualist outlook is all about Man; hardly at all about
   God.
   rchbishop Lang's Committee on

SPIRITUALITY

1   By aspiring to a similitude of God in goodness, or love,
neither man nor angel ever transgressed, or shall transgress.
Francis Bacon *Advancement of Learning*

2   I am certainly convinced that it is one of the greatest impulses
of mankind to arrive at something higher than a natural state.
James Baldwin *Nobody Knows My Name*

3   I have found the evil weakening in me and the good raised up.
Robert Barclay 'Apology for the True Christian Divinity'

4   Justice is of the spirit, not of the outside world.
Hilda Clark *Spiritual Experiences of Friends*

5   Physical things depend on spiritual things and not the
opposite.
The Cloud of Unknowing

6   We need a spirituality to direct our freedom and make it
fruitful, so that human lives can gain something of the nothing-
wasted integrity and completeness of a work of art.
Don Cupitt *Taking Leave of God*

7   It is good if man can bring about that God sings within him.
Rabbi Elimelekh of Lizhensk Jewish spirituality

8   True spirituality seeks for bitterness rather than sweetness in
God, inclines to suffering rather than to consolation.
St John of the Cross *The Ascent of Mount Carmel*

9   There is no good in trying to be more spiritual than God. God
never means man to be a purely spiritual creature . . . He likes
matter. He created it.
C.S. Lewis *Mere Christianity*

10   'I am your life,' says the Lord, 'your bread, your source. If
you drink of this water you'll never thirst, if you eat of this
bread you will live forever.'
    I suffer from spiritual malnutrition.
Michel Quoist *With Open Heart*

11   If I had two loaves of bread, I would sell one and buy
hyacinths, for they would feed my soul.
The Qur'an

12   Man's difficulty today is that he is so immersed in the temporal
that he has lost sight of the spiritual, has lost sight of God.
Gilbert Shaw *Spiritual Warfare*

1 We are in Christ to serve the world and each other — never to dominate. Our freedom is the sword of the Spirit, a very different thing from the sword of Caesar.
> Gilbert Shaw *Spiritual Warfare*

2 However well of Christ
You talk and preach
Unless He lives within
He is beyond your reach.
> Angelus Silesius *The Book of Angelus Silesius*

3 His safest haven was prayer, not prayer of a single moment or idle or presumptuous prayer, but prayer of long duration, full of devotion, serene in humility.
> Thomas of Celano *Life of St Francis*

4 It is a splendid habit to laugh inwardly at yourself. It is the best way of regaining your good humour and of finding God without further anxiety.
> Abbé de Tourville *Letters of Direction*

5 Teach me, like you, to drink creation whole
And casting out myself, become a soul.
> Richard Wilbur *Advice to a Prophet*

6 Nuns fret not at their convent's narrow room,
And hermits are contented with their cells.
> William Wordsworth 'Nuns Fret Not'

SPRING

7 Of all things the beginning
Was on an April morn
In spring the earth remembereth
The day that she was born.
> *Mediaeval Latin Lyrics* Trans. Helen Waddell

8 To be interested in the changing seasons is a happier state of mind than to be hopelessly in love with Spring.
> George Santayana

STEADFASTNESS

9 And therefore, you are to strike the thick cloud of unknowing with the longing darts of love and never to retreat, no matter what comes to pass.
> *The Cloud of Unknowing*

STRENGTH

1 For ordinary occasions, it is right to husband one's strength and make it go as far as one can and count the cost, and with such and such power meet such and such claims.
> Fr Andrew SDC *Letters of Fr Andrew SDC*

2 Nothing is so strong as gentleness, nothing so gentle as real strength.
> St Francis de Sales

3 As thy days, so shall thy strength be.
> *Holy Bible* Deuteronomy Chap. 33 v. 25

4 Soldiers of Christ, arise,
And put your armour on,
Strong in the strength which God supplies
Of his eternal son.
> Charles Wesley *Hymns and Sacred Poems*

SUBMISSION

5 There is no happiness where there is no wisdom: no wisdom but in submission to the gods.
> Sophocles *Antigone*

SUCCESS

6 We are prone to judge success by the index of our salaries or the size of our automobiles, rather than by the quality of our service and our relationship to humanity.
> Martin Luther King *The Words of Martin Luther King*

7 Let us work as if success depends on ourselves alone, but with the heartfelt conviction that we are doing nothing and God everything.
> St Ignatius Loyola

SUFFERING

8 If suffering went out of life, courage, tenderness, pity, faith, patience and love in its divinity would go out of life, too.
> Fr Andrew SDC *Life and Letters*

9 There are those who suffer greatly, and yet, through the recognition that pain can be a thread in the pattern of God's weaving, find the way to a fundamental joy.
> Anon

1   We are created from and with the world
To suffer with and from it day by day.
   W.H. Auden 'Canzone'

2   Suffering is a form of gratitude to experience, or an
opportunity to experience evil, and change it into good.
   Saul Bellow *Hertzog*

3   It is infinitely easier to suffer in obedience to a human
command than to accept suffering as free, responsible men.
   Dietrich Bonhoeffer *Letters and Papers from Prison*

4   There is no point in being overwhelmed by the appalling total
of human suffering; such a total does not exist. Neither
poverty nor pain is accumulable.
   Jorge Luis Borges *Other Inquisitions*

5   Each thorn among those blackberries
Has pierced the hand that made it.
   Jack Clemo *The Child Traitor*

6   We cannot live, sorrow or die for somebody else, for suffering
is too precious to be shared.
   Edward Dahlberg *Because I Was Flesh*

7   He is in agony till the world's end. And we must never sleep
during that time.
   David Gascoigne *Ecce Homo*

8   If you suffer, thank God — it is a sure sign you are alive.
   Elbert Hubbard *Epigrams*

9   God will not look you over for medals, degrees or diplomas,
but for scars.
   Elbert Hubbard *The Note Book*

10   Nobody can love suffering, but we can love to suffer.
Instinctively we recoil from suffering but we can learn to suffer
for a positive dynamic reason.
   Cardinal Basil Hume OSB *Searching for God*

11   Although the world is full of suffering it is also full of the
overcoming of it.

12   Character cannot be developed in ease and quiet. Only
through experience of trial and suffering can the soul be
strengthened, vision cleared, ambition inspired, and success
achieved.
   Helen Keller

1   We feel and weigh soon enough what we suffer from others, but how much others suffer from us, of this we take no heed.
> Thomas à Kempis *The Imitation of Christ*

2   If a man in truth *wills* the Good then he must be willing to suffer *for* the Good.
> Søren Kierkegaard *Purity of Heart*

3   We must somehow believe that unearned suffering is redemptive.
> Martin Luther King *The Words of Martin Luther King*

4   It is cruel and false to brand every sufferer as a sinner: much suffering and sickness is due to the sin either of other persons or of society in general.
> Lambeth Conference Report 1958

5   Are you laying a feather-bed for me, no that shall not be.
My Lord was stretched on a hard and painful tree.
> St Lawrence Quoted *Butler's Lives of the Saints*

6   Creative suffering can shake the world and prayer, exercised in patience, is that which fuels it.
> Robert Llewelyn *A Doorway to Silence*

7   Know how sublime a thing it is
To suffer and be strong.
> Henry Wadsworth Longfellow *Voices in the Night* 'The Light of the Star'

8   When Heaven is about to confer a great office on any man, it first exercises his mind with suffering, and his sinews and bones with toil.
> Meng-Tze *The Book of Meng-Tze*

9   Even the most innocent of men's affairs seem doomed to cause suffering. Pushing the lawn-mower through tall wet grass, and enjoying the strong aroma of the morning, I found that the blades had cut a frog in half. I have not forgotten his eyes.
> Christopher Morley *Inward Ho!*

0   God is in all men, but not all men are in God — and that is why they suffer.
> Jawaharlal Nehru

1   As deeply as a man looketh into life, so deeply also doth he look into suffering.
> Friedrich Nietzsche *Thus Spake Zarathustra*

1 What is deservedly suffered must be borne with calmness.
   Ovid *Heroides*

2 Man's grandeur stems from his knowledge of his own misery.
   A tree does not know itself to be miserable.
   Blaise Pascal *Pensées*

3 Suffering passes: having suffered never passes.
   Jean Péguy

4 There is no suffering in the world but ultimately comes to be
   endured by God.
   A.T. Quiller-Couch

5 Nothing begins, and nothing ends,
   That is not paid with moan;
   For we are born in other's pain,
   And perish in our own.
   Francis Thompson 'Daisy'

6 O Christ, I see thy crown of thorns in every eye, thy bleeding,
   naked, wounded body in every soul; thy death liveth in every
   memory; thy crucified Person is embalmed in every affection;
   thy pierced feet are bathed in everyone's tears; and it is my
   privilege to enter with thee into every soul.
   Thomas Traherne

7 Activity of mind fails before the incommunicability of man's
   suffering.
   Lionel Trilling *The Liberal Imagination*

8 God calls you to suffer for the gospel; He does not call you to
   sickness.
   Colin Urquhart *Receive Your Healing*

9 If I am called upon to suffer let me be the well-bred beast that
   goes away and suffers in silence.
   HRH The Prince of Wales 'Prayer' Quoted in *This England*
   Summer 1987

SUICIDE

10 There is but one truly serious philosophical problem, and that
   is suicide. Judging whether life is, or is not worth living,
   amounts to answering the fundamental question of philosophy.
   Albert Camus *The Myth of Sisyphus*

1   Not only is suicide a sin, it is THE sin. It is the ultimate and absolute evil, the refusal to take the oath of loyalty to life.

2   The man who kills a man, kills *a* man. The man who kills himself kills all men; as far as he is concerned he wipes out the whole world.
     G.K. Chesterton *Orthodoxy*

3   There are many who dare not kill themselves for fear of what the neighbours might say.

4   There is no suicide for which all society is not responsible.
     Cyril Connolly *The Unquiet Grave*

5   Doesn't suicide seem a little like going where you haven't been invited?
     Richard Eberhart *How It Is*

6   Self-compassion . . . it must be that saves from suicide.
     George Gissing *The Private Papers of Henry Ryecroft*

7   Man is a prisoner who has no right to open the door of his prison and run away. A man should wait, and not take his own life until God summons him.
     Plato *Dialogues*

8   I am the only man in the world who cannot commit suicide.
     The Revd Chad Varah, founder of the Samaritans

SUNDAY

9   Sunday clears away the rust of the whole week.
     Joseph Addison *The Spectator*

10   Asked to comment on the new campaign, an official of the Lord's Day Observance Society said last night: 'We do not give statements on Sunday.'
     News Chronicle Quoted Michael Bateman *This England*

11   God ended all the world's array,
    And rested on the seventh day.
    His holy voice proclaimed it blest,
    And named it for the Sabbath rest.
     The Venerable Bede

12   There are many people who think that Sunday is a sponge to wipe out all the sins of the week.
     Henry Ward Beecher

1 The young people were taught to observe the Sabbath; they might not cut out things nor use their paint-box on Sunday. One treat only was allowed them — on Sunday evenings they might choose their own hymns.
   Samuel Butler *The Way of All Flesh*

2 Some keep the Sabbath going to Church —
   I keep it staying at Home —
   With a Bobolink for a Chorister —
   And an Orchard, for a Dome.
   Emily Dickinson *Complete Poems*

3 'Tis a strange thing that among us people can't agree the whole week because they go different ways on Sunday.
   George Farquhar

4 Sundays the pillars are,
   On which heaven's palace arched lies.
   George Herbert *The Temple* 'Sunday'

5 The cheerful Sabbath bells, wherever heard,
   Strike pleasant on the sense, most like the voice
   Of one, who from the far-off hills proclaims
   Tidings of good to Zion.
   Charles Lamb 'The Sabbath Bells'

6 Golf may be played on Sunday, not being a game within the view of the law, but being a form of moral effort.
   Stephen Leacock *Other Fancies* 'Why I Refuse to Play Golf'

7 Socialists don't hold meetings on Sunday, not if they've got any sense. Only God holds meetings on Sundays.
   James Mitchell 'When the Boat Comes In' BBC TV 10 March 1981

8 The feeling of Sunday is the same everywhere, heavy, melancholy, standing still. Like when they say 'As it was in the beginning, is now, and ever shall be, world without end.'
   Jean Rhys *Voyage in the Dark*

SUPERNATURAL

9 Religion has made an honest woman of the supernatural.
   Christopher Fry *The Lady's Not For Burning*

10 The supernatural is the natural not yet understood.
   Elbert Hubbard *The Note Book*

SUPERSTITION

1 It were better to have no opinion of God at all than such an opinion as is unworthy of him.
   Francis Bacon *Essays* 'Of Superstition'

2 Superstition is the religion of feeble minds.
   Edmund Burke 'Reflections on the Revolution in France'

3 Superstition is the only religion of which base souls are capable.
   Joseph Joubert

4 I miss my daily Mass, and have a superstitious feeling that anything may happen on the days I don't go. However, nothing in particular has.
   Rose Macaulay *Letters to a Friend*

SURRENDER

5 No man can do properly what he is called upon to do in this life unless he can learn to forget his ego and act as an instrument of God.
   W.H. Auden

6 Surrender of self applies as much to the daily affairs of life as it does to the affairs of the soul. They cannot be separated. We are all of a piece.
   Brother Roger CR *So Easy to Love*

SURVIVAL

7 I will live and survive and be asked
   How they slammed my head against a trestle,
   How I had to freeze at nights
   How my hair started to turn grey ...
   I will smile. And will crack some joke
   And brush away the encroaching shadow
   And I will render homage to the dry September
   That became my second birth.
   And I'll be asked: 'Doesn't it hurt you to remember?'
   Irina Ratushinskaya 'Suffering and Hope'

8 How fleeting is this world ...
   Yet it survives.
   It is ourselves that fade from it
   And our ephemeral lives.
   Angelus Silesius *The Book of Angelus Silesius*

SUSPICION

1   Suspect a man, and he will soon merit your suspicion.
       Tubby Clayton, founder of Toc H

SYMPATHY

2   Next to love, sympathy is the dimmest passion of the human
     heart.
       Edmund Burke

3   Pity may represent no more than the impersonal concern
     which prompts the mailing of a cheque, but true sympathy is
     the personal concern which demands the giving of one's soul.
       Martin Luther King *Strength to Love*

4   I believe sympathy is one of the most helpful helps one can
     bestow upon one's fellow creatures; and it seems a great pity
     that so many people feel it is their duty to criticize rather than
     sympathize.
       Hannah Whithall Smith

5   The world has no sympathy with any but positive grief. It will
     pity you for what you lose, never for what you lack.
       Madame Swetchine *The Writings of Madame Swetchine*

6   My need for sympathy has often induced me to seek it from
     people who, instead of strengthening me, unnerved me.
       Vincent Van Gogh *Dear Theo*

7   And whoever walks a furlong without sympathy walks to his
     own funeral dressed in a shroud.
       Walt Whitman *Leaves of Grass* 'Song of Myself'

8   His morality is all sympathy, just what morality should be.
       Oscar Wilde *De Profundis*

TEACHING

1 Christianity cannot be taught. All that you can do is clear the young mind and put it in a fit state to receive the Holy Spirit.
> Sir Richard Acland Quoted Llew Gardner *Sunday Express* 10 December 1961

2 What can only be taught by the rod and with blows will not lead to much good; they will not remain pious any longer than the rod is behind them.
> Martin Luther *The Great Catechism, Second Command*

3 Teach your son to love and fear God whilst he is still young, that the fear of God may grow up with him; and the same God will be a husband to you, and a father to him — a husband and father which cannot be taken from you.
> Sir Walter Raleigh to his wife, from the Tower of London, on the eve of his execution

TEARS

4 Tears are often the telescope by which men see far into heaven.
> Henry Ward Beecher

5 What soap is for the body, tears are for the soul.
> Jewish proverb

TEMPERANCE

6 Abstinence is as easy to me, as temperance would be difficult.
> Samuel Johnson Quoted Hannah More *Anecdotes*

7 We should thank God for beer and Burgundy by not drinking too much of them.
> G.K. Chesterton *Orthodoxy*

TEMPLE

1 God builds his temple in the heart on the ruins of churches
and religions.
    Ralph Waldo Emerson *Worship*

2 No temple can still the personal griefs and strifes in the breasts
of its visitors.
    Margaret Fuller *Summer on the Lake*

3 The chief sanctity of a temple is that it is a place to which men
go to weep in common.
    Miguel de Unamuno *The Tragic Sense of Life* 'The Man of Flesh
    and Bone'

TEMPTATION

4 It is good to be without vices, but it is not good to be without
temptation.
    Walter Bagehot *Biographical Studies*

5 All men are tempted. There is no man that lives that cannot
be broken down, provided it is the right temptation, put in the
right spot.
    Henry Ward Beecher *Proverbs from a Plymouth Pulpit*

6 The Devil tempted Christ, but it was Christ who tempted the
Devil to tempt him.
    Samuel Butler

7 Your foolish fears about the future come from the devil. Think
only of the present, abandon the future to Providence. It is the
good use of the present that assures the future.
    Jean-Pierre de Caussade SJ *The Flame of Divine Love*

8 What we most want to ask of our maker is an unfolding of the
divine purpose in putting human beings into conditions in
which such numbers of them would be sure to go wrong.
    Oliver Wendell Holmes *Over the Teacups*

9 Get thee behind me, Satan.
    Holy Bible St Matthew Chap. 16 v. 23

10 There is a certain degree of temptation which will overcome
any virtue. Now, in so far as you approach temptation to a
man, you do him an injury, and if he is overcome, you share
his guilt.
    Samuel Johnson Quoted Boswell's *Life of Johnson*

1   You are much more likely to make your man a sound drunkard by pressing drink on him as an anodyne when he is dull and weary than by encouraging him to use it as a means of merriment among his happy and expansive friends.

     C.S. Lewis *The Screwtape Letters*

2   Blessed is he who has never been tempted for he knows not the frailty of his rectitude.

     Christopher Morley *Inward Ho!*

3   I always despised Adam because he had to be tempted by the woman, as she was by the serpent, before he could be induced to pluck the apple from the tree of knowledge. I should have swallowed every apple on the tree the moment the owner's back was turned.

     George Bernard Shaw Quoted Hesketh Pearson *Bernard Shaw*

4   Have you ever wanted to run away with your neighbour's wife? If you have not then do not condemn the man who does — you might have done likewise.

     Rev. H.R.L. Sheppard Broadcast sermon 1924

5   I can resist everything except temptation.

     Oscar Wilde *Lady Windermere's Fan*

TENSION

6   The tension between the call to the desert and to the market place arises not from the greater presence of God in one or the other, but from our varying psychological needs to apprehend him in different ways.

     Sheila Cassidy Quoted *Prayers for Peace* 'The Peace of God'.

7   Nervous tension may be sent by God as a trial of faith and courage, it is not something to be courted as a sign of generous purpose. Nerves are a plague like any other, and more self-inspecting than most.

     Hubert van Zeller *Leave Your Life Alone*

THANKSGIVING

8   If the Church IS IN CHRIST, its initial act is always the act of thanksgiving, of returning the world to God.

     Alexander Schmemann *For the Life of the World. Sacraments and Orthodoxy*

THEOLOGY

1   'God saw everything that He had made and behold, it was
    very good' (Genesis 1.31). This is the foundation of Western
    religion. The afterthought − that it is not after all so very good
    − leads to theology.
    Gerald Brenan *Thoughts in a Dry Season*

2   I have only a small flickering light to guide me in the darkness
    of a thick forest. Up comes a theologian and blows it out.
    Denis Diderot

3   The cure for false theology is mother-wit. Forget your books
    and traditions, and obey your moral preceptions at this hour.
    Ralph Waldo Emerson *The Conduct of Worship*

4   Theologians are like wives. One at a time is a pretty good rule;
    two are certain death in circumlocution.
    Dennis Hackett *The Times* 'Countdown to God' 12 October 1981

5   Theology is an attempt to explain a subject by men who do not
    understand it. The intent is not to tell the truth, but to satisfy
    the questioner.
    Elbert Hubbard *The Philistine*

6   Only a minority of the religions of the world have a theology.
    There was no systematic series of statements which the Greeks
    agreed in believing about Zeus.
    C.S. Lewis 'Is Theology Poetry?'

7   A Theologian is born by living, nay dying and being damned,
    not by thinking, reading and speculating.
    Martin Luther *Table Talk*

8   Theology is the effort to explain the unknowable in terms of
    the not worth knowing.
    H.L. Mencken *Prejudices*

9   The point is, could God pass an examination in Theology?
    Malcolm Muggeridge BBC TV 26 February 1981

10 The most important quality in a person connected with
    religion is absolute devotion to the truth.
    Albert Schweitzer *Out of My Life and Thought*

11 Men should consider that raising difficulties concerning the
    mystery of religion cannot make them more wise, learned or
    virtuous; better neighbours or friends.
    Jonathan Swift

1 The clergy moves back and forth between the poles, the eternal truth of its foundation and the temporal situation in which the eternal truth must be received.
   Paul Tillich *Systematic Theology*

2 Theological religion is the source of all imaginable follies and disturbances: it is the parent of fanaticism and evil discord. It is the enemy of mankind.
   Voltaire *Philosophical Dictionary of Religion*

3 All your western theologies, the whole mythology of them, are based on the concept of God as a senile delinquent.
   Tennessee Williams *The Night of the Iguana*

THOUGHT

4 In much of your talking, thinking is half-murdered.
   Kahlil Gibran *The Prophet*

5 All things are at odds when God lets a thinker loose on this planet.
   Edith Hamilton *The Greek Way*

6 It is the very energy of thought
   Which keeps thee from thy God.
   John Henry, Cardinal Newman *The Dream of Gerontius*

7 Thinking is the talking of the soul with itself.
   Plato

8 Human thought, like God, makes the world in its own image.
   Adam Clayton Powell *Keep the Faith Baby*

9 As soon as man does not take his existence for granted, but beholds it as something unfathomably mysterious, thought begins.
   Albert Schweitzer *The Teaching of Reverence for Life*

10 Men suffer from thinking more than anything else.
   Leo Tolstoy *Sevastopol*

11 Thoughts alone cause the round of a new birth and a new death; let a man therefore strive to purify his thoughts. What a man thinks, that he is; this is the old secret.
   The Upanishads

12 Thoughts whose very sweetness yieldeth proof
   That they were born for immortality.
   William Wordsworth 'Inside King's College Chapel'

TIME

1   Time is a sort of river of passing events and strong is its
current; no sooner is a thing brought to sight than it is swept
by and another takes its place, and the two will be swept away.
   Marcus Aurelius *Meditations*

2   Take good care of time, how you spend it, for nothing is more
precious than time. In one little moment, short as it is, heaven
may be won or lost.
   The Cloud of Unknowing

3   Men's curiosity searches past and future
And clings to that dimension.
   T.S. Eliot *Four Quartets* 'The Dry Salvages'

4   Time will bring healing.
   Euripides *Alcestis*

5   Dost thou love life? Then do not squander time, for that's the
stuff life is made of.
   Benjamin Franklin *Poor Richard*

6   Time and thinking tame the strongest grief.
   W.C. Hazlitt 'English Proverbs'

7   Time's waters will not ebb nor stay.
   John Keble *The Christian Year* 'First Sunday after Christmas'

8   If you picture Time as a straight line along which we have to
travel, then you must picture God as the whole page on which
the line is drawn.
   C.S. Lewis *Mere Christianity*

9   Lives of great men all remind us
We can make our lives sublime,
And, departing, leave behind us
Footprints on the sands of time.
   Henry Wadsworth Longfellow 'A Psalm of Life'

10 Pythagoras, when he was asked what time was, answered that
it was the soul of this world.
   Plutarch *Morals*

11 Make use of time if thou lov'st eternity.
   Francis Quarles *Enchiridion*

12 The moment passed is no longer; the future may never be; the
present is all of which man is the master.
   Jean-Jacques Rousseau

1 Timelessness is so much a part of you, of me
We cannot hope to find the self
Until aware of our eternity.
Angelus Silesius *The Book of Angelus Silesius*

2 The old men ask
for more time, while the young
waste it. And the philosopher
smiles, knowing there is none
there. But the hero stands
sword drawn at the looking glass
of his mind, aiming at that
anonymous face over his shoulder.
R.S. Thomas 'Patterns'

TOLERANCE

3 Toleration is the cause of many evils and renders diseases and
distempers in the state more strong and powerful than any
remedies.
Archibald Campbell, 1st Marquis of Argyll, on religious
toleration

4 More and more people care about religious tolerance as fewer
and fewer care about religion.
Alexander Chase *Perspectives*

5 If you don't like people, put up with them as well as you can.
Don't try to love; you can't, you'll only strain yourself.
E.M. Forster *Two Cheers for Democracy*

6 All religions must be tolerated. Every man must get to heaven
in his own way.
Frederick the Great

7 Give to every other human being every right that you claim
yourself.
Robert G. Ingersoll *Limitations of Toleration*

8 Grant us that we may never forget, O Lord, that every man is
the Son of a King.
Jewish spirituality

9 By hook, by crook, by hair of head,
By scruff of neck and seat of pants,
Our stubborn infants shall be led
Along the path of tolerance.
Phyllis 𝘾Ginley *Primary Education* 'A Pocketful of Wry'

1 We must respect the other fellow's religion, but only in the sense and to the extent that we respect his theory that his wife is beautiful and his children smart.
   H.L. Mencken *Minority Reports*

2 The fallacy of the liberal mind has been to see God in everything. This has been of great assistance to the devil.
   Malcolm Muggeridge *Sunday Times* 19 April 1981

3 O God, help us not to despise or oppose what we do not understand.
   William Penn

4 Let your precept be 'Be easy.'
   Sir Richard Steele *The Spectator* No. 196

TONGUES

5 The Holy Spirit is composer and conductor. He gives each member of the worshipping congregation sounds — which He weaves together in heavenly harmony.

6 'Tongues' is a heart to heart language. As a baby lies in his mother's arms and babbles to his mother — they both understand what he means. So we lie in God's arms and babble to Him. And we both understand.
   Fr John Harper 'Sermons: St John-in-the-Fields, St Ives'

TRACTARIAN MOVEMENT

7 The Tracts were written for wide distribution. They were intended to be sold in hawkers' baskets. So the movement began. It was not in the least concerned with the revival of ceremonial — that came later, but before all else the Tractarian leaders were bent on the recovery of sound doctrine and godly discipline.
   C.B. Mortlock *Daily Telegraph* 7 July 1933

TRADITION

8 Christian work is constantly crippled by clinging to blessings and traditions of the past. God is not the God of yesterday. He is the God of today. Heaven forbid that we should go on playing religious games in one corner when the cloud and fire of God's presence have moved to another.
   David Watson *Through the Year with David Watson*

TRANQUILLITY

1   The time of business does not differ from the time of prayer; and in the noise and clutter of my kitchen, while several persons are at the same time calling for different things, I possess God in as great tranquillity as if I were upon my knees at the Blessed Sacrament.

     Br Lawrence *The Practice and Presence of God*

TRANSATLANTIC EVANGELICALS

2   To Jewellers — A Simple Pearl of Great Price! This inestimable Jewel may be obtained by application to Jesus Christ at the extremely low price of 'All that a man Hath.'

     The Circular — Journal of the Perfectionists Quoted Charles Nordoff *The Communistic Societies of the US*

3   Jimmy Swaggart's speciality is rigid moral fervour and eternal damnation. He once said Mother Teresa would go to hell if she were not born again.

     Simon Hoggart *Observer* 21 February 1988

4   Mistrust of godless higher education is a constant theme of the evangelicals. 'You can educate yourself right out of a relationship with God' (Tammy Faye Bakker).

     Observer 28 February 1988

5   My choicest political adviser is God who told me to run for the Presidency.

     Rev. Pat Robertson Quoted Douglas Brown *Church Times* March 1988

6   There is no soul under heaven that's going to walk through that gate of pearl unless they are born again by the blood of Jesus Christ.

     Jimmy Swaggart Quoted *Observer* 28 February 1988

TRANSGRESSION

7   All we like sheep have gone astray; we have turned every one to his own way.

     Holy Bible Isaiah Chap. 53 v. 6

8   He was numbered with the transgressors; and he bare the sins of many, and made intercession for the transgressors.

     Holy Bible Isaiah Chap. 53 v. 12

TRINITY

1 The divine nature is really and entirely identical with each of the three persons, all of whom can therefore be called one. I and the Father are one.
   St Thomas Aquinas

2 Among all things called One, the Unity of the Divine Trinity holds the first place.

3 How can plurality consist with unity, or unity with plurality? To examine the fact closely is rashness, to believe it is piety, to know it is life, and life eternal.
   St Bernard of Clairvaux

4 The unity of the Father, Son and Spirit is a unity of operation and revelation in which they are involved as three very diverse factors, to be described at best in analogical terms.
   Hans Küng

5 The Holy Trinity, pervading all men from first to last, from head to foot, binds them all together. The saints in each generation are joined to those who have gone before, and filled like them with light to become a golden chain in which each saint is a separate link, united to the next by faith, works and love. So in the one God they form a single chain which cannot be broken.
   St Simeon the New Theologian *Centauris*

TROUBLE

6 People with great troubles talk about little ones, and the man who complains of the crumpled rose leaf very often has his flesh full of thorns.
   G.K. Chesterton *Tremendous Trifles*

7 If we examine the sources of our troubles and agitations, we find that they almost invariably spring from a desire of appreciation or a fear of contempt.
   James, Cardinal Gibbons *The Ambassador of Christ*

8 Man is born unto trouble, as the sparks fly upward.
   Holy Bible Job Chap. 5 v. 7

9 There are no troubles in my own life except the troubles inseparable from being a spirit living in the flesh.
   George Santayana

1   Trouble will rain on those who are already wet.
    Spanish proverb

2   The usual excuse of those who cause others trouble is that they
    wish them well.
    Marquis de Vauvenargues *Maxims and Reflections*

TRUST

3   Thou shalt not be afraid for any terror by night: nor for the
    arrow that flieth by day.
    Book of Common Prayer Psalm 91 v. 5

4   I would rather work with God in the dark than go alone in the
    light.
    Mary Gardiner Brainard *Not Known*

5   When we trust as far as we can, we often find ourselves able to
    trust at least a little further.
    Mark Gibbard SSJE *Jesus, Liberation and Love*

6   Trust ye in the Lord for ever: for in the Lord Jehovah is
    everlasting strength.
    Holy Bible Isaiah Chap. 26 v. 4

7   Trust ... in the living God.
    Holy Bible 1 Timothy Chap. 6 v. 17

8   To be trusted is a greater compliment than to be loved.
    George Macdonald *The Marquis of Lossie*

9   O Lord, put no trust in me; for I shall surely fail if Thou
    uphold me not.
    St Philip Neri

10 The Lord is my strength, my strength and my salvation — in
    him I trust, in him I trust.
    Taizé Community Office Book

TRUTH

11 Truth is the secret of eloquence and of virtue, the basis of
    moral authority; it is the highest summit of art and life.
    H.F. Amiel *Journal*

12 What God's Son has told me, take for true I do;
    Truth himself speaks truly or there's nothing true.
    St Thomas Aquinas

1 Truth sits upon the lips of dying men.
>Matthew Arnold 'Sohrab and Rustum'

2 Be so true to thyself, as thou be not false to others.
>Francis Bacon *Essays* 'Of Wisdom for a Man's Self'

3 No pleasure is comparable to the slandering upon the vantage-ground of truth.

4 What is truth? said Jesting Pilate and would not stay for an answer.
>Francis Bacon *Essays* 'Of Truth'

5 A truth that's told with bad intent
Beats all the lies you can invent.
>William Blake 'Auguries of Innocence'

6 Truth can never be told so as to be understood, and not be believed.
>William Blake *The Marriage of Heaven and Hell* 'Proverbs of Hell'

7 The commandment of absolute truthfulness is really only another name for the fulness of discipleship.
>Dietrich Bonhoeffer *The Cost of Discipleship*

8 He shall defend thee under his wings, and thou shalt be safe under his feathers: his faithfulness and truth shall be thy shield and buckler.
>*Book of Common Prayer* Psalm 91 v. 4

9 Truth exists. Only lies are invented.
>Georges Braque *Thoughts on Art*

10 Truth is the highest thing that man may keep.
>Geoffrey Chaucer *Canterbury Tales* 'The Franklin's Tale'

11 Truths turn into dogmas the moment they are disputed.
>G.K. Chesterton *Heretics*

12 I have kept my truths; but I have discovered not that they were not truths, but that they were not mine. When I fancied I stood alone I was really in the position of being backed up by all Christendom.
>G.K. Chesterton *Orthodoxy*

13 They who know the truth are not equal to those who love it, and they who love it are not equal to those who delight in it.
>Confucius *Analects*

1   All truth is precious, if not all divine.
     William Cowper 'Charity'

2   As time goes on, new and remote aspects of truth are discovered, which can seldom or never be fitted into creeds that are changeless.
     Clarence Day *The Simian World*

3   Though truth and falsehood be
Near twins, yet truth a little elder is.
     John Donne *Sermons*

4   If God were able to backslide from truth I would fain cling to truth and let God go.
     Meister Eckhart Quoted Richard Harries *Turning to Prayer*

5   Ethical axioms are found and tested not very differently from the axioms of science. Truth is what stands the test of experience.
     Albert Einstein *Out of My Later Years*

6   Men turn this way and that in their search for new sources of comfort and inspiration, but the enduring truths are to be found in the word of God.
     Queen Elizabeth, the Queen Mother

7   God offers to every mind its choice between truth and repose.
     Ralph Waldo Emerson *Essays* 'Intellect'

8   No man speaks the truth or lives a true life two minutes together.
     Ralph Waldo Emerson *Journals*

9   Face to face the truth comes out.
     Thomas Fuller *Gnomologia*

10   Truth never damages a cause that is just.
     Gandhi *Non-Violence in Peace and War*

11   Say not, 'I have found the truth' but rather, 'I have found a truth.'
     Kahlil Gibran *The Prophet*

12   The truths of life are not discovered by us. At moments unforeseen, some gracious influence descends upon the soul, touching it to an emotion which, we know not how, the mind transmutes into thought.
     George Gissing *The Private Papers of Henry Ryecroft*

1 Truth is the god of the free man.
  Maxim Gorky *The Lower Depths*

2 Don't be so arrogant as to suppose that the truth is no bigger
  than your understanding of it.
  Michael Green *Jesus Spells Freedom*

3 Truth is a torch which gleams in the fog, but does not dispel it.
  Claude-Adrien Helvétius 'Of the Spirit'

4 He that trusts in a lie shall perish in truth.
  George Herbert *Jacula Prudentum*

5 Come, my Way, my Truth, my Life!
  Such a Way as gives us breath,
  Such a Truth as ends all strife,
  Such a Life as killeth Death.
  George Herbert *The Temple* 'The Call'

6 Ye shall know the truth, and the truth shall make you free.
  Holy Bible St John Chap. 8 v. 32

7 It is the customary fate of new truths to begin as heresies and
  end as superstitions.
  Thomas Henry Huxley *The Coming of Age of the Origin of
  Species*

8 A man had rather have a hundred lies told of him, than one
  truth which he does not wish should be told.

9 It is more from carelessness about truth than from intentional
  lying, that there is so much falsehood in the world.
  Samuel Johnson Boswell's *Life of Johnson*

10 When speculation has done its worst, two and two still make
   four.
   Samuel Johnson *The Idler*

11 A Church which abandons the truth abandons itself.
   Hans Küng *The Church*

12 Truth does not lie beyond humanity, but is one of the products
   of human mind and feeling.
   D.H. Lawrence *The Rainbow*

13 To love truth for truth's sake is the principal part of human
   perfection in this world, and the seed-plot of all other virtues.
   John Locke 'Letter to Anthony Collins'

1 Superstition, idolatry and hypocrisy have ample wages, but truth goes a-begging.

Martin Luther *Table Talk*.

2 In religion above all things the only thing of use is objective truth. The only God that is of use is a being who is persona, supreme and good, and whose existence is as certain as that two and two make four.

W. Somerset Maugham *The Summing Up*

3 To be mistaken is a misfortune to be pitied, but to know the truth and not to conform one's actions to it is a crime which Heaven and Earth condemn.

Giuseppe Mazzini *The Duties of Man*

4 The smallest atom of truth represents some man's bitter toil and agony; for every ponderable chunk of it there is a brave truth-seeker's grave upon some lonely ashdump and a soul roasting in hell.

H.L. Mencken *Prejudices*

5 Though all the winds of doctrine were let loose to play upon the earth, so Truth be in the field, we do ingloriously, by licensing and prohibition, to misdoubt her strength.

John Milton *Areopagitica*

6 I speak the truth, not my fill of it, but as much as I dare to do so, a little more as I grow old.

Montaigne *Essays*

7 Rabbi Simeon said: The punishment of the liar is that he isn't believed even when he is telling the truth.

Avoth de-Rabbi Nathan *Gemora*

8 It is obvious that to be in earnest in seeking the truth is an indispensable requisite for finding it.

John Henry, Cardinal Newman *Oxford University Sermons*

9 The love of truth has its reward in Heaven, and even on earth.

Friedrich Nietzsche *Beyond Good and Evil*

10 To me the truth is something which cannot be told in a few words, and those who simplify the universe only reduce the expansion of its meaning.

Anais Nin *Diary* 'Winter'

11 We know the truth, not only by the reason, but also by the heart.

Blaise Pascal *Pensées*

1   Truth often suffers most by the heat of its defenders than from
    the arguments of its opposers.
       William Penn *Some Fruits of Solitude*

2   Do not veil the truth with falsehood, nor conceal the truth
    knowingly.
       The Qur'an

3   Speak the truth and shame the Devil.
       François Rabelais

4   Truth is given, not to be contemplated, but to be done. Life is
    an action, not a thought.
       F.W. Robertson *Sermons*

5   I think the most important quality in a person concerned with
    religion is absolute devotion to truth.
       Albert Schweitzer *Out of My Life and Thought*

6   Truth is like life; it has to be taken in its entirety or not at all.
    Isolated truths will not do.
       Fulton J. Sheen *Lift Up Your Hearts*

7   It is the calling of great men, not so much to preach new
    truths, as to rescue from oblivion those old truths which it is
    our wisdom to remember and our weakness to forget.
       Sydney Smith

8   The truth is almost the strongest argument.
       Sophocles *Phaedra*

9   A lie travels round the world while Truth is putting on her
    boots.
       Charles Haddon Spurgeon *Truth and Falsehood*

10 The truth is here! Go where you will — to Benares or to
    Mathura; until you have found God in your own soul, the
    whole world will seem meaningless to you.
       Rabindranath Tagore

11 Truth is such a precious article, let us all economise in its use.
       Mark Twain

12 Any human being can penetrate the kingdom of truth, if only
    he longs for truth and perpetually concentrates all his attention
    upon its attainment.
       Simone Weil

1 Christ likes us to prefer truth to him because, before being Christ, he is truth. If one turns aside from him to go towards the truth, one will not go far before falling into his arms.
   Simone Weil *Waiting for God*

2 The ugliness of the script is not the ugliness of the divine scribe.
   The Wisdom of the Sufis Compiled by Kenneth Cragg

3 It is one thing to wish to have truth on our side, and another to wish sincerely to be on the side of truth.
   Richard Whately *On the Love of Truth*

4 I believe that in the end truth will conquer.
   John Wycliffe, to the Duke of Lancaster 1381

TYRANNY

5 I have sworn upon the altar of God eternal hostility against every form of tyranny over the mind of man.
   Thomas Jefferson *Writings*

6 First they came for the Jews. I was silent. I was not a Jew. Then they came for the Communists. I was silent. I was not a Communist. Then they came for the trade unionists. I was silent. I was not a trade unionist. Then they came for me. There was no one left to speak for me.
   Martin Niemoller Quoted *Morning Has Broken*

UBIQUITY

1 God is seated in the hearts of all.
   Bhagavad Gita

2 In every place where you find the imprint of men's feet there
   am I.
   The Talmud

ULTRA CATHOLIC

3 The music we perform at Mass is Verdi and Scarlatti.
   Assorted females form the choir; I wish they weren't so catty.
   Two flutes, a fiddle and a harp assist them in the gallery;
   The organist left years ago, and so we save his salary.

   I am an Ultra-Catholic — No 'Anglo', I beseech you!
   You'll find no trace of heresy in anything I teach you.
   The clergyman across the road has whiskers and a bowler,
   But I wear buckles on my shoes and sport a feriola.
   Fr Eric Mascall *Pi in the High*

UNCERTAINTY

4 Wherever you turn there is uncertainty; only death is sure, but
   even the day of your death is uncertain.
   St Augustine of Hippo 'Psalm 38'

5 Watch therefore, for ye know neither the day nor the hour
   wherein the Son of man cometh.
   Holy Bible St Matthew Chap. 25 v. 13

UNDERSTANDING

6 Understanding is the reward of faith. Therefore seek not to
   understand that thou mayest believe, but believe that thou
   mayest understand.
   St Augustine of Hippo *St John's Gospel*

1   God is not what you imagine or what you think you
    understand. If you understand you have failed.
        St Augustine of Hippo *De Trinitate*

2   Such good things as pass man's understanding.
        Book of Common Prayer Collect for Sixth Sunday after Trinity

3   Of course understanding of our fellow beings is important. But
    this understanding becomes fruitful only when it is sustained
    by sympathetic feeling in joy and sorrow.
        Albert Einstein *Ideas and Opinions*

4   Understanding a person does not mean condoning; it only
    means that one does not accuse him as if one were God or a
    judge placed above him.
        Erich Fromm *Man for Himself*

5   Understanding is the beginning of approving. To negate with
    conviction one must never have looked at what one negates.
        André Gide *The Journals of André Gide*

6   The fear of the Lord is the beginning of wisdom: a good
    understanding have all they that do his commandments.
        Holy Bible Psalm 111 v. 10

7   With all thy getting get understanding.
        Holy Bible Proverbs Chap. 4 v. 7

8   When we talk about understanding, surely it takes place only
    when the mind listens completely — the mind being your
    heart, your nerves, your ears — when you give your whole
    attention to it.
        Krishnamurti *You Are in the World*

9   O Lord, give me understanding concerning Thyself, for I
    cannot understand Thee except by means of Thee.
        Sufi spirituality

10 If one is master of one thing and understands one thing well,
    one has at the same time insight into and understanding of
    many things.
        Vincent Van Gogh *Dear Theo*

11 The language of the mystics cannot meet the language of
    science or reason, but nevertheless in a world that craves
    experimental testimonies it will always be one of the roads by
    which our contemporaries can find God.
        René Voillaume *Contemplation in the Church in Our Time*

UNHAPPINESS

1 No sooner is it a little calmer with me that it is almost too calm. As though I have a true feeling of myself only when I am unbearably unhappy. That is probably true, too.
   Franz Kafka *The Diaries of Franz Kafka*

2 By becoming more unhappy, we sometimes learn how to be less so.
   Madame Swetchine *The Writings of Madame Swetchine*

3 Those who are unhappy have no need for anything in this world but people capable of giving them their attention.
   Simone Weil *Waiting for God*

UNION

4 Prayer oneth the soul to God.
   Julian of Norwich

5 Making my will one with the will of God, this is the union which I myself desire and should like to see in everyone, and not just a few of those raptures, however delightful, which go by the name of union.
   St Teresa of Avila *Foundations*

UNITARIANISM (Boston-style)

6 We believe in the Fatherhood of God, the brotherhood of man, and the neighbourhood of Boston.
   Anon The formula by which the Boston Unitarians explain their easy-going ecumenism and patrician membership

UNITY

7 The whole Christian life is that we are totally one with each other in his Church, that Christ has given himself totally to us in this oneness.
   Fr Peter Ball CGA Clergy Conference at Swanwick 1985

8 Behold, how good and how pleasant it is for brethren to dwell together in unity.
   Holy Bible Psalm 133 v. 1

9 One Lord, one faith, one baptism, one God and Father of all, who is above all, and through all, and in all.
   Holy Bible Ephesians Chap. 4 vv. 5—6

UNIVERSE

1   The universe begins to look more like a great thought in the
    mind of God, than like a great machine.
       Sir James Jeans *The Mysterious Universe*

2   The universe is not on the side of frugality; the stars were
    hurled, broadcast from the hand of God.
       Don Marquis *Prefaces*

3   The cosmos is a gigantic fly-wheel making 10,000 revolutions a
    minute. Man is a sick fly taking a dizzy ride on it. Religion is
    the theory that the wheel was designed and set spinning to give
    him a ride.
       H.L. Mencken *Prejudices*

4   One God, one law, one element,
    And one far-off divine event,
    To which the whole creation moves.
       Alfred, Lord Tennyson *In Memoriam*

5   The children of God should not have any other country here
    below but the universe itself, with the totality of all the
    reasoning creatures it has ever contained, contains, or ever
    will contain. That is the native city to which we owe our love.
       Simone Weil *Waiting for God*

UNKNOWN

6   Behind the dim unknown,
    Standeth God within the shadow, keeping watch above his
       own.
       James Russell Lowell 'The Present Crisis'

7   We are ignorant of the Beyond because this ignorance is the
    condition *sine qua non* of our own life. Just as ice cannot know
    fire except by melting, by vanishing.
       Jules Renard *Journal*

UNSELFISHNESS

8   Neighbours praise unselfishness because they profit by it.
       Friedrich Nietzsche

9   There is nothing in Christianity or Buddhism that quite
    matches the sympathetic unselfishness of an oyster.
       Saki (H.H. Munro) *Chronicles of Clovis*

1 Lord, grant that I may seek to comfort rather than be
comforted; to love rather than be loved.
> Mother Teresa of Calcutta Quoted Kathryn Spink *For the
> Brotherhood of Man Under the Fatherhood of God*

UTOPIA

2 Religion wisely assumes misfortune and so survives, when
earthly Utopian hopes, which must inevitably be disappointed,
soon perish.
> Malcolm Muggeridge *Tread Softly For You Tread on My Jokes*

3 Not in Utopia — subterranean fields, —
Or some secreted island, Heaven knows where!
But in the very world, which is the world
Of all of us, — the place where in the end
We find our happiness, or not at all!
> William Wordsworth *The Prelude* Book XI

VALOUR

1 How strangely high endeavours may be blessed,
Where piety and valour jointly go.
    John Dryden

VANITY

2 And the name of that town is Vanity: and at the town there is
a fair kept called Vanity Fair.
    John Bunyan *The Pilgrim's Progress*

3 A vain man can never be utterly ruthless; he wants to win
applause and therefore he accommodates himself to others.
    Goethe

4 All is vanity, and discovering it — the greatest vanity.
    John Oliver Hobbes (Pearl Mary Teresa Craigie) *The Sinner's
Comedy*

5 Most of us retain enough of the theological attitude to think
that we are little gods.
    Oliver Wendell Holmes *The Mind and Faith of Justice Holmes*

6 Vanity of vanities; all is vanity.
    Holy Bible Ecclesiastes Chap. 1 v. 2

7 There is no arena in which vanity displays itself under such a
variety of forms as in conversation.
    Blaise Pascal

8 The greatest magnifying glasses in the world are a man's own
eyes when they look upon his own person.
    Alexander Pope

9 Most of us would be far enough from vanity if we heard all the
things that are said of us.
    Joseph Rickaby *Waters That Go Softly*

1 The primary sin of man today is not to see redemption, not to
  see the Lord, but to set up his own standard.
  > Gilbert Shaw *Homily*

VESPERS

2 God that madest earth and heaven, darkness and light
  Who the day for toil has given
  For rest the night
  Guard us waking, guard us sleeping and when we die
  May we in thy mighty keeping
  All peaceful lie.
  > R. Heber

3 Glory to thee, my God, this night
  For all the blessings of the light;
  Keep me, O keep me, King of Kings,
  Beneath thy own almighty wings.
  > Thomas Ken

VESTMENTS

4 For me, I neither know nor care
  Whether a Parson ought to wear
  A black dress or a white dress;
  Filled with trouble of my own, −
  A Wife who preaches in her gown,
  And lectures in her night-dress!
  > Thomas Hood 'The Surplice Question'

5 I go to church; and this day the parson hath got one to read
  with a surplice on; I suppose himself will take it up hereafter
  for a cunning fellow he is as any of his coat.
  > Samuel Pepys *Diary*

6 The Puritan hostility to time and money spent on apparel
  displeased Queen Elizabeth I, who said to the Puritan
  President of Magdalen: 'Master Doctor, that loose gown
  becomes you well. I wonder your notions should be so narrow.'
  > Peter G. Watkins Quoted *Church Times* March 1988

VICE

7 We make a ladder of our vices, if we trample those same vices
  underfoot.
  > St Augustine of Hippo *Sermons*

1   For the better cure of vice they think it necessary to study it,
    and the only efficient study is through practice.
        Samuel Butler

2   Half the vices which the world condemns most loudly have
    seeds of good in them and require moderate use rather than
    abstinence.
        Samuel Butler *The Way of All Flesh*

3   It is the function of vice to keep virtue within reasonable
    bounds.
        Samuel Butler *Notebooks*

4   We are more apt to catch the vices of others than their virtues,
    as disease is far more contagious than health.
        Charles Caleb Colton *Lacon*

5   Men wish to be saved from the mischiefs of their vices, but not
    from their vices.

6   There is a capacity of virtue in us, and there is a capacity of
    vice to make your blood creep.
        Ralph Waldo Emerson *Journals of Ralph Waldo Emerson*

7   It is the restrictions placed on vice by our social code which
    make its pursuit so peculiarly agreeable.
        Kenneth Grahame *Pagan Papers*

8   The vices are never so well employed as when combating each
    other.
        William Hazlitt

9   I find that the best good I have has some tincture of vice.
        Montaigne *Essays*

10 Vice, like virtue,
    Grows but by small steps, and no true innocence
    Can ever fall at once to deepest guilt.
        Jean Racine *Phèdre*

VICTORY

11 Even victors are by victories undone.
        John Dryden *Epistles* 'To John Driden of Chesterton'

12 There is a way of winning by losing, a way of victory in defeat
    which we are going to discover.
        Laurens van der Post *A Bar of Shadow*

VIOLENCE

1 The violence of Jesus is deep love, not the sword or the prison, which is how we always want to resolve the problems which seem insoluble to us.
   Carlo Carretto *The God Who Comes*

2 God hates violence. He has ordained that all men fairly possess their property, not seize it.
   Euripides *Helen*

3 No doubt religion has to answer for some of the most terrible crimes in history. But that is the fault not of religion but of the ungovernable brute in man.
   Gandhi

4 The Church condemns violence, but it condemns indifference more harshly. Violence can be the expression of love, indifference never.
   Graham Greene *The Comedians*

5 Violence ends by defeating itself. It creates bitterness in the survivors and brutality in the destroyers.
   Martin Luther King *The Words of Martin Luther King*

6 The modern choice is between Non-Violence and Non-Existence.
   Martin Luther King

7 Much violence is based on the illusion that life is a property to be defended and not a gift to be shared.
   Henri Nouwen

8 Violence can only be concealed by a lie, and the lie can only be maintained by violence. Any man who has once proclaimed violence as his method is inevitably forced to take the lie as his principle.
   Alexander Solzhenitsyn Nobel Prize Lecture 1973

VIRGIN

9 She [St Agnes] was still too young for punishment, but already ripe for victory, too young for battle, yet ready to win the crown. Her tender age was a disadvantage, but she won the trial of virtue.
   St Ambrose

10 Virginity is a life of angels, the enamel of the soul.
   Jeremy Taylor *Holy Living*

VIRTUE

1 If there's a power above us,
   (And that there is all nature cries aloud
   Through all her works) he must delight in virtue.
     Joseph Addison *Cato*

2 Virtue is more clearly shown in the performance of fine actions
   than in the non-performance of base ones.
     Aristotle *Nicomachean Ethics*

3 Virtue is nothing but well directed love.
     St Augustine of Hippo

4 Waste no time arguing what a good man should be; be one.
     Marcus Aurelius

5 Virtue is like precious odours — most fragrant when they are
   incensed or crushed.
     Francis Bacon *Essays* 'Of Adversity'

6 Virtue is like a rich stone — best plain set.
     Francis Bacon *Essays* 'Of Beauty'

7 There is no road or ready way to virtue.
     Sir Thomas Browne *Religio Medici*

8 Virtue is not the absence of vices or the avoidance of moral
   dangers; virtue is a vivid and separate thing, like pain or a
   particular smell.
     G.K. Chesterton *Tremendous Trifles*

9 The existence of virtue depends entirely upon its use.

10 Many wish not so much to be virtuous, as to seem to be.
      Cicero *De Republica*

11 The two virtues, humility and charity, are good examples and
    may stand for the others. Whoever has these clearly needs no
    more. For he has them all.

12 Virtue is nothing else but an ordered and measured affection
    directed towards God for his sake alone.
      The Cloud of Unknowing

13 Virtue is not left to stand alone. He who practises it will have
    neighbours.

14 If a superior man abandons virtue how can he fulfil the
    requirements of that name?
      Confucius *Analects*

1   Silver and gold are not the only coin,
Virtue too passes current all over the world.
> Euripides *Oedipus*

2   Do not think that you have acquired virtue, unless you have
struggled for it to the point of shedding your blood.
> Evagrius of Pontus *On Prayer*

3   Let us belong to God even in the thick of the disturbance
stirred up round about us by the diversity of human affairs.
True virtue is not always nourished in external calm any more
than good fish are always found in stagnant waters.
> St Francis de Sales

4   The virtue that requires to be ever guarded is scarcely worth
the sentinel.
> Oliver Goldsmith *The Vicar of Wakefield*

5   The measure of any man's virtue is what he would do if he had
neither the laws nor public opinion, nor even his own
prejudices, to control him.
> William Hazlitt *Characteristics*

6   Virtue never grows old.
> George Herbert *Jacula Prudentum*

7   I don't believe the Devil would give half as much for the
services of a sinner as he would for those of one of those folks
that are always doing virtuous acts in a way to make them
unpleasing.
> Oliver Wendell Holmes *The Professor at the Breakfast Table*

8   Through virtue lies the one and only road to a life of peace.
> Juvenal *Satires*

9   Make a virtue of necessity.
> Br Lawrence *Ma Bonne Mère*

10   Virtue is an angel, but she is a blind one, and must ask of
Knowledge to show her the pathway that leads to her goal.
> Horace Mann *Thoughts for a Young Man*

11   I cannot praise a fugitive and cloistered virtue, unexercised
and unbreathed, that never sallies out and sees her adversary,
but slinks out of the race where that immortal garland is to be
run for, not without dust and heat.
> John Milton *Areopagitica*

1   There is no man so good that if he places all his actions and
    thoughts under the scrutiny of the law he would not deserve
    hanging ten times in his life.
    Montaigne *Essays*

2   He who dies for virtue does not perish.
    Plautus

3   We are never so virtuous as when we are ill. It is then that a
    man recollects that there are gods, and that he himself is
    mortal, and he resolves that if he has the luck to recover, his
    life shall be passed in harmless happiness.
    Pliny the Younger *Epistles*

4   We bestowed the Book on those of our servants whom We
    have chosen. Some of them sin against their souls, some follow
    a middle course, and some, by Allah's leave, vie with each
    other in charitable works: this is the supreme virtue.
    The Qur'an

5   The chief cause of our misery is less the violence of our
    passions than the feebleness of our virtues.
    Joseph Roux *Meditations of a Parish Priest*

6   I am not impressed by external devices for the preservation of
    virtue in men and women. Marriage laws, the police, armies
    and navies are the mark of human incompetence.
    Dora Russell *The Right to Be Happy*

7   The glory that goes with wealth and beauty is fleeting and
    fragile, virtue is a possession glorious and eternal.
    Sallust *Catiline*

8   There is but one Virtue — the eternal sacrifice of self.
    George Sand

9   When men grow virtuous in their old age they only make a
    sacrifice to God of the devil's leavings.
    Jonathan Swift *Thoughts on Various Subjects*

VISION

10 I was created to see God, and I have not yet accomplished that
    for which I was made.
    St Anselm

11 Who is narrow of vision cannot be large of heart.
    Chinese proverb

1 ... an ocean of darkness and death, but an infinite ocean of
light and love flowed over the ocean of darkness. And in that
also I saw the infinite Love of God.
George Fox *Journal*

2 Where there is no vision, the people perish.
Holy Bible Proverbs Chap. 29 v. 18

3 Man has two eyes. One only sees what moves in fleeting time,
the other what is eternal and divine.
Angelus Silesius *The Book of Angelus Silesius*

4 If ye do not recognise God, at least recognise his signs.
Sufi spirituality

5 What we call our Religious Experiences are genuine if
fragmentary glimpses of the Divine Reality.
Evelyn Underhill *Spiritual Life*

VOCATION

6 Men are called to meet the Lord insofar as they constitute a
community, a people. It is a question not so much of a
vocation to salvation as a convocation.
Gustavo Gutierrez *A Theology of Liberation*

7 Condescend to all weaknesses and infirmities of your fellow
creatures, cover their frailties, love their excellencies,
encourage their virtue, relieve their wants, rejoice in their
prosperities, compassionate their distress, receive their
friendship, overlook their unkindness, forgive their malice and
condescend to do the lowest offices to the lowest of mankind.
William Law *A Serious Call to a Devout and Holy Life*

8 O God, You have appointed me to watch over the life and
death of Your creatures. Here I am, ready for my vocation.
Maimonides Quoted *Oxford Book of Prayer*

9 I want to go and be a Cowley Father
I do not want to run away to sea
I won't be a policeman or a fireman
And an actor's life is not for me.
I will not be a gangster in Chicago
For the Vicar says such men are very bad
So order me a cassock and a girdle
For I want to go and be a Cowley dad.
Fr Eric Mascall *Pi in the High*

1 For each individual soul there is a vocation as real as if that
   soul were alone upon the planet.

   Mark Rutherford *The Deliverance of Mark Rutherford*

2 The vocation of every man and woman is to serve other
   people.

   Leo Tolstoy *War and Peace*

3 A 'religious vocation' if it is real must be an attraction to a life,
   not a work. The truest vocation would be best described as a
   supernatural attraction to the Cross.

   Fr William of Glasshampton SDC *A Franciscan Revival*

WAITING

1 He went to the Garden of Gethsemane to wait upon the outcome. Waiting can be the most intense and poignant of all human experiences — the experience which, above all others, strips us of our needs, our values and ourselves.
   W.H. Vanstone *The Stature of Waiting*

WANT

2 As long as I have a want, I have a reason for living. Satisfaction is death.
   George Bernard Shaw *Overruled*

3 Hundreds would never have known want if they had not first known waste.
   Charles Haddon Spurgeon

WAR

4 The Church knows nothing of a sacredness of war. The Church which prays the 'Our Father' asks God only for peace.
   Dietrich Bonhoeffer *No Rusty Sword*

5 There is nothing that war has ever achieved we could not better achieve without it.
   Havelock Ellis *Selected Essays*

6 There never was a good war, or a bad peace.
   Benjamin Franklin Letter to Quincey, 11 September 1783

7 War is kinder than a Godless peace.
   G.A. Studdert-Kennedy *The Unutterable Beauty*

8 Weapons of war are tools of evil; those who truly admire them are murderers at heart.
   Taoist spirituality

1 War is the greatest crime man perpetrates against man.
>   Zarathustra

WASTE

2 ... as water spilt on the ground, which cannot be gathered up
again.
>   *Holy Bible* 2 Samuel Chap. 14 v. 14

WEAKNESS

3 All hands shall be feeble, and all knees shall be weak as water.
>   *Holy Bible* Ezekiel Chap. 7 v. 17

4 And he said unto me, My grace is sufficient for thee: for my
strength is made perfect in weakness.
>   *Holy Bible* 2 Corinthians Chap. 12 v. 9

5 We should keep up in our hearts a constant sense of our own
weakness, not with a design to discourage the mind and
depress the spirits, but with a view to drive us out of ourselves,
in search of the Divine assistance.
>   Hannah More *Practical Piety*

WEALTH

6 Theirs is an endless road, a hopeless maze, who seek for goods
before they seek for God.
>   St Bernard of Clairvaux *De Diligendo Deo*

7 The splash of wealth can distance the rich from the needs of
the poor and make them forget their humanity.
>   Christopher Bryant SJ *The Heart in Pilgrimage*

8 Increase of material comforts, it may be generally laid down,
does not in any way whatsoever conduce to moral growth.
>   Gandhi Quoted *News Chronicle* Obituary 31 January 1948

9 Unto whomsoever much is given, of him shall be much
required.
>   *Holy Bible* St Luke Chap. 12 v. 48

10 No man takes with him to Hades all his exceeding wealth.
>   Theognis *Elegies*

11 Wealth consists not in having possessions but in having few
wants.
>   Esther de Waal *Seeking God: The Way of St Benedict*

WHOLENESS

1 To be 'whole' is to be spiritually, emotionally and physically healthy. Jesus lived in perfect wholeness.
Colin Urquhart *Receive Your Healing*

WICKEDNESS

2 When the wicked man turneth away from his wickedness that he hath committed, and doeth that which is lawful and right, he shall save his soul alive.
Book of Common Prayer Sentence of Scripture before Evening Prayer

3 A belief in a supernatural source of evil is not necessary; men alone are quite capable of every wickedness.
Joseph Conrad *Under Western Eyes*

4 Even as the holy and the righteous cannot rise beyond the highest which is in each of you, so the wicked and the weak cannot fall lower than the lowest which is in you also.
Kahlil Gibran *The Prophet*

5 There is no peace, saith the Lord, unto the wicked.
Holy Bible Isaiah Chap. 48 v. 22

6 The wicked are like the troubled sea, when it cannot rest, whose waters cast up mire and dirt.
Holy Bible Isaiah Chap. 57 v. 20

7 Wickedness is always easier than virtue, for it takes the short cut to everything.
Samuel Johnson Quoted James Boswell *Tour to the Hebrides*

WILL

8 I was kept fast bound, not with exterior chains or irons, but with my own iron will. The enemy held my will and of it he had made a chain which fettered me fast.
St Augustine of Hippo Quoted *Butler's Lives of the Saints*

9 Not my will, but thine, be done.
Holy Bible St Luke Chap. 22 v. 42

10 If it's GOT to be a battle of wills, I'll fight the devil himself, as long as the necessity lasts. But it's not my idea of life.
D.H. Lawrence *Selected Letters of D.H. Lawrence*

WINE

1 Take counsel in wine, but resolve afterwards in water.
    Benjamin Franklin *Poor Richard*

2 Wine that maketh glad the heart of man.
    Holy Bible Psalm 104 v. 15

3 The best wine ... that goeth down sweetly, causing the lips of
    those that are asleep to speak.
    Holy Bible The Song of Solomon Chap. 7 v. 9

4 Drink no longer water, but use a little wine for thy stomach's
    sake.
    Holy Bible 1 Timothy Chap. 5 v. 23

WISDOM

5 The first key to wisdom is assiduous and frequent questioning.
    For by doubting we come in enquiry and by enquiry we arrive
    at the truth.
    Peter Abelard

6 A wise man will make more opportunities than he finds.
    Francis Bacon *Essays 'Of Ceremonies and Respects'*

7 They live in freedom who have gone beyond the dualities of
    life. Competing with no one, they are alike in success and
    failure and content with whatever comes to them.
    Bhagavad Gita

8 There is a deep wisdom inaccessible to the wise and prudent
    but disclosed to babes.
    Christopher Bryant SJ *The Heart in Pilgrimage*

9 First then, fear God: for His fear is wisdom and being wise,
    thou canst not err.
    Cervantes *Don Quixote*

10 Knowledge is proud that he has learned so much;
    Wisdom is humble that he knows no more.
    William Cowper *Poems*

11 Let my heart be wise. It is the god's best gift.
    Euripides *Medea*

12 If a man empties his purse into his head, no one can take it
    from him.
    Benjamin Franklin

1 The price of wisdom is above rubies.
Holy Bible Job Chap. 28 v. 18

2 Wisdom is the principal thing; therefore get wisdom: and with all thy getting get understanding.
Holy Bible Proverbs Chap. 4 v. 7

3 A wise man is strong; yea, a man of knowledge increaseth strength.
Holy Bible Proverbs Chap. 24 v. 5

4 Therefore whosoever heareth these sayings of mine, and doeth them, I will liken him unto a wise man, which built his house upon a rock.
Holy Bible St Matthew Chap. 7 v. 24

5 Be ye therefore wise as serpents, and harmless as doves.
Holy Bible St Matthew Chap. 10 v. 16

6 The wisdom of this world is foolishness with God.
Holy Bible 1 Corinthians Chap. 3 v. 19

7 Common sense suits itself to the ways of the world. Wisdom tries to conform to the ways of heaven.
Joseph Joubert *Pensées*

8 To have a low opinion of our own merits, and to think highly of others, is an evidence of wisdom. All men are frail, but thou should'st reckon none as frail as thyself.
Thomas à Kempis *The Imitation of Christ*

9 He who knows others is learned; he who knows himself is wise.
Lao-Tze *Character of Tao*

10 The wise man does not lay up treasure.
Lao-Tze

11 Neither despise, nor oppose, what thou dost not understand.
William Penn Quoted *A Little Book of Life and Death*

12 Accumulated knowledge does not make a wise man. Knowledgeable people are found everywhere, but we are cruelly short of wise people.
Michel Quoist *With Open Heart*

13 Though a man be wise,
It is no shame for him to live and learn.
Sophocles

flesh

1   The sublimity of wisdom is to do those things living which are
to be desired when dying.
> Jeremy Taylor

2   When a man lacks wisdom
His mind is always restless, and his senses are wild horses
Dragging the driver hither and thither.
But when he is full of wisdom
His mind is collected
And his senses become tamed horses
Obedient to the driver's will.
> *The Upanishads*

3   The wisdom of life consists in the elimination of non-essentials.
> Lin Yutang *The Wisdom of China and India*

WITNESS

4   I call heaven and earth to witness against you this day.
> *Holy Bible* Deuteronomy Chap. 4 v. 26

5   It is in simply being itself and living its own supernatural
life that the Church performs its greatest service to the
world.
> Fr Eric Mascall *Corpus Christi*

6   Because Christ bears witness to Scripture, we believe it.
Because Scripture bears witness to Christ, we go to Him.
> John R. Stott *Christ, the Controversialist*

WOMAN

7   As Father Adam first was fool'd,
A case that's still too common,
Here lies a man a woman rul'd —
The Devil ruled the woman.
> Robert Burns 'Epitaph on a Hen-Pecked Country Squire'

8   If God considered woman a fit helpmeet for man, he must
have had a very poor opinion of man.
> Samuel Butler *Notebooks*

9   Male religious authority reinforces male secular authority and
gives it a mystical unquestionable basis.
> Wendy Collins, Ellen Friedman, Agnes Pinot *The Directory of
> Social Change*

1   I'm not denyin' that women are foolish; God Almighty made
    'em to match the men.
        George Eliot *Adam Bede*

2   Only if we women and men are able to live in non-sexist
    Christian communities, to celebrate non-sexist Christian
    liturgies and to think in non-sexist theological terms and
    imagery will we be able to formulate a genuine Christian
    feminist spirituality.
        Elizabeth Fiorenza Quoted Carol Christ *Woman's Spirit
        Rising — A Feminist Reader in Religion*

3   As far as I know there is only one place for women in the
    church, and that is on their knees, either praying or scrubbing.
        Fr Hack Quoted Colin Stephenson *Merrily on High*

4   The plain ones be as safe as churches.
        Thomas Hardy *Tess of the D'Urbervilles*

5   It is better to dwell in a corner of the housetop, than with a
    brawling woman in a wide house.
        Holy Bible Proverbs Chap. 21 v. 9

6   Who can find a virtuous woman? for her price is far above
    rubies.
        Holy Bible Proverbs Chap. 31 v. 10

7   Women are liars since the world began.
        John Masefield 'The Widow in the Bye Street'

8   If God is male, not female, then men are intrinsically better
    than women. It follows then, that until the emphasis on
    maleness in the image of God is redressed the women of the
    world cannot be entirely liberated. For if God is thought of as
    simply and exclusively male, then the very cosmos seems
    sexist.
        Paul Moore *Take a Bishop Like Me*

9   Many committed churchwomen are crying 'What do I have to
    do to be taken seriously as a WOMAN by the Church?' The
    answer does not lie in priesthood but in ministry. Women who
    try to follow Christ do not challenge the Church and the world
    for status, but seek ways to minister to both.
        Jean Oddy Letter to *Church Times* 11 March 1988

10 Silence gives grace to woman.
        Sophocles *Ajax*

1   The one certain way for a woman to hold a man is to leave him for religion.

      Muriel Spark *The Comforters*

2   God save us all from wives who are angels in the street, saints in the church and devils at home.

      Charles Haddon Spurgeon *John Ploughman*

3   An Anglican Deaconess is seen as an ecclesiastical social worker, a lay reader, a visitor of the sick, an honorary clergy wife, or as a kind of nun. Even if they value her ministry, everyone in the parish knows that the 'real' clergy are men.

4   Most churches on either side of the ocean see women as playing only a 'supportive', if any, role in their congregations. Men preach, women listen. Men pray, women say Amen. Men study theology, women sew for the bazaar. Men make decisions, women make the tea.

5   The consensus appears to be that as it is presented and practised in our churches the gospel is NOT Good News for women.

      Elaine Storkey *What's Right with Feminism*

6   Whatever you say against women, they are better creatures than men, for men were made of clay, but woman was made of man.

      Jonathan Swift *Polite Conversation*

7   Ten measures of speech descended on the world; women took nine and men one.

      The Talmud

8   Women today are innovators, organisers and leaders to a degree previously unknown in Western culture. We are the richer for it.

      Br Terry Tastard SSF *Church Times* 'Communities in Crisis' 6 February 1987

WONDER

9   Wonder is the basis of worship.

      Thomas Carlyle *Sartor Resartus*

10   The world will never starve for want of wonders; but only for want of wonder.

      G.K. Chesterton *Tremendous Trifles*

1 God moves in a mysterious way
His wonders to perform;
He plants his footsteps in the sea,
And rides upon the storm.
William Cowper *Olney Hymns*

2 Wonders will never cease.
David Garrick *Correspondence*

3 To work a wonder, God would have her shown,
At once, a bud, and yet a rose full-blown.
Robert Herrick 'The Virgin Mary'

4 A man who has lost his sense of wonder is a man dead.
William of St Thierry Quoted Mark Gibbard *Guide to Hidden Springs*

WORDS

5 Good words are worth much, and cost little.
George Herbert *Jacula Prudentum*

6 He that hath knowledge spareth his words.
Holy Bible Proverbs Chap. 17 v. 27

7 Be not rash with thy mouth ... let thy words be few.
Holy Bible Ecclesiastes Chap. 5 v. 2

8 Sorrowful words become the sorrowful, angry words the passionate, jesting words the merry, and solemn words the grave.
Horace *Ars Poetica*

9 Sincere words are not grand.
Lao-Tze *The Simple Way*

10 Apt words have power to suage
The tumours of a troubled mind,
And are as balm to festered wounds.

11 He's gone, and who knows how may he report
Thy words by adding fuel to the flame?
John Milton *Samson Agonistes*

WORK

12 We do the works, but God works in us the doing of the works.
St Augustine of Hippo

1   One may do much [work] or one may do little; it is all one,
    provided he directs his heart to heaven.
        Berakoth Jewish Reform Prayer

2   Arouse yourself, gird your loins, put aside idleness, grasp the
    nettle and do some hard work.
        St Bernard of Clairvaux *Letters*

3   He who labours as he prays lifts up his heart to God with his
    hands.
        St Bernard of Clairvaux 'On Loving God'

4   Renunciation and activity both liberate.
    But to work is better than to renounce.

5   What is work and what is not work is a question that perplexes
    the wisest of men.
        Bhagavad Gita

6   Free men freely work: whoever fears God fears to sit at ease.
        Elizabeth Barrett Browning *Aurora Leigh*

7   The 'wages' of every noble work do yet lie in heaven or else
    nowhere.
        Thomas Carlyle *Past and Present*

8   Establish thou the work of our hands upon us; yea, the work
    of our hands establish thou it.
        Holy Bible Psalms 90 v. 17

9   I must work the works of him that sent me, while it is day: the
    night cometh, when no man can work.
        Holy Bible St John Chap. 9 v. 4

10 Every man's work shall be made manifest.
        Holy Bible 1 Corinthians Chap. 3 v. 13

11 Every child should be taught that useful work is worship and
    that intelligent labour is the highest form of prayer.
        Robert G. Ingersoll *How to Reform Mankind*

12 The greatness of work is inside man.
        Pope John Paul II *Easter Vigil and Other Poems*

13 The trivial round, the common task,
    Would furnish all we ought to ask;
    Room to deny ourselves, a road
    To bring us daily nearer God.
        John Keble 'New Every Morning'

1   You cannot be a true Martha abroad unless you are a true Mary at home.

     John Mason Neale 'Direction to a Religious Community of Sisters'

2   Good for the body is the work of the body, good for the soul is the work of the soul, and good for either the work of the other.

     Henry David Thoreau *Journal*

3   O Lord, let us not live to be useless, for Christ's sake.

     John Wesley

4   Work will be prayer only if there is also prayer which is not work.

     Edward Yarnold *The Theology of Christian Spirituality* 'The Study of Spirituality'

WORLD

5   I can show them that a vigorous and constant soul can live in the world without receiving ANY worldly taint, can find springs of sweet piety in the midst of the briny waters of the world.

     St Francis de Sales *The Devout Life*

6   We live together in a world that is bursting with sin and sorrow.

     Samuel Johnson *Miscellanies*

7   This world is full of beauty, as other worlds above;
    And if we did our duty, it might be full of love.

     Gerald Massey *The World is Full of Beauty*

WORSHIP

8   There is only one perfect act of worship ever offered and that was the life of Jesus Christ himself. From his conception to his ascension, he ever offers that life to the Father as the perfect act of worship in Heaven, and when we worship all we do is to join him.

     Fr Peter Ball CGA Clergy Conference at Swanwick 1985

9   He simply wanted to be loved, nothing more. Of course, there are those who love him, even among Christians. But they are not numerous.

     Albert Camus *The Fall*

1   Does not every true man feel that he is himself made higher by
    doing reverence to what is really above him?
      Thomas Carlyle *Heroes and Hero Worship*

2   God builds his temples in the heart on the ruins of churches
    and religions.
      Ralph Waldo Emerson *The Conduct of Life* 'Worship'

3   My God and my all.
      St Francis of Assisi Quoted *The Little Flowers of Assisi*

4   The various modes of worship, which prevailed in the Roman   *Scholars*
    world, were all considered by the people as equally true; by
    the philosopher, as equally false; and by the magistrate as
    equally useful.
      Edward Gibbon *Decline and Fall of the Roman Empire*

5   Men are idolators, and want something to look at and kiss and
    hug, or throw themselves down before; they always did, they
    always will, and if you don't make it of wood you must make it
    of words.
      Oliver Wendell Holmes *The Poet at the Breakfast Table*

6   For where two or three are gathered together in my name,
    there am I in the midst of them.
      Holy Bible St Matthew Chap. 18 v. 20

7   God is a Spirit: and they that worship him must worship him in
    spirit and in truth.
      Holy Bible St John Chap. 4 v. 24

8   Even the poor Pagan's homage to the Sun
    I would not harshly scorn, lest even there
    I spurned some elements of Christian prayer.
      Thomas Hood 'Ode to Rae Wilson, Esq.'

9   My father considered a walk among the mountains as the
    equivalent of church-going.
      Aldous Huxley *Those Barren Leaves*

10   It cannot be that the instinct which has led to the erection of   *writers*
    cathedrals, and of churches in every village, is wholly mistaken
    and misleading. There must be some great truth underlying
    the instinct for worship.
      Sir Oliver Lodge

11   And learn there may be worship without words!   ] *poets*
      James Russell Lowell 'The Cathedral'

1 More worship the rising than the setting sun.
   Pompey Quoted *Plutarch's Lives*

2 He worships God who knows Him.
   Seneca *Letters to Lucilius*

3 God respects me when I work, but he loves me when I sing.
   Rabindranath Tagore

4 To worship is to quicken the conscience by the Holiness of
      God
   To feed the mind with the Truth of God
   To purge the imagination by the Beauty of God
   To devote the will to the Purpose of God.
   Archbishop William Temple 'St John's Gospel'

5 Now let us do something beautiful for God.
   Mother Teresa of Calcutta, in a letter to a friend

6 St Francis ordered a plot to be set aside for the cultivation of
   flowers when the convent garden was made, in order that all
   who saw them might remember the Eternal Sweetness.
   Thomas of Celano *Life of St Francis*

7 God prefers bad verses recited with a pure heart, to the finest
   verses possible chanted by the wicked.
   Voltaire *Philosophical Dictionary*

8 The worship of God is not a rule of safety — it is an adventure
   of the spirit, and flight after the unattainable.
   Alfred North Whitehead *Science and the Modern World*

9 Apollo said that everyone's true worship was that which he
   found to be in use in the place where he chanced to be.
   Xenophon *Recollections of Socrates*

WORTH

10 A man passes for that he is worth. What he is engraves itself
    on his face in letters of light.
    Ralph Waldo Emerson *Essays* 'Spiritual Laws'

11 Slow rises worth by poverty depressed.
    Samuel Johnson 'London'

12 The worth of a State, in the long run, is the worth of the
    individuals composing it.
    John Stuart Mill *On Liberty*

WOUNDS

1 Open thy gate of mercy, gracious God!
My soul flies through these wounds to seek out Thee.
    William Shakespeare *Henry VI Part III* Act I Sc. 4

WRATH

2 Envy and wrath shorten the life.
    Apocrypha Ecclesiasticus Chap. 30 v. 24

3 I was angry with my friend:
I told my wrath, my wrath did end.
I was angry with my foe:
I told my wrath, my wrath did grow.
    William Blake 'A Poison Tree'

4 Wrath killeth the foolish man.
    Holy Bible Job Chap. 5 v. 2

5 A soft answer turneth away wrath: but grievous words stir up anger.
    Holy Bible Proverbs Chap. 15 v. 1

6 Let not the sun go down upon your wrath.
    Holy Bible Ephesians Chap. 4 v. 26

YEAR

1   A thousand years in thy sight are but as yesterday when it is
past, and as a watch in the night.
    Holy Bible Psalm 90 v. 4

2   We spend our years as a tale that is told.
    Holy Bible Psalm 90 v. 9

YEARNING

3   The heavens are still; no sound
Where then shall God be found?
    Shao Tung Shinto spirituality

4   O Lord, to find Thee is my desire
But to comprehend Thee
Is beyond my strength ...
I call upon Thee night and day.
    Sufi spirituality

YESTERDAY

5   Oh God, Put back Thy Universe and give me yesterday.
    Henry Arthur Jones *Silver King*

YOUTH

6   I felt so young, so strong, so sure of God.
    Elizabeth Barrett Browning *Aurora Leigh*

7   Rejoice, O young man, in thy youth; and let thy heart cheer
thee in the days of thy youth.
    Holy Bible Ecclesiastes Chap. 11 v. 9

8   Remember now thy Creator in the days of thy youth while the
evil days come not.
    Holy Bible Ecclesiastes Chap. 12 v. 1

1 How it does my heart good, visiting at that bleak hill,
  When limber liquid youth, that to all I teach
  Yields tender as a pushed peach,
  Hies headstrong to its wellbeing of a self-wise will.
    Gerard Manley Hopkins 'The Bugler's First Communion'

2 Praise youth and it will prosper.
    Irish proverb

3 Myself when young did eagerly frequent
  Doctor and Saint, and heard great argument
  About it and about: but evermore
  Came out by the same door as in I went.
    Omar Khayyam *Rubaiyat* Trans. Edward Fitzgerald

4 One other thing stirs me when I look back at my youthful
  days, the fact that so many people gave me something or were
  something to me without knowing it.
    Albert Schweitzer *Memories of Childhood and Youth*

5 What's to come is still unsure:
  In delay there lies no plenty;
  Then come kiss me, sweet and twenty,
  Youth's a stuff will not endure.
    William Shakespeare *Twelfth Night* Act II Sc. 3

6 Like a kite
  Cut from the string
  Lightly the soul of my youth
  Has taken flight.
    Ishikawa Takuboku 'Song of my Youth'

7 Bliss was it in that dawn to be alive,
  But to be young was very heaven!
    William Wordsworth 'French Revolution'

ZEAL

1 If our zeal were true and genuine we should be much more angry with a sinner than a heretic.
   Joseph Addison *The Spectator*

2 Zeal without knowledge is always less useful and effective than regulated zeal, and very often it is highly dangerous.
   St Bernard of Clairvaux

3 Zeal is fit only for wise men, but is found mostly in fools.

4 Zeal without knowledge is fire without light.
   Thomas Fuller *Gnomologia*

5 They have a zeal of God, but not according to knowledge.
   Holy Bible Romans Chap. 10 v. 2

6 Mistrust your zeal for doing good to others.
   Abbé Huvelin

7 We are often moved with passion, and we think it to be zeal
   Thomas à Kempis *The Imitation of Christ*

8 Had I but serv'd my God with half the zeal
   I serv'd my king, he would not in mine age
   Have left me naked to mine enemies
   William Shakespeare *Henry VIII* Act III Sc. 2

9 Press bravely onward! — not in vain
   Your generous trust in human-kind;
   The good which bloodshed could not gain
   Your peaceful zeal shall find.
   John Greenleaf Whittier 'To the Reformers of England'

SUBJECT INDEX

INDEX OF AUTHORS AND MAJOR WORKS